REMEDIES

REMEDIES

Inns of Court School of Law

Institute of Law, City University, London

OXFORD
UNIVERSITY PRESS

OXFORD
UNIVERSITY PRESS

Great Clarendon Street, Oxford OX2 6DP

Oxford University Press is a department of the University of Oxford.
It furthers the University's objective of excellence in research, scholarship,
and education by publishing worldwide in

Oxford New York

Auckland Bangkok Buenos Aires Cape Town Chennai
Dar es Salaam Delhi Hong Kong Istanbul Karachi Kolkata
Kuala Lumpur Madrid Melbourne Mexico City Mumbai Nairobi
São Paulo Shanghai Singapore Taipei Tokyo Toronto

and an associated company in Berlin

Oxford is a registered trade mark of Oxford University Press
in the UK and certain other countries

Published in the United States
by Oxford University Press Inc., New York

A Blackstone Press Book

British Library Cataloguing in Publication Data
Data available

Library of Congress Cataloging in Publication Data
Data available

ISBN 0-19-925506-7

1 3 5 7 9 10 8 6 4 2

Typeset by L. K. Murdoch, Tonbridge, Kent
Printed in Great Britain
on acid-free paper by
Ashford Colour Press, Gosport, Hampshire

FOREWORD

These manuals are designed primarily to support training on the Bar Vocational Course, though they are also intended to provide a useful resource for legal practitioners and for anyone undertaking training in legal skills.

The Bar Vocational Course was designed by staff at the Inns of Court School of Law, where it was introduced in 1989. This course is intended to equip students with the practical skills and the procedural and evidential knowledge that they will need to start their legal professional careers. These manuals are written by staff at the Inns of Court School of Law who have helped to develop the course, and by a range of legal practitioners and others involved in legal skills training. The authors of the manuals are very well aware of the practical and professional approach that is central to the Bar Vocational Course.

The range and coverage of the manuals have grown steadily. All the manuals are updated annually, and regular reviews and revisions of the manuals are carried out to ensure that developments in legal skills training and the experience of our staff are fully reflected in them.

This updating and revision is a constant process and we very much value the comments of practitioners, staff and students. Legal vocational training is advancing rapidly, and it is important that all those concerned work together to achieve and maintain high standards. Please address any comments to the Bar Vocational Course Director at the Inns of Court School of Law.

With the validation of other providers for the Bar Vocational Course it is very much our intention that these manuals will be of equal value to all students wherever they take the course, and we would very much value comments from tutors and students at other validated institutions.

The enthusiasm of the publishers and their efficiency in arranging production and publication of the manuals is much appreciated.

The Hon. Mr Justice Elias
Chairman of the Advisory Board of the Institute of Law
City University, London
August 2002

CONTENTS

PREFACE

In every problem or situation presented by a client, there is one question which will always be uppermost in his or her mind — what remedy can I hope to obtain? Students may be familiar with excellent books which argue remedial principles from an academic approach but which do not address problems from a practical point of view. Practitioners will be familiar with texts on remedies within a specific area of law, rather than providing an overview. Borrowing from each, the aim of this Manual is to focus the study of remedies on practical application and to provide a sourcebook which also covers how to calculate damages, and obtain an overview of possible remedies in a variety of legal areas. Substantive law is not ignored but takes its place alongside the practical implications of identifying and choosing a remedy for a particular problem. The Manual also contains many examples of common problems which arise in a particular area, with answers given on how to identify and pursue appropriate remedies. The word 'practical' appears frequently. Despite its possible overuse, the authors of the Manual have sought to focus on real problems, real solutions, to provide a sourcebook that will be valuable in everyday practice.

The first part covers the general principles of tort and contract remedies, and gives in-depth instruction on the calculation of damages. in particular for personal injury and fatal accident cases. It also covers eight areas of law, providing a legal framework and possible remedies which should be considered.

To appreciate and choose appropriate remedies requires an understanding of the financial implications involved and the second section of this Manual covers this increasingly important area. In addition to providing an understanding of tax, there is instruction on basic accounting principles and a section on insolvency.

Students at the Inns of Court School of Law will have the opportunity to work on many of the problems found in the last section of the Manual. It is hoped that readers will use these as study tools and have a similar chance to discuss the range of remedies suggested by the problems, and weigh the benefits and disadvantages of seeking a particular solution. It is through the process of identifying a whole range of possible relief and acquiring an ability to differentiate between the options that allows a choice to be made which best fulfils the client's objectives. It is hoped that the practical approach to the study of remedies in this Manual will stimulate the thought processes to enable students and practitioners alike to obtain the best 'practical' solution to difficult problems.

There is a long list of contributing authors to this Manual from current practitioners to members of the academic staff of the Inns of Court School of Law. Their combined experience from years of practice and teaching have produced a highly informative and useful sourcebook. All students and practitioners who are faced daily with the challenge of identifying, choosing and calculating remedial relief will give thanks for their combined efforts.

TABLE OF CASES

TABLE OF STATUTES

European primary and secondary legislation

PART I

PRINCIPLES AND APPLICATION OF REMEDIAL RELIEF

ONE

INTRODUCTION

1.1 Role and Context of Remedies

It is usually in the first months of practice that barristers come face to face with the realities of dealing with the problems and objectives of clients. Armed with a considerable amount of textbook law, practitioners soon discover that the task of finding a resolution or remedy to a specific problem demands additional skills: a knowledge of the range of major remedies, the ability to recognise which remedy can be sought in any situation and the likelihood of success of a particular remedy, how to choose between alternative remedies, and an understanding of how to calculate damages.

For most students, academic training has focused on substantive law: researching, classifying and analysing legal arguments. Such analysis has a central role in the barrister's work. However, to the client, it is of secondary importance. The client's crucial and primary question for you, as legal adviser, will be what solution the law offers to the client's problem, i.e., what is the remedy? It is not uncommon to hear former students say that they simply had not appreciated the importance of knowing how to go about *solving* a problem, i.e., what damages to claim, whether or not to seek an injunction, and how to find appropriate remedies in an unfamiliar area of law.

The term 'remedy' is wide-ranging and can include any positive solution to a client's problem. The Civil Procedure Rules 1998 use the term 'remedy' rather than 'relief', for example permitting a party to apply for remedy from sanctions previously ordered by the court. As an adviser you will wish to take an overview of all possible remedies including routes which do not involve court intervention, such as self-help remedies, exhausting internal complaints procedures or filing complaints with agencies such as the Commission for Racial Equality. This Manual will focus on remedies which a court can give, the most common being (a) the judgment of a money award of damages and (b) orders that defendants refrain from certain acts or restore the position the claimant was in before the cause of the claim arose. Though the study of remedies involves both substantive law principles and rules of procedure and enforcement, it does not lie squarely in either of these areas. Substantive law is decided by the court and answers the question, 'Is the defendant liable?' Procedural rules govern the issue, 'How can that liability be enforced?' The law of remedies falls between them, overlapping but distinct. Having determined that the defendant is liable, it answers the question, 'What remedy will the law permit?'

1.2 Classifying Remedies

While not all of the wide range of available remedies fit into set categories, most will fall into general areas and it is helpful to start with an understanding of these.

(a) *Compensatory remedies.* These compensate the claimant for losses suffered. The most common compensatory remedy is damages, i.e., a sum of money to put the claimant in as good a position as before the harm and recognition of loss. If a defendant fails to satisfy a judgment ordering payment of damages, there are various methods of enforcement available against the defendant's assets and wages (see ***Civil Litigation Manual***). A winning claimant will normally be awarded costs and, although these compensate for costs expended, they are not heemed to be part of the damages award.

(b) *Coercive remedies.* These aim to prevent harm from occurring or re-occurring. The most common preventative remedy is an injunction, which is an order by the court that the defendant do or refrain from doing a certain act to prevent harm occurring. An injunction, by itself, normally does not involve compensation to the claimant. In addition to injunctions, courts have a variety of specialised orders, e.g., an order for specific performance of a contract, which requires the defendant to perform contractual obligations. Failure to obey a court order is contempt of court for which the court may order payment of a fine and/or a period of imprisonment and/or sequestration of assets.

(c) *Declaratory remedies.* These interpret documents such as wills and contracts, and resolve disputes about the parties' rights. The most common is the declaration. In one sense a declaration can be a preventative remedy in that it will resolve uncertainty about the parties' rights or legal ownership before either side has taken steps based on an (erroneous) view of the matter. In another sense these types of remedies can be seen as indirectly 'coercive' in that a declaration puts the parties on notice of the legal interpretation of the matter. If either side subsequently acts contrary to that interpretation, the courts are likely to award compensation to the injured party and possibly an injunction preventing further acts.

(d) *Exemplary or punitive remedies.* These aim to punish the offending party for deliberate or particularly grave wrongful acts. The most common is an order requiring a defendant to pay a sum of money as exemplary or punitive damages. This remedy is distinct as it does not 'compensate' in the sense of restoring the claimant's position. Nor is it coercive in the sense of requiring the defendant to do or refrain from doing an act. Rather it is to penalise the defendant through civil rather than criminal litigation, and is often done to send a clear message of the court's view of particular conduct.

Remedies can also be categorised as either legal or equitable. Damages are the most common legal remedy. The most frequently used equitable remedies are injunctions and specific performance, although the list is extensive and includes *quantum meruit*, rescission, rectification, constructive trust, subrogation, contribution and receivership. Traditionally there were separate courts of law and equity, each providing their own specific type of remedies. Although the merger of modern courts diffused the distinction, it remains important in at least one respect: a claimant will often be denied an equitable remedy if the legal remedy (e.g., an award of monetary damages) would be adequate (see ***Civil Litigation Manual***).

1.3 Further Sources of Information

In addition to the information contained in this Manual, the course Manuals on specialist areas of law will assist with an in-depth study of remedies relevant to those areas. A list of practitioners' works on specific subjects can also be found in the legal research section of the ***Case Preparation Manual***. Increasingly texts are appearing in electronic form which may also be helpful. The following practitioner texts are of particular interest:

Burrows, A., *Remedies for Torts and Breach of Contract*, 2nd edn, Butterworths, 1994.
Chase, G., *Taxation Treatment of Compensation and Damages*, Butterworths, 1994.
Goff and Jones, *The Law of Restitution*, 5th edn, Sweet & Maxwell, 1998.
Goldrein and De Haas, *Structured Settlements: A Practical Guide*, 2nd edn, Butterworths, 1997.

Judicial Studies Board, *Guidelines for the Assessment of General Damages in Personal Injury Cases*, 5th edn, Blackstone (OUP), 2000.
Kemp and Kemp, *Quantum of Damages*, Sweet & Maxwell, looseleaf.
McGregor, H., *Damages*, 16th edn, Sweet & Maxwell, 1999.
Munkman, J., *Damages for Personal Injuries and Death*, 10th edn, Butterworths, 1996.

TWO

WHO TO SUE?

2.1 Introduction

When considering the remedies available to your client, it is important to consider the client's legal status and that of the person from whom the remedy is sought. This involves an awareness of the different types of legal persons and the limits on some persons' legal capability and liability.

2.2 Legal Personality

2.2.1 GENERAL

Where the claimant and defendant are individuals acting on their own behalf, you will need to consider whether they are treated differently before the law. For example, there are limits placed on the legal capacity of minors or persons suffering from mental disorder.

The claimant or defendant may be a group of people acting together, e.g., a business which wishes to sue a supplier for breach of contract or a sports club seeking damages for the negligence of builders. You will need to determine precisely who the legal persons are for whom you are acting and against whom you are seeking a remedy. The three principal legal forms which the group may take are: a trust, a corporation and an unincorporated association. These different forms may be used for a variety of purposes from running a business to a local social club.

Once you have determined the legal status of the claimant and defendant you need to consider what, if any, limits are placed on the capacity of such legal persons and who can bind the group (i.e., how do the rules of agency apply to this type of legal status).

2.2.2 TRUSTS

When dealing with a problem which involves a trust, you need to ensure that you are clear on the distinct roles of the settlor, trustees and beneficiaries. The legal ownership of any property is vested in the trustees, who are under a duty to hold it for the benefit of the beneficiaries. Thus, for example, when acting for the trust, you will need to ensure that whatever action is being proposed is within the trustees' power both in equity and under the specific terms of the trust.

2.2.3 CORPORATIONS

A corporation is a legal person separate from its members. A corporation may be formed (a) by Royal Charter, e.g., the BBC, (b) by statute, e.g., local authorities, or (c) under the Companies Acts as a private or public company. You will need to ensure that you are clear which individual(s) have the legal authority to act on behalf of the corporation.

2.2.4 UNINCORPORATED ASSOCIATIONS

Unincorporated associations have no legal personality separate from their members. The principal legal effect is that one member may be liable for the acts of another member. The three main types of such associations are (a) trade unions and employers' associations, (b) clubs (where the difference between a proprietary and a members' club is important), and (c) partnerships. You will need to ensure that you know what type of unincorporated association you are dealing with and who has the authority to act for it.

2.3 Business Associations

Although the different forms of legal person may be used for a variety of reasons, e.g., a club may incorporate as a limited company, the main use of incorporation is to trade. It is important to understand the different legal forms used to trade: (a) sole trader (an individual who sets up in business and trades in his own name), (b) partnership (persons carrying on a business in common with a view of profit), and (c) a company (a corporation created by registration under Companies Act 1985 (CA 1985)).

2.3.1 FORMATION

2.3.1.1 Sole traders

No formalities are required to set up as a sole trader and the personality of the 'trader' is indistinguishable in law from that of the individual. The debts of the business are the liability of the sole trader personally and without limit. For accounting purposes, however, the sole trader will distinguish between assets 'owned' by the business and personal assets.

2.3.1.2 Partnerships

No formalities are required to form a partnership. It will exist if it satisfies the definition in s. 1(1) of the Partnership Act 1890 (PA 1890) 'the relation which subsists between persons carrying on a business in common with a view of profit' (companies are expressly excluded by s. 1(2)). There are few restrictions on the formation of partnerships although the business must be lawful and CA 1985, s. 716, prohibits partnerships of more than 20 partners, unless exempt, which many professionals (e.g., solicitors, accountants) are.

The Limited Liability Partnership Act 2000 (in force from 6 April 2001) creates a new form of legal entity known as a limited liability partnership. Forming such a partnership requires similar formalities to those needed to form a company (see **2.3.1.3**), i.e., registration with the Registrar of Companies and filing of certain documents with the Registrar. As with a company, the liability of the partnership itself will be unlimited and the liability of the individual partners will be limited to contribute to the assets on the winding up of the partnership to such extent as set out in the Act. The 2000 Act specifically provides that the law relating to partnerships does not apply to a limited liability partnership and that the law relating to companies on relevant matters such as registration, insolvency and winding up shall be applied to such partnerships. These entities will be more like companies than partnerships. It is not known how many will choose to use this new form of entity to trade. Although the limitation on partners liability is attractive, the price paid is disclosure of information about the partnership including financial matters.

2.3.1.3 Companies

A company can only be formed by complying with the formalities set out in the CA 1985, which requires certain documents including the memorandum (the company's constitution) and the articles (the rules for the conduct of internal affairs) to be filed with the Registrar of Companies who will issue a certificate of incorporation, enter it in the register of companies and open a file for the new company at Companies House.

A company exists as a legal person distinct from its members from the date in the certificate of incorporation. The principal effect of this is that the company alone is liable for its debts. While the company has unlimited liability for its debts (i.e., can be liquidated to obtain assets to pay creditors), the members are not liable for the debts of the company, and their liability to contribute to the company's assets, to enable it to pay its creditors, may be limited by share or guarantee.

Companies can be categorised on the following basis:

(a) The liability of members to contribute to assist the company to pay its debts:

  (i) company limited by shares — members' liability to contribute (at any time) limited to nominal value and any premium on shares (mostly used for trading purposes);

  (ii) company limited by guarantee — members' liability to contribute (on liquidation only) limited to amount of guarantee given (mostly used for non-trading organisations, e.g., educational institutions);

  (iii) unlimited company — members' liability to contribute (on liquidation only) is unlimited (rare).

(b) The ability to offer its securities (shares and debentures) to the public:

  (i) public company — the memorandum states that it is a public company and the name must end with the words 'Public Limited Company' (or 'plc').

  (ii) private company — any other company. Unless it is an unlimited company, the name of a private company must end with the word 'Limited' (or 'Ltd'). All unlimited companies and companies limited by guarantee must be private. Some guarantee companies are exempt from the requirement that the name must end with the word 'Limited'.

A group of companies exists where one company controls one or more other companies, either through voting rights of members or determining the composition of the board of directors. The holding (controlling) company is (usually) the principal shareholder of the subsidiary (controlled) company. The law, for most purposes, treats the various companies in the group as distinct legal persons with liability only for their own debts.

2.3.2 INTERNAL MANAGEMENT AND CONTROL OF THE ASSOCIATION

2.3.2.1 Sole traders

A sole trader is free to employ others and whatever 'say' is given to others in the running of the organisation is a matter between them; the law has no impact here, save to provide contractual remedies if appropriate.

2.3.2.2 Partnerships

The term 'partner' is usually used to describe an 'equity' partner (i.e., one with full rights). Other types of partners usually have very limited if any 'partnership' rights, e.g., 'sleeping' partners (who take no active part in management) or 'salaried' partners (usually in fact employees).

The equity partners own the firm (i.e., have invested their capital) and manage the business (i.e., have the right to attend meetings and participate in the decision-making process running the business). The rights of the partners should be set out in a partnership agreement. However, PA 1890 implies terms into any partnership in so far as they are not inconsistent with what has been agreed. Section 24 contains most of these provisions, which include the right to take part in the management and have access to the books and that differences may be decided by simple majority of the partners (except a change in the nature of the business, introduction and expulsion of a partner, all of which require unanimity). Section 24 is subject to agreement to the contrary, express or implied (except expulsion of a partner which must be express), and s. 19 provides that the rights and duties of partners may be varied by consent of all the partners, express or inferred by conduct.

PA 1890, ss. 28 to 30, require partners to act in good faith towards one another, e.g., give full information and account for benefits derived from the firm. Although not expressly stated in PA 1890, partners have a duty to act within their actual authority.

2.3.2.3 Companies

A company as a legal person must make decisions but this must be done by the individuals controlling it. It is necessary to determine what decisions are decisions of the company and not just of the individuals. The members, as owners, make decisions collectively by voting in general meeting (on most matters a simple majority is sufficient but some decisions, mostly those which relate to the company's constitution, require a 75 per cent majority). Such decisions will be decisions of the company. CA 1985 requires certain formalities for such meetings which are more stringent for public than private companies. Decisions made without following the proper procedures can be challenged as irregular and invalid.

It is impractical for members to have general meetings to make all the decisions necessary to run the business. Much of the decision-making power is therefore delegated to the directors who must also act collectively through decisions at board meetings unless the power to sub-delegate has been given. There are thus two decision-making organs of the company, the general meeting and the board. As a general rule, once members have delegated their decision-making powers to the board, they cannot simultaneously exercise the delegated powers. In most public companies, the members and directors will not be the same people, and ownership (which is with the members) is therefore separated from the management powers (which are with the directors). This can cause problems where there is disagreement about the manner in which the business should be conducted. Small private companies are more likely to have a few members who are also directors of the company (i.e., the same people own and control the business).

Directors' powers are limited by the general law applicable to fiduciaries, which requires them to act in the best interests of the company as a whole (i.e., the shareholders collectively), to exercise their powers for proper purpose (i.e., in accordance with the memorandum of association and articles) and not to put themselves in a position where their duty to the company conflicts with their own personal interests (e.g., restrictions are placed on their contracting with the company, particularly substantial property transactions, without consent of the members, and there are outright prohibitions on certain loans). Directors also owe a duty of care and can be sued in negligence if they fall below the requisite standard.

Members' rights are contained in the articles of association, which are deemed to be a contract by CA 1985, s. 14. The articles usually have detailed provisions on calling of meetings, appointment, removal and powers of directors, paying of dividends etc. A company limited by shares can adopt a model form of articles (Table A) set out in a statutory instrument.

Where directors act wrongfully or some other person commits a wrong against the company, it is the company which must sue (*Foss* v *Harbottle* [1935] 2 KB 113). The power to institute proceedings is usually delegated to the directors. If the directors refuse, the members may be permitted to take collective action on behalf of the company but will have to do this collectively (i.e., a majority of the members will have to agree to initiate action and follow the proper rules, usually by calling a meeting of members and putting the matter to a vote, to make the decision valid). While this option appears attractive, it has not been favoured in more recent cases; see *Breckland Group Holdings Ltd* v *London and Suffolk Properties Ltd* [1989] BCLC 100. A simple majority of members can always dismiss directors with whom they disagree, Only in very rare circumstances can an individual member bring an action on behalf of the company.

CA 1985, s. 459, affords some protection to members by enabling them to petition the court for an order where the company's affairs are conducted in a manner which is unfairly prejudicial to them. In addition, the DTI has the power to investigate a company in a variety of circumstances.

2.3.3 CONTRACTUAL CAPACITY AND AGENCY RULES

2.3.3.1 Sole traders

The contractual capacity of a sole trader is determined by the general rules for contractual capacity of the individual in the law of contract.

General agency rules will apply to acts of employees and the sole trader will be personally liable for torts and breaches of contract committed in the course of business. The assets available to satisfy judgment debts will be the personal and business assets of the trader.

2.3.3.2 Partnerships

As with sole traders, there is no limit on the contractual capacity of partners except the general rules of contract law.

Normal agency rules have been applied to partnerships and codified in PA 1890, ss. 5 to 18. Each partner is both agent and part of the principal. Acts of individual partners carrying on the business of the partnership in the usual way will bind all the partners unless the partner is acting outside his authority and the third party is aware of this or is not aware of dealing with a partner (s. 5). Case law has established that all partners will have usual authority to buy and sell goods and pay debts, give receipts and draw cheques but that the 'usual' authority of partners in trading partnerships is wider than non-trading (e.g., professional) partnerships and includes borrowing money. Where limits are placed on a partner's authority, the firm will still be bound unless the third party has notice of the limitation (ss. 5 and 8). Section 6 deals specifically with acts done and instruments executed in the firm's name and s. 7 with pledging the firm's credit.

Tortious liability is covered by ss. 10 and 11. Section 10 makes the firm liable for loss or damage caused in the ordinary course of business or with the authority of co-partners. Under s. 11 the firm is liable to make good loss suffered from misapplication of money or property received by a partner within his apparent authority or by the firm in the course of business.

The combined effect of ss. 14, 17 and 36 on the liability of incoming and outgoing partners is that partners are not liable for acts done before or after the time they were partners unless they have been held out to be partners outside this period (s. 14), e.g., by having their names on the letterhead as partners or by failing to give proper notice of retirement from the partnership under s. 36. They remain liable for debts and obligations incurred while a partner even after their retirement (unless discharged by agreement of all the parties).

Although it enjoys no separate legal status, a firm (i.e., the partners), may sue or be sued in the firm name (RSC, O. 81, preserved in CPR, sch. 1), in which case all the partners who were partners at the date of the action will be parties (see ***Civil Litigation Manual***).

2.3.3.3 Companies

A company's contractual capacity is limited to activities authorised by the objects clause of its memorandum, which sets out the purpose for which the company was formed, e.g., to make and sell bicycles. Any contract not within the scope of this clause is theoretically *ultra vires* and void. The theory behind the rule was to protect the investors (at the expense of the outsider dealing with the company) in that their money could only be used for the stated purposes. However, the effect of this rule has been almost eradicated (a) by companies having very broad objects clauses (under CA 1985, s. 3A, companies can incorporate with the object 'to carry on any trade or business whatsoever'), (b) because companies can easily change their objects (CA 1985, s. 4), and (c) because statute gives considerable protection to outsiders. CA 1985, s. 35, allows both the company and the outsider to enforce an *ultra vires* act but retains the right of members to restrain proposed *ultra vires* acts and makes directors liable for them.

2.3.3.4 Business Names Act 1985

Whether acting for or against a business association, it is important to get the legal name correct. This will not be difficult where the business name is the legal name of the person running it; in the case of sole traders and partners, their surnames and, in the case of a company, its corporate name (in the memorandum). However, the business may use a 'trade' name (i.e., not the legal name of the person running it). In these circumstances, the Business Names Act 1985 requires disclosure of the legal name on correspondence, at business premises etc.

2.3.4 CESSATION OF BUSINESS: TERMINATION OF ASSOCIATION

2.3.4.1 Sole traders

A sole trader may cease trading at any time for any reason. If there are business debts on cessation, she or he will remain personally liable for them.

2.3.4.2 Partnerships

PA 1890, s. 32, provides that a partnership formed for a fixed term will end at the end of the term and a partnership at will (i.e., without a fixed term) may be ended by any partner giving notice to the others of intention to dissolve, the partnership being dissolved from the date in the notice. Section 32 is subject to agreement to the contrary, e.g., that dissolution may occur only by mutual agreement of all the partners, in which case a single partner cannot terminate by notice. The court does have power to order dissolution on one of the grounds in PA 1890, s. 35, which include a partner being in wilful or persistent breach of the agreement. Resort will be made to this provision only where the partners have no power to dissolve or cannot reach agreement to dissolve.

2.3.4.3 Companies

A company ceases to exist when the name is removed from the register of companies. It may be liquidated voluntarily by the members passing a resolution. The court may order the company to be liquidated if one of the grounds set out in the Insolvency Act 1986, s. 122, is proved. These grounds include that it would be 'just and equitable'.

2.3.4.4 Insolvency

Insolvency may result in the cessation of business (sole trader, partnership or company) and dissolution of any association (see **Chapter 21**).

THREE

LIABILITY FOR BREACH OF CONTRACT

3.1 Introduction

A claim for damages arises in circumstances where there has been a failure to perform, without lawful excuse, one or more of the obligations (whether conditions, warranties, or innominate or intermediate terms) contained in a contract. The innocent party may also have the right to rescind (terminate) the contract or choose to affirm. A failure to perform in this sense includes a refusal to perform, defective performance, delayed performance, and action taken which prevents performance.

3.1.1 PERFORMANCE

Generally, failure to perform amounts to breach of contract. However, where obligations are concurrent, each party's right to the other's performance depends on being able to show readiness, willingness and ability to perform. One party may be contractually bound to perform fully before the other party is under any obligation to perform at all (sometimes known as an entire contract). However, the doctrine of part performance provides that where one party has substantially performed but not completed performance of the contractual obligations, the other party cannot assume a discharge of obligations and a counterclaim can be made to compensate for minor discrepancies in performance. Alternatively, a claim for *quantum meruit* can be made where it is possible to infer a fresh agreement between the parties that payment will be made for the performance completed because a benefit has been conferred by it, provided that it is possible for the benefit of the performance to be accepted or rejected and one party is preventing the other from completing performance.

In cases where the parties agree otherwise, or where the contract is frustrated or the contract provides for the situation which has occurred or the limitation period has run out, there will be no actionable breach of contract for non-performance.

The right of the innocent party to *terminate* for breach of contract arises where the other has repudiated the contractual duty to perform, either before the time for performance falls due (known as an 'anticipatory breach' of contract) or whilst the contract remains only partly performed, or where the breach of contract complained of goes to the root of the contract. Repudiation can be express or implied reasonably from the circumstances, which must show either an intention to renounce the obligations under the contract or an absolute refusal to perform. It entitles the other party to an immediate cause of action, although if preferred, that party can choose to wait until the time for performance falls due.

3.1.2 WHAT IS THE EFFECT OF A REPUDIATORY BREACH OR A BREACH WHICH GOES TO THE ROOT OF THE CONTRACT?

The innocent party can *affirm* the contract or choose to *rescind* (terminate or discharge) it.

If affirmation is chosen, the contract remains alive, and the 'guilty' party can repent the breach and complete the performance as originally agreed, whilst the 'innocent' party can claim damages to compensate for any loss remaining. If the contract remains unperformed, the 'innocent' party can claim damages for that failure at the date when performance falls due. Where damages are calculated by reference to market price, the damages payable may be more or less than would have been payable at the date when the breach could have been anticipated.

If rescission is chosen, then, once communicated to the 'guilty' party, that election is final and terminates all the contractual obligations as to the future, such that the guilty party is, as a rule of construction, not entitled to take advantage of the wrong by relying on any of the terms in the contract (see *Briggs* v *Oates* [1991] 1 WLR 407).

Parties can agree to avoid the normal consequences of the common law, so the contract can provide for termination for a minor breach or without cause.

The consequences of a breach as to time for performance will depend upon whether time is of the essence. Time will be of the essence when the parties have expressly agreed that it will be so, when reasonable notice is given to make time of the essence or where the circumstances or subject matter of the contract make it imperative.

Where one party offers to perform all obligations under the contract and the other refuses to accept performance, the first party will be discharged from all further performance.

3.1.3 WHAT ARE THE TERMS OF A CONTRACT?

Express terms are those which the court finds as a fact were agreed orally between the parties, and those which were stated in writing. The parol evidence rule states that agreed terms not included in a written contract between the parties must be ignored. There are several exceptions to this rule and, in limited circumstances, a written contract can be rectified if it was executed by both parties under a common mistake. Some contracts may be made partly in writing and partly by word of mouth and whether or not a court will accept this will depend on the intention of the parties. Distinguish a *mere* representation from an express term.

Implied terms are those which will be included in a contract:

(a) because there is a custom of the trade to that effect and nothing in the contract contradicts their implication, or

(b) because they are implied by statute, such as the terms implied under the Sale of Goods Act 1979 (as amended by the Sale and Supply of Goods Act 1994) and the Supply of Goods and Services Act 1982, or

(c) because the parties must have intended to include them. Such terms must have been obvious — the officious bystander test — or necessary so as to give the transaction the business efficacy which the parties intended it to have or be those which the 'nature of the contract itself implicitly requires' (*Liverpool City Council* v *Irwin* [1977] AC 239).

3.1.4 WHAT IS THE RELATIVE IMPORTANCE OF CONTRACTUAL TERMS?

Although a claim for damages will be available for any breach of any term of a contract, the importance of the term broken will determine the availability of the remedy of rescission. A breach of a *condition* will entitle the innocent party to claim *rescission and damages*, whereas the breach of a *warranty* will entitle the innocent party to claim only damages. The parties can agree on which terms are to be conditions of the contract, or the court can decide, by looking at the consequences of breach, whether the term concerned did, in the events which have happened, go to the root of the contract.

3.2 Preliminary Issues

3.2.1 THE BREACH OF CONTRACT MUST HAVE CAUSED THE LOSS

The breach must be the effective or dominant cause of loss rather than providing merely an opportunity to sustain loss. It is for the court to exercise common sense in assessing whether a breach was the cause or merely the occasion for the loss. The breach must be the dominant or effective cause of the loss. The 'but for' test is insufficient (see *Galoo Ltd* v *Bright Grahame Murray* [1994] 1 WLR 1360). The claimant must be able to prove that *but for* the defendant's breach of contract there would have been no loss (see *Banque Bruxelles Lambert SA* v *Eagle Star Insurance Co. Ltd* [1995] QB 375). Where the breach is one of a number of causes of the loss, and all have had an equal impact in causing that loss, the breach will be taken to have caused the loss (see *Monarch SS* v *Karishamns* [1949] AC 196).

Where the breach partly causes the loss and the loss is otherwise due to the actions of a third party, liability for breach will arise if the acts of that party were contemplated by the defendant (see *De La Bere* v *Pearson Ltd* [1908] 1 KB 48; *Beoco Ltd* v *Alfa Laval Co. Ltd* [1994] 3 WLR 1179).

3.2.2 WHAT IS THE STANDARD OF PROOF?

The general rule is that the claimant must prove both the fact of damage and its amount, although where it is clear that a loss has been caused, difficulty in actually assessing that loss will not bar relief (see *Chaplin* v *Hicks* [1911] 2 KB 786).

It is said that the standard of proof is therefore one of *reasonable* certainty. What is required is evidence from which the existence of damage can be reasonably inferred and which provides adequate data for calculating the amount (see *McGregor on Damages*). Where absolute certainty is possible, detailed and precise evidence will be required.

Difficult cases are those where the claim is necessarily somewhat speculative, for example, a claim for loss of profit. In *E. Bailey and Co. Ltd* v *Balholm Securities Ltd* [1973] 2 Lloyd's Rep 404, it was suggested that a claim for loss of profit will be reasonably certain where the claimant has lost the opportunity of making profit in circumstances where there was no equal exposure to the risk of loss — for example, in commodity trading the chance of profit is entirely speculative and hence there is insufficient certainty of loss for a claim to be successful. There must be a substantial chance or probability, a mere possibility must be ignored (see *Obagi* v *Stanborough*, *The Times*, 15 December 1993).

Case law suggests that there is a sufficient degree of certainty in claims for loss of reputation arising from a loss of publicity. For example, cases where an actor or author is denied, in breach of contract, the chance of enhancing his reputation, and cases where the whole purpose of the contract is for publicity, i.e., advertising contracts, where the breach causes a loss of business.

Where the loss depends upon a large number of contingencies a claim can be made for the value of the chance which the claimant has lost. The greater the number of contingencies, the lower the value of that chance (see *Chaplin* v *Hicks* [1911] 2 KB 786).

3.2.3 CAN THE PARTIES TO A CONTRACT PLAN FOR ITS BREACH?

Sophisticated contracts often plan for a breach of contract through clauses aimed at, for example, limiting, restricting or excluding liability.

3.2.4 CAN LIABILITY FOR BREACH BE EXCLUDED OR RESTRICTED?

The first issue in relation to exclusion and exemption clauses is whether the clause has been *incorporated* into the contract (see *Chitty on Contracts*, vol. 1, part 3).

If the clause is found to be a part of the contract the court will then have to *construe* the clause to see whether it covers the damage which has been suffered and operates in the circumstances which have occurred. The *contra proferentem* rule applies, i.e. where there is any ambiguity, the clause will be strictly construed against the party for whose benefit it was inserted. Such clauses, if intended to cover negligence, must do so expressly or be capable of no other interpretation.

In some cases the power to exclude liability is prevented or is made subject to court review by statute, for example, the Unfair Contract Terms Act 1977 (UCTA 1977). The main protections which are afforded by the Act as they apply here are to be found in ss. 2–7 and 11. The Act only applies to business liability and prevents, in any circumstances, an attempt to exclude, etc., liability for death or personal injury arising from negligence. Negligence is defined as a failure to exercise reasonable care and skill. Otherwise, if a party to a contract attempts to rely on an exclusion clause to excuse a negligent performance of the contract or, in cases involving consumers or contracts in a standard form, a failure to perform substantially or at all or to exclude or restrict liability, the clause will be subjected to the *test of reasonableness*, as defined in s. 11. The burden of proving reasonableness rests with the party seeking to rely on the clause.

The Unfair Terms in Consumer Contracts Regulations 1999 (SI 1999/2083) supplement UCTA 1977. They apply in a broad range of areas, e.g., retail, banking, mortgage agreements and real property transactions including tenancies. Under the 1999 Regulations an unfair term in a contract between a seller or supplier and a consumer is not binding on the consumer. It is unfair if it has not been individually negotiated (i.e., it is a standard term of the seller or supplier) and, contrary to the requirement of good faith, it causes a significant imbalance in the parties' rights and obligations arising under the contract to the detriment of the consumer. A seller or supplier is obliged to ensure that any written term is expressed in plain intelligible language, and if there is doubt as to the meaning of a term, the interpretation most favourable to the consumer prevails.

The parties can agree that different or additional remedies to those provided by the common law should be applicable, for example, liquidated damages clauses, forfeiture clauses, repossession clauses and arbitration clauses. Such clauses may need to be construed by the court to establish their precise ambit.

A liquidated damages clause specifies the amount of damages to be paid in the event of a particular breach. Apart from consideration under UCTA 1977, in these cases the issue is whether such a term will be enforced by the court, or whether it will fail because it is found to be a penalty clause. In *Dunlop Pneumatic Tyre Co. Ltd* v *New Garage and Motor Co. Ltd* [1915] AC 79 it was held that the resolution of this issue depends upon the intention of the parties at the time when the contract was made. In construing that intention the court will have regard to the following matters:

(a) Was the clause intended to terrorise the other party into performing or was it a genuine pre-estimate of the damage likely to be suffered?

(b) Was it extravagant or unconscionable?

(c) Did it provide for the payment of a sum which is greater than the loss suffered?

(d) Did it provide for the payment of a single sum upon the occurrence of any of many different events?

See *Philips Hong Kong* v *Attorney-General of Hong Kong* (1990) 61 BLR 41.

FOUR

LIABILITY IN TORT

4.1 Introduction

There are three torts whose practical significance is so great that we need to reintroduce them to you from a practitioner's point of view.

The commonest by far of all tortious claims is the action for damages for personal injury. Such claims will almost always be founded on negligence, occupiers' liability or breach of statutory duty. Although you will have studied these at the academic stage, you are likely to have done so in a rather academic way, and some practical notes on these three important causes of action now follow.

4.2 Negligence

4.2.1 INGREDIENTS OF THE TORT OF NEGLIGENCE

These are:

(a) the existence of a duty of care;

(b) the duty owed to the claimant;

(c) negligence, i.e., breach of the duty of care;

(d) causation of damage;

(e) damage not too remote.

As well as these ingredients, in many cases the court is concerned with the question of quantum, i.e., the extent of the damage recoverable in financial terms.

4.2.2 THE PRACTITIONER'S VIEW OF NEGLIGENCE

At the academic stage you will largely have been concerned with the duty situation, the principles of reasonable foreseeability etc. The practitioner is largely concerned with breach of duty, i.e., negligence. The situations in which a duty of care is owed by one person to another are on the whole so well established that in practice it is rare for an issue to arise as to duty. It is only in the comparatively rare cases where there is no clear authority on whether a duty is owed, or a claimant seeks to establish a new situation, that a court will be concerned with this aspect of the tort. A general practitioner is, however, concerned almost every day with the question of whether someone has been negligent or not.

4.2.3 DUTY SITUATIONS

Particularly common and important duty of care situations in practice are:

(a) The duty owed by users of the highway to other users and to those beside the highway.

(b) The duty owed by manufacturers of products to users or consumers of these products. This has now largely been superseded by product liability under Part I of the Consumer Protection Act 1987.

(c) The duty owed by professional persons to their clients: such duties are usually contractual as well as tortious, but may arise in tort alone, particularly in cases of medical negligence.

(d) The duty owed by builders (and others responsible for safety in buildings) to owners and occupiers of buildings. Specific cases have severely restricted the scope of these duties (see *D & F Estates Ltd* v *Church Commissioners* [1989] AC 177, and *Murphy* v *Brentwood District Council* [1991] 1 AC 398, in which the House of Lords held that *Anns* v *Merton London Borough Council* [1978] AC 728 was wrongly decided).

(e) The duty owed by employers to their employees. Frequently known as the threefold duty laid down by *Wilson's and Clyde Coal Co. Ltd* v *English* [1938] AC 57, it is strictly a single duty, but for practical purposes it is a duty with five identifiable limbs:

   (i) to provide a safe place of work,

   (ii) to provide a safe system of work,

   (iii) to provide effective supervision,

   (iv) to provide proper plant and materials,

   (v) to provide a competent staff of men.

The duty arises both in tort and contract, but for practical purposes treat it as a tortious duty. It is a duty of reasonable care, not an absolute duty, but the standard of care expected can be surprisingly high on occasions. The duty is non-delegable: that is to say no one can discharge it but the employer, who cannot avoid liability by appointing someone else to discharge it.

4.2.4 OTHER IMPORTANT OR CURRENT TOPICS UNDER THE GENERAL HEADING OF NEGLIGENCE

(a) Limits on the scope of the duty with regard to the recoverability of economic loss (see **6.1.3**).

(b) The development of the doctrine of 'assumption of responsibility' in determining whether a duty of care is owed and the scope of such a duty. The leading case is *Henderson* v *Merrett Syndicates Ltd* [1994] AC 145. Other recent cases showing the application of the doctrine are: *Williams* v *Natural Life Health Foods Ltd* [1998] 2 All ER 577; *Costello* v *Chief Constable of the Northumbria Police* [1999] 1 All ER 550; *Leach* v *Chief Constable of Gloucestershire Constabulary* [1999] 1 All ER 215; and *Watson* v *British Board of Boxing Control* [2001] 2 WLR 1256.

(c) The issue of whether a duty of care can be owed by a statutory body which acts negligently in the discharge of its statutory functions. The leading case is *X* v *Bedfordshire County Council* [1995] 3 All ER 353. Other recent cases involving local authorities are: *Barrett* v *Enfield LBC* [1997] 3 All ER 171; *O'Rourke* v *Camden LBC* [1997] 3 All ER 23; *Clunis* v *Camden & Islington Health Authority* [1998] 3 All ER 180; *W* v *Essex County Council* [1998] 3 All ER 111 and [2000] 2 All ER 237; *Harris* v *Evans* [1998] 3 All ER 522; *Barrett* v *Enfield LBC* [1999] 3 All ER 193; *Phelps* v *Hillingdon LBC* [2000] 4 All ER 504; and *S* v *Gloucestershire CC* [2000] 3 All ER 346. Other cases involving emergency services are: *Capital and Counties plc* v *Hampshire CC* [1997] 2 All ER 865; *OLL Ltd* v *Secretary of State for Transport* [1997] 3 All ER 897; *Kent* v *Griffiths* [2000] 2 All ER 474; and *Bailey* v *HSS Alarms Ltd*, *The Times*, 20 June 2000.

(d) Limits on the scope of the duty with regard to causing nervous shock in someone other than the primary victim. The leading case is *Alcock* v *Chief Constable of South Yorkshire Police* [1992] 1 AC 310. Other recent cases are: *Vernon* v *Bosley* [1997] 1 All ER 577; *Frost* v *Chief Constable of South Yorkshire Police* [1997] 1 All ER 540; *Hunter* v *British Coal* [1998] 2 All ER 97; *White* v *Chief Constable of South Yorkshire Police* [1999] 1 All ER 1; and *Greatorex* v *Greatorex* [2000] 4 All ER 769.

(e) The duty owed by solicitors drafting a will to potential beneficiaries. The leading case is *White* v *Jones* [1995] 2 AC 207. Other recent cases are: *Carr-Glynn* v *Frearsons* [1998] 4 All ER 225; and *Gibbons* v *Nelsons*, *The Times*, 21 April 2000. An analogous situation arises in respect of pensions: *Gorham* v *British Telecom* [2000] 4 All ER 867.

(f) The abolition of the immunity from civil liability of advocates (including barristers): *Arthur J.S. Hall* v *Simons* [2000] 3 All ER 673.

(g) The principle of *res ipsa loquitur*. This is frequently pleaded, but rarely successful. It raises a presumption of negligence on the defendant's part in certain circumstances, in the absence of any evidence of negligence. It is always preferable to prove negligence by evidence rather than rely on *res ipsa loquitur*. It is therefore very much a last resort for a claimant in difficulties.

(h) Causation: see **6.1.2**.

(i) Remoteness: see **6.1.4**.

(j) The defence of *volenti non fit injuria*. This is not frequently raised and not easy to establish. For a fairly recent example of a successful defence of *volenti*, see *Morris* v *Murray* [1991] 2 QB 6. The defence cannot be relied upon where the defendant has a duty to protect the claimant against himself (*Reeves* v *Metropolitan Police Commissioner* [1999] 3 All ER 897).

(k) Contributory negligence. Frequently raised, frequently established, and very important in practice. See **6.3.1**.

(l) Vicarious liability. Nowadays it is very rare for an employee or agent to be outside the scope of his employment. The test in *Harrison* v *Michelin Tyre Co. Ltd* [1985] 1 All ER 918 is very difficult to satisfy. Particular difficulties arise where the employee has committed a crime or some other wholly unauthorised act while employed by the defendant. The test to be applied in such cases was recently considered by the House of Lords in *Lister* v *Helsey Hall Ltd* [2001] UKHL 22, [2001] 2 All ER 769. In practice the majority of tortious actions are probably founded on vicarious rather than direct liability.

(m) Limitation periods. These are particularly important in cases of latent injury and damage. See the ***Civil Litigation Manual*, Chapter 23**.

4.3 Occupiers' Liability

The liability of occupiers to visitors and non-visitors is statutory. The liability to lawful visitors is laid down by the Occupiers' Liability Act (OLA) 1957 which imposes a duty of care similar in standard and scope to the common law duty of care. Liability to non-visitors or trespassers is governed by the Occupiers' Liability Act 1984, which imposes no general duty but lays down the circumstances in which a duty will arise, and then defines a duty of a lower standard and narrower scope than that owed to lawful visitors.

Liability under the 1957 Act is based on negligence, i.e., breach of a duty of reasonable care. The statutory guidelines and defences included within the Act equate occupiers' liability with common law negligence to a considerable extent. Although the Act covers the relationship of employer and employee, it is not usually appropriate in such circumstances. Where the occupier is the employer of the visitor, a claim will usually be brought in negligence or for breach of statutory duty rather than under the OLA 1957.

Liability under the 1984 Act is very difficult to establish. Until recently the only successful claimant trespassers had all been children. However, in *Tomlinson* v *Congleton BC* [2002] All ER (D) 213, the Court of Appeal held that a council was liable to an adult trespasser who was fully aware of the danger. This decision, which is somewhat surprising on its facts, contains a useful analysis of s. 1 of the OLA 1984.

4.4 Breach of Statutory Duty

4.4.1 INTRODUCTION

Breach of statutory duty has considerably more importance in practice than it does to an academic studying the law of tort. There are thousands and thousands of specific duties imposed upon various people, usually employers, with regard to safety and health in various places of work, industrial processes and commercial premises. A great many injuries are suffered by people in the course of their work. In most cases of industrial injury, a claim is likely to be brought not only in negligence, but also under a statute or statutory regulation.

Statutory duties are to be found covering more or less any workplace, work situation or industrial process you can think of. They are laid down by statute (e.g., the Factories Act 1961) or by statutory instrument (e.g., the Construction (General Provisions) Regulations 1961). Most statutes and regulations are currently in the process of being replaced by new regulations based on European Directives.

The relevant directives and statutory provisions are gathered together in the major reference work *Redgrave's Health and Safety*, 3rd edn by J. Hendy and M. Ford (London: Butterworths, 1998) where you will find such delights as the Manufacture of Cinematograph Film Regulations 1928, the Genetically Modified Organisms Regulations 1992 and the Equipment and Protective Systems Intended for Use in Potentially Explosive Atmospheres Regulations 1996.

The duties laid down by statute are unlike common law duties. They are not general, but highly specific. They do not, for the most part, involve any principles of negligence or reasonable foreseeability. Three broad types of duty can be identified.

4.4.2 ABSOLUTE DUTIES

Many duties are absolute. They require that something 'shall be done' without further qualification. They are very strictly construed, and breach of an absolute duty will give rise to liability even where there is no fault on the part of the defendant. So, for example, it is no defence that compliance with a duty would mean the defendant could not operate machinery at all (*John Summers & Sons Ltd* v *Frost* [1955] AC 740), or that all the evidence showed that the accident which in fact happened was an impossibility (*Galashiels Gas Co. Ltd* v *O'Donnell* [1949] AC 275).

4.4.3 DUTIES OF REASONABLE CARE

Such duties require persons to act with reasonable care; the standard of care is similar to the common law standard, and a reasonable foreseeability test will be applied. In such cases the word 'reasonably' usually appears in the statute: e.g., a duty to prevent something happening 'so far as is reasonably practicable'; a duty to 'take such steps as are reasonable in all the circumstances to ensure that' something does or does not happen.

4.4.4 HYBRID DUTIES

These are duties which are less than absolute, but which require more than reasonable care: for example, a duty to 'take such steps as may be necessary to prevent . . .'; or to 'take all appropriate precautions'. There is no single test for breach of such duties. The standard of care required is a question of the interpretation of each individual statutory section or regulation. Words which tend to indicate a hybrid duty are words such as: adequate, secure, appropriate, sufficient, necessary, practicable.

4.4.5 TO ESTABLISH LIABILITY

There are as many as eight conditions to be satisfied before a claimant can succeed in a claim for damages for breach of statutory duty.

(a) That the legislation applies. The statutes are not of general application. For example, the Workplace (Health, Safety and Welfare) Regulations 1992 (SI 1992/3004) only apply to workplaces as defined in reg. 2. It may well be that the defendant has done something prohibited by the Regulations, but if it was not done in a workplace there will be no liability. Always check the application of the statute or regulations. This will usually be found in the legislation itself.

(b) That the duty is imposed upon the defendant or upon someone for whom the defendant is vicariously liable. Somewhere in the regulations or statute will be a section or regulation stating upon whom the duties are imposed. Different duties are imposed on different people: e.g., under the Railway Safety (Miscellaneous Provisions) Regulations 1997, some duties are imposed upon Railtrack, others upon train operators, and yet others on employers contracted to work on the railway. Always make sure you are suing the right person.

(c) That the duty is owed to the claimant. The statute or regulations may state to whom a duty is owed, or it may be a matter of construction. The duty will usually be owed to the person(s) whose safety the statute is intended to protect. Others may be injured by a breach of statutory duty, but will be unable to claim (e.g., *Hartley* v *Mayoh & Co.* [1954] 1 QB 383).

(d) That breach of the legislation gives rise to civil liability. Not every statute or regulation aimed at safety will give rise to civil liability. Either it must expressly state that it does so, or it must be construed by the court as doing so. There will usually be no difficulty where the claimant has suffered the harm the statute was intended to prevent; but there may well be doubt where the statute imposes a criminal sanction, though this is not necessarily fatal. Modern statutes usually make this point clear (see, e.g., Health and Safety at Work etc. Act 1974, s. 47). For older statutes, check in *Redgrave*.

(e) That the defendant is in breach of duty. This sounds obvious, but it may need careful examination of the facts and the legislation. Regulations are specific, not general. The defendant is only in breach if he has done exactly what he is forbidden to do; conversely he will be in breach unless he has done *exactly* what is required. Note that where a regulation requires a defendant to do something so far as 'practicable' or 'reasonably practicable' the claimant need not show that it was practicable or reasonably practicable, only that it was not done. It is for the defendant to show that it was not practicable or reasonably practicable. See, for example, *Larner* v *British Steel plc* [1993] 4 All ER 102.

(f) That the claimant has suffered damage. This must usually amount to personal injury or death. There are few, if any, statutory duties giving rise to liability for damage to property.

(g) That the damage is of the kind the statute was intended to prevent. There is no liability if the damage is of a different kind from that which was contemplated (*Gorris* v *Scott* (1874) LR 9 Ex 125). But the damage need not have been caused in the precise manner anticipated.

(h) That the breach of statutory duty caused the damage. Causation is obviously an essential requirement, as in negligence. But there are some particularly important aspects of causation, explained in the next paragraph.

4.4.6 CAUSATION

Causation is established by applying the 'but for' test. This results in the important principle that the defendant will have a good defence if he can establish that the claimant would still have been injured even if the defendant had fulfilled his statutory duty (*McWilliams* v *Sir William Arrol & Co. Ltd* [1962] 1 WLR 295). Where the duty is to provide a safety device, and the defendant has failed to provide it, there will still be no liability if the defendant shows that even if he had provided the safety device, the claimant would probably not have used it.

A further particular difficulty of causation arises where the duty is imposed not only on the defendant but also on the claimant. Some duties are imposed not only upon employers, but also upon employees: both may therefore be in breach of the same duty. If the only reason that the defendant is in breach of an absolute duty is that the claimant put the defendant in breach by his own breach, should the defendant be liable? The answer is a qualified no.

If the defendant's breach is coextensive with and consists of the claimant's own wrongful act and nothing more, then the defendant will not be liable for his own breach (*Ginty* v *Belmont Building Supplies Ltd* [1959] 1 All ER 414). But this is a strict rule and it involves the defendant establishing that there is absolutely no fault on his part beyond the technical breach of an absolute duty brought about by the claimant's own, unpreventable act.

More usually, however, a claimant will be able to establish some fault on the part of the defendant which makes the defendant's breach wider and so not coextensive with the claimant's breach. This can usually be done by showing that the defendant has not done all that he reasonably could to prevent the breach occurring, and so has caused or permitted it to happen, as well as having implicitly committed it himself (e.g., *Boyle* v *Kodak Ltd* [1969] 1 WLR 661). In practice you can frequently get round the *Ginty* principle on this basis.

The coextensive breach principle does not even arise where the duty is imposed not upon the defendant directly, but upon someone for whom he is vicariously liable. In such a case, the defendant's liability will depend on whether the tortfeasor for whom he is vicariously liable could have raised a defence of *volenti non fit injuria* against the claimant. If so, the defendant may also raise that defence; if not, he will be liable (*Imperial Chemical Industries Ltd* v *Shatwell* [1965] AC 656). This is an exception to the general rule that *volenti* is *not* a defence to breach of statutory duty where the duty is imposed on the defendant himself (*Wheeler* v *New Merton Board Mills Ltd* [1933] 2 KB 669).

Contributory negligence is a good partial defence to breach of statutory duty, however.

FIVE

DAMAGES IN CONTRACT

5.1 The Legal Remedy: Damages

Where a contract has been breached, damages are available as a matter of right. Even where loss cannot be proved, nominal damages may be claimed, although cases of this type are relatively rare. The underlying principle of the damage award is to compensate the claimant for his losses, rather than measure the award by the amount of gain derived by the defendant. In a few situations the defendant's gain may also be taken into account, for example, where a defendant in the position of a fiduciary is required to account for the profit made by his acts. Compensation for the claimant can also be measured by lost opportunity, for example, where the defendant in breach of contract uses the claimant's car, the defendant may be required to pay a reasonable rental value for the use of the car for the relevant period, notwithstanding that the claimant would not have used it or otherwise leased it to someone else during the period.

A claimant's 'loss' includes any harm to the person or property of the claimant including any diminution of the claimant's assets caused by the breach. However, in calculating the total 'loss', any benefits which the claimant has enjoyed (or savings made) as a result of the breach must be set off against (reduce) the loss. The court will not generally award damages which will put the claimant in a better position than he would have been in if the breach had not occurred, although the practical effect of some damage awards may do just that.

There are three basic methods of calculating 'loss':

(a) expectation (or loss of bargain) basis;

(b) reliance (or wasted expenditure) basis; and

(c) restitution.

The choice of which basis to use in calculating the claim for damages will depend on the kind of loss which has occurred as a result of the breach, and which method achieves the most advantageous result for the client.

5.1.1 EXPECTATION (LOSS OF BARGAIN) BASIS

Damages for loss of bargain are forward looking (*Robinson* v *Harman* (1848) 1 Ex 850) and are intended to put the claimant into the position in which he would have been if the contract had actually been performed. This includes both the loss of the promised performance and the loss of profit resulting from not being able to put the performance to use. For example, if C purchases a car for business from D and D cancels at the last minute, C has lost the benefit of the car itself, but has also lost the chance to use it in his or her business until he or she can secure another car, i.e., a loss of profit.

All losses which are not too remote from the breach may be recovered, provided that the claimant has acted reasonably to mitigate his or her loss.

5.1.1.1 How is expectation loss quantified?

There are two alternative ways of calculating the amount of damages necessary to compensate for the loss of bargain: the cost of cure measure (reinstatement cost); or the difference in value measure (diminution in value). Which of these two measures is the appropriate one seems to depend largely on common sense. Consideration should be given to why the performance was wanted, what impact the claimant's duty to mitigate has had, and whether the court believes that the claimant, awarded damages on the cost of cure basis, either has carried out or will carry out the cure.

In *Radford* v *De Froberville* [1977] 1 WLR 1262 a contract for the sale of land required a wall to be built separating the land sold from that belonging to the claimant. In a claim for damages for breach of contract the claimant was held entitled to receive the cost of building the wall as compensation from the defendant because the claimant genuinely wanted the work done and convinced the court that the money would be used for that purpose, even though the land had not been diminished in value by the failure to carry out the contractual obligation.

In *Tito* v *Waddell (No. 2)* [1977] Ch 106 a mining company had agreed to replant land after it had been mined and had then failed to do so. It was held, in an action for damages seeking the cost of replanting, that the claimants could not succeed since there was no evidence that they intended to use the money to carry out the contractual obligation. Instead, damages were assessed on the basis of the diminution in the value of the land — a much smaller sum of money.

Where a claim for negligent performance of a contract is made against a surveyor, the rule is that the correct measure of damages is normally diminution of value. However this is not an absolute and invariable rule and will not be followed if its application would manifestly not do justice in the case (see *Hipkins* v *Jack Cotton Partnership* [1989] 2 EGLR 157).

Where a finance company lends money on the basis of a negligent valuation of the property, it is entitled to recover, as part of the measure of damages, interest at a proper rate of interest but not necessarily the rate provided by the loan. (See *Swingcastle Ltd* v *Alastair Gibson* [1991] 2 AC 223.)

Subject to the principles of remoteness and mitigation, damages arising from some common breaches of contract are quantified in the ways illustrated by **Table 5.1**. See further **6.2.5**.

Table 5.1 Damages arising from some common breaches of contract

Type of contract	Where a claim is made against the person who confers the benefit			Where the claim is against the person who receives the benefit
	Non-performance	*Delayed performance*	*Defective performance*	*Non-performance*
Transfer of property or goods	(a) The difference between the cost of buying the same goods in the market and the contract price if it has not been paid. (b) Or, if there is no market, then the loss of user profit. (The rule in *Bain* v *Fothergill*, relating to sale of land, that only expenses can be recovered has been abolished so now normal expectation damages will be available.)	(a) The difference between the market value at the due date for delivery and the market value at the date of actual delivery. (b) Or, if intended to be used, then the loss of profit which could have been expected from that use. (The rule in *Bain* v *Fothergill*, relating to sale of land, that only the expenses which have been incurred can be recovered, has been abolished so now normal expectation damages will be available.)	Where the goods are defective, or are not of contract quality, then the value of the goods in their expected or intended condition less their market value in the defective condition (diminution of value), and, if wanted for use, the loss of user profit. However, if the defect can be cured, then the measure is the cost of cure. Betterment will be ignored.	(a) Where there is a failure to pay or accept the goods, then the difference between the contract price and the selling price on the market. (b) Or, if there is no market, then the loss of profit suffered.
Contract for a loan	The difference between the contract cost of the loan and the market cost of the loan.	Same as for non-performance.		
Contract for services	The difference between the market cost of the same service and the contract cost, less the contract price if it has not already been paid.	The value of the service if rendered on the due date, less its value on the date when rendered.	Where the value of the property is reduced, then the diminution in the value of that property. However, if reasonable, the cost of cure measure will be awarded instead if the work has been or will be done. If there is no reduction in value, then such consequential losses as arise.	Where there is a failure to accept a service: (a) A failure to supply cargo in a contract of carriage, then the difference between the contract rate and the market rate for carriage. (b) In a wrongful dismissal, the difference between the contract wage and any substitute wage. (c) Where there is a failure to allow work to proceed, then the contract price less the costs saved by not having to carry out the work.

Source: Table compiled from *McGregor on Damages* and Burrows, *Remedies for Tort and Breach of Contract*

5.1.2 RELIANCE (OR WASTED EXPENDITURE) BASIS

Reliance loss arises where the claimant has expended money which is then wasted in preparation for, or in partial performance of, the contract. It covers out-of-pocket expenses. Like the expectation loss basis, the reliance loss method aims to put the claimant in as good a position as he was in before the contract was made (see Fuller and Perdue, 'Reliance Interest in Contract Damages' (1936) 46 *Yale Law Journal* 52).

Reliance loss will be claimed in cases where expectation loss is too speculative to recover (see, e.g., *McRae* v *Commonwealth Disposals Commission* (1950) 84 CLR 377; *Anglia Television Ltd* v *Reed* [1972] 1 QB 60).

Common examples of reliance expenses are for collection of goods (where the buyer is required by the contract to collect the goods and after incurring charges the seller repudiates the contract), storage and transport charges. According to *Anglia Television Ltd* v *Reed*, pre-contractual expenses are recoverable as part of the reliance loss, provided 'it was such as would reasonably be in the contemplation of the parties as likely to be wasted if the contract was broken' (per Lord Denning MR at p. 64).

5.1.3 RESTITUTION (UNJUST ENRICHMENT)

The third basis of calculating loss is where the claimant, in performing his obligations under the contract, has conferred a benefit on the defendant and wishes to claim back the benefit (or the value) given. For example, where the claimant has paid in advance for a product which is not delivered, he is entitled to the return of the money paid. The 'loss' to the claimant is measured by reference to the amount of benefit (including the reasonable value of services) given to the defendant, rather than focusing on the amount of claimant's loss, although in some cases this may be the same amount. In breach of contract cases, actions based on a claim for restitution may be for *quantum meruit*, and where there has been a total failure of consideration (failure to perform), the action will be for the recovery of money had and received.

The effect of a restitutionary claim is to restore both parties to the position they would have been in if the contract had never been made. This differs from the expectation basis which is meant to put the claimant in the position he would have been in if the contract had been performed. It also differs from the reliance basis in that a restitution claim assumes that no contract had been made but the party in breach may be left in a worse position. Damages for breach of contract which are awarded purely for restitutionary loss have been rare (see *Wrotham Park Estate Co. Ltd* v *Parkside Homes Ltd* [1974] 1 WLR 798). It is important to bear in mind that claims for restitution are not limited to cases of breach of contract and are frequently part of claims for other equitable remedies (see later in this chapter and **Chapter 13**).

5.1.4 CHOOSING BETWEEN EXPECTATION, RELIANCE AND RESTITUTION

Generally the claimant will be permitted to choose the method on which to base his or her claim, and the defendant is not entitled to insist that the claimant must pursue one basis over another. There are, however, several guiding principles which will apply. First a claimant will not be permitted to claim damages for a reliance loss where this would compensate him, in effect, for a bad bargain, thereby putting him in a better position than he would have been in had the contract been performed. Where the loss flows from having entered into the contract rather than from its breach, only the lower expectation loss will be recoverable. (See *CCC Films (London) Ltd* v *Impact Quadrant Films Ltd* [1985] QB 16 and *C & P Haulage* v *Middleton* [1983] 1 WLR 1461.)

A claimant will not be permitted to claim for expectation losses that are too speculative to be capable of satisfactory proof. In such a case, the claim will be limited to reliance losses and the value of any restitutionary claim.

A claim in restitution will only be permitted if the breach is a serious one which amounts to a total failure of consideration. If this is proved, restitution may be claimed even if the result is to leave the claimant in a better position than he would have been if the contract had been performed. This is a complex area and practitioners are advised to consult specialist texts on contract law.

The various bases may also be combined within one claim provided the losses are not duplicated, allowing the claimant to recover twice for the same loss. It is possible to have a situation where the claimant paid in advance for a product, and incurred installation expenses. After installation the product was found to be defective. The claimant may recover the money paid for the product (in restitution) and the costs of installation (incurred in reliance). If expected profits were also lost as a result of the breach, the net (not the gross) profits could be recovered as well.

5.2 When Can Loss of Profit Be Claimed?

A claim for loss of profit will arise in cases where the business use of the goods or service contracted for is lost or delayed as a result of the breach of contract.

Where there is no difference between the market price and the contract price, a claim for loss of profit will succeed only if it can be established that there was a market — that is, that the supply of the goods or services in question outstripped the demand for them — otherwise only nominal damages will be available (see *W.L. Thompson Ltd* v *Robinson (Gunmakers) Ltd* [1955] Ch 177; *Lazenby Garages Ltd* v *Wright* [1976] 1 WLR 459). Whether or not there is an available market depends upon whether there is an available buyer who is prepared to pay a fair price on that day. Where there is only a hypothetical sale, there is an available market only where, on the relevant day, there were sufficient possible traders in touch with each other to evidence a market in which the goods could have been sold (see *Shearson Lehman Hutton Inc.* v *Maclaine Watson & Co. Ltd (No. 2)* [1990] 3 All ER 723).

Where there has been an inadequate repair causing an explosion, and thereby loss of profit, that loss of profit cannot be claimed because the further damage arises from another cause. Damages will then be limited to the replacement of the defective equipment and to the loss of profit while the repair is being effected.

5.3 Can Incidental Losses Be Included in the Assessment of Damages?

Such items as the cost of stopping delivery, holding goods in store, defending a sub-buyer's claim etc. are included in the assessment of damages and can be recovered.

5.4 When Can Damages Be Obtained for Loss of Reputation?

The general rule is that damages cannot be awarded for loss of reputation caused by wrongful dismissal or because a wrongful dismissal may make it more difficult to find alternative employment (see *Addis* v *Gramophone Co. Ltd* [1909] AC 488). However, in cases where the obtaining of publicity is the main purpose of the contract, damages for the lost chance of enhancing reputation will be recoverable (breaches of actors' contracts, and breach of advertising contracts). Equally, dishonouring a trader's cheque in breach of contract will entitle the trader to damages for lost reputation and, where goods or services are provided directly to the claimant's customers but are not of contract quality, again, damages for lost reputation can be recovered.

5.5 When Can Damages Be Obtained for Distress and Disappointment?

The general rule is that damages for distress are not available in an action for breach of contract. However, recent cases suggest some slackening in the strictness of this rule, so that in contracts entered into for purposes of enjoyment (see *Jarvis* v *Swans Tours Ltd* [1973] QB 233) damages will be available for disappointment, and in contracts entered into to avoid distress or to gain peace of mind damages will be available for the failure to prevent that distress (see *Heywood* v *Wellers* [1976] QB 446). The scope of this exception has now been extended by the House of Lords in *Farley* v *Skinner* [2001] 4 All ER 801. It is not necessary that the very purpose of the contract should have been to provide pleasure, relaxation or peace of mind; it is sufficient that this was a major or important part of the contract. However, damages under this head should be restrained and modest. The House of Lords regarded £10,000 as right on the upper limit.

Damages for distress can also be claimed as consequential to physical inconvenience because this is taken to be obviously within the contemplation of the parties at the time of contracting (see *Perry* v *Sydney Phillips and Son* [1982] 1 WLR 1297). Damages for distress arising out of wrongful dismissal from a contract of employment cannot be recovered (*Addis* v *Gramophone Co. Ltd* [1909] AC 488, recently reaffirmed in *Johnson* v *Unisys Ltd* [2001] UKHL 13, [2001] 2 All ER 801). No claim for inconvenience or stress can be made by a company (see *Firststeel Cold Rolled Products* v *Anaco Precision Pressings, The Times*, 21 November 1994).

5.6 Exemplary or Punitive Damages

Exemplary damages are not available for breach of contract claims (see *Addis* v *Gramophone Co. Ltd* [1909] AC 488).

5.7 When Are Damages Assessed?

The general rule is that damages are assessed at the time of breach (the date of the accrual of the cause of action), that is, at the date when the damage occurs, because the innocent party is required to act reasonably (to mitigate) by going to the market to replace the goods or services as soon as is possible after the breach (see *C. Sharpe & Co. Ltd* v *Nosawa* [1917] 2 KB 814). However, where it appears probable that the defendant may make good his default, then damages will be assessed at the time when that probability ceases.

This general rule fails to take account of the problems caused by inflation and the consequent variability of the cost of goods and services, or of the changing world value of money. The rule is now often ignored where it would 'give rise to injustice, [and] the court has power to fix such other date as may be appropriate in the circumstances' (see *Johnson* v *Agnew* [1980] AC 367). However, *The Folias* [1979] AC 685 and *Attorney-General of the Republic of Ghana* v *Texaco Overseas Tankships Ltd* [1994] 1 Lloyd's Rep 473 held that if the contract discloses no intention as to the currency in which damages for breach are to be payable, they should be calculated in the currency in which the claimants incurred the loss.

So, where the price of the contract has already been paid, and it may not be reasonable to expect the innocent party to replace the goods or services by going to the market, since he or she may not have the money to do so (that party has not got the opportunity to act), damages will be assessed by reference to the market value at the time of judgment. Equally, a buyer of land is entitled to seek specific performance of the contract of sale and, if damages are awarded instead of specific performance, those damages will be assessed at the date of judgment rather than at the date of breach (see *Wroth* v *Tyler* [1974] Ch 30).

In cases where foreign currency liability arises, the sum in sterling to be paid is the applicable rate for exchange on the date of payment (see *Miliangos* v *George Frank (Textiles) Ltd* [1976] AC 443).

Where an anticipatory breach of contract occurs, the innocent party has the option of accepting the breach or continuing to press for performance. In the former situation there is an immediate obligation to mitigate and damages will be assessed at that time. However, in the latter case, damages will be assessed as at the date when performance should have taken place.

See further **6.2.2**.

5.8 Taxation of Damages

In assessing damages for a breach of contract, to what extent will a deduction be made for taxation?

The general rule is that where the loss which is compensated for by the payment of damages is loss of income, the tax which would have been paid on that income if earned in the normal way will be deducted from the damages awarded (see *British Transport Commission* v *Gourley* [1956] AC 185). This rule applies only if the damages are not themselves subject to taxation. Now, since sums in excess of £30,000 awarded for wrongful dismissal are taxable, the *Gourley* principle no longer applies to sums in excess of that amount (see *Shove* v *Downs Surgical plc* [1984] 1 All ER 7). The easiest way to calculate the correct sum to be paid by way of damages is to use the net effect approach.

The appropriate principles are set out in **Chapter 20**.

5.9 Limitations on Compensatory Damages

5.9.1 LOSS IN THE CONTEMPLATION OF THE PARTIES

Compensatory damages are subject to the limitation imposed by the rules preventing claims for losses which are deemed to be too remote from the breach.

The test in contract is whether the loss was in the reasonable contemplation of the parties. In *Hadley* v *Baxendale* (1854) 9 Ex 341 two limbs to the test for judging whether the damage is too remote were identified: first, damage which arises naturally, that is, according to the usual course of things from such breach of contract (see further *Banque Keyser Ullmann SA* v *Skandia (UK) Insurance Co. Ltd* [1991] 2 AC 249); or second, such as may reasonably be supposed to have been in the contemplation of both parties, at the time they made the contract, as a probable result of the breach of it. (See further *Victoria Laundry (Windsor) Ltd* v *Newman Industries Ltd* [1949] 2 KB 528, *The Heron II* [1969] 1 AC 350, and *H. Parsons (Livestock) Ltd* v *Uttley Ingham & Co. Ltd* [1978] QB 791, which suggests that in contract there must be a serious possibility of the loss arising, whereas in the law of tort a slight risk of the loss is enough.)

5.9.2 THE CLAIMANT IS UNDER A DUTY TO MITIGATE THE LOSS

The general rule is that the claimant is required to take reasonable steps to reduce the loss and to avoid taking action which may increase the loss suffered (see *Payzu Ltd* v *Saunders* [1919] 2 KB 581 and *Banco de Portugal* v *Waterlow and Sons Ltd* [1932] AC 452). Where the effect of the mitigating act is to wipe out the loss from the breach, according to *British Westinghouse Co.* v *Underground Electric Railways Co. of London* [1912] AC 673 the claimant will be entitled to nominal damages only. (Note that no such duty arises in relation to claims for misrepresentation, see *Hussey* v *Eels* [1990] 2 QB 227.)

5.9.3 OTHER RESTRICTIONS ON THE RIGHT TO CLAIM DAMAGES

If the claimant saves the cost of performance as a result of the breach, these savings will be deducted from the overall award of damages, as will any sums of money earned from new employment in a claim for wrongful dismissal.

Loss which results purely from the claimant's own impecuniosity is generally irrecoverable (see *Owners of Dredger Liesbosch* v *Owners of Steamship Edison* [1933] AC 449). However, it would seem that if the claimant's impecuniosity prevents him from mitigating the loss, this will not affect the claim for damages (see *Perry* v *Sydney Phillips and Son* [1982] 1 WLR 1297 and *Alcoa Minerals of Jamaica* v *Broderick* [2000] 3 WLR 23).

Where a contract entitles the defendant to perform in a number of alternative ways, then it will be assumed that the defendant will choose to perform in the way most advantageous to him and damages will be assessed on that basis.

5.9.4 WHAT IS THE EFFECT OF CONTRIBUTORY NEGLIGENCE ON A CLAIM FOR DAMAGES FOR BREACH OF CONTRACT?

There are three classes of case:

(a) Those where liability arises both in contract and tort coextensively, in which case the Law Reform (Contributory Negligence) Act 1945 applies and damages will be reduced to take account of any contributory negligence on the part of the claimant (see *Forsikringsaktieselskapet Vesta* v *Butcher* [1989] AC 852).

(b) Those where the breach does not amount to a tort as well, in which case the 1945 Act does not apply and any contributory negligence on the part of the claimant can be disregarded (see *Lambert* v *Lewis* [1982] AC 225).

(c) Those where there is both strict liability in contract and coextensive liability in contract and tort. In such a case there can be no defence of contributory negligence (*Barclays Bank plc* v *Fairclough Building Ltd* [1995] 1 All ER 289).

5.9.5 WHEN IS INTEREST ON DAMAGES RECOVERABLE?

The Supreme Court Act (SCA) 1981, s. 35A and the County Courts Act (CCA) 1984, s. 69, give the court discretion to award interest on all or any part of damages for all or any part of the period from the date of the cause of action until the date of payment or judgment. If the contract itself fixes interest, the court has no power to fix any different rate. Any claim for interest must be mentioned specifically in the appropriate statement of case.

5.10 Other Remedies

5.10.1 ACTION FOR AN AGREED SUM

This remedy is available where there is a duty to pay the sum of money agreed and the action providing the right to claim exists. For example, the Sale of Goods Act 1979, s. 49, provides that an action for the price only arises once the property in the goods has passed to the buyer, even though the duty to pay arises as soon as the seller is willing and able to deliver.

If the injured party elects to affirm the contract, he can claim the agreed sum if all that is necessary has been done to make the action available or, arguably, if he can complete doing that which is necessary to make the action available (see *White & Carter (Councils) Ltd* v *McGregor* [1962] AC 413).

5.10.2 QUASI-CONTRACT — THE LAW OF RESTITUTION

Quasi-contract is sometimes described as an action for money had and received or unjust enrichment or benefit. This occurs: first 'where the claimant has been compelled to pay money for which the defendant is liable, he may sue the defendant for the money so paid' (*Cheshire, Fifoot and Furmston*, p. 631). Second, where money has been paid under a mistake which, had it been true, would have required the payment of the money. It is no longer necessary to distinguish a mistake of fact from a mistake of law (*Kleinwort Benson Ltd* v *Lincoln City Council* [1998] 4 All ER 513). Third, where money is paid where there has been a total failure of consideration or where money is paid in pursuance of a void contract. Money paid in pursuance of an illegal contract is rarely recoverable in quasi-contract. Fourth, where one party is bound to pay a sum of money to another and agrees to pay that money to a third party and has informed that third party of the intention to pay, that party is liable in quasi-contract to make the payment. Fifth, where a wrongful (tortious) act has been committed against the claimant who, as a consequence has suffered loss, the claimant may be entitled to recover for the loss in quasi-contract — where action can be brought in tort, the claims are alternatives to each other. Sixth, a claim to *quantum meruit* for reasonable remuneration for work done or services rendered where no price was fixed or where a new contract has been substituted for the old.

For an interesting analysis see *Rover International Ltd* v *Cannon Film Sales Ltd (No. 3)* [1989] 3 All ER 423. See also *Lipkin Gorman* v *Karpnale* [1991] AC 548 for an example of unjust enrichment.

This area is developing rapidly as a method by which redress can be sought. See *D.O. Ferguson and Associates* v *Sohl* (1992) 62 BLR 95.

SIX

DAMAGES IN TORT

6.1 Liability

To establish liability on the part of the defendant, in order to recover damages, a claimant must show:

(a) The elements of the tort.

(b) Causation.

(c) Loss and damage.

(d) Loss and damage not too remote.

6.1.1 ELEMENTS OF THE TORT

To go into the elements of all the various torts is beyond the scope of this chapter. Many, but not all, torts involve the breach of some duty owed by the defendant to the claimant, e.g., negligence, breach of statutory duty. Others involve the performance of some deliberate act calculated or likely to cause harm to the claimant, e.g., assault and battery, conversion, defamation. Yet others are torts of strict liability, e.g., *Rylands* v *Fletcher* liability, product liability. Whatever the elements of the tort may be, each of them must be made out.

6.1.2 CAUSATION

The claimant must show causation — that the tortious act caused his or her injury, loss or damage. It need not have been the sole cause. It is usual to apply the 'but for' test: the claimant must show that *but for* the defendant's tortious act he or she would not, on the balance of probabilities, have suffered the injury or loss. It may be sufficient in some circumstances to show that the tortious act increased the likelihood of damage occurring (*McGhee* v *National Coal Board* [1973] 1 WLR 1), but it must still have caused the injury on the balance of probabilities (*Kay* v *Ayrshire and Arran Health Board* [1987] 2 All ER 417). There is no claim in respect of a tortious act which has increased the likelihood of damage if it still would have occurred in any event on the balance of probabilities (*Hotson* v *Fitzgerald* [1987] AC 750).

Causation may be broken by a supervening act or event, in which case the claimant's claim will fail. The supervening act may come between the defendant's tortious act and damage, in which case the chain of causation may be broken altogether, but whether it is broken is a question of fact and degree. If the supervening act was reasonably foreseeable and/or made little difference to the chain of events, the chain is probably not broken. If, on the other hand, it was not reasonably foreseeable and was a wholly new event, the chain of causation may be broken even if the 'but for' test is still satisfied. If the supervening act was one which the defendant had a duty to prevent, then the chain of causation is not broken (*Reeves* v *Metropolitan Police Commissioner* [1999] 3 All ER 897). Alternatively, the supervening event may occur after the claimant has suffered damage, and its effect is to add to the claimant's damage. In such circumstances the question is whether the second event was natural, in which case causation is broken (*Jobling* v *Associated Dairies Ltd* [1982] AC 794), or whether it was a tortious act, in which case causation is not broken (*Baker* v *Willoughby* [1970] AC 467). The principle of *Baker* v *Willoughby*, that the second tortfeasor should be liable only for the additional harm caused to a claimant who had already been injured by the first tortfeasor, was upheld in *Murrell* v *Healy* [2001] 4 All ER 345, where the court had to consider what loss of earnings would have flowed from the first accident even though it had been superseded by the second accident which caused a complete loss of earnings.

Where the supervening event was brought on by a second tortious act, but was such that it might well have resulted in due course from the first tortious act, the second tortfeasor will not be fully liable for the consequences of the event; rather, a discount should be made (*Heil* v *Rankin*, *The Times*, 20 June 2000).

6.1.3 LOSS AND DAMAGE

The claimant must establish loss and damage in order to recover damages (with the exception of trespass to land, which is actionable without proof of loss). He or she does not, however, have to establish the extent of his or her loss, so long as he or she can prove it does exist: the court will then assess the damage as best it can. Difficulty of assessment is no bar to recovery. On this principle damages can be recovered for loss of a chance or opportunity.

There may, however, be some limitation in law as to the type of loss in respect of which damages can be recovered. The primary example is pure economic loss in negligence. Although the House of Lords ruled in *Junior Books Ltd* v *Veitchi & Co. Ltd* [1983] 1 AC 520 that there is no fundamental rule that pure economic loss is not recoverable, consistent lines of case law show that such loss is in most cases not recoverable in negligence (e.g., *Leigh & Sillavan Ltd* v *Aliakmon Shipping Co. Ltd* [1986] AC 785; *Peabody Donation Fund* v *Sir Lindsay Parkinson & Co. Ltd* [1985] AC 210). Even damage that at first sight appears to be damage to property may in fact be deemed pure economic loss (*D & F Estates Ltd* v *Church Commissioners* [1989] AC 177; *Murphy* v *Brentwood District Council* [1991] 1 AC 398). The major exception is economic loss resulting from negligent misstatement or negligent professional advice (*Hedley Byrne & Co. Ltd* v *Heller and Partners Ltd* [1964] AC 465; *Caparo Industries plc* v *Dickman* [1990] 2 AC 605; *Henderson* v *Merrett Syndicates Ltd* [1994] AC 145).

Nevertheless, it should not be thought that economic loss is not generally recoverable in tort as a whole. Many torts result solely or primarily in pure economic loss to the claimant: misrepresentation, deceit, procuring breach of contract, conspiracy, slander of title, slander of goods, conversion, breach of copyright, infringement of patent. In all these cases damages for pure economic loss may be recovered.

6.1.4 REMOTENESS

Broadly speaking, the test for remoteness in tort is reasonable foreseeability: it must have been reasonably foreseeable that the damage suffered by the claimant might result from the defendant's act. With what degree of likelihood is not entirely clear, but the cases tend to suggest only a slight degree of likelihood is required in tort, with rather more likelihood in contract (e.g., *H. Parsons (Livestock) Ltd* v *Uttley Ingham & Co. Ltd* [1978] QB 791).

It is not necessary that the precise damage suffered should have been foreseeable; the broad type of damage will suffice. It is not necessary that the damage should have come about in precisely the foreseeable manner. It is not necessary that the actual seriousness or quantum of damage should have been foreseeable. Reasonable foreseeability appears to be the correct test for all torts, except torts of strict liability and deceit (see **7.4.3**).

6.2 Quantum of Damages

6.2.1 COMPENSATORY NATURE OF DAMAGES

Damages in tort are compensatory in nature and are designed to put the claimant into the position he or she would have been in had the tort not been committed. This means that a claimant may prima facie receive damages both in respect of any loss directly caused by the tortious act and in respect of any consequential loss, provided the rules of causation and remoteness are satisfied.

6.2.2 TIME OF ASSESSMENT

Strictly speaking, damages are to be assessed at the date when damage occurs. This will frequently, but not necessarily, be the same as the date when the cause of action arose. However, courts are also bound to take account of all events which occur prior to trial, which would tend to suggest that damages should be valued as at the date of trial. This latter approach is adopted in cases of personal injury and death. In cases of damage to property and economic loss the courts seem to adopt a more discretionary and flexible approach. In *Dodd Properties (Kent) Ltd* v *Canterbury City Council* [1980] 1 All ER 928, it was held that damages for the cost of repair to property should be assessed at the date when it was reasonable for the claimant to undertake the repairs: this may be as late as the date of trial. The same result was achieved in *Alcoa Minerals of Jamaica* v *Broderick* [2000] 3 WLR 23.

6.2.3 MODE OF ASSESSMENT: GENERAL

The mode of assessing damages varies greatly according to the tort, the nature of the loss etc. Without considering each tort separately, one can nevertheless identify certain types of damage and consider how they are quantified in general terms:

(a) Personal injury.

(b) Economic loss consequent on injury or death.

(c) Other kinds of personal non-financial damage.

(d) Damage to property.

(e) Interference with property.

(f) Pure economic loss.

Most torts are capable of giving rise to several of these different types of damage all at once. There may be some special rules as to how each type of damage is to be quantified in respect of the particular tort that has caused it: reference should be made to specialist textbooks, e.g., *Clerk and Lindsell on Torts*; *McGregor on Damages*.

Personal injury and economic loss consequent on injury and death are dealt with in **Chapters 11** and **12**. This chapter will concentrate on the remaining four types of damage.

6.2.4 OTHER KINDS OF PERSONAL NON-FINANCIAL DAMAGE

This includes, for example, loss of liberty, mental distress, damage to reputation, and inconvenience and discomfort. It is not difficult to see how such damage may arise. Loss of liberty may result from false imprisonment, malicious prosecution, or negligence (see *Meah* v *McCreamer* [1985] 1 All ER 367). Mental distress, or injury to feelings, which amounts to suffering is a personal injury and is dealt with under that head. Mental distress that falls short of suffering (e.g., fear, grief and anguish) is prima facie not recoverable in tort but may be 'tacked on' to damages for defamation, malicious prosecution, assault, deceit and nuisance. Damage to reputation obviously results from defamation, but it can also result from defamation of goods, malicious prosecution, negligence, deceit, misrepresentation or breach of copyright. Inconvenience and discomfort can result from virtually any tort, and may be recoverable as a separate head where it does not overlap with loss of amenity.

Such losses are assessed with very little to go on but the judge's or jury's own intuitive judgment and comparison with awards in previous cases (so far as they can be ascertained), much as pain, suffering and loss of amenity are assessed in personal injury cases. Some observations can be made:

(a) Damages for loss of liberty, mental distress and inconvenience obviously overlap and may well be assessed together.

(b) Damages for injury to feelings involving mental distress are very similar to damages for pain and suffering and can be assessed in the same way.

(c) Damages for loss of reputation may be substantial in cases of defamation. In most other cases the loss of reputation may well be treated as future economic loss and assessed accordingly.

(d) Damages for inconvenience and discomfort (when not included in loss of amenity in a personal injury claim) are likely to amount to a modest sum.

6.2.5 DAMAGE TO PROPERTY

6.2.5.1 The two modes of assessing damages

Broadly speaking, wherever damage is done to the claimant's property a choice has to be made between two alternative modes of assessing damages. One is the cost of cure basis, i.e., awarding the claimant the cost of repairing the damaged property or replacing the destroyed property; the other is the diminution in value basis, i.e., awarding the claimant the value of the property destroyed or the difference between its value today and its value before it was damaged. There is no fixed rule as to which measure is correct; it depends on what is reasonable in all the circumstances. To recover damages for the cost of cure, the claimant must show that reinstatement of the damaged property, as opposed to the acquisition of a substitute, is what is required to make good his or her damage. He or she must show that he or she genuinely intends to reinstate and that it is reasonable to do so (subject to the duty to mitigate) (*Ruxley Electronics and Construction Ltd* v *Forsyth* [1996] 1 AC 344, HL).

6.2.5.2 Making the choice

Once the facts of a case are known it is not usually too difficult to make a choice. In the case of land, contrast the two cases mentioned above. In the case of goods, more than anything else the value of the chattel will be the deciding factor: a court, or an insurance company, will award whichever is the lesser of the cost of repairing a damaged motor car or its value just before it was damaged. Where property is kept for its value (e.g., a painting), damages will usually be limited to its value. Where property is kept for use (e.g., a ship), the claimant may well be able to recover its replacement cost (*Owners of Dredger Liesbosch* v *Owners of Steamship Edison* [1933] AC 449). However, a claimant whose working crane was destroyed was able to recover its resale value, not the cost of obtaining a replacement crane (*Southampton Container Terminals Ltd* v *Hansa Schiffahrts GmbH* [2001] 2 Lloyd's Rep 275). Where a chattel is merely damaged the choice may be three-way — cost of repairs, diminution in value, or cost of replacement less residual value. In such a case, particularly where the chattel is a ship, the decision depends on what is reasonable.

6.2.5.3 Consequential economic loss

Consequential economic loss can also usually be recovered. Where property is destroyed the claimant may recover damages for loss of its use until it is replaced: where it is damaged the claimant may recover damages for loss of its use while it is being repaired. This may include the cost of hiring an alternative, so long as this is reasonable.

Care must be taken where the chattel is a profit-earning chattel (e.g., a ship available for charter). If damages are awarded on a cost of repair or replacement basis, then an additional sum can be recovered for loss of profit in the interim. But if damages are assessed on the basis of its market value at the date of destruction, this value would include its profit-earning potential and so damages cannot be awarded for loss of profit as well (though there have been cases where damages in respect of loss of profit on fixed future engagements have been recovered). If a profit-earning building is destroyed, similar care must be taken to avoid double recovery (see *Dominion Mosaics and Tile Co. Ltd* v *Trafalgar Trucking Co. Ltd* [1990] 2 All ER 246).

6.2.5.4 Negligent valuation of property

In cases of negligent survey reports, on the basis of which the claimant has bought property at a price above what he or she would have paid if the report were correct, the measure of damages is diminution in value, not cost of cure. The claimant can recover the difference between the price he or she paid and the actual value of the property, but not the cost of repairs, even if he or she has reasonably carried out those repairs (*Watts* v *Morrow* [1991] 1 WLR 1421). Consequential expenses may however be recovered (*Patel* v *Hooper & Jackson* [1999] 1 All ER 992).

6.2.6 INTERFERENCE WITH PROPERTY

6.2.6.1 Goods

Loss caused by interference with goods arises particularly in cases of conversion and trespass. If the claimant has been permanently deprived of goods, damages will be assessed on the same alternative bases as if they were destroyed: the claimant may either recover the value of the goods lost, or the cost of replacing them, whichever is reasonable. He or she may also recover consequential damages for loss of use. If the deprivation is temporary, damages are likely to be simply for loss of use. The rules of mitigation may well require the claimant to replace lost goods within a reasonable time in order to minimise loss. If he or she does not do so because he or she cannot afford to, the full loss may not be recovered (*Owners of Dredger Liesbosch* v *Owners of Steamship Edison* [1933] AC 449 — a much criticised decision which has been distinguished, arguably ignored, wherever possible: see, for example, *Alcoa Minerals of Jamaica* v *Broderick* [2000] 3 WLR 23).

The date of assessment is also within the court's discretion. The general rule, re-affirmed in *BBMB Finance (Hong Kong) Ltd* v *Eda Holdings Ltd* [1990] 1 WLR 409 is that the value of goods lost is to be assessed at the date of loss or conversion. However the rule is not absolute, and in other cases, particularly where damages are being awarded under the Torts (Interference with Goods) Act 1977, s. 3, as an alternative to return of the goods, a later date may be appropriate (*IBL Ltd* v *Coussens* [1991] 2 All ER 133).

6.2.6.2 Land

Where the case involves trespass to land, damages are recoverable without proof of loss. If the claimant can show financial loss deriving from the loss of use of his or her land, damages are likely to be assessed on that basis. Otherwise they may be assessed on the basis of what would have been a fair rent for the land (*Swordheath Properties Ltd* v *Tabet* [1979] 1 WLR 285) or a fair sum for granting an easement (*Bracewell* v *Appleby* [1975] Ch 408). Where a nuisance has caused loss of enjoyment of land damages are likely to be assessed on a loss of amenity basis. If the nuisance cannot be stopped by injunction, damages in lieu may well be quantified on a diminution in value basis.

6.2.7 PURE ECONOMIC LOSS

Pure economic loss is by nature measurable, even if only with difficulty, and so can be quantified on a financial basis. Where there is an element of future loss, a degree of informed speculation may be required. Some of the possible approaches to this are dealt with in **Chapter 11**. It may also be necessary for a court to quantify a chance in order to award damages for lost opportunity.

6.3 Reduction of Damages

6.3.1 CONTRIBUTORY NEGLIGENCE

6.3.1.1 Statutory basis

The power of the court to reduce damages to take account of the claimant's contributory negligence derives from the Law Reform (Contributory Negligence) Act 1945, s. 1(1), which reads:

> *Where any person suffers damage as a result partly of his own fault and partly of the fault of any other person or persons, a claim in respect of that damage shall not be defeated by reason of the fault of the person suffering the damage, but damages recoverable in respect thereof shall be reduced to such extent as the court thinks just and equitable having regard to the claimant's share in the responsibility for the damage.*

'Fault' is defined in s. 4 as:

> *negligence, breach of statutory duty, or other act or omission which gives rise to a liability in tort or would, apart from this Act, give rise to the defence of contributory negligence.*

Contributory negligence is therefore a partial defence, and accordingly a factor which reduces damages where the claim is made in tort. It appears to be applicable to all torts, except deceit (see **7.6**) and conversion (Torts (Interference with Goods) Act 1977, s. 11). Contributory negligence is for the defendant to raise and prove. Once established, the court is obliged to apportion responsibility in some way.

6.3.1.2 Apportionment of responsibility

How apportionment is to be made is entirely within the court's discretion and depends on the facts of each case. The court will take into account not only negligence by the claimant which was a partial cause of the accident, but also negligence which was a partial cause of the injury, or which exacerbated the injury (such as failure to wear a seat belt). It is not just the extent to which the claimant caused his or her own injury that is relevant, but the extent to which he or she is blameworthy. Two claimants, both injured in the same accident and both guilty of the same omission, may not necessarily have to bear the same degree of responsibility for their own injury. The more culpable the defendant, the less responsibility on the claimant's part.

What is being measured is the extent to which the claimant is responsible for his or her own damage as opposed to anyone else. So if, for example, the claimant and two companions lawfully enter the defendant's premises, where the claimant is injured as a result of negligence attributable partly to the defendant, partly to his or her own companions and partly to himself or herself, it is nonsense to say contributory negligence cannot be more than 25% simply because three other people are involved. Contributory negligence may be 50% or more. In *Fitzgerald* v *Lane* [1989] AC 328 the judge found the claimant and two defendants in a road accident 'all three equally at fault', and assessed damages on the basis of one-third contributory negligence. The House of Lords held that the judge's finding of fact meant that contributory negligence was 50% as against each defendant.

6.3.1.3 The form of assessment

Contributory negligence is always assessed as a percentage or fraction and is a round number, e.g., 20%, 25% (one-quarter), one-third, 40%, one-half etc. The normal minimum is 10% — anything below that is likely to be ignored by the court.

6.3.2 APPORTIONMENT OF LIABILITY

6.3.2.1 Apportionment between two defendants

Where a court has found two defendants to be liable to the claimant, or when the defendant has successfully claimed a contribution from a third party, a decision has to be made as to what proportion of the claimant's damages each should pay.

It must be remembered, however, that liability in tort is joint and several. So if the court holds two defendants equally liable, either of them is liable for 100% of the claimant's loss and will have to pay the full amount if the other cannot. But if both defendants are able to pay, the court will apportion damages as it sees fit, considering the different degrees of fault, blameworthiness and causation. If there is more than one claimant, apportionment may be different in respect of each claimant (see, for example, *Wright* v *Lodge* [1993] 4 All ER 299).

6.3.2.2 Apportionment between two defendants and a claimant

Care needs to be taken in the apportionment of liability between defendants when there has also been a finding of contributory negligence by the claimant. The proportion of contributory negligence must be dealt with first, and only then is apportionment made between the defendants. That is why the net result in *Fitzgerald* v *Lane* [1989] AC 328 (see **6.3.1.2**) was that the claimant had to bear 50% of his or her loss himself or herself, and each defendant was liable for 25%.

If a court holds the claimant 10% to blame and apportions liability two-thirds to the first defendant and one-third to the second defendant, the first defendant will pay 60% of the claimant's loss (i.e., two-thirds of 90%) and the second defendant will pay 30%.

If a court holds the claimant 20% to blame and the second defendant 25% to blame, the second defendant will pay 20% of the claimant's loss (i.e., one-quarter of 80%). Similarly if a court orders a third party to make a 25% contribution.

Sometimes a court apportions liability between the parties in such a way as to produce a total of 100%. If, for example, the court holds the claimant 10% to blame, the defendant 50% and the third party 40%, the claimant will recover 90% of his or her loss from the defendant, who will then receive a contribution of four-ninths from the third party.

6.3.2.3 Apportionment between two causes

Where the claimant's injury is the result of more than one cause, and he claims against a defendant who can be shown to be liable for some, but not all of that injury, then the court must make an apportionment, attempting to assess what proportion of the claimant's injury the defendant can be said to be responsible for. This may be a difficult task, but it must be undertaken as best it can (*Holtby* v *Brigham & Cowan (Hull) Ltd* [2000] 3 All ER 421).

6.3.3 MITIGATION

6.3.3.1 The positive requirement

The claimant has a duty to mitigate. This does not mean that he or she is required to minimise his or her loss at all costs, rather that he or she must take all reasonable steps to do so. If the claimant fails to do what he or she could reasonably have done to minimise his or her loss, damages will be assessed on the basis of what the loss would have been had he or she taken those reasonable steps. Any reasonable expense incurred in order to be able to mitigate may be recovered as damages. Indeed, if it was reasonable for the claimant to incur that expense in an attempt to mitigate, it will be recoverable even if, in fact, no mitigation is achieved.

6.3.3.2 The negative requirement

The claimant is also under a duty not to do anything unreasonable subsequent to the damage which might exacerbate it, and not to incur any unreasonable expense which increases the extent of his or her loss. If he or she does so, damages will be assessed on the basis of what the loss would have been had he or she not taken that action or incurred that expense. However, a claimant is not deemed to have the benefit of hindsight: the test is simply whether it was reasonable for the claimant to have behaved as he or she did at the time.

6.3.3.3 The test is subjective

When dealing with mitigation the courts apply the test of what is reasonable subjectively, i.e., the question is whether it was reasonable for this claimant in all the circumstances to have behaved as he or she did, not whether a reasonable person would have behaved in that way. The courts are particularly lenient in cases of personal injury. There is a willingness, for example, to hold that it is reasonable for the parents of an injured child to give up their jobs in order to stay at home to care for their child, even though their financial loss would have been far less had they employed a nurse and a nanny.

6.3.4 INTEREST ON DAMAGES

Interest can be awarded on damages recovered in tort under SCA 1981, s. 35A. By s. 35A(1), the award of interest is discretionary; but it becomes prima facie mandatory in cases of personal injury and death, unless there are special reasons why it should not be awarded (s. 35A(2)). Because of this there are particular rules for claims for personal injury (see **11.16**) and fatal accidents (see **12.2.6** and **12.9**).

In other cases, both the rate of interest and the period for which it is awarded are within the court's discretion. However, the discretion to award interest is generally exercised in cases of financial loss; the rate will usually be based on current market rates — the usual maximum being the current Judgments Act 1838 rate. The period will usually be date of loss to date of trial.

6.4 Exemplary Damages

Exemplary, or punitive, damages can be awarded in tort in the three situations laid down in *Rookes* v *Barnard* [1964] AC 1129, and confirmed in *Cassell & Co. Ltd* v *Broome* [1972] AC 1027. These are:

(a) Where there has been oppressive or unconstitutional action by the servants of the government. These can include, for example, civil servants, politicians, local government officers, county councillors, and the police.

(b) Where the defendant's conduct has been calculated to make a profit which may well exceed the compensation payable to the claimant. This is not confined to strictly financial profit, but may include other benefits, e.g., the eviction of a tenant.

(c) Where such damages are expressly authorised by statute. There do not appear to be any major examples of this.

Exemplary damages are recoverable for trespass, false imprisonment, malicious prosecution, assault, defamation, private nuisance, interference with business, intimidation, misfeasance in public office and possibly breach of copyright, but not for negligence, public nuisance, breach of statutory duty or deceit. The view that exemplary damages were strictly limited to those torts for which they had been held recoverable before *Rookes* v *Barnard* is incorrect (see *Kuddus* v *Chief Constable of Leicestershire Constabulary* [2001] 3 All ER 193 (which added misfeasance in public office to the above list)).

The quantum of exemplary damages, where awarded, is highly arbitrary and within the discretion of the judge or jury. However, the defendant's means must be taken into account.

In *Thompson* v *Commissioner of Police of the Metropolis* [1997] 2 All ER 762 the House of Lords laid down some ground rules for cases involving misconduct by the police. The judge must give the jury guidance with regard to quantum, and indicate a range for exemplary damages of £5,000 to £50,000.

6.5 Aggravated Damages

Aggravated damages can be awarded in a case of malicious falsehood (see *Khodaparast* v *Shad* [2000] 1 All ER 545). Such damages go beyond merely compensating the claimant for loss, but include an element of damages for injury to feelings caused by the defendant's conduct and malicious intent.

SEVEN

LIABILITY AND DAMAGES FOR MISREPRESENTATION

7.1 General

The law provides remedies in certain situations where one person has made a false representation to another who has then acted to his or her detriment in reliance upon that representation. This will usually, but not invariably, mean that the representee has entered into a contract with the representor. It will also usually, but not invariably, mean that the representee has suffered loss.

Remedies are available at common law, in equity and by statute. An action may be brought in some circumstances in tort and in other circumstances in contract. The remedies available are damages and rescission. The historical development of the law has resulted in substantial overlap between the actions and remedies available.

7.2 What Makes a Misrepresentation Actionable?

Various conditions must be satisfied to make a misrepresentation actionable:

(a) There must be a statement made by the representor or his or her agent. The statement may be oral or written, or by conduct. It may be express or implied.

(b) The statement must be a statement of fact, past or present, as opposed to a statement of opinion, intention or law (but see **7.3.6**). However, it is not always possible to draw a clear dividing line, and what may at first sight appear to be a statement of opinion or intention can sometimes be shown to be a statement of fact. Silence can amount to a representation.

(c) The representation must be made to the representee, directly or indirectly, or to a class of which the representee is a member. This class may be the public at large.

(d) The representee must reasonably have been induced by the representation or reasonably acted in reliance upon it, believing it to be true. The representation need not be the only inducement. Once this is established, no further element of causation is required (*Downs* v *Chappell* [1996] 3 All ER 344). The result will usually be that the representee has entered into a contract.

(e) The representor must either have intended the representee to act upon the statement, or at least the facts must be such that he or she ought to have realised that the representee might do so.

(f) The representation must be false. No more is prima facie required. Whether the misrepresentation was fraudulent, negligent or innocent affects the cause of action and remedy available.

7.3 The Causes of Action Available

There are six causes of action available with regard to misrepresentation.

7.3.1 DECEIT

This is a tortious action, available where the misrepresentation was made fraudulently. The definition of fraud is laid down by *Derry* v *Peek* (1889) 14 App Cas 337: the defendant must have made the representation knowing it to be false, or not believing it to be true, or with reckless dishonesty, not caring whether it was true or false (see *Thomas Witter Ltd* v *TBP Industries Ltd* [1996] 2 All ER 573). It is enough that the claimant has acted in reliance upon the representation — no contract is necessary. The remedies available are:

(a) Rescission, if the claimant has been induced to enter into a contract.

(b) Damages, if the claimant has suffered loss.

(c) Both rescission *and* damages, if appropriate.

7.3.2 STATUTORY MISREPRESENTATION

This is a tortious action under the Misrepresentation Act 1967, s. 2(1) where the misrepresentation was made negligently. The claimant need show only that the representation was false, that he or she entered into a contract in reliance on it, and that he or she suffered loss thereby. The burden of proof then shifts onto the defendant to show (if possible) that he or she reasonably believed the representation to be true, both when it was made and at the time the contract was made. The remedy is damages.

7.3.3 MISREPRESENTATION IN EQUITY

This is an action for rescission of the contract, available in cases of fraudulent, negligent or innocent misrepresentation, whether or not the representation has become a term of the contract (MA 1967, s. 1(a)). The claimant need show only that he or she entered into a contract in reliance on the defendant's misrepresentation. The remedy is rescission, but the court can award damages in lieu of rescission (MA 1967, s. 2(2)).

7.3.4 BREACH OF CONTRACT

This is available as a cause of action where the representation has become a term of the contract. Whether it has done so is a question of fact. Breach of contract is proved by showing the representation to be false. The remedy is damages.

7.3.5 BREACH OF COLLATERAL WARRANTY

This cause of action arises where the representation was of contractual effect, but did not become a term of the contract, usually because the representation was oral and the contract written. There is then an implied collateral contract: in consideration of the warranty made by the representor, the representee agreed to enter into the main contract. The remedy is damages.

7.3.6 NEGLIGENT MISSTATEMENT

This is a common law action in negligence following *Hedley Byrne & Co. Ltd* v *Heller and Partners Ltd* [1964] AC 465. The claimant must prove the existence of a duty of care, breach of the duty (negligence) and loss. This cause of action will usually arise, but not necessarily so, when there is *no* contract between the claimant and defendant, though the loss usually flows from a contract between the claimant and a third party.

The scope of negligent misstatement is somewhat wider than negligent misrepresentation and may include not just misstatement of fact, but also the giving of negligent opinions and advice. The remedy is damages.

7.4 Damages

The measure of damages is subject to different principles and is likely to vary according to the cause of action giving rise to the remedy. There is, however, a fundamental distinction between tortious and contractual damages.

7.4.1 DAMAGES IN TORT

Tortious damages are designed to put the claimant into the position in which he or she would have been had the tort not been committed. Where the tortious act is the making of a misrepresentation, then damages are designed to put him or her in the position he or she would have been in had the misrepresentation not been made. What that position is, is a question of fact, but the courts will usually assume that the claimant would not have entered into the contract, and so damages will put him or her into the position in which he or she would have been had the contract never been made.

Broadly speaking, therefore, the claimant can recover the contract price and any consequential loss, but not loss of bargain — the profit he or she would have made on the contract if the misrepresentation had been true. From the contract price must be deducted the value today of any property the claimant has received under the contract. The damages are the difference between what the claimant paid and what he or she has left now (as opposed to what he or she actually got for his or her money at the time: *Naughton* v *O'Callaghan* [1990] 3 All ER 191). Where but for the misrepresentation the claimant would still have entered into a contract but at a lower price, the damages are the difference between what was paid and what would have been paid.

7.4.2 DAMAGES IN CONTRACT

Contractual damages are designed to put the claimant into the position in which he or she would have been had the contract not been breached. Where the breach of contract consists of the representation being false, then damages are designed to put him or her into the position in which he or she would have been had the representation been true.

Broadly speaking, therefore, the claimant can recover damages for loss of bargain and any consequential loss, but not the contract price. Damages for loss of bargain are the difference between what was promised and what was actually received. In many cases this will result in greater damages than in tort, but not where the contract in fact would have resulted in a bad bargain for the claimant, or where the rules of remoteness would limit contractual damages to a greater extent than tortious damages.

7.4.3 DAMAGES FOR DECEIT

These will be assessed on tortious principles (*Doyle* v *Olby (Ironmongers) Ltd* [1969] 2 QB 158). The damages are therefore designed to compensate the claimant for his or her loss flowing from the fraudulent representation and to put him or her into the position he or she would have been in if the deceit had not been committed, rather than if the representation had been true, so lost profits will not normally be recoverable. However, the claimant can recover damages in respect of the profit he or she would have made elsewhere had he or she not been the victim of the deceit (see *East* v *Maurer* [1991] 2 All ER 733). If as a result of the deceit the claimant has entered into a profitable contract with the defendant, but if there had been no fraudulent misrepresentation would have entered into an even more profitable contract, then he or she can still claim the difference between the profit he or she would have made and the profit he or she has in fact made (*Clef Aquitaine* v *Laporte Materials (Barrow) Ltd* [2000] 3 All ER 493).

However, the remoteness test of reasonable foreseeability does not apply. A claimant is entitled to recover all loss directly flowing from the deceit, including consequential loss, whether or not it was foreseeable. The quantum will be what is required to compensate the claimant for the deceit, even if some part of the loss is loss that might have been sustained even if there had been no deceit (see *Smith New Court Securities Ltd* v *Scrimgeour Vickers (Asset Management) Ltd* [1997] 4 All ER 769).

The measure of damages where the deceit has deprived the claimant of his or her property is the value of the property, not the cost of replacing it (*Smith Kline & French Laboratories Ltd* v *Long* [1988] 3 All ER 887).

7.4.4 DAMAGES UNDER MA 1967, S. 2(1)

After some initial doubt, it is now clear that these will be assessed on tortious principles, since they are akin to damages for deceit (*André & Cie SA* v *Michel Blanc et Fils* [1977] 2 Lloyd's Rep 166; *Sharneyford Supplies Ltd* v *Edge* [1986] Ch 128). It has also been established that damages under s. 2(1) are not subject to a test of reasonable foreseeability, but are recoverable on the same basis as damages for deceit (*Royscot Trust Ltd* v *Rogerson* [1991] 2 QB 297).

7.4.5 DAMAGES FOR BREACH OF CONTRACT OR BREACH OF COLLATERAL WARRANTY

These will be assessed according to contractual principles, applying the remoteness rule in contract (*Hadley* v *Baxendale* (1854) 9 Ex 341; *Heron II* [1969] 1 AC 350), which, if anything, is somewhat stricter than the rule in tort (*H. Parsons (Livestock) Ltd* v *Uttley Ingham & Co. Ltd* [1978] QB 791).

7.4.6 DAMAGES FOR NEGLIGENT MISSTATEMENT

These will be assessed according to tortious principles at common law and will depend on the scope of the duty under *Hedley Byrne* v *Heller* and the reasonable foreseeability test.

7.4.7 DAMAGES IN LIEU OF RESCISSION UNDER MA 1967, S. 2(2)

Damages in lieu of rescission are in the discretion of the court, apparently irrespective of the wishes of either party. The option is available whenever the innocent party could have rescinded the contract at some time after it was made, not only if the remedy remains available at the time of the court's order (*Thomas Witter Ltd* v *TBP Industries Ltd* [1996] 2 All ER 573).

The measure of damages under s. 2(2) also appears to be within the court's discretion, but on a strict reading of the Act it seems likely that damages will be simply alternative to rescission, i.e., the tortious measure of what is sufficient to return the claimant to his or her pre-contractual position, and may not even include any consequential loss, which will have to be recovered, if possible, under s. 2(1) or for breach of contract. There is no sound authority on this issue.

7.5 Rescission

7.5.1 WHEN IS RESCISSION FOR MISREPRESENTATION AVAILABLE?

Rescission is available as a remedy, in principle at least, wherever the representee has been induced by the representation to enter into a contract, even if the representation has become a term of the contract (MA 1967, s. 1(a)). However, rescission, being an equitable remedy, is within the court's discretion, and the court has a further discretion to award damages in lieu of rescission.

7.5.2 THE 'RIGHT' TO RESCIND

Rescission is not simply a remedy granted by the court. Where a representee has a 'right' to rescind (i.e., the circumstances have arisen in which a court would have the discretion to order rescission), he or she may do so by giving notice of this to the representor. It may then not be necessary to apply to the court at all, though the court's assistance may be required to enforce rescission.

7.5.3 WHAT DOES RESCISSION INVOLVE?

Rescission simply involves putting the parties into the position they were in before the contract was made, with the repayment of the contract price and the return of goods, if appropriate.

7.5.4 BARS TO RESCISSION

The court's discretion to order rescission will not be exercised where any of the bars to rescission have arisen. The main bars are:

(a) Where *restitutio in integrum* is no longer possible.

(b) Where the claimant has affirmed the contract.

(c) Where a third party has acquired an interest in the subject matter of the contract.

(d) Where there has been an unreasonable lapse of time.

The bars to rescission are dealt with more fully in **8.3.5**.

7.6 Contributory Negligence

In cases of misrepresentation, the question sometimes arises whether a defendant will be liable if the claimant could, with reasonable diligence, have discovered the falsity of the representation and could reasonably have been expected to do so. In the case of fraudulent misrepresentation, this is no defence (*Alliance & Leicester Building Society* v *Edgestop Ltd* [1994] 2 All ER 38). It must follow that the position is the same where a claim is made under MA 1967, s. 2(1), on the basis of *Royscot Trust Ltd* v *Rogerson* [1991] 2 QB 297.

However, where there is concurrent liability in negligence at common law and under MA 1967 s. 2(1), damages under both heads may be reduced for the claimant's contributory negligence (*Gran Gelato Ltd* v *Richcliff (Group) Ltd* [1992] Ch 560, applying the same rule as that established for concurrent liability in tort and contract in *Forsikringsaktieselskapet Vesta* v *Butcher* [1986] 2 All ER 488).

For breach of contract contributory negligence is no defence. In negligence, at common law, contributory negligence is in principle available as a defence. But it must be remembered that the duty under *Hedley Byrne & Co. Ltd* v *Heller and Partners Ltd* [1964] AC 465 arises only where it was reasonably foreseeable that the claimant would rely on the defendant's statement, and it would be odd in such circumstances to hold that the claimant was at fault in relying upon it: see, for example, *Gran Gelato* v *Richcliff*.

7.7 Exclusion of Liability for Misrepresentation

Any contract term which purports to exclude or restrict liability for misrepresentation or limit the remedy available is of no effect, unless it satisfies the reasonableness test in UCTA, s. 11 (MA 1967, s. 3, as amended).

EIGHT

EQUITABLE REMEDIES IN CONTRACT

8.1 Introduction

In contract cases, and in particular for breach of contract, the primary remedy is damages. However, there are in certain situations a range of equitable remedies available, both to remedy a breach of contract and to enforce contractual rights. Three are dealt with in this section: specific performance, rescission, and rectification. They have certain features in common Injunctions are of particular importance and have a chapter to themselves (**Chapter 9**).

(a) *Equitable remedies are discretionary.*
Equitable remedies are not available as of right: they will only be granted in the exercise of the court's discretion in accordance with certain well-established principles.

(b) *Common law remedies must be inadequate.*
An equitable remedy will be granted only if damages would not in all the circumstances of the case be an adequate remedy for the claimant.

(c) *The maxims of equity apply.*
The famous maxims 'You must come to equity with clean hands' and 'Equity does not act in vain' are to be taken seriously. The court will not exercise its discretion in favour of a claimant who is himself or herself in breach of contract, or grant an injunction which could never be enforced.

8.2 Specific Performance

8.2.1 WHAT IS SPECIFIC PERFORMANCE?

Specific performance is an order requiring a party to a contract to perform or complete the performance of his or her obligations under the contract. The effect of the order is therefore to put the parties into the position they would have been in had the contract been performed, and it is the equitable equivalent of damages in respect of the claimant's expectation loss.

The remedy is discretionary, but the circumstances in which it will or will not be granted are to a considerable extent certain. Rather than attempting to define when specific performance will be granted, the courts have defined the bars to the granting of an order, and tend to approach the exercise of discretion negatively: if there is nothing *against* the making of an order, it will be made. There are numerous possible bars, the most important of which is designed to prevent the common law remedy of damages and the equitable remedy of specific performance overlapping.

8.2.2 ADEQUACY OF DAMAGES

8.2.2.1 Basic rule

The first and principal hurdle for a claimant to overcome is to show that *damages would not be an adequate remedy*. In most cases, damages are adequate and so specific performance will not be ordered. In order to show that they are not adequate, the claimant will usually have to demonstrate either the uniqueness of the thing contracted for, and/or the financial ineffectiveness of damages.

8.2.2.2 Uniqueness

Contracts, broadly speaking, are for the sale of property or the performance of services.

In contracts for the sale of property, the adequacy of damages may well depend on the uniqueness of the thing which the claimant contracted to buy. It may be unique either because there is no other thing in existence like it, or because, however ordinary the thing is, the claimant if awarded damages would be unable to obtain another thing like it from anywhere else.

Commodities and shares are usually considered not to be unique; they are readily available on the market. So, a contract for the sale of shares will not be specifically enforced (*Cuddee* v *Rutter* (1720) 1 P Wms 570) because damages would enable the claimant to buy other identical shares. But it would be different if substitute shares were not available (e.g., where the breach deprived a claimant of a majority shareholding) (*Harvela Investments Ltd* v *Royal Trust Co. of Canada (CI) Ltd* [1986] AC 207).

Land is, on the other hand, considered unique, however ordinary a simple house and garden may appear to be, and contracts for the sale of land are routinely enforced by specific performance. This tradition is so deeply rooted that the remedy may be regarded as virtually automatic, unless any of the other bars arises.

Goods and chattels fall somewhere in the middle of the uniqueness spectrum. Ordinary goods are not unique and specific performance will not be granted where substitutes can readily be obtained. But if the goods have some special or rare quality, an order may be granted: however, the courts are reluctant to recognise sentimental value as rendering goods unique. Ordinary goods may become unique if in all the circumstances no substitute can in fact be obtained: in *Sky Petroleum Ltd* v *VIP Petroleum Ltd* [1974] 1 WLR 576 an order was made requiring the defendants to deliver petrol to the claimants at a time of petrol shortage. Section 52 of the Sale of Goods Act 1979 gives the court a discretion to order specific performance of a contract for the sale of specific or ascertained goods, but does not seem in effect to have made such orders any more common than they would have been at common law.

Contracts for the performance of services are likely to be unique only where there is a personal service involved, in which case they are unlikely to be enforced for other reasons (see **8.2.3.4**). Where the services could be performed by anyone, damages are likely to be an adequate remedy.

8.2.2.3 Financial ineffectiveness

There are various ways in which damages may not provide effective compensation, but that fact does not necessarily mean that the court will deem damages to be an inadequate remedy.

The fact that damages would be difficult to assess does not necessarily mean that damages would be an inadequate remedy. Older cases accepted the idea that difficulty in assessment of damages should point towards specific performance being granted, but later cases have shown reluctance on the part of the courts to follow this line. In this respect courts are more lenient in granting injunctions than specific performance.

The defendant's inability to pay may be a relevant consideration.

Damages may not be adequate where the defendant's obligation is a continuing one, lasting beyond the date of judgment, such that an award of damages now will only compensate the claimant for his or her loss so far and a further action might be required in the future.

Where damages, if awarded, would be purely nominal, they may be considered to be an inadequate remedy, on the ground that specific performance would in such circumstances be the more appropriate remedy (e.g., *Beswick* v *Beswick* [1968] AC 58).

Although a contract requiring the defendant to pay money will normally not be specifically enforceable, because damages would be an adequate remedy, *Beswick* v *Beswick* shows that it may be enforceable where payment is to be made to a third party or where the payment is in the form of an annuity or other periodical payment, which is a continuing obligation.

8.2.3 OTHER BARS

8.2.3.1 Contracts requiring supervision

Traditionally, the court would not order specific performance where the enforcement of the order would require the court's constant supervision (e.g., *Ryan* v *Mutual Tontine Association* [1893] 1 Ch 116). More recent authority suggests that this principle is exaggerated (e.g., *Posner* v *Scott-Lewis* [1987] Ch 25).

Arguably, the difficulty of supervision is no longer a bar to specific performance, but rather a factor going to the court's discretion (*Tito* v *Waddell (No. 2)* [1977] Ch 106). It may be that the need for supervision, even constant supervision, will not prevent specific performance being granted where it is important to protect the claimant's interest and where it is clear from the contract and/or order what the defendant is required to do.

8.2.3.2 Contract too vague

Specific performance will not be granted where the terms of the contract are so vague that it is impossible for the order to state exactly what the defendant is required to do, or for the defendant to know what should be done to comply with the order, or for the court to say whether the defendant has complied with the order or is in contempt.

8.2.3.3 Building contracts

The court will not normally make an order requiring a builder to erect or complete a building, on three grounds:

(a) Damages would be adequate if another builder could do the work.

(b) It is likely to be difficult to specify exactly what the builder must do.

(c) Constant supervision may be required.

However, in modern conditions, particularly where the contract is in a detailed form, specific performance may be granted if three conditions are satisfied:

(a) The work is precisely defined by the contract.

(b) Damages will not adequately compensate the claimant.

(c) The defendant is in possession of the land on which the building is to be done (*Wolverhampton Corporation* v *Emmons* [1901] 1 QB 515; *Carpenters Estates* v *Davies* [1940] Ch 160).

8.2.3.4 Contracts involving personal services

It is well established that the court will not order specific performance of a contract involving personal services, or service contracts which are personal in nature. The prime example is the contract of employment. With regard to the employee's services, the rule is now statutory and absolute (Trade Union and Labour Relations (Consolidation) Act 1992, s. 236). In all other circumstances the rule remains discretionary, but is nevertheless well entrenched. The rule applies not only to contracts of personal service in the strict sense, but also to contracts involving the performance of services of a personal nature.

The greater the personal element involved in the contract, the less likely it is that specific performance will be ordered. However, the rule is not absolute and the courts are unwilling to make it so (e.g., *C.H. Giles & Co. Ltd* v *Morris* [1972] 1 WLR 307). Modern conditions of employment may make it possible for an employee to get an order against an employer (*Hill* v *C.A. Parsons & Co. Ltd* [1972] Ch 305). Where the contract requires the performance of services which are not personal in nature, there is no bar, even if the services are to be performed by a particular individual.

8.2.3.5 Contracts to carry on a business

The court will not normally specifically enforce a contract in such a way as to require a person to carry on a business. This long-standing principle was recently affirmed by the House of Lords in *Co-operative Insurance Society Ltd* v *Argyll Stores (Holdings) Ltd* [1997] 3 All ER 297. This will be so even where damages may strictly not be an adequate remedy. The original reason was because such an order would require the constant supervision of the court, but it probably exists now as a principle in its own right, justified on the basis that it is against the public interest to require someone to carry on a busines at a loss if a plausible alternative exists.

8.2.3.6 Equity will not act in vain

Specific performance will not be granted where it would be in vain to do so, for example, where once the order was made the defendant could still lawfully terminate the contract at any time (*Sheffield Gas Consumers Co.* v *Harrison* (1853) 17 Beav 294); or where the defendant would be incapable of fulfilling his or her obligations (*Castle* v *Wilkinson* (1870) LR 5 Ch App 534).

8.2.3.7 Coming to equity with clean hands

A claimant will not be granted specific performance of a contract unless he or she has performed all his or her obligations under the contract hitherto and remains ready and willing to perform any future obligations. This willingness must be pleaded and proved. A claimant who is himself or herself in breach of contract will not normally be granted specific performance of it, though this bar may not arise if the breach is trivial (*Dyster* v *Randall and Sons* [1926] Ch 932). How clean the claimant's hands are is a matter of the court's judgment and goes to its discretion.

8.2.3.8 Delay

There is no statutory limitation period barring claims for specific performance, but unreasonable delay will amount to a bar in equity. This is known as the *doctrine of laches*, and is again a matter of the court's discretion. How long a delay is unreasonable depends on the facts of the case, but in most circumstances not long is allowed. It was generally thought that one year was the upper limit for most cases, but this may be too strict. A delay of over two years was held not unreasonable in *Lazard Bros* v *Fairfield Properties* (1977) 121 SJ 893.

8.2.3.9 Want of mutuality

The doctrine of mutuality traditionally required an order for specific performance to be refused against a defendant where the defendant could not have enforced the contract by specific performance against the claimant. However, it is now clear that the doctrine can be waived by the court, which must judge mutuality at the time of judgment as opposed to the time of the contract (*Price* v *Strange* [1978] Ch 337).

8.2.3.10 Hardship

Specific performance will be refused where it would cause severe hardship to the defendant. This is simply part of the court's overriding discretion to refuse specific performance where it would be unjust to grant it. However, in a case of hardship, the hardship must be severe, not be brought about by the defendant's own acts, and lead to injustice. See, for example, *Patel* v *Ali* [1984] Ch 283.

8.2.3.11 Contract only partly specifically enforceable

Where the court cannot grant specific performance of the contract as a whole, it will not grant specific performance only of that part of the contract which is specifically enforceable (*Ryan* v *Mutual Tontine Association* [1893] 1 Ch 116). However, where a contract can be divided into one or more separate agreements, one part of the contract can be specifically enforced while the others are not.

8.2.4 DAMAGES IN LIEU OF SPECIFIC PERFORMANCE

Damages originally obtainable in lieu of or in addition to specific performance under Lord Cairns' Act can now be obtained by virtue of SCA 1981, s. 50. Such damages will be assessed on the same basis as damages at common law (*Johnson* v *Agnew* [1980] AC 367).

8.3 Rescission

8.3.1 WHAT IS RESCISSION?

Rescission is an equitable remedy whereby a contract made between two parties is set aside, and they are restored to the position they would have been in had the contract never been made. The contract is in effect voidable: valid until it is rescinded, and thereafter treated as if it had never taken effect. Rescission is the equitable equivalent of damages in respect of the claimant's reliance loss.

8.3.2 WHEN IS RESCISSION AVAILABLE?

There are three main situations in which rescission is available as a remedy:

(a) misrepresentation;

(b) mistake; and

(c) undue influence.

Its availability as a remedy for misrepresentation is dealt with in **Chapter 7**.

Rescission is available for mistake in certain circumstances in which the contract is valid as opposed to void at common law, but it is nevertheless just to rescind it. Such circumstances would, however, appear to be rare. It is the only effective remedy where a contract has been obtained by improper pressure amounting to undue influence. Rescission has no use where a contract is void at common law, e.g., for illegality, duress or mistake.

8.3.3 THE ACT OF RESCISSION

Rescission is not just a judicial remedy: a party to a contract may rescind it for misrepresentation, mistake or undue influence by giving notice to the other party, and, if accepted by the other party, the contract will be at an end with no recourse to the courts necessary. However, a court order either for rescission or to declare the validity of the claimant's act of rescission may be necessary where there is a dispute between the parties, and an order for enforcement may also be required and involve application to the court.

8.3.4 REPUDIATION DISTINGUISHED FROM RESCISSION

Rescission is not to be confused with repudiation of a contract (which is a *breach* of contract) or with the claimant's right to accept a defendant's repudiatory breach as a discharge from the contract (which is sometimes referred to as 'rescission').

Where there has been a breach of contract, repudiatory or not, the claimant is entitled to seek damages to put him or her into the position he or she would have been in had the contract been performed. Where the claimant seeks rescission, he or she is asking to be put into the position he or she would have been in had the contract not been made: this may involve a claim for damages for consequential loss, but there can be no claim for damages in respect of the claimant's expectation loss.

8.3.5 EQUITABLE BARS TO RESCISSION

Rescission is a discretionary remedy and there are equitable bars that will prevent its being granted. There are four bars in particular.

8.3.5.1 *Restitutio in integrum* is not possible

Restitutio in integrum is the process by which the parties return and recover benefits gained under the contract. The contract will cease to be capable of rescission if the parties can no longer be restored to their original positions. The most likely reason for this is that the subject matter has changed so much that the party who gave it will not get back the same thing that he or she originally had (for example, goods have been destroyed or seriously damaged, or business assets have been disposed of). If the subject matter has merely diminished in value, this will not bar rescission, unless the loss is due to the acts of the buyer.

Nevertheless, equity does not require that restitution should be precise. There will be no bar, so long as it can be achieved substantially and fairly, so that a party gets back substantially the same thing he or she parted with and the change does not result in injustice. This will be so particularly if a financial adjustment can be made to take account of the alteration of the subject matter (*Erlanger* v *New Sombrero Phosphate Co.* (1878) 3 App Cas 1218). The court will not apply the bar too strictly in cases of undue influence involving a breach of fiduciary relationship (*O'Sullivan* v *Management Agency and Music Ltd* [1985] QB 428).

8.3.5.2 Third party acquiring rights

The right to rescind is lost if an innocent third party has acquired an interest under the contract for value before the claimant seeks to rescind. This is an application of the basic principle that equity will not defeat the bona fide purchaser for value without notice ('equity's darling'). There is, of course, no bar if the third party is a volunteer or the defendant's trustee in bankruptcy.

8.3.5.3 Affirmation

If the claimant, with knowledge of his or her right to rescind, nevertheless affirms the contract, his or her right to rescind is waived. He or she may affirm either expressly, by informing the defendant that he or she intends to proceed with the contract, or by conduct, for example, by continuing to take the benefit of it or by doing something which would suggest an intention not to rescind or seek rescission. However, the claimant can affirm only after he or she has discovered the truth. This means not only that the claimant must be aware of the facts of which he or she was previously unaware (for example, that the defendant's representation was false), but that he or she must also be aware of his or her legal rights and his or her option to rescind (*Peyman* v *Lanjani* [1985] Ch 457).

Failing to give notice of rescission within a reasonable time after discovering the truth may amount to affirmation. On the other hand, once notice has been given, continuing to perform the contract until trial, where there is no real alternative, does not constitute affirmation.

8.3.5.4 Delay

Delay between discovery of the truth and seeking to rescind may also evidence affirmation. An intention to rescind must always be communicated to the defendant. As a matter of practice a claimant should be advised to communicate this intention at the earliest moment. If the first notice of rescission is the service of proceedings, there is a good chance the claimant will be held to have affirmed.

Delay between the date of the contract and seeking rescission may, however, amount to a bar in itself, even where there is no question of affirmation. It will never do so in a case of fraud or breach of fiduciary duty, but it may do so in other cases (*Leaf* v *International Galleries* [1950] 2 KB 86).

8.3.5.5 **Damages in lieu of rescission**

Damages in lieu of rescission may be recovered for misrepresentation under the Misrepresentation Act 1967, s. 2(2). See **Chapter 7**.

8.4 Rectification

8.4.1 WHAT IS RECTIFICATION?

Rectification is a discretionary equitable remedy for mistake in contract. Where two parties have agreed the terms of a contract, but they are then incorrectly set down in or excluded from a document which purports to contain the full terms of the contract, the court may order the rectification of that document. It is the *writing* which is being put right, not the contract itself.

8.4.2 WHAT IS REQUIRED?

The mistake must be the mistake of both parties. If the mistake is that of one party only, or one party was indifferent as to the detail that the claimant wants rectified, rectification will not be ordered. The exception is where the omission or error is due to the defendant's fraud. If terms are omitted from a document, it will be rectified to include them only if they were expressly agreed by the parties or are customary terms which could be implied in any event. A document which accurately records an oral agreement made by mistake cannot be rectified.

8.4.3 STANDARD OF EVIDENCE REQUIRED

Clear evidence is required before rectification will be ordered; there must be strong and convincing evidence that the document failed accurately to record the intention of the parties. It is most unlikely that rectification will be ordered solely on the claimant's oral evidence.

8.4.4 BARS TO RECTIFICATION

Rectification is barred by delay; where a third party has acquired rights for value; and where judgment has been obtained in an action in which rectification could have been sought, but was not.

8.5 Account of Profits

It was established by the decision of the House of Lords in *Attorney-General* v *Blake* [2000] 4 All ER 385 that there is another equitable remedy available for breach of contract: an account of profits. In an exceptional case, the court is not limited to the remedies of damages, specific performance and injunction, but may order the defendant to account for all or some of the profits he or she has made through his or her breach of contract. The case is likely to be exceptional where the contractual obligation is very close to being a fiduciary obligation. The remedy will be granted where the court thinks it just in all the circumstances.

It remains to be seen whether the remedy will be granted in other cases. Although not limited in principle, it may be that the exceptional circumstances required will arise only in cases of the kind in *Blake*, which involved a convicted spy.

NINE

INJUNCTIONS

9.1 Introduction

An injunction is an equitable remedy by which the court makes an order to the defendant telling him or her to do or not to do a specific act. It is widely available in contract, tort and family law, subject to certain requirements established by case law.

9.2 Prohibitory and Mandatory Injunctions

An injunction may be prohibitory or mandatory. A prohibitory injunction restrains the defendant from doing something; a mandatory injunction requires the defendant to do something. Whether an injunction is mandatory or prohibitory is strictly speaking a matter of substance, not of the form of words used. So, an order restraining the defendant from not doing something is 'mandatory'; an order requiring the defendant to stop doing something is 'prohibitory'. The distinction may be significant, because a claimant is supposed to couch a mandatory order in positive terms; but a mandatory order is generally harder to obtain than a prohibitory order. In practice, therefore, the almost invariable tendency is to phrase injunctions prohibitively wherever possible, e.g., an order restraining the defendant from allowing a state of affairs to continue.

In contract, a mandatory injunction to stop a breach is very rare, because in most cases it is to all intents and purposes an order of specific performance and will be sought as such. However, there is no such thing as interim specific performance, and in the pre-trial stages of a claim an interim mandatory injunction may occasionally be sought.

9.3 Final and Interim Injunctions

A final injunction, sometimes known as a perpetual injunction (even if limited in time), is an order made at trial. However, most injunctions are sought as a matter of some urgency: the claimant cannot wait until trial. It may be that the defendant's alleged wrongdoing will cause the claimant irreparable continuing damage pending trial or the damage will have been done by the time the case comes on for trial. The claimant will then seek an interim injunction, which will last only for a temporary period, until trial at the latest. Such an injunction, in cases of extreme urgency, may be sought without notice to the defendant, but if sought without notice will usually only be granted with permission to the defendant to apply to set it aside, or for a short time.

The principles applicable to the grant of interim injunctions are basically procedural rather than equitable and are very different from the principles governing the grant of final injunctions.

9.4 Injunction for Breach of Contract

9.4.1 SUPPORT OF CONTRACTUAL RIGHTS

An injunction can only be granted in support of a legal or equitable right. If the claimant has no such right which needs protecting, or has no *locus standi* to bring the action to protect the legal rights of others, no injunction can be granted. In contract, it is the claimant's contractual rights which are being supported. The claimant must therefore show a valid contract and a breach by the defendant.

9.4.2 ACTUAL OR THREATENED BREACH

Where the breach is actual, it will be relatively easy to prove. An injunction can readily be granted to restrain a continuing breach or to prevent the repetition of a breach. But sometimes the breach is merely threatened and lies in the future. In such circumstances a *quia timet* injunction may be granted to restrain the apprehended breach, but a high degree of proof is required. The claimant will have to prove a high probability of the breach occurring, and the likelihood of substantial damage resulting (*Attorney-General* v *Manchester Corporation* [1893] 2 Ch 87; *Fletcher* v *Bealey* (1885) 28 ChD 688).

Take care not to confuse an anticipatory breach (which is actual) and a threatened breach (which is not).

9.4.3 PREVENTION OF BREACH OF A NEGATIVE STIPULATION

As explained in **9.2**, injunctions to restrain a breach of contract are almost always prohibitory unless interim. It follows that the need for an injunction arises where the defendant has done or threatens to do something he or she promised in the contract not to do: the injunction will be in support of a negative stipulation in the contract. Such a stipulation will normally be express, but an injunction can be granted to prevent a breach of an implied negative stipulation, provided that it does not amount to specific performance by the back door (see **9.6**). An injunction will not, however, be granted in support of an implied negative stipulation in a contract of employment or personal service (*Mortimer* v *Beckett* [1920] 1 Ch 571).

9.4.4 WHEN IS A FINAL MANDATORY INJUNCTION APPROPRIATE?

The only circumstance in which a final mandatory injunction may be appropriate for breach of contract is where it is necessary to undo the effects of a breach by the defendant of a negative promise. For example, the claimant sells the defendant part of his or her land and the contract contains a covenant that the defendant will not erect a building on the land which is out of keeping with the houses in the neighbourhood. The defendant builds a Japanese pagoda and the claimant seeks a mandatory injunction requiring it to be pulled down.

9.4.5 THE TERMS OF THE INJUNCTION

The terms of any injunction for breach of contract must be carefully drawn. The claimant's rights are defined by the contract and so the claimant cannot get an order any wider in scope than that which the contract entitles him or her to, unless the defendant's acts amount also to a tort or some other wrong.

9.5 The Grant of an Injunction

9.5.1 IN GENERAL

Being an equitable remedy, an injunction will only be granted in the discretion of the court, and the usual equitable bars apply. However, the hurdles are not on the whole as difficult to overcome as they are for an order of specific performance. A prohibitory injunction to restrain a breach of an express negative stipulation will normally be granted, the important exception being where this would indirectly amount to specific performance of a contract which would not be specifically enforced in equity (see **9.6**).

9.5.2 INADEQUACY OF DAMAGES

The claimant must, of course, show that damages would not be an adequate remedy, but this is a much lower hurdle where he or she seeks to prevent the defendant doing something rather than where he or she requires him or her to do something: in the case of a prohibitory injunction to restrain a breach of contract, damages are not likely to be considered adequate (*Doherty* v *Allman* (1878) 3 App Cas 709). However, damages may be adequate where the likely harm would be trivial, and a much stiffer test will be applied where the claimant seeks a mandatory injunction (*Shepherd Homes Ltd* v *Sandham* [1971] Ch 340).

9.5.3 OTHER BARS

Other bars will prevent the grant of an injunction in the same way as they prevent an order for specific performance:

(a) *Contract too vague* An order will not be made if it does not allow the defendant to understand precisely what he or she may or may not do (see **8.2.3.2**).

(b) *Equity will not act in vain* An injunction will not be made if it would have no effect (see **8.2.3.6**).

(c) *Clean hands* An injunction will not normally be granted to prevent a breach of contract by the defendant if the claimant is also in breach; and the claimant must show himself or herself ready and willing to perform all his or her future obligations (see **8.2.3.7**).

(d) *Delay* Delay may lead to an injunction being refused, but this is by no means as serious a bar as it is to specific performance. Where, however, the claimant's delay effectively amounts to acquiescence in the defendant's breach, an injunction may not be granted (e.g., *Sayers* v *Collyer* (1884) 28 ChD 103) (see **8.2.3.8**).

(e) *Hardship* See **8.2.3.10**.

9.6 Back-door Specific Performance

9.6.1 GROUND FOR REFUSAL OF AN INJUNCTION

An important additional ground for the refusal of an injunction arises where a prohibitory injunction, if granted, would in effect amount to an order for specific performance of the contract, but an order for specific performance would not be made. In other words, a claimant who is not entitled to specific performance cannot get it by the back door of an injunction. Where the injunction would have the same effect as an order for specific performance, the decision whether to grant it will be made on specific performance criteria, e.g., *Sky Petroleum Ltd* v *VIP Petroleum Ltd* [1974] 1 WLR 576, *Hill* v *C.A. Parsons & Co. Ltd* [1972] Ch 305.

9.6.2 CONTRACTS OF PERSONAL SERVICE AND BACK-DOOR SPECIFIC PERFORMANCE

The issue arises most commonly in cases involving a contract of personal service, which cannot be specifically enforced and so cannot be indirectly enforced by an injunction restraining the defendant from withdrawing his or her services. However, where there is an express negative stipulation in the contract, typically a restraint of trade clause, this may be enforced by an injunction. So, although the claimant may not be able to compel the defendant to perform services for him or her, he or she may be able to prevent him or her performing services for someone else (*Lumley* v *Wagner* (1852) 1 De G M & G 604).

However, even an order restraining the defendant from working for someone else may still in effect amount to specific performance if the defendant would have no other means of earning a living. Accordingly, an injunction will not be granted in support of an express negative stipulation in a personal service contract if the end result will be that the defendant is still compelled to work for the claimant (*Rely-a Bell Burglar Alarm Co.* v *Eisler* [1926] Ch 609) or is given the stark choice of working for the claimant or being unemployed (*Warner Bros Pictures Inc.* v *Nelson* [1937] 1 KB 209). Some alternative means of earning a living must be open to the defendant before an injunction will be granted. The same principle applies where the contract is one of personal service by the claimant to the defendant (*Page One Records Ltd* v *Britton* [1968] 1 WLR 157).

If a claimant is prevented by this rule from obtaining an injunction against the person to whom he or she is contracted, he or she cannot get round it by instead seeking an injunction to restrain a third party from inducing a breach of the contract (*Warren* v *Mendy* [1989] 3 All ER 103).

An injunction will never be granted in support of an implied negative stipulation in a contract of personal service.

9.7 Injunctions in Tort

9.7.1 INTRODUCTION

An injunction can only be granted in support of a legal right. Since a tort is a legal wrong the claimant has a right to prevent that legal wrong if it has caused, is causing or will cause damage to him or her or if he or she has *locus standi* to prevent damage to the public at large. Injunctions are particularly useful in tort to restrain trespass, nuisance, defamation, inducing breach of contract, and all the torts involving intellectual property. Except in cases of trespass and nuisance, interim injunctions are likely to be sufficient.

9.7.2 PROHIBITORY INJUNCTIONS

9.7.2.1 The primary remedy

Although, strictly speaking, an injunction can only be granted where damages would not be an adequate remedy, when the claimant seeks to prevent a tort the granting of an injunction is more or less automatic. Injunction has become the primary remedy. Unless the claimant is barred, once his or her legal right is established an injunction will be granted, unless:

(a) the injury to the claimant's legal rights is small;

(b) the injury is assessable in money;

(c) a small money payment would be adequate compensation; and

(d) it would be oppressive to the defendant to grant an injunction (*Shelfer* v *London Electric Lighting Co.* [1895] 1 Ch 287; *Kennaway* v *Thompson* [1981] QB 88).

However, where these conditions are made out, damages are likely to be awarded in lieu (*Jaggard* v *Sawyer* [1995] 1 WLR 269).

9.7.2.2 Appropriateness of an injunction

An injunction has in effect become a right to which the claimant is entitled unless there are special circumstances (*Pride of Derby and Derbyshire Angling Association*

Ltd v *British Celanese Ltd* [1953] Ch 149). This is because an injunction is so obviously appropriate and because damages will rarely be adequate. Damages can only compensate a claimant for past damage; they will never prevent future recurrence. And if damages are relatively small, a defendant might simply regard them as the price to be paid for the right to commit a tort.

9.7.2.3 Refusal of injunctions

The equitable bars to the granting of an injunction have the same meaning in tort as in contract. Injunctions may be refused where the conditions set out in **9.7.2.1** above are satisfied and/or the claimant is barred in equity by delay, acquiescence, or his or her own conduct. But in a serious case, injunctions are rarely refused. This is so, even if considerable hardship may be caused to the defendant (*Redland Bricks Ltd* v *Morris* [1970] AC 652), or if the interest of the public at large is overwhelmingly greater than the private interest of the claimant (*Attorney-General* v *Birmingham Borough Council* (1858) 4 K & J 528).

9.7.3 MANDATORY INJUNCTIONS

9.7.3.1 Nature

In tort, a mandatory injunction orders the defendant to undo the wrong. It will usually be sought in a case of trespass, to require the defendant to remove something from the claimant's land, or which causes a nuisance. The leading case is *Redland Bricks Ltd* v *Morris* [1970] AC 652.

9.7.3.2 Difficulty of obtaining a mandatory injunction

Mandatory injunctions are much harder to obtain than prohibitory injunctions. Their grant is certainly not automatic. Damages in lieu will usually be regarded as the primary remedy, and the adequacy of damages hurdle is not easy to cross.

A mandatory order will not be made where hardship may be caused to the defendant. The bars are similar to those to specific performance; or arguably stricter. A mandatory injunction may be refused not only where serious hardship would be caused to the defendant, but simply where the hardship suffered would on balance be greater than that suffered by the claimant if the order were refused.

9.7.4 *QUIA TIMET* INJUNCTIONS

Either prohibitory or mandatory *quia timet* injunctions may be granted to restrain a tort, usually nuisance. A high degree of proof is required: the claimant must show, on good evidence, that the tort is highly likely to occur and to occur imminently (*Attorney-General* v *Manchester Corporation* [1893] 2 Ch 87; *Fletcher* v *Bealey* (1885) 28 ChD 688).

9.8 Interim Injunctions

9.8.1 JURISDICTION

Jurisdiction to grant interim injunctions in the High Court derives from the SCA 1981, s. 37.

County court jurisdiction to grant interim injunctions derives from the CCA 1984, ss. 38(1), which allows the court to make any order which could be made by the High Court if the proceedings were in the High Court. See ***Civil Litigation Manual*, Chapter 14**.

9.8.2 PRINCIPLES

As stated earlier, the principles applicable to the granting of interim injunctions are largely procedural. A summary of the relevant principles is set out below. A more detailed explanation may be found in the ***Civil Litigation Manual*, Chapter 14**.

9.8.2.1 The *American Cyanamid* guidelines

While the granting of an injunction lies within the discretion of the court, the guidelines applicable to such applications are found in the leading case of *American Cyanamid Co.* v *Ethicon Ltd* [1975] AC 396. Generally the factors which the court will consider may be approached as a series of steps and the case for an injunction may fall at any point in the sequence:

(a) *Is there a serious question to be tried?* If the answer is yes (and it is often a fairly easy threshold to meet):

(b) *Would damages be an adequate remedy, i.e., if the claimant succeeds at trial would he or she be adequately compensated by a (monetary) award?* If damages would be inadequate:

(c) *If the defendant succeeded at trial, i.e., he or she demonstrated a right to do the act(s) which the claimant sought to enjoin, would he or she be adequately compensated by the claimant's undertaking as to damages?*

(d) *Where does the balance of convenience lie?* The factors which the court will take into consideration and the weight attached to each will vary with each case.

(e) Where factors appear to be evenly balanced the court will consider preserving the *status quo*. This means the state of affairs immediately before the issue of the writ, unless the claimant has delayed, in which case the *status quo* will be that existing immediately before the application. See *Garden Cottage Foods Ltd* v *Milk Marketing Board* [1984] AC 130, HL.

In some established areas the *American Cyanamid* approach is not strictly adhered to in determining whether to grant the injunction. Various factors may be of more or less importance depending on the nature of the dispute or third parties who may be affected by the granting of the injunction. Some of these areas are industrial disputes, defamation cases, actions against public authorities (where the public interest is an important factor in determining the balance of convenience), and covenants in restraint of trade.

9.8.2.2 Where granting an interim injunction would dispose of the action

It is important to distinguish between injunctions intended to be temporary in nature, i.e., effective until later trial, and those which would, in effect, dispose of the dispute because there are no further issues between the parties which need to be determined at a later trial. If this is the case, the *American Cyanamid* guidelines on the balance of convenience are not applied. Rather it is appropriate for the court to consider the degree of likelihood that the claimant would have succeeded in establishing his or her right to an injunction at a trial on the merits. An injunction will only be granted if the claimant's case is overwhelming. See ***Civil Litigation Manual*, Chapter 14**, and *Cayne* v *Global Natural Resources plc* [1984] 1 All ER 225, CA.

9.8.3 PROCEDURE

Applications for interim injunctions are governed by CPR, Parts 23 and 25. An application must be made by application notice, supported by written evidence, usually in the form of a witness statement. This evidence should set out the facts on which the applicant relies. Under normal circumstances the application notice should be served not less than three clear days before the hearing. However, in urgent cases applications can be made without notice, even before the issue of a claim form. In these circumstances an injunction can be made without the respondent being heard. However, the order made will only last until a return date, when there will be a further hearing.

A more detailed explanation of the relevant procedure will be found in the ***Civil Litigation Manual*, Chapter 14** and a more detailed explanation of the relevant documents will be found in the ***Drafting Manual*, Chapter 19**.

TEN

BAILMENT AND INTERFERENCE WITH GOODS

10.1 Definition

We can define bailment as being the delivery of goods on an express or implied condition that they shall be restored by the bailee to the bailor (or dealt with according to the bailor's directions) as soon as the purpose for which they are bailed has elapsed or has been performed.

Bailment is an area of law which combines elements of property law in addition to those of contract and tort.

10.2 When Does Bailment Arise?

Bailment arises whenever one person (the bailee) is voluntarily in possession of goods belonging to another person (the bailor).

Although bailment is usually created by a contract, this does not necessarily have to be the case, as the legal relationship of bailor and bailee can arise independently of any contractual agreement.

The element common to all types of bailment is the imposition of an *obligation*. This arises when the bailee takes goods into his or her possession and thereby assumes responsibility for their safe keeping.

For bailment to arise, the actual or constructive possession of the goods must be relinquished by:

(a) the owner of the goods, or

(b) the bailor, or

(c) an agent who is duly authorised for the purpose,

to the bailee, who then either keeps the goods or performs some act with them.

Every bailee has a common law duty to take reasonable care of the bailor's goods and not to convert them to his or her own use (*Morris* v *C.W. Martin and Sons Ltd* [1966] 1 QB 716). The standard of care to be applied is the standard demanded by the circumstances of each particular bailment.

10.3 Classification

Bailment has in the past been categorised in many ways, with fine distinctions between them. However, for present purposes, there are two basic types: gratuitous bailment and bailment for reward.

10.3.1 GRATUITOUS BAILMENT

Gratuitous bailment arises when a chattel is deposited with the bailee who simply retains it until its return is demanded. Because the bailee does not receive any reward for his or her services, neither party acquires any rights or assumes any obligations until there is actual delivery and acceptance of the chattel. It is only then that the bailee becomes obliged to carry out his or her promise.

This category includes situations where property is lent to another for a specific purpose, without charge.

Examples

(a) Joe asks Fred, as an unpaid favour, to look after his hi-fi for him whilst he goes on holiday. Fred agrees. If Fred was to change his mind at any time prior to receiving the hi-fi, there is nothing that Joe can do about it. However, once Fred accepts delivery of the goods, he is bound to look after them, and to return them to Joe upon demand.

(b) Joe lends Fred his hi-fi to use at his birthday party. Fred is entitled to use it for that purpose only, and then is obliged to return it.

10.3.2 BAILMENT FOR REWARD

Bailment for reward covers situations where a chattel is pawned or pledged as security for a loan, or the performance of an obligation; or where goods are hired for reward.

Examples

(a) Anna borrows £100 from Tim, to be repaid in six months' time together with 10 per cent interest. She leaves her watch with Tim as security. Tim is the bailee of the watch.

(b) Sue hires a motor mower from Gardenhire Ltd, for seven days, at a cost of £20. She becomes a bailee of the mower.

10.3.3 TERMINATION OF BAILMENT

Bailment will usually determine at the end of the period agreed between the parties. At the conclusion of the bailment, the bailor has the right to immediate possession of the goods. When this arises will depend on the circumstances of the individual case or on the terms of the contract if there is one.

10.4 Torts (Interference with Goods) Act 1977

Bailment, and the remedies available in respect of breach by bailor or bailee as well as the rights of third parties are now governed by the Torts (Interference with Goods) Act 1977, which basically protects the right to possession of and title to the goods.

Apart from a new tort of statutory conversion under s. 2(2), the 1977 Act does not create any new torts and so previous case law regarding pre-existing torts is still relevant.

10.4.1 CAUSES OF CLAIM

Section 1 of the 1977 Act defines the torts for which a defendant may be liable if he or she wrongfully interferes with a claimant's chattels or goods. These are:

(a) conversion (s. 2(1)(a)),

(b) trespass (s. 1(1)(b)),

(c) negligence (so far as it results in damage to goods or to an interest in goods) (s. 1(1)(c)),

(d) any other tort as far as it results in damage to goods (s. 1(1)(d)).

These subdivisions are not mutually exclusive: conduct by a particular defendant may fall into one or more of the above categories.

Conversion is the most common tort and the main textbooks should be consulted for detailed guidance on this complex subject. However, some of the basic principles are set out below.

10.4.2 CONVERSION

10.4.2.1 Definition

Anyone who, without authority, takes possession of another person's goods, with the intention of asserting some right or dominion over them, is *prima facie* guilty of a conversion, provided that there is an intention on the part of the person so dealing with them to assert a right inconsistent with the rights of the owner. This can include (but is by no means limited to) wrongfully taking or parting with possession of goods, wrongfully retaining them, denying the title of the person entitled to possession, or, when acting as a bailee, so neglecting them that they are destroyed or totally lost. More particular examples are set out below.

The general rule is that the right to bring a claim for conversion belongs to the person who can prove that he or she had, at the time of the conversion, either actual possession or the immediate right to possess the goods.

The injury suffered by the claimant in such a case is twofold:

(a) an injury to the claimant's right to possession,

(b) an injury to the claimant's title in the goods.

10.4.2.2 An alternative definition

Conversion is a deliberate act of dealing by a defendant with a chattel in a manner inconsistent with the claimant's right which deprives the claimant of the use and possession of the chattel. One exception to the proposition that conversion is a deliberate act is contained in s. 2(2) of the 1977 Act, namely, where a bailee is in breach of his or her duty to his or her bailor and thereby allows the goods to become lost or destroyed.

10.4.2.3 Conduct amounting to conversion

For liability to be established in conversion it is sufficient that the conduct of the defendant is inconsistent with the rights of the claimant. It follows that a whole range of acts can amount to conversion, from total abrogation of the claimant's rights in the goods to lesser conduct which may or may not amount to deprivation of the claimant's right in the goods depending upon the particular circumstances.

The following are the most common situations when conversion may arise:

(a) *Conversion by wrongful taking*
Peter wrongfully takes a watch belonging to Mary. Peter's intention must be either to deny Mary's rights or to assert a right which is inconsistent with her ownership. In the latter case the assertion of the right need not be that of full ownership: it is sufficient if assertion of the right is inconsistent with Mary's true entitlement.

(b) *Conversion by transfer*
This occurs when the defendant purports to give the claimant's goods to a third party along with some right over the goods which actually belongs to the

claimant. To extend the above example, Peter gives Mary's watch to Antonia as a present.

(c) *Conversion by wrongful sale*
When property is wrongfully sold so that the property and the title to it are passed to a third party, irrespective of whether or not the goods are actually delivered to the buyer. Thus, if Peter sells Mary's watch to William, who buys it in good faith, Peter is guilty of conversion.

(d) *Conversion by taking*
There must be detention of the goods which is adverse to the rights of the true owner. A demand by the claimant and a refusal by the defendant must be shown. If Mary lends Peter her watch, but he thereafter refuses to return it when asked, Peter has committed an act of conversion.

(e) *Conversion by destruction*
Conversion will occur when the chattel is dealt with in such a manner that its original identity is destroyed. The destruction must be wilful. If Peter accidentally drops and treads on Mary's watch, no act of conversion is committed. If, however, he deliberately throws it into the river, the tort has been committed.

(f) *Conversion by loss*
Loss of someone else's chattel may amount to an abuse of possession (and therefore to conversion) if it is other than purely accidental.

(g) *Conversion by denial of right*
This can be considered to be a residual category embracing activities which do not fall into any of the above categories. This form of conversion occurs when a defendant deals with goods in a manner which amounts to denial of the true title. However, even absolute denial of title is not *per se* sufficient to amount to conversion because there must in addition be some further dealing with the goods; in other words some positive conduct on the part of the defendant, such as actively barring the claimant access to his or her goods whilst also repudiating the claimant's right to his or her goods.

The essential element in conversion is dealing with the goods in a manner which is altogether inconsistent with the title of the true owner. Therefore a defendant may be liable for conversion of goods notwithstanding the fact that he or she has never been in possession of them or physically handled them. However, the categories of conversion are not closed and in many cases it will be a matter of judicial discretion whether to treat the act as sufficiently inconsistent with the true owner's rights for a conversion to have taken place.

10.4.3 SUBJECT MATTER OF CONVERSION

By s. 14(1) of the 1977 Act:

> *... unless the context otherwise requires ... 'goods' includes all chattels personal other than things in action and money.*

The definition does not purport to be exhaustive or all-embracing.

It is generally considered that the exclusion of money is limited to money in the sense of currency, so that valuable or antique coins can be converted (*Moss* v *Hancock* [1899] 2 QB 111).

10.4.4 WHO MAY BRING A CLAIM FOR CONVERSION AND AGAINST WHOM?

10.4.4.1 Claimant

The right to bring a claim for conversion belongs to the person who is able to establish that at the time of conversion he or she either had:

(a) actual possession of the goods or

(b) the immediate right to possess the goods.

It is doubtful whether an equitable right is sufficient to ground a claim in conversion (*The Future Express* [1993] 2 Lloyd's Rep 542).

10.4.4.2 Defendants

(a) *The immediate tortfeasor.* This should be self-explanatory.

(b) *Agents.* In order for an agent to be liable in conversion, it is necessary to consider the agent's actual or constructive knowledge of the true ownership of the goods. This is a detailed area of law beyond the scope of this chapter.

10.4.5 MORE THAN ONE CLAIMANT

The policy behind the 1977 Act is that a claimant should only recover his or her own actual loss and no more, and that multiplicity of actions should be avoided.

10.4.5.1 Double liability

Section 7(1) defines the scope of double liability which may arise where:

(a) two or more rights of claim for wrongful interference are founded on a possessory title (s. 7(1)(a)), or

(b) the measure of damages in a claim for wrongful interference founded on a proprietary title is or includes the entire value of the goods, although the interest is one of two or more interests in the goods (s. 7(1)(b)).

Section 7(2) provides that where there are two or more claimants in the same claim against one defendant the relief granted will be such as to avoid double liability of the defendant towards the claimants.

Section 7(3) provides that if there are two claimants but only one claimant is a party to the claim and that claimant receives more than he or she would have if s. 7(2) applied then that claimant must account to any other person having a claim for that excess.

Section 7(4) protects a defendant who overpays in the event of double liability by permitting a defendant to recover overpayment from a claimant to the extent that that claimant has been unjustly enriched by the overpayment. Therefore if a bailor and bailee both have the right to sue for conversion they cannot both exercise such rights and thereby obtain double recovery from a defendant. Either bailor or bailee may sue and whoever is the first person to obtain damages will conclude the case (*Nicolls* v *Bastard* [1825–42] All ER Rep 429 at p. 430). The successful claimant must then account to the other party for the proportion of damages representing his or her interest in the goods.

10.4.5.2 Competing rights to the goods

Section 8(1) of the Act permits a defendant to plead by way of a defence to the claimant's claim that a third party has title to the goods which is equal to, or superior to, that of the claimant.

10.4.5.3 Co-owners

If two or more people own a chattel then one co-owner cannot bring a claim against another co-owner for interference with his or her right to possession because each co-owner has a right to possession which is lawful. However, if one co-owner goes further and performs an act which could only be permitted if he or she alone had exclusive possession of the goods then a claim by the other co-owner or co-owners will be permitted. Such a claim is only allowed if there has been 'a destruction of the particular chattel or something equivalent to it' (s. 10(1)).

Section 10(1) of the 1977 Act affirms the well-established proposition that one co-owner cannot maintain an action against another co-owner.

10.4.6 FORMS OF REMEDY

10.4.6.1 Nature of the remedy

The appropriate remedy is often prescribed by the state of the goods. If the goods have been destroyed or disposed of then the claimant's remedy will be confined to judgment for a sum of money. However, if the goods are still in the possession or control of the defendant then the remedies available to an aggrieved claimant are somewhat wider.

10.4.6.2 Available remedies

Where the goods are in the possession or control of the defendant, s. 3(1) of the 1977 Act provides the following remedies:

(a) an order for specific delivery of the goods and payment of any consequential damages (s. 3(2)(a)),

(b) an order for delivery of the goods but also giving the defendant the option of paying damages by reference to the value of the goods in addition to payment of any consequential damages (s. 3(2)(b)),

(c) damages, including the assessed value of the goods in addition to any consequential loss (s. 3(2)(c)).

A remedy may only be given under one of these heads (s. 3(3)(a)) and furthermore a remedy under s. 3(2)(a) is at the discretion of the court whereas a remedy under s. 3(2)(b) or s. 3(2)(c) is at the election of the claimant (by virtue of s. 3(3)(b)).

(d) On application by any person the court has a discretionary power to make an order for delivery up of the goods which either are or may become the subject matter of subsequent proceedings (for example, see *Howard E. Perry & Co. Ltd* v *British Railways Board* [1980] 1 WLR 1375 and s. 4 of the 1977 Act). Such an application may be made under the court's power to grant interim remedies under CPR, r. 25.1(1).

We will examine each of the above remedies in turn.

10.4.6.3 Specific delivery

Section 3(2)(a) of the 1977 Act. This order is made at the discretion of the court and thus will not usually be made in respect of ordinary articles which have no special value either intrinsically or for the claimant, because in such cases damages would provide adequate compensation.

If the court makes an order for specific delivery, a duty is imposed on the defendant to ensure that the goods are ready for collection by the claimant. The order may contain conditions regarding delivery of the goods. The order may be enforced by writ of specific delivery to recover the goods or their assessed value.

If it can be shown to the court that an order for specific delivery has not been complied with then the court may proceed to revoke that order or any relevant part of the order and instead order payment of damages which will be assessed on the value of the goods.

10.4.6.4 Judgment for delivery or damages

Section 3(2)(b) of the 1977 Act. Here the claimant has an election between delivery or damages together in either case with payment of any consequential damages.

Damages will be assessed by reference to the value of the goods.

The provisions allowing the court to impose conditions on specific delivery under s. 3(2)(a) apply equally under s. 3(2)(b). Such order may be enforced as under s. 3(2)(a).

10.4.6.5 Damages

A claimant may recover all such damages as are the direct and natural result of the conversion.

The 1977 Act is silent as to the time when damages should be assessed apart from a reference in s. 6(1) regarding improvements to the goods. We must therefore rely on previously established rules.

A claimant who seeks damages for conversion based upon the value of the goods will be limited to the value of the goods at the time of conversion. If the value of the converted goods decreases after conversion, the claimant is still entitled to their original value and consequently receives a windfall (*Solloway* v *McLaughlin* [1938] AC 247).

A subsequent rise in the value of goods since the time of conversion is recoverable as consequential damages provided the increase in value was foreseeable at the time of conversion (*The Playa Larga* [1983] 2 Lloyd's Rep 171, CA).

10.4.6.6 Basis of assessment

If there is a market price for the goods, the value of the goods is to be taken as the market price at the time of conversion. However, if there is no market price, the basis for assessing damages will be the cost of replacement as determined by the evidence.

If the value of the goods is fluctuating, the measure of damages may depend upon the claimant's awareness of the conversion.

10.4.6.7 Taxation

When considering damages for conversion, the principles in *British Transport Commission* v *Gourley* [1956] AC 185 are thought to be applicable. Therefore, any tax liability which would have accrued to the claimant had the claimant's goods not been converted should be taken into account in the quantification of damages.

10.4.6.8 Aggravated and exemplary damages

Aggravated damages may be awarded if the court considers they are justified by the circumstances of the conversion (*Owen and Smith* v *Reo Motors (Britain) Ltd* (1934) 151 LT 274).

The availability of exemplary damages was severely curtailed by the judgment of Lord Devlin in *Rookes* v *Barnard* [1964] AC 1129. Essentially such damages will only be awarded in cases where the court considers that the tortfeasor should be taught a lesson and are generally reserved for exceptional cases of misconduct.

10.4.6.9 Special damage

Where a defendant is aware that the chattel converted by him or her is required by the claimant for a particular purpose (for example, to be hired out for profit), the defendant may be liable to pay special damage for failure of that purpose by reason of his or her conversion. See, for example, *Bodley* v *Reynolds* (1846) 8 QB 779, in which a workman deprived of his tools recovered loss of wages.

10.4.6.10 Effect

If a defendant satisfies a judgment for damages for conversion of goods, the claimant's title is transferred to the defendant (*Ellis* v *John Stenning & Son* [1932] 2 Ch 81).

10.4.7 IMPROVEMENT OF THE GOODS

Section 6(1) of the 1977 Act restates the common law rules and provides that a person who improved goods, honestly believing that he or she had good title to them, is to be entitled to the value of the goods attributable to the improvement. This is known as the principle of allowance and is based upon the fact that the true owner should not be compensated for more than the value of the goods which he or she originally lost. Generally, any expenditure of work or materials which enhances saleability will constitute an improvement.

Section 6(2) extends the availability of the allowance from the original wrongdoer who effects the improvement to a bona fide purchaser who has obtained his or her supposed title from the improver who is in this case the defendant.

Section 6(4) applies the principle of allowance to any person who acquires a limited interest in goods by way of bailment or otherwise.

10.4.8 LIMITATION

The Limitation Act 1980 provides that once the period of limitation, namely six years from the date of first conversion, has expired, the right to bring proceedings expires. This is an absolute bar, which is different from the basic limitation rule which does not expressly bar the *right* to sue, but merely affords a complete defence to anyone taking the limitation point.

10.4.9 DEFENCES

Liability in conversion is strict (*Marfani & Co. Ltd* v *Midland Bank Ltd* [1968] 1 WLR 956 at p. 971). However, if a defendant can invoke any of the exceptions to the *nemo dat quod non habet* rule, he or she may escape liability for conversion.

10.4.10 TRESPASS

10.4.10.1 Definition

Trespass may be defined as an intentional or negligent direct interference with goods in the possession of the claimant. It is concerned with *direct and immediate* interference with the claimant's possession of a chattel.

The tort of trespass includes not only the taking away, or removal out of the claimant's possession, of his or her goods but also any unpermitted contact with or impact upon another's chattel. Mere touching is sufficient as long as it causes damage.

10.4.10.2 Elements

Whilst a claim in conversion can be founded by a claimant who has the right to possession, though not actual possession, by contrast, a claim in trespass can only be brought by the claimant if he or she is actually in possession at the time of the interference. There are exceptions to this rule as regards executors and administrators and trustees, but these are beyond the scope of this chapter.

10.4.10.3 Nature of the interference

The interference must be of a direct nature and in addition there must be a blameworthy state of mind in the trespasser. Accidental interference of a non-negligent nature will not constitute a trespass.

10.4.10.4 Remedies

Damages and/or an injunction are available if the defendant is no longer in possession or control of the goods. If the defendant is in possession or control of the goods, the same remedies are available as for conversion.

Where the goods are damaged by trespass but the claimant is not actually deprived of them, the claimant will only be entitled to damages which represent the loss actually suffered as a direct result of the trespass.

10.4.11 NEGLIGENCE RESULTING IN DAMAGE TO GOODS

This covers negligent damage to goods and the usual remedies for negligence apply, namely damages and/or an injunction, irrespective of whether the defendant has the goods in his or her possession or control. Orders for specific delivery or delivery and damages are not available.

10.4.12 OTHER TORTS

Section 1(d) of the 1977 Act applies the Act to any other tort so far as it results in damage to goods or to an interest in goods. This would cover, for example, non-natural user under the rule in *Rylands* v *Fletcher*, slander of title to goods and passing off. The scope of s. 1(d) is not precisely defined although it is considered to embrace negligent damage, loss or destruction of goods not covered by s. 1(c).

10.4.13 CONTRIBUTORY NEGLIGENCE

Section 11(1) precludes contributory negligence as a defence in proceedings for wrongful interference which are founded on conversion or intentional trespass. However, there is internal inconsistency in the 1977 Act because such a defence is permitted for negligence and other torts, in other words, for proceedings brought under s. 1(c) or (d) of the Act

10.4.14 REVERSIONARY INJURY

A person who is entitled to goods, but has neither immediate possession nor the right to possession, is unable to sue a wrongdoer for conversion or for trespass. However, a claim will lie if the wrong committed deprives the person, either temporarily or permanently, of the benefit of his or her reversionary interest. The act must affect the person's reversionary interest in the goods.

The remedy for reversionary injury is confined to damages and the claimant cannot obtain an interim order for delivery up of the goods. Apart from these distinctions the procedural provisions relating to conversion contained in the 1977 Act apply.

10.5 Exercises

10.5.1 EXERCISE 1

Problem

Ben is a supplier of fresh fruit and owner of two fruit stores from which Pamela often buys fruit. Ben hires a motor car to Pamela for six weeks whilst he goes on holiday. He normally uses the car for fresh fruit deliveries to his two shops on a daily basis. Pamela collects the motor car and signs a contract whereby she will hire the car from Ben for six weeks at £120 per week. After four weeks Pamela can no longer afford the rent and decides to sell the car at an auction. James buys the car at the auction.

(a) Discuss liability and remedies.

(b) What difference would it make if Pamela had not signed a contract to hire the motor car but instead just borrowed it from Ben's premises with his permission?

Solution

By hiring the motor car to Pamela a situation of bailment is created whereby Ben is the bailor and Pamela is the bailee. Because a contract of hire is signed between Pamela and Ben, the conditions of bailment are contained in a contract. If Pamela had not signed a contract, a situation of bailment between Pamela and Ben would still exist because Ben has entrusted goods (his car) to Pamela upon condition that she return them in the original state after six weeks. However, bailment would only exist when Pamela took delivery of the car from Ben.

By selling the motor car at an auction, Pamela has committed the tort of conversion because she has only hired the car from Ben. The ownership of the car vests in Ben. By selling the car, Pamela is asserting a right which she does not have, namely that of ownership of the car, and secondly she is also asserting a right which is inconsistent with the right of the true owner, namely Ben's right to possession of the car.

The remedies for conversion are contained in s. 3 of the 1977 Act. An order for specific delivery under s. 3(2)(a) of the 1977 Act is only granted at the discretion of the court and will generally only be granted where the court considers that damages are inadequate as a remedy. However Ben may seek an order under s. 3(2)(b) of the 1977 Act for delivery of the goods and also giving the defendant the option of returning the goods any time before execution of the judgment. Because Pamela has sold the car at an auction to James, recovery of the car may be difficult if not impossible from James, who bought the car in the belief that the car once sold was his. The most appropriate remedy for Ben would be damages, which would be assessed by reference to the value of the goods lost. Furthermore because Ben uses the car for his occupation as a fruit supplier, he will be able to claim special damage from Pamela for loss of business. However, for such damages to be recoverable, Pamela must have been aware that the car was used by Ben for this purpose. Because she shops regularly at Ben's shop this requirement would be met.

Furthermore, Ben would have a claim for damage for breach of contract, namely the two weeks' rent that Pamela has failed to pay.

10.5.2 EXERCISE 2

Problem

Frank and his wife Mary jointly own a computer which they lend to Tracey for six weeks. Tracey does not return the computer to Frank and Mary because she threw it against a wall in a fit of rage when she lost some work stored on the hard disk. The entire computer is smashed and has been assessed by a computer specialist as being beyond economical repair.

(a) What remedies are available to Frank and Mary and which is the most appropriate in this case?

(b) What steps should they take to obtain such remedy?

(c) If Frank alone recovers the value of the computer what steps can Mary take to recover her share of the value of the computer?

ELEVEN

QUANTUM OF DAMAGES FOR PERSONAL INJURY

11.1 The Barrister's Involvement

When representing a client in a claim for damages for personal injury a barrister will be closely involved, not only with the issues of liability, but also with the process of quantifying damages. If the issue of quantum goes to trial, you will present evidence on and argue the question of 'how much' before the court. If a settlement is reached you are likely to be involved in, or even to conduct, the negotiation. Even at the earliest stages of your involvement in the case you are likely to be asked to advise on quantum, i.e., to state how much in your opinion a judge would be likely to award. A preliminary view on quantum needs to be taken before the claimant can decide whether to bring his or her claim in the High Court or County Court. By virtue of CPR, PD 7, para. 3.6, if a claim for personal injury is started in the High Court, the claim form must state that the claimant expects to recover £50,000 or more.

It follows that you must understand the principles on which damages are quantified, the process by which a court would arrive at a final figure, and the practical steps to be taken in advising on quantum.

11.2 The Law

11.2.1 BASIS OF THE LAW

The law in this area is largely judge-made, with occasional legislative assistance or interference. It has grown up in a piece-meal fashion over the last 70 years or so and has no overall coherence, logic or rationale. It is not very scientific, and its overall effect tends to be to undercompensate those who have suffered serious injuries. In *Lim Poh Choo* v *Camden and Islington Area Health Authority* [1980] AC 174 Lord Scarman said:

> Lord Denning MR in the Court of Appeal declared that a radical reappraisal of the law is needed. I agree . . . I would suggest to your Lordships that such a reappraisal calls for social, financial, economic and administrative decisions which only the legislature can take. The complexities of the present case . . . emphasise the need for reform of the law.

Few lawyers would disagree with this. Several statutory reforms have been made since 1980, but none of them constitute the radical overhaul suggested. However some recent legislation, and the decision of the House of Lords in *Wells* v *Wells* [1998] 3 All ER 481 have made some very significant steps towards a more scientific calculation of damages, which should lead to claimants being more properly compensated in future. For a fuller explanation see **11.10.3**.

11.2.2 THE RATIONALE OF THE LAW

There is no force of law behind most of the rules for the quantification of damages. In theory, at least, a court may assess damages in any way it sees fit in order to do justice to the parties. However, there are two very important constraints:

(a) The method of assessment is limited by the powers of the court. In particular, except where there is a claim for provisional damages (for which see **11.5**), the court can only ever make one order, at the date of trial, which cannot later be varied in the light of subsequent developments. So the court cannot adopt a wait-and-see approach to future uncertainties. It must assess damages in a way that will so far as possible do justice today for the claimant tomorrow. This will almost always be by the payment of a single lump sum. The only exceptions, both of which require the parties' consent, are that the court can now make an order for periodical payments under s. 2 of the Damages Act 1996 (see **11.18**), and that it can approve a structured settlement agreed by the parties themselves (see **11.19**).

(b) There is a vital principle behind the assessment of damages, which is that parties must be able to predict as closely as possible the damages that a court would award. If they cannot do so, there is little chance of their agreeing on a sum in settlement of a claim, and every case would have to go to trial. Such a result would be most undesirable. So, if parties are to be able to predict the likely damages, courts must be consistent in their approach. That is why the rules for assessment that follow are universally applied by the courts, however unsatisfactory they may seem to individual judges or in particular cases.

11.2.3 SOURCES

The practitioner's 'bible' is Kemp & Kemp, *The Quantum of Damages*. Also useful is *Butterworths Personal Injury Litigation Service;* also essential is regular reference to *Current Law*. Valuable on-line services are Lawtel–PI Quantum Reports and Personal Injury Interactive; and Butterworths PI Online.

11.3 Basic Principles

11.3.1 APPLICATION OF THE COMPENSATORY PRINCIPLE

The aim of an award of damages is to compensate the claimant for the loss caused to him or her by his or her injuries and to place him or her, so far as it is possible to do so, in the position he or she would have been in had those injuries not been suffered. The claimant must be compensated, therefore, not only for the injuries themselves, but also for the effect they have had on him or her emotionally, intellectually and financially. This cannot be done, of course, simply by the payment of money; but money is all the law has to give, and so some arbitrary yet fair relationship has to be found between the injury and the compensation.

Not all loss can be measured in money, but it still has to be assessed in financial terms.

11.3.2 MEASUREMENT OF LOSS

Such loss as *can* be measured in money, is so measured. Loss that can only partially be measured in money is assessed arithmetically to a certain extent. Wholly non-financial loss is assessed according to conventional guidelines.

11.3.3 TIME OF ASSESSMENT

Although the cause of action accrues at the date of the injury, and all damage that flows from the injury is deemed to have been suffered at that time, nevertheless to all intents and purposes damages are assessed as at the date of the trial.

In the case of financial loss already incurred, the court will take the total amount so far; and in the case of future financial loss, the court will give any item recoverable the value it bears at the date of trial. The court will also take account of all facts about the extent of the claimant's injury or its effect on him or her that are known at the date of trial, and of any supervening events, such as the claimant's death or redundancy, or the onset of some disease, even if these facts or supervening events were unpredictable at the time of the injury (see *Jobling* v *Associated Dairies Ltd* [1982] AC 794).

11.4 Two Broad Heads of Damages

Damages are either special or general. In any ordinary case there will be a claim for both special and general damages.

11.4.1 SPECIAL DAMAGES

11.4.1.1 Nature and proof of special damage

Special damages represent the claimant's actual pecuniary loss between the date of injury and the date of trial; in other words, those losses that are strictly measurable in money and susceptible to precise calculation.

Every item of special damage must be specifically pleaded and specifically proved. This does not mean that every item can be given a value which is certain; rather, that every item can be given a value which is ascertainable, either by proof, by agreement between the parties, or by decision of the court. A schedule of loss and expenses, setting out the special damages claimed, must be served with particulars of claim for damages for personal injury (CPR, PD 16, para. 4.2).

11.4.1.2 Examples of items of special damage

There is in principle no limit to the range of items that can be recovered as special damages, provided they are within the rules of causation, remoteness and the duty to mitigate, but the following list shows those items most commonly recovered:

(a) Incidental damage to property, e.g., damage to a motor vehicle, damage to clothing, a broken wrist watch.

(b) Medical expenses. All reasonable medical expenses may be recovered. A claimant is not obliged to mitigate his or her loss by having treatment under the National Health Service (Law Reform (Personal Injuries) Act 1948, s. 2(4)).

(c) Associated expenditure, e.g., cost of travel to and from hospital, prescription charges.

(d) Cost of nursing care, whether in a residential institution or at home.

(e) Cost of other paid help, e.g., housekeeper, nanny, baby sitter, gardener, etc.

(f) Reasonable necessary expenditure: e.g., special equipment (crutches, wheelchair); purchase of special car, or conversion of car to hand controls; purchase of new house, special accommodation; cost of converting present or new home for claimant's special needs (e.g., building extension, enlarging bathroom, putting in a lift, ramps instead of steps, lowering work surfaces in kitchen).

(g) Increases in ordinary expenditure: e.g., additional transport costs, heating costs, holiday costs, cost of employing someone to do work the claimant previously did on a D-I-Y basis.

(h) Loss of earnings from date of injury to date of trial. This is usually the major item of special damages.

(i) Loss of other fringe benefits from the claimant's employment, e.g., free goods, services, use of company car for private purposes, private health scheme etc.

(j) Loss of social security benefits. A claimant who was unemployed at the date of the accident and in receipt of social security benefits can recover the benefits he or she would have received but for the accident (*Neal* v *Bingle* [1998] 2 All ER 58).

(k) Other miscellaneous losses, e.g., cancellation of a holiday.

(l) Costs incurred by members of the claimant's family visiting him or her in hospital, looking after him or her etc., including their lost earnings. These are recoverable as part of the claimant's own loss (*Kirkham* v *Boughey* [1958] 2 QB 338).

(m) The value of unpaid care provided by a friend or relative. Surprising as it may seem at first sight, a reasonable sum can be recovered by the claimant for the notional cost of employing someone to care for him or her, even where that care is being provided gratuitously, irrespective of any legal liability to pay (*Cunningham* v *Harrison* [1973] QB 942; *Donnelly* v *Joyce* [1974] QB 454). This is so whether or not the relative has given up paid employment to look after the claimant; and even where the relative has given up paid employment and the claim is valued on that basis, the loss is still viewed as the claimant's, not the relative's, loss. However the loss is not recoverable where it is the defendant himself or herself who is providing the voluntary care (*Hunt* v *Severs* [1994] AC 350).

(n) The above principle does not however apply to a relative who does gratuitous work for the claimant in his or her business. No damages are recoverable for the value of such work (*Hardwick* v *Hudson* [1999] 3 All ER 426).

(o) A claimant may also recover damages for the value of care which he used to provide gratuitously to a member of his family, but which as a result of his injury he is no longer able to provide (*Lowe* v *Guise* [2002] All ER (D) 353).

(p) Court of Protection fees; costs of administering a trust fund. Where the claimant is unable to look after his or her own affairs, a receiver will need to be appointed and remunerated; where the claimant is a minor a trust fund may be required. Such administrative costs are recoverable.

11.4.1.3 The schedule of loss and expense

CPR, PD 16, para. 4.2, requires the claimant to 'attach to his particulars of claim a schedule of details of any past and future expenses and losses which he claims'. Note that what is required is a full setting out of the sums claimed, not only by way of past, but also of future loss and expense. Do not be confused into thinking that future losses and expenses are special damages.

11.4.2 GENERAL DAMAGES

11.4.2.1 Nature and proof of general damages

General damages represent the loss to the claimant that cannot be precisely quantified, that is, past and future non-financial loss and future financial loss.

General damages do not have to be specifically pleaded, though any material facts giving rise to a claim for general damages should be pleaded (e.g., the injuries, loss of employment, handicap on the labour market). Nor do general damages need to be specifically proved: they can be implied to a certain extent. However, evidence is required, and in practice as much evidence as is available should be presented. A medical report must be served with the claimant's particulars of claim (CPR, PD 16, para. 4.3).

11.4.2.2 Heads of general damages

Heads of general damages are as follows:

(a) Pain and suffering.

(b) Loss of amenity.

(c) Hybrid heads.

(d) Future loss of earnings.

(e) Loss of earning capacity.

(f) Loss of pension rights.

(g) Future expenses (including value of future unpaid help).

A further head of general damages, loss of expectation of life, was abolished by the Administration of Justice Act 1982 (AJA 1982), s. 1.

Heads of damages may occasionally overlap, and where this happens care must be taken to avoid double recovery. There are various rules that have been developed by the courts to deal with overlap situations which are explained below, where they arise.

11.5 Provisional Damages

11.5.1 WHEN MAY A CLAIMANT CLAIM PROVISIONAL DAMAGES?

A claimant may in certain circumstances claim provisional damages rather than damages. Section 32A of SCA 1981 (inserted by AJA 1982, s. 6) provides:

> *(1) This section applies to a claim for damages for personal injuries in which there is proved or admitted to be a chance that at some definite or indefinite time in the future the injured person will, as a result of the act or omission which gave rise to the cause of action, develop some serious disease or suffer some serious deterioration in his physical or mental condition.*
> *(2) Subject to subsection (4) below, as regards any action for damages to which this section applies in which a judgment is given in the High Court, provision may be made by rules of court for enabling the court, in such circumstances as may be prescribed, to award the injured person —*
> *(a) damages assessed on the assumption that the injured person will not develop the disease or suffer the deterioration in his condition; and*
> *(b) further damages at a future date if he develops the disease or suffers the deterioration.*
> *(3) Any rules made by virtue of this section may include such incidental, supplementary and consequential provisions as the rule-making authority may consider necessary or expedient.*

The same provisions appear as s. 51 of the County Courts Act 1984, for actions in the County Court.

The relevant rules mentioned in s. 32A(3) are to be found in CPR, Part 41.

The circumstances in which a court will make an award of provisional damages were considered in *Willson* v *Ministry of Defence* [1991] 1 All ER 638. The judge held that:

(a) the chance of serious disease or deterioration must be measurable rather than fanciful;

(b) the 'serious deterioration' must be something distinct and beyond the ordinary deterioration that is a normal part of the claimant's condition;

(c) the risk of further injury in the future will not give rise to a provisional award where that risk of injury and its likely consequences are purely speculative.

11.5.2 EFFECT OF A CLAIM FOR PROVISIONAL DAMAGES

A claim for provisional damages will result in an initial award which will be lower than an award of damages on a once-and-for-all basis, but with the possibility of a further award in the future which, when taken together with the initial award, will produce a total sum greater than an award of damages on a once-and-for-all basis would have been. The reasons for this will be explained when we see how damages are quantified.

A claim for provisional damages affects only the general damages, not the special damages. A claimant may claim provisional damages or damages in the alternative. If a claimant claims damages, it is not open to a defendant to argue that the claimant should be awarded provisional damages.

11.5.3 PROVISIONAL DAMAGES ARE NOT INTERIM PAYMENTS

Be sure not to confuse provisional damages with interim payments in respect of damages under CPR, Part 25. See the ***Civil Litigation Manual*, Chapter 13**.

11.6 Quantification of Damages — Introduction

The quantification of damages is a five-stage process:

Stage 1: Quantify special damages.

Stage 2: Quantify general damages.

Stage 3: Make any necessary deductions.

Stage 4: Contributory negligence.

Stage 5: Add interest.

11.7 Stage 1: Quantify Special Damages

11.7.1 A MATTER OF ARITHMETIC

Since special damages represent the claimant's quantifiable financial loss, this is basically just a matter of arithmetic. The claimant has to prove both the item of loss and its value. The court will therefore award such losses as are proved. If the claimant fails to prove that an item of expenditure is reasonable, the court will either not award it, or will award such sum as would have been reasonable.

11.7.2 ADVISING ON QUANTUM

If you are advising on quantum, look at the special damages that have been incurred, decide whether in your opinion they are reasonable, exclude what you think the claimant cannot prove or what is unreasonable, and take the result. Where the claimant is claiming the value of voluntary services, a reasonable figure for this must be claimed and proved.

Do not look into the future with special damages. Although the cut-off point for a court is the date of trial, when negotiating a settlement or advising on quantum, take the cut-off date as today, calculate special damages so far, and treat the continuing expenditure in the future as general damages. Do not invent a notional date of trial.

11.7.3 ASSESSING SPECIAL DAMAGES

The assessment of most items of special damage is straightforward once the figures are known: medical expenses, damage to property, costs of nursing care, paid help, items of expenditure, items of increased expenditure, value of fringe benefits, miscellaneous losses, costs incurred by, and lost earnings of, claimant's relatives, Court of Protection fees — all these can simply be added up taking the exact figures that have been ascertained.

Some items of special damages are a little more complicated to assess, however, and the method for such items is as follows.

11.7.4 ASSESSING LOST EARNINGS

11.7.4.1 Basis of assessment

Except where the claimant is very seriously injured and the cost of caring for him or her is expensive, the major item of special damages is likely to be lost earnings. These are assessed not just on the basis of what the claimant was earning at the date of the accident, but on the basis of what he or she would have earned between accident and trial. So if, for example, the claimant is able to show that, but for his or her injuries, he or she would have had a chance of an increase in earnings, or promotion, or moving on to better paid employment, or advancing his or her career, or building up his or her business, etc., then damages will be awarded taking account of these increased earnings. The claim is for the loss of a chance. This means that the claimant does not have to show that he or she probably would have had an increase in earnings, only that he or she has lost the chance of such an increase; but damages will be assessed in accordance with the chance, so if the chance was 75%, the claimant will recover 75% of what the increase would have been.

Similarly, any likely decreases in income must be taken into account (e.g., because of retirement, redundancy, ailing business).

11.7.4.2 Methods of calculation

Where the claimant was a regular wage earner, the lost earnings can be calculated by reference to someone else doing the same job. If he or she received regular amounts of commission, bonuses, overtime, then again his or her loss can be assessed in this way. Where however, his or her earnings fluctuated, then an average will be taken over an appropriate period. The norm is to average the last six pay-packets, though a longer period may need to be taken (if, for example, he or she had overtime in summer but not in winter).

11.7.4.3 Taxation to be taken into account

The claimant's lost earnings are always calculated net, not gross. That is to say, you base the calculations on what the claimant earned or would have earned after deductions of tax and national insurance. This is the rule in *Gourley's* case (*British Transport Commission* v *Gourley* [1956] AC 185).

Since the claimant will not be liable to tax on the award of damages (Income and Corporation Taxes Act 1988, s. 148 and sch. 11, para. 3), tax must be taken off the amount received in compensation for lost earnings, otherwise the claimant will be better off than he or she would have been but for his or her injury. Both basic rate and higher rate tax is taken into account. Where the claimant's claim is for a partial, rather than total, loss of earnings, the earnings lost are deemed to be the top slice of his or her income. For further guidance see **Part II** of this Manual.

11.7.4.4 The *Gourley* principle and pension contributions

The *Gourley* principle also applies to an employee's compulsory contributions to a pension scheme, and earnings are taken net of such contributions, if no pension rights have been lost (*Dews* v *National Coal Board* [1987] 2 All ER 545). If the non-payment of pension contributions *has* led to a diminished pension, then usually the claimant will claim damages for lost pension rights (see below **11.12**) and so must deduct his or her pension contributions to avoid double recovery.

11.7.4.5 Expenses incurred in connection with employment

On the same principle, it is necessary to set against the claimant's lost earnings any expenses he or she would have incurred in order to be able to earn that income but which have been saved, e.g., the cost of travel to and from work, special clothing etc. Obviously no such deduction needs to be made if the claimant still incurs these expenses in order to earn a lesser income.

11.7.5 THE COST OF A NEW HOME

There is no difficulty where the claimant is simply paying more in rent for his or her new accommodation: the measure is simply the increase in rent.

But where the claimant purchases new accommodation, the process is not as simple as might have been thought. The claimant cannot be awarded the capital cost of the new house less the sale value of his or her old house, because there will be a windfall effect for his or her family, dependants and heirs. What he or she has actually lost is the use of his or her capital tied up in the new house, and so he or she should be awarded the interest he or she could have gained by investing that sum (*Roberts* v *Johnstone* [1989] QB 878). It was decided in *Wells* v *Wells* [1998] 3 All ER 481 that this should be taken as 3% per year; but since a discount rate has been set under the Damages Act 1996 (see **11.10.3.4** to **11.10.3.9** below), it should now be taken as 2.5% per year. So calculate the loss by taking the difference in capital value (cost of new house less sale price of old) and award the claimant 2.5% of this sum per year. No deduction needs to be made for the 'Rolls Royce' effect — the fact that the claimant may incidentally be enjoying better amenities (larger garden, closer to shops), or improved quality of life ('better' area, quieter neighbourhood) than he or she otherwise would, providing the new house was a reasonable purchase.

Costs involved in the purchase, e.g., estate agent's fees, conveyancing costs and removal costs and any increased outgoings on the new house are also recoverable.

11.7.6 THE COST OF CONVERTING A HOME

The claimant may not only have had to purchase new accommodation, but may also have had to convert it, or his or her existing home, for his or her special needs. Such a cost is therefore recoverable additionally to the cost of any new home. However, an adjustment must be made to take account of any change in the value of the house brought about by the conversion work (*Roberts* v *Johnstone*).

Not all the money spent on conversion will have had an effect on house value. Ignore any expenditure which has not, and consider only the expenditure which has had an effect. Suppose the claimant has spent £30,000 on conversion, £20,000 of which has had no effect on the value of the house, and £10,000 of which has had the effect of increasing its value. He or she will recover £20,000 in any event. If the value of the house has increased by £10,000 or more, he or she cannot recover the £10,000 conversion cost. If the value has increased by less than £10,000, deduct the increase in value from the £10,000 and award the difference.

If the conversion work has decreased the value of the house, then the loss in value can be recovered as well as the conversion cost.

11.7.7 LOSS OF USE OF COMPANY CAR

The value of this item will depend on the extent to which the claimant was permitted to and did use the car for private purposes, and what sort of car it was. Figures provided by motoring organisations can be found in *Butterworths Personal Injury Litigation Service*, section XIV [50]. Expect a sum in the area of £2,000–£5,000 per year, even substantially more if the claimant did a high mileage in a large car. Take care to establish whether the claimant or the company paid for petrol for private use. Be careful to avoid any overlap with a claim for increased travel costs.

11.7.8 VALUE OF UNPAID CARE

The method of assessing this item is discretionary, and will depend to some extent on who the relative providing the care is and what he or she has given up in order to be able to do so. One common approach is to award the cost of employing a professional or professionals to provide the services being valued. If the claimant's spouse nurses him or her round the clock, then the value will be the cost of 24-hour nursing attendance, less an allowance for the amount of care he or she would have provided in any event as a spouse. Alternatively damages may be assessed on the basis of the relative's lost earnings, if he or she has given up work to look after the claimant. If the relative has reasonably given up work to care for the claimant, the lost earnings are likely to be recoverable in full, even if the care is strictly less valuable. There may even be an added value if the relative is providing services over and above those that giving up work has enabled him or her to provide.

The courts frown upon artificial 'contracts' between the claimant and the carer, and will not take the amount in the contract as reliable evidence of the value of the services.

Although this item of damages is not precisely quantifiable in financial terms and is a matter of assessment, nevertheless it is strictly part of the special damages.

11.7.9 AGREEMENT ON QUANTUM

The quantum of special damages will usually be agreed between the parties, subject to liability. Certainly, the court will expect special damages to be agreed and, if they are not will want to know why not. Even if there is a dispute as to an item of special damages, the quantum can still be agreed on an either/or basis. See *Practice Direction (Damages: Personal Injury Actions)* [1984] 1 WLR 1127.

11.8 Stage 2: Quantify General Damages

11.8.1 INTRODUCTION

Each head of damages is quantified in an entirely different way, so we must look at them separately. However, the first two heads can be taken together.

11.9 Heads 1 and 2: Pain and Suffering and Loss of Amenity

11.9.1 A SINGLE AWARD

These are usually quantified together; that is to say, a single award will be made for pain and suffering and loss of amenity as a composite, without any indication from the court as to how much is awarded under each head.

This award will simply be a round sum, apparently plucked out of the air. Pain and suffering and loss of amenity are by their nature wholly non-financial losses, and the compensation cannot possibly be calculated, it can only be evaluated on some basis. The basis chosen for evaluation is basically convention, coupled with comparison with previous awards, experience, and sheer intuition. The process is not as arbitrary as it may sound, however. Before we look at it, we should distinguish pain and suffering and loss of amenity, which are closely connected, and sometimes overlap, yet which are not quite the same thing.

11.9.1.1 Damages for pain and suffering

Damages for pain and suffering compensate the claimant for the physical pain and the emotional and intellectual suffering caused by the injury. Shock is included, as are anxiety, embarrassment and emotional injury. It is strictly speaking not the injury itself for which the claimant is being compensated, so a claimant who suffers multiple injuries, and is thereby rendered immediately and permanently unconscious, recovers nothing under this head, because although he or she has been injured, he or she feels no pain and is not experiencing any mental suffering as a result of his or her injuries. Nevertheless, it is the injury itself which will form the starting point for evaluating pain and suffering, so the exact nature and extent of the injury is important. The more serious the injury, the longer it lasts, the greater the award. A claimant who makes a complete recovery gets less than one who is permanently handicapped or disfigured.

Emotional distress, e.g., fear, horror, anguish and grief, which is not connected to physical or psychiatric injury, does *not* by itself give rise to a claim under this head.

It is necessary to look at the particular claimant and his or her individual circumstances. A claimant who is distressed by a scar on his or her face suffers more than one who is not. The claimant's age and life expectancy are relevant. The shorter his or her expected life, the shorter the period of pain and suffering and the less he or she will recover in damages, even where it is the injuries themselves that have reduced his or her life expectancy. However, the claimant's suffering may be increased by knowledge that his or her life expectancy has been reduced, and this must be taken into account (AJA 1982, s. 1(1)(b)).

11.9.1.2 Damages for loss of amenity

Damages for loss of amenity compensate the claimant for his or her lost or reduced enjoyment of life. Loss of amenity can be general — for example, where the injuries have affected the claimant's general sense of well-being or cheerful disposition; or specific — for example, where the claimant is no longer able to enjoy a game of football or play the piano. Other examples of loss of amenity include loss of brain function, loss of any of the five senses, loss of sex-life, loss of mobility, loss of ability to do one's job, loss of job satisfaction, loss of ability to form friendships or relationships, loss of marriage prospects, breakdown of marriage, and loss of enjoyment of a holiday. In this case it is the loss of amenity itself for which the claimant is being compensated, not the suffering caused by awareness of it, so a claimant who is in a coma or so severely brain-damaged as to have no realisation of his or her plight can recover damages under this head (*Wise* v *Kaye* [1962] 1 QB 638; *Lim Poh Choo* v *Camden and Islington Area Health Authority* [1980] AC 174).

Loss of amenity, even more than pain and suffering, is highly subjective and specific to the claimant. As with pain and suffering, the claimant's age and life expectancy will make a difference, and the shorter the life expectancy the *shorter* the loss of amenity. But it does not follow that the shorter the life expectancy the less the loss of amenity. An injury may diminish the quality of life of an older claimant far more than it does that of a younger claimant. You must look to see precisely how each claimant has been affected by his or her injuries. For example, loss of hearing may be more serious for a musician than a painter; a permanent limp may be more serious for an athlete than a bank manager; a broken nose may be more serious for a model than a builder.

11.9.1.3 The difficulty of separating the two heads of damage

In the end pain and suffering and loss of amenity have to be taken together because it is usually impossible to say where one ends and the other begins. If, for example, a claimant has an injured leg and can walk only half a mile before it starts to hurt, there is pain, there is suffering, and there is loss of amenity, but one cannot say they are three separate items of loss. The pain causes loss of mobility; inability to enjoy a walk produces suffering. It is necessary for the court to award a single lump sum.

11.9.2 ARRIVING AT A FIGURE FOR PAIN AND SUFFERING AND LOSS OF AMENITY

11.9.2.1 The first stage

The starting point for the court in selecting that figure is the evidence presented to it — medical evidence and the evidence of the claimant. A barrister's starting point in advising on quantum will be the medical reports and information contained within the claimant's statement. The first stage is to ascertain as accurately as possible the nature and extent of the injuries, the degree of pain and suffering and the loss of amenity. Where the evidence is contradictory, the court will have to decide what evidence to accept; in advising all you can do is bear that conflict in mind.

11.9.2.2 The second stage

The next stage is to look up the awards that have been made in past cases of a similar nature. These are found in *Kemp & Kemp*, volumes 3 and 4, in *Butterworths PILS* and in *Current Law*, categorised according to the broad nature of the injury; also on Lawtel and Butterworths Online, where you need to search for keywords. There is a conventional tariff or a guideline range for each type of injury. The tariffs used by judges are published by the Judicial Studies Board and can be found in *Kemp & Kemp* and *Guidelines for the Assessment of General Damages in Personal Injury Cases*, 5th edn, London: Blackstone Press (OUP), 2000. You should certainly make use of these, but they are not sufficient by themselves. First try to ascertain the correct range for the type of injury you are dealing with, then try to ascertain whereabouts in the range your case falls, by comparing the facts of your case with those reported and making such value judgments as seem right, taking particular account of your claimant's individual circumstances, suffering and losses of amenity. It is not a precise art, but it is possible to get quite close. This is what a judge will do, and it is what you do in negotiating a settlement or advising on quantum.

11.9.2.3 Example

Compare the awards made to the claimants in the following two cases. Do you think they were about right? What factors do you think explain the difference? The relevant *JSB Guidelines* (5th edition) are: moderate whiplash injuries where the period of recovery has been fairly protracted and where there remains an increased vulnerability to further trauma — £3,750 to £7,000; minor soft tissue and whiplash injuries and the like where symptoms are moderate and a full recovery takes place within at most two years — up to £3,750.

Case A — November 2000 — Damages £6,750
Female, aged 38 at the time of the accident and 42 at trial, sustained injury when her car was struck from behind with some force by the defendant's vehicle. She was taken to hospital where a whiplash type injury was diagnosed. She was given a collar and painkillers and was off work for six weeks. She saw her GP on a couple of occasions and was referred for physiotherapy. Although her symptoms improved over time, they never disappeared. At the date of trial she continued to experience intermittent pain at the base of her neck radiating into her left shoulder. Although she had been able to resume aerobics after a short break she now avoided exercises requiring her to raise her left arm above the horizontal. Heavier housework or a change in weather would also bring on symptoms in her shoulder. The opinion of the joint expert was that she had sustained a classic whiplash with partial tearing of the ligaments of the neck. The expert anticipated further gradual recovery until about five years after the accident. Thereafter she would be left with intermittent symptoms which, although permanent, would be no more than a minor nuisance.

Case B — November 2000 — Damages £3,000
Male, aged 32 at the date of the road traffic accident and 33 at trial, sustained injury in a head-on collision. He struck his head on the car door pillar suffering a mild head injury and sustained a whiplash type injury to his neck and back. He visited his GP who referred him for four sessions of physiotherapy. He also took painkillers and was off work for three weeks. Thereafter he had headaches at work when concentrating on his computer screen. He was unable to go swimming for several months due to neck and back pain and had not returned at all to playing football. At the date of trial, his back problems had resolved. However, he was still experiencing a dull ache in his neck associated with certain activities and headaches, albeit with decreasing frequency. Medical opinion was that there would be a full resolution of symptoms within 12 months of the accident.

11.9.2.4 *Heil* v *Rankin*

The process of comparing awards in previous cases must be performed in the light of the decision of the Court of Appeal in *Heil* v *Rankin* [2000] 3 All ER 138. In that case (and seven others considered at the same time) the Court took account of a recent Law Commission Report to the effect that awards for pain, suffering and loss of amenity were too low, and decided that an increase was required in all awards that would previously have been over £10,000. Awards under £10,000 did not need increasing. The increase should be on a sliding scale, with the highest (those over £150,000) increasing by a third. By way of indication, the Court increased an award of £40,000 by 10%, an award of £45,000 by 11%, an award of £80,000 by 19%, an award of £110,000 by 25% and an award of £135,000 by 30%. This has become known as the *Heil* v *Rankin* uplift.

The 5th edition of the *JSB Guidelines* (July 2000) has taken this adjustment into account, and so no uplift needs to be made when using the Guidelines as a starting point for assessing damages. Nor will there be any need to add an uplift when using a case decided after 23 March 2000 as a comparison. But when looking at a case before that date, in which damages were more than £10,000, it will be necessary to add a *Heil* v *Rankin* uplift to see what would have been awarded today.

This may be done approximately, using the Court of Appeal's examples as a guide; or it may be done rather more precisely, using this formula, explained in *Quantum*, 18 April 2000:

> If £A is the value of an award in March 2000, immediately prior to *Heil* v *Rankin*, then the award after the uplift will be £A + [(£A − 10,000)/420,000 × £A]. The part in square brackets is the uplift.

But this will only be one part of a calculation which also has to take account of inflation: see below.

11.9.2.5 Inflation

It is particularly important to look at recent awards and take account of the effect of inflation on the value of money. The tariffs for each type of injury, and the actual sums awarded, gradually increase more or less in line with inflation. The need to take accurate account of inflation was recognised by the Court of Appeal in *Housecroft* v *Burnett* [1986] 1 All ER 332. Before that decision, awards had been lagging behind inflation for some years.

The most accurate assessment can be made when one can find a comparable very recent award. *Current Law*, Lawtel and Butterworths Online are particularly helpful here, but *Kemp & Kemp* and *Butterworths PILS* are also updated regularly. In the absence of a recent comparable award, one needs to look at earlier awards and multiply them by the appropriate inflation factor. A table of such multipliers can be found in *Kemp & Kemp* at the front of volumes 3 and 4 and in each monthly part of *Current Law*. Be very cautious however of adopting this approach to awards prior to *Housecroft* v *Burnett*, since an inaccurate result may be obtained. Generally speaking, awards more than ten years old are of little practical help.

Additional account will need to be taken of the *Heil* v *Rankin* uplift where the value of the award was over £10,000 in March 2000. This can lead to some fairly complex calculations, and so not surprisingly at the present time more than usual reliance is being placed on the *JSB Guidelines* and very recent cases wherever possible. But not all types of injury are covered by the Guidelines, and there is not always a comparable recent award, so such calculations will sometimes be necessary. As the years pass, and more and more recent awards are reported, it will be possible in due course to forget about the uplift. Some sample calculations follow.

11.9.2.6 Sample calculation — inflation only

Suppose you want to find out what the value of an award of £7,500 made in June 1995 is in April 2002. The size of the award is such that no *Heil* v *Rankin* uplift will be involved. So the adjustment needs to be made for inflation only. There are two ways of doing the calculation.

The shorter, less accurate method is to use the table in *Kemp & Kemp*, IT–101. At the time of writing, this was up-to-date only to January 2001. You will see that if you apply a multiplier of 1.17 to an award made in January 1995 you will get the value in January 2001. You can be a bit more accurate if you look also at the multiplier for January 1996, which is 1.14, and make a rough and ready guess that for June 1995 the multiplier might be about half way between the two, so 1.155. You then notice that in recent years the multiplier has increased by about 0.025 a year, so you can estimate that this should be added on to give you the value of the award up to January 2002. Then £7,500 × 1.18 gives you £8,850. You ignore inflation from January to April 2002. This calculation will usually do for advisory purposes where only an approximate sum is required.

A fuller, more accurate calculation can be made using the monthly Retail Prices Index tables in *Kemp & Kemp*, IT–102. First look up the RPI for June 1995, which is given as 149.8. Then look up the RPI for April 2002. You may find that the table in *Kemp & Kemp* doesn't go that far (it's usually a few months behind), so try *Current Law*. In the June 2002 issue you will find that the RPI for April 2002 was 175.7. You then do the calculation £7,500 × 175.7 ÷ 149.8 which gives you £8,797, which you would probably round to £8,800.

You can always find the most recent RPI figure on-line at www.statistics.gov.uk/instantfigures.asp.

11.9.2.7 Sample calculation — inflation and *Heil* v *Rankin* uplift

Suppose you want to find out what the value of an award of £60,000 made in June 1995 is in April 2002. You will need to do the calculation in three stages.

First you must update the award for inflation to March 2000. Using the RPI tables and the method explained above, the sum will be £60,000 × 168.4 ÷ 149.8 = £67,450.

Next you must give this sum the *Heil* v *Rankin* uplift. Using the formula set out in **11.9.2.4**, the sum is £67,450 + [(£67,450 − 10,000) ÷ 420,000 × £67,450]. This produces an uplift of £9,226 and so an adjusted sum of £76,676.

Finally you must update this sum for inflation between March 2000 and April 2002. Using the RPI table again, the sum is £76,676 × 175.7 ÷ 168.4 = £80,000, a nice round number. This then is your answer.

11.9.2.8 Criminal Injuries Compensation Board awards

Awards made by the Criminal Injuries Compensation Board have in the past been assessed in the same way as awards made by courts. Many of the cases reported are CICB awards and they are generally comparable and can be used to help assess damages in similar cases. From 8 November 1995 the Criminal Injuries Compensation Act 1995 introduced a new scheme of compensation, based not on common law damages but on fixed tariffs laid down by the Home Secretary. Such awards are not likely to be reliable or helpful and should not be used.

11.9.2.9 The final figure

In the end the figure arrived at is chosen by judgment based upon careful research and informed experience. When advising on quantum, a barrister will frequently, having formed a preliminary view, test it out on other members of chambers before setting down his or her final conclusion. That opinion may be expressed as a range 'in the range £25,000–£30,000' — or as an approximate figure — 'about £12,000'. It is probably better to give an approximate figure if you can, especially if an attempt at settlement is to be made. If you give a range, indicate what circumstances will put the award at the bottom and the top end of the range.

11.9.3 THE PROBLEM OF FUTURE UNCERTAINTY AS REGARDS PAIN AND SUFFERING AND LOSS OF AMENITY

A particular problem arises in quantifying damages for pain, suffering and loss of amenity where the prognosis is uncertain. This will in fact almost always be the case to some extent, except where the claimant has wholly recovered from his or her injury. It is to the claimant's advantage usually to try and delay trial or settlement until the future is as certain as it is going to be, but this may not be possible. For example, it may not be certain whether the claimant's condition will deteriorate; whether he or she has recovered as far as he or she is going to or whether he or she will continue to improve; whether osteoarthritis will set in in ten years' time; whether an apparent obstacle has been overcome permanently or temporarily; whether a female claimant will be able to give birth to children or not. In such circumstances the court has to assess the chance and value it. Broadly speaking, if there is a 10% chance of an unfavourable development, the court will award 10% of any increase in damages that that development would attract.

Alternatively, where the uncertainty is as to whether the claimant's condition will seriously deteriorate, or whether some serious disease will set in (but *not* in the case of any other uncertainty) the claimant has the option of claiming provisional damages under SCA 1981, s. 32A and CCA 1984, s. 51. This will result in a lower award now, but with the certainty of a further award in the future if the serious deterioration or disease occurs. This has to be balanced against the advantages of a once-and-for-all settlement which evaluates the chance, produces a greater sum now and brings the litigation to an end. It is a tactical decision.

11.9.4 HYBRID HEADS

11.9.4.1 Overlap between loss of amenity and financial loss

There are certain miscellaneous heads of damages which are sometimes seen as losses of amenity and sometimes as financial losses. Occasionally there is an element of both loss of amenity and financial loss, and care must be taken to avoid overlap. Some common examples of hybrid heads follow. This list is not exhaustive.

11.9.4.2 Loss of congenial employment

Awards are increasingly often being made under this head. Such damages compensate the claimant for his or her loss of job satisfaction. If the claimant was previously employed or earning his or her living in a way which brought him or her particular pleasure, enjoyment, pride or responsibility, and as a result of his or her injury is now employed in a more boring or mundane job, even if there is no loss of earnings, there is a recoverable loss under this head. It ought strictly to be part of the claimant's loss of amenity, but has come to be treated as a separate head of damages for which a lump sum of up to about £5,000 might be awarded. If there is also a claim for loss of earnings, care must be taken not to take account of loss of job satisfaction twice. A table in *Kemp & Kemp* (para. 5–251) shows some sample awards.

11.9.4.3 Loss of housekeeping ability

This head was established by *Daly* v *General Steam Navigation Co. Ltd* [1981] 1 WLR 120. It is strictly a claim for financial loss. If a claimant has suffered an impairment of his or her ability to do housework, to the extent that this has diminished his or her happiness, it can be taken account of as part of the general loss of amenity. But otherwise it is essentially a claim for the cost of a housekeeper and is valued on that basis, both for special damages and general damages (see **11.13.3**).

11.9.4.4 Loss of marriage prospects

Under this head there is truly an element of both loss of amenity and financial loss. It arises where a young claimant's injury has diminished or destroyed his or her chances of marriage. To the extent that this affects his or her happiness, it is a loss of amenity. But there is also a financial loss. Only female claimants have in the past succeeded in claiming this financial loss, which is the financial support a husband would probably have provided. However such a loss could in theory be established by a man who was engaged to a wealthy woman at the time of the accident. How a female claimant is compensated under this head is dealt with in **11.10.5.2**.

11.9.4.5 Breakdown of marriage

Sometimes a claimant's injuries can lead to his marriage breaking down. This is something to be taken account of in the award for loss of amenity, but there may also be a financial loss. Provided it is not too remote, an award can be made under this head, for example, for the loss of a spouse's services. The breakdown of the marriage may also result in significant extra expenditure, particularly if there is a divorce. Unfortunately there are conflicting authorities on whether such loss is recoverable: *Jones* v *Jones* [1985] QB 704; *Pritchard* v *J.H. Cobden Ltd* [1988] Fam 22.

11.10 Head 3: Future Loss of Earnings

This head of damages arises where there is at the date of trial or settlement an annual loss of earnings which is measurable at today's values, and evidence that it will continue into the future. If at the date of trial there is no measurable annual loss, but nevertheless evidence that some loss is likely to accrue in the future, then an award under the next head, loss of earning capacity (see **11.11**) may be more appropriate.

11.10.1 THE MULTIPLIER AND THE MULTIPLICAND

Damages are calculated on a multiplier/multiplicand basis. This means that two separate figures must be arrived at in turn and then multiplied together to produce the result. The multiplicand represents the aspect of the claimant's loss that is reasonably certain and measurable in financial terms, i.e., his or her current annual loss. The multiplier represents that aspect of the loss that is uncertain and not precisely ascertainable, i.e., how long into the future such a loss will continue.

11.10.2 CALCULATING THE MULTIPLICAND

This is basically the claimant's net annual loss of earnings as at the date of trial, or as at the date on which you are advising on quantum. In calculating special damages, account has already been taken of any likely pay increases, promotion, career moves, business developments etc., and these factors obviously also affect what the claimant would have been earning today. The *Gourley* principle again applies and all calculations should be done using net sums. The calculation is simply, what the claimant would have been earning net annually, minus what he or she is now earning net annually (if anything), minus annual expenses saved. What you are left with is the multiplicand.

This calculation of the multiplicand is straightforward where the claimant's loss of earnings is likely to continue at more or less the same level until the age at which he or she would have retired. But what if there is evidence that the claimant was likely to have been promoted, or that his or her earnings would have increased for some other reason, for example a new job, or the expansion of his or her business; or alternatively evidence that he or she would have been likely to lose his or her job or suffer a decrease in earnings at some point in the future? The traditional approach to these problems was to make no adjustment to the multiplicand, but rather to make an adjustment to the multiplier to take account of any future uncertainties. But as we shall see in **11.10.3** when we look at multipliers, the approach these days is likely to be more scientific, and there may well be a reluctance to make speculative adjustments to the multiplier. If so, then the court has two alternative approaches open to it. One is to decide on a multiplicand which represents not the annual loss of earnings today, but the average annual loss of earnings over the period to be measured, applying a single multiplier. The other approach will be for the court to look at the evidence, and find as a fact, for example, that the claimant's earnings would probably have increased by £x in about five years' time, and make a split award, using two or even three, multiplicands, and a multiplier divided into two (or three) parts. See **11.10.4**.

11.10.3 THE MULTIPLIER

11.10.3.1 What is the multiplier?

The multiplier represents the number of years for which the claimant is to be awarded his or her net annual loss of earnings. It is sometimes known as the 'number of years' purchase'. It is important to realise that the multiplier is *not a real number of years*. If a claimant were to be given his or her loss for a real number of years, the effect of accelerated receipt (i.e., the fact that he or she receives the money earlier than he or she would have done had he or she earned it) would be to over-compensate him or her massively. Think, for example, of a male claimant aged 25 at the date of his accident, with a net annual loss of £10,000. He would have retired at 65 and so has lost 40 years of income. But a multiplier of 40 produces a lump sum of £400,000, from which the claimant would be able to derive an annual income far in excess of £10,000.

The multiplier is therefore an artificial figure. It takes account of accelerated receipt. It also takes account of all the variables and uncertainties with regard to the future. It is specific to the individual claimant.

11.10.3.2 The old approach to selecting the multiplier

Until recently, multipliers were selected in a rather artificial way. The starting points were the claimant's age, sex, state of health before the accident and the nature of the employment lost. The more secure the job, the higher the retirement age, the higher the multiplier would be. There was then an assumption made that the claimant, when investing his or her lump sum award of damages, would be able to achieve a net rate of return on his or her investment of 4 to 5% per year. To take account of accelerated receipt, therefore, the total lump sum needed to be reduced by about 4.5% a year, and the multiplier would be arrived at on this basis. This was not generally done by accurate calculation, but rather by reference to tables in *Kemp & Kemp* which showed the multipliers used in other cases, and conventional wisdom, which told us that the appropriate multiplier, for example, was 13 for 20 years of real time, 15 for 25 years of real time, etc. The multiplier selected was almost always a whole number of years, and the court would move the figure first arrived at up or down by a year or so to take account of contingencies like promotion, unemployment etc.

11.10.3.3 The development of a new approach

This method had however become rather out of date. The 4.5% discount rate assumed that the claimant would invest his or her damages to a substantial extent in higher-risk investments, such as equities, or at least ought to. If he or she invested in a safer way, for example in Index-Linked Government Securities (ILGS), he or she would probably only achieve an annual net rate of return of 2 to 3%. Very few claimants actually invested their damages in anything more adventurous than a deposit account, and so ended up under-compensated. Further, the method ignored the existence of what are called the 'Ogden Tables'. These are actuarial tables compiled by a working party under Sir Michael Ogden and first published in 1983. The fourth edition (2000) can be found in *Kemp & Kemp*, chapter 8, appendix 1, *Butterworths PILS* Part [XIV] 86 and on Lawtel. The tables set out the multipliers that should be adopted to measure various periods of the future for claimants of every age, at different discount rates, based on statistical evidence of the population's life expectancy and mortality rate. These tables make it possible to select multipliers in a much more accurate way.

The Law Commission in 1994 made two recommendations: that the Ogden Tables should become admissible in evidence, and that multipliers should be based on an annual discount rate of 3% rather than the conventional 4.5%. Parliament accepted these recommendations and enacted s. 10 of the Civil Evidence Act 1995, and the Damages Act 1996. However case law intervened.

11.10.3.4 Civil Evidence Act 1995, s. 10

This section provides that the Ogden Tables should be admissible in evidence. This obviates the need to call expert evidence to prove them in every case. Section 10 has not yet been brought into force, but in the light of the decision in *Wells* v *Wells* (see **11.10.3.7**), this is no longer of any importance. It may now never be brought into force.

11.10.3.5 Damages Act 1996

Section 1 of the Damages Act 1996 reads:

> (1) *In determining the return to be expected from the investment of a sum awarded as damages for future pecuniary loss in an action for personal injury the court shall, subject to and in accordance with rules of court made for the purposes of this section, take into account such rate of return (if any) as may be prescribed by an order made by the Lord Chancellor.*
>
> (2) *Subsection (1) above shall not however prevent the court taking a different rate of return into account if any party to the proceedings shows that it is more appropriate in the case in question.*
>
> (3) *An order under subsection (1) may prescribe different rates of return for different classes of case.*
>
> (4) *Before making an order under subsection (1) above the Lord Chancellor shall consult the Government Actuary and the Treasury; and any order under that subsection shall be made by statutory instrument subject to annulment in pursuance of a resolution of either House of Parliament.*
>
> (5) . . .

The effect of this section is to enable the Lord Chancellor to prescribe a rate of return lower than 4.5%. It also enables the parties to argue for any rate of return they think is appropriate in the light of the current state of the market and the facts of the case. Once the appropriate rate of return on investment is prescribed, it becomes possible to find the correct multiplier to be taken as a starting point by reference to the Ogden Tables.

The Damages Act 1996 came into force on 24 September 1996, but it was not until June 2001 that the Lord Chancellor prescribed a rate. He was initially waiting for the decision of the House of Lords in *Wells* v *Wells* [1998] 3 All ER 481, but nearly two years passed before a consultation paper was issued by the Lord Chancellor's Department in March 2000, which stated that the Lord Chancellor intended at last to prescribe a rate, and at the same time to bring s. 10 of the Civil Evidence Act 1995 into force. Responses to the consultation were invited by June 2000, and on 27 June 2001 the Lord Chancellor prescribed a rate. But before we consider the effect of this order, we need to look at what happened in the meantime.

11.10.3.6 *Wells* v *Wells* — the background

In 1994 and 1995 several claimants were successful in persuading judges to assume a rate of return on investment of damages of 3% or even less, thus obtaining a multiplier substantially greater than that which would have been applied using the conventional discount. They were able to do so with expert evidence on investment and the use of the Ogden Tables. Several of these cases went to the Court of Appeal and were reported under the name of the first, *Wells* v *Wells* [1997] 1 All ER 673.

The Court of Appeal came down emphatically in favour of retaining the conventional approach to multipliers, and assuming a rate of return on investment of about 4.5%, thus putting the common law in clear conflict with the intention of the Law Commission and the Damages Act 1996. There was then more than a year's delay before the case went to the House of Lords.

11.10.3.7 The House of Lords' decision in *Wells* v *Wells*

The House of Lords decided that the conventional rate of discount of 4.5% should no longer be used when selecting multipliers, and that a rate reflecting the likely rate of return when investing in ILGS should be used instead. This rate should be a standard rate, to be applied in every case until a new rate was set. This would facilitate the settlement of claims, and avoid the need to call expert evidence at trials. The rate should for the time being be 3% until either there was a very considerable change in economic circumstances and/or the Lord Chancellor set a different rate under s. 1(3) of the Damages Act 1996. The House of Lords invited him to do this as soon as possible, to avoid uncertainty. Thereafter the rate should always be set by the Lord Chancellor under the Act, so as to avoid the need for the courts to reconsider the issue. The rate should always be set to within 0.5 of a percentage point (i.e. 2.5%, 3%, 3.5% etc.), so as to make it possible for the Ogden Tables always to be used in practice.

The standard rate should not however be regarded as absolutely fixed. It was accepted by the House of Lords in *Hodgson* v *Trapp* [1989] AC 807, and anticipated by s. 1(2) of the Damages Act 1996, that there may be exceptional circumstances in which an argument can be made out for assuming a different rate of return on investment, particularly where higher rate tax is likely to be payable on income. But it is likely to be rare that such an argument will succeed.

The House of Lords also held that the correct approach in future to selecting a multiplier should be to use the Ogden Tables. Once the correct rate of discount (the assumed net rate of annual return of investment) is known, the tables will provide the correct multiplier, or at least the correct starting point. At this point therefore a new approach to selecting the multiplier came into effect, and the use of the Ogden Tables had official sanction, even though s. 10 of the Civil Evidence Act 1995 was not yet in force.

11.10.3.8 After *Wells* v *Wells*

While the Lord Chancellor continued to delay setting a rate under the Damages Act 1996, pressure mounted for the courts to adopt a rate lower than 3%. Sir Michael Ogden argued in an article in *The Times* that the rate should be set at 2%, and in one case a judge decided to do so, but the Court of Appeal in *Warren* v *Northern General Hospital Trust, The Times*, 10 April 2000, held that the courts could not alter the 3% discount rate until the Lord Chancellor made an order.

11.10.3.9 The rate set by the Lord Chancellor

In June 2001 the Lord Chancellor prescribed a rate of 2.5%. He accepted the need to have a single rate to cover all types of case, so he did not exercise his power under s. 1(3) of the Damages Act 1996. He also accepted the view of the House of Lords that the rate should be set as a multiple of 0.5%, and that the rate of 2.5% should remain unchanged for the foreseeable future.

It remains the case under the Damages Act 1996, s. 1(2), that a party may seek to persuade the court to adopt a different rate where appropriate on the facts of the case. However, following the decision in *Warriner* v *Warriner* [2002] All ER (D) 202, it is hard to envisage in what circumstances a party will succeed in doing so. In that case the Court of Appeal held that the different rate must be more appropriate in the light of the reasons given by the Lord Chancellor for setting the rate at 2.5%. So, in effect, it must be shown that there are circumstances to the case which were not considered by the Lord Chancellor. A very long life expectancy and very large damages are not such circumstances.

We therefore now have a settled approach to the selection of multipliers, which is explained in the next paragraphs. Remember that if the rate does change in the future, this will make very little difference to the process of calculation of damages. The principles by which multipliers are selected will remain unchanged; it is only the appropriate column in the Ogden Tables which will alter.

11.10.3.10 Selecting a multiplier — the new approach

The starting point in finding the multiplier for a loss of future earnings claim will be the appropriate Ogden Table. You will notice that there are two matching sets of tables: 1–18 and 19–36. Tables 1–18 are based on official mortality statistics published by the government, based on the period 1990–92. Tables 19–36 are based on projected statistics for the year 1998. Since life expectancy is gradually rising, the second set of tables gives slightly higher multipliers. Paragraph 9 of the text to the Ogden Tables suggests that all judges in practice are using tables 19–36.

Assuming that tables 19–36 are to be used, for loss of earnings tables 21–28 are the relevant ones. Choose the table appropriate to the claimant's sex and likely retirement age, then all you need to know is the claimant's age today, and the correct discount rate (2.5%) and the multiplier can be read off. In the event of non-standard retirement ages simply adjust the claimant's age. If the claimant is a 35-year-old male but would not have retired until the age of 67, use table 25 but treat the claimant as aged 33.

11.10.3.11 Discount for contingencies

As explained above, account has to be taken of uncertainties with regard to job security and any other contingencies other than mortality. The House of Lords in *Wells* v *Wells* recognised that this practice needed to continue in the case of multipliers for loss of future earnings. The unscientific approach of the past (add or subtract a year or two by guesswork) does not mix well with the actuarial approach and will doubtless be abandoned. There are two ways of dealing with contingencies.

The first is that advocated by the Ogden Working Party and explained in paragraphs 30–44 of the Explanatory Notes to the Tables, and also recommended by *Kemp & Kemp*. That is to use Tables A, B and C, with the further adjustments set out in paragraphs 40–44, in order to discover the factor by which the multiplier initially selected should be adjusted. So for example, in the case of a male aged 35, who would have retired at 65, Table 25 gives us a multiplier of 20.56 and Table A shows that this multiplier should be reduced by a factor of 0.96 (for the moment it is accepted that the 'medium' column is appropriate). If the job was a 'safe' one, increase the factor by 0.01 (see paragraph 41); if it was a 'risky' one reduce it by 0.01 (see paragraph 42). If the claimant lives in the South East, increase the factor by 0.01; if he lives in the North West, reduce it by 0.01. So, if the claimant was in a risky job in the North West, the multiplier would be 0.96 − 0.01 − 0.01 = 0.94 × 20.56 = 19.33.

The other way of dealing with contingencies is much more rough and ready. It is simply to reduce the multiplier by 10%. This was the conventional method before *Wells* v *Wells*, and it appears that it is still widely followed in practice. It is too soon to say whether it will die out.

11.10.3.12 Other contingencies

There are still circumstances in which the court will or may make further adjustments to the multiplier from that suggested by the Ogden Tables. If there is evidence that the claimant was in poor health before his or her accident, such that his or her likely earnings were not typical of a person of his or her age, or if his or her employment prospects were particularly poor, it is still open to the court to decide that the multiplier should be further reduced, and the reduction is likely to be made in the old-fashioned, rather arbitrary way of deducting a certain number of years.

Previously, there were other contingencies that could affect the multiplier, particularly factors like the claimant's actual earning capacity following the accident, or prospects of improving his or her earnings in the future. It seems unlikely that such contingencies will affect the multiplier in future. If they are to be taken account of, they will affect the multiplicand, maybe giving rise to a split award.

11.10.3.13 Factors which do not affect the choice of multiplier

(a) Future inflation. It has often been argued that in times of high inflation multipliers should be adjusted upwards to take account of the fact that the lump sum awarded to the claimant will diminish in value in real terms more quickly. However, high inflation is usually accompanied by higher interest rates and so no adjustment needs to be made (*Lim Poh Choo* v *Camden and Islington Area Health Authority* [1980] AC 174). The theory is that inflation is already taken account of in the conventional multiplier selected. It was thought for a time that there was an exception where the award was so great that the income it produced when invested would attract tax at higher rates and not merely basic rate, but this exception was all but ruled out by the House of Lords in *Hodgson* v *Trapp* [1989] AC 807.

(b) Foreign tax. The fact that a foreign claimant is liable to pay tax in his own country at a higher rate than he would pay in this country is not a justification for altering the discount rate or the multiplier (*Van Oudenhoven* v *Griffin Inns Ltd* [2000] 1 WLR 1413).

(c) The period between injury and trial. The length of time between injury and trial is not to be taken into account in the selection of the multiplier (*Pritchard* v *J. H. Cobden Ltd* [1988] Fam 22), though of course the court looks to the number of working years lost at the date of trial, not at the date of the injury. The rule is the opposite to the rule that applies in claims under the Fatal Accidents Act (see **12.5.2.8**) and does operate slightly in favour of claimants who are slow in bringing their cases to trial.

11.10.4 SPLIT AWARDS

Split awards for loss of future earnings are those where more than one multiplicand is worked out, and a separate multiplier applied to each. Following *Wells* v *Wells* it is likely that such awards will become a lot more common in future. It is the most effective way of calculating loss where the claimant's earnings or losses are likely to change in the future. If for example there is evidence that the claimant would have been promoted in about 10 years, with a corresponding increase in salary, the court is likely to take two multplicands and split the multiplier.

For example, let us assume a female claimant aged 43, who would have been promoted at the age of 50 and retired at the age of 60. The multiplier according to Ogden Table 24 is 13.65, reduced in accordance with Table C by a factor of, say, 0.91, making 12.42. The judge calculates two multiplicands, one for her existing loss — £35,000 per year, the other for her loss after promotion — £42,000 per year. The multiplier for her existing loss should measure a real period of 7 years. Ogden Table 38 helps here — for a fixed period of 7 years the multiplier is 6.43. So for the period before promotion the claimant is awarded 6.43 × £35,000 = £225,050. For the loss after promotion, she gets £42,000 × the remainder of the multiplier (12.42 − 6.43 = 5.99) = £251,580.

It is even possible that in appropriate cases the court will split the multiplier into three periods, with three different multiplicands, for example where the claimant is a young man in his early twenties who had a very long and promising career ahead of him. A split award will also always be necessary in lost years cases; see **11.10.7.3** below.

11.10.5 FEMALE CLAIMANTS AND FUTURE LOSS OF EARNINGS

11.10.5.1 Possible lower awards

A female claimant may not recover damages for loss of future earnings assessed on the basis of Ogden Table 22, 24, 26 or 28. This is because the court must take account of the possibility that she would have given up or interrupted her employment at some time in the future in order to have children and raise a family. If she is able to satisfy the court that she would not have done so, then of course the multiplier will be unaffected. But in the absence of such evidence, the court must evaluate the chance, and it remains a statistical probability that an unmarried woman will get married, and will have children, and will give up or interrupt her employment for some years at least; so a reduced award will result.

11.10.5.2 Loss of marriage prospects

However, an unmarried female claimant may very well also have suffered a loss of marriage prospects. This is not just a loss of amenity, it is also a financial loss — she has lost the financial support her husband would have provided had she given up work to raise a family. Although to make an award for lost marriage prospects and loss of future earnings may amount to double recovery, one can cancel the other out. In *Moriarty* v *McCarthy* [1978] 1 WLR 155 the court reduced the award for loss of future earnings on the ground that the claimant might have given up work to raise a family, but made an award of an amount equal to the reduction for loss of marriage prospects. More simply, the court in *Hughes* v *McKeown* [1985] 1 WLR 963 made no award for loss of marriage prospects, but used the same multiplier in the claim for loss of future earnings as would have been applied in the absence of any loss of marriage prospects.

11.10.6 CHILD CLAIMANTS AND FUTURE LOSS OF EARNINGS

When the claimant is a child who has not yet started work or chosen a career, particular difficulties arise. There can never be a measurable annual loss and so damages assessed on a multiplier/multiplicand basis are not prima facie appropriate. Indeed, where the claimant is very young, and where his or her earning capacity has been reduced rather than destroyed by the injury, the court is likely to make an award for loss of earning capacity rather than loss of future earnings (e.g., *Joyce* v *Yeomans* [1981] 1 WLR 549). But if the claimant has lost any chance of career or employment, the court may well assess damages on a multiplier/multiplicand basis (e.g., *Croke* v *Wiseman* [1981] 3 All ER 852).

The court will first of all need evidence of what the child's likely earnings would have been. If there is good evidence that the child's background was such that he or she would have been a high earner, then the court may take quite a large multiplicand (or series of multiplicands, for a split award). In the absence of such evidence, national average earnings are likely to form the basis of the multiplicand.

The multiplier will depend on the age at which the child would probably have started work. Treat the child as if that were its age in looking up the appropriate multiplier in the Ogden Tables. Reduce it for contingencies in accordance with Tables A–C, and then turn to Ogden Table 37 to determine the extra effect of accelerated receipt before the age of 18. So if for example the claimant is a 5-year-old boy who would probably have started work at the age of 18 and retired at the age of 65, the multiplier will be 27.14 according to Ogden Table 25. This will be reduced by a factor of 0.98 in accordance with Table A, making 26.60. But the money will be received 13 years in advance, so Table 37 shows that the multiplier must be discounted further by a factor of 0.7254. 26.60 × 0.7254 gives a final multiplier of 19.30.

11.10.7 LOST YEARS

11.10.7.1 Basis of assessment

What if, as a result of his or her injury, the claimant's life expectancy has been reduced? Is the multiplier in the claim for loss of earnings to be based on his or her actual, reduced, life expectancy, or on what his or her life expectancy would have been but for his or her injury? The answer, laid down in *Pickett* v *British Rail Engineering Ltd* [1980] AC 136, is that the claimant can claim loss of future earnings, not only for the period he or she will survive, but also for the years he or she has lost, unless that loss is too remote to be measurable. It was thought to be too remote to be measurable if, for example, the claimant was a very young child (*Croke* v *Wiseman* [1981] 3 All ER 852) or if the years that had been lost could have had only a negligible effect on the choice of multiplier (e.g., a 20-year-old whose remaining life expectancy has been reduced from 50 to 40 years). However, following the adoption of the Ogden Tables as the normal starting point, it is now arguable that such a loss is always measurable, even if small.

11.10.7.2 Deduction for living expenses

But in a lost years case a deduction will have to be made from the multiplicand to take account of the claimant's living expenses over those lost years; living expenses which he or she will no longer incur and so which cannot be recovered. 'Living expenses' includes all that the claimant would have spent exclusively on himself or herself — both needs (food, clothing, travel, etc.) and pleasures (beer, cigarettes, entertainments etc.) — but not what he or she would have saved or spent on the support of his or her dependants, or others, such as friends. Expenditure which would have been both for his or her own and his or her dependants' benefit (e.g., rent, mortgage interest, council tax, heating, electricity, gas, TV rental, the cost of running a car) has to be apportioned and a share taken from the multiplicand as the claimant's living expenses (*Harris* v *Empress Motors Ltd* [1983] 3 All ER 561).

11.10.7.3 Two awards

It follows that in a lost years case there will usually be two awards for loss of future earnings, each with a different multiplicand and multiplier: one in respect of the period that the claimant is likely to survive, using a multiplicand from which living expenses have not been deducted; and one in respect of the lost years, using a reduced multiplicand. For the method of calculation, see **11.10.4**.

11.10.8 PROVISIONAL DAMAGES FOR FUTURE LOSS OF EARNINGS

The court may in appropriate cases make a provisional award for future loss of earnings under SCA 1981, s. 32A or CCA 1984, s. 51. Normally uncertainties with regard to the future are taken account of by evaluating the chance. But where the uncertainty is as to whether the claimant's condition will seriously deteriorate, causing him or her to lose their job, the court can assess damages initially on the basis that his or her loss of earnings will continue at its present level, and award a further sum in the future if the loss increases due to the deterioration in condition.

11.11 Head 4: Loss of Earning Capacity

11.11.1 THE NATURE OF THE AWARD

This head of damages arises where there is clear evidence that the claimant will not earn as much in the future as he or she would have done but for the injury, but there is nevertheless no measurable annual loss to found an award for loss of future earnings on a multiplier/multiplicand basis. Instead an award for loss of earning capacity may be made. This is commonly known as a '*Smith* v *Manchester*' award, from *Smith* v *Manchester Corporation* (1974) 17 KIR 1. It compensates the claimant, not so much for lost earnings, but rather for lost earning capacity or the 'handicap on the labour market', and is assessed as a single lump sum.

11.11.2 WHEN IS AN AWARD OF THIS KIND APPROPRIATE?

It is possible to identify various situations in which an award of this kind is appropriate:

(a) Where the claimant is back in pre-accident employment, or in work of equal value, so that there is no immediate loss, but nevertheless, as a result of the injury, he or she will at some time in the future be forced into an early retirement or a less well paid job. If there is a real, or substantial, risk of this, a lump sum award can be made (*Moeliker* v *A. Reyrolle & Co. Ltd* [1976] ICR 252).

(b) Where the claimant is back in pre-accident employment and is not likely to lose it, but nevertheless the injury has damaged prospects of promotion, ability to advance the career or chances of moving on to higher paid employment.

(c) Where the claimant is handicapped on the labour market by the injury. For example, he or she was not in settled employment or was unemployed at the date of the accident, or is not yet back at work but will be soon, and is now going to find work harder to come by, or will find that the range of jobs open to him or her is narrower than it was. In all these instances a *Smith* v *Manchester* award is appropriate.

(d) Where the claimant is a child who has not yet entered the labour market (see **11.10.6**).

11.11.3 QUANTIFICATION OF AN AWARD FOR LOSS OF EARNING CAPACITY

The award is quantified as a round lump sum which is chosen on a fairly arbitrary basis, with some reference to awards in previous cases. A table in *Kemp & Kemp*, para. 6–700 gives some guidance and shows that awards under this head are generally not particularly high. A typical working basis for assessment is to take one to two years' net pay, but a higher sum may be appropriate; see, e.g., *Foster* v *Tyne and Wear County Council* [1986] 1 All ER 567, where a lump sum of five times annual net pay was approved.

11.11.4 AWARDS COMBINING HEADS 3 AND 4

Judges do not always draw a clear distinction between damages for loss of earnings and loss of earning capacity, and occasional hybrid awards can be found where damages for future loss of earnings have been assessed as a lump sum, or where damages for lost earning capacity have been quantified by means of a speculative multiplicand and multiplier. It is likely that this tendency will be more marked following *Wells* v *Wells*, with judges seeking to use a multiplier/multiplicand basis whenever possible.

The two heads are normally alternative to each other, but there are cases where an award under each head is appropriate, e.g., where the claimant has not yet gone back to work but is expected to do so in, say, a year's time; he or she will then resume pre-accident employment but will still be handicapped on the labour market or have lower prospects of promotion. In such a case the court would probably award one year's loss of earnings and a small lump sum. The courts are increasingly willing to recognise that there is a distinction between the two heads and to make an award both for future loss of earnings and for handicap on the labour market.

11.11.5 PROVISIONAL DAMAGES AND LOSS OF EARNING CAPACITY

If the claimant has claimed provisional damages, this may well preclude an award being made under this head. If, for example, there is uncertainty as to whether the claimant's condition will deteriorate, but certainty that if it does the claimant will be forced into early retirement, the court will assess damages initially on the basis that there is no loss of earning capacity, and any later award, if there is deterioration, is likely to be on a multiplier/multiplicand basis.

11.12 Head 5: Loss of Pension Rights

11.12.1 BASIS OF THE AWARD

It is often the case that if a claimant has lost his or her employment as a result of their injury, or employment has been interrupted, he or she has also lost their employers' contributions towards a retirement pension, which will accordingly be reduced. Damages can be awarded to compensate for this loss.

11.12.2 OLD METHOD OF CALCULATING DAMAGES UNDER THIS HEAD

Damages used to be calculated as follows (see *Auty* v *National Coal Board* [1985] 1 All ER 930):

(a) Assuming no change in the value of money, what annual pension would the claimant have received on retirement had he or she not been injured and had there been no interruption to the pension contributions?

(b) What annual pension will the claimant in fact receive, again assuming no change in the value of money?

(c) The difference between (a) and (b) is the annual loss. Multiply it by an appropriate multiplier representing the number of years for which he or she is likely to receive the pension (or, in a lost years case, would have received it).

(d) Discount the lump sum arrived at by 4% or 5% per annum for accelerated receipt. This calculation is on a year on year basis.

11.12.3 NEW METHOD OF CALCULATION

Following *Wells* v *Wells* it must now be appropriate to use an actuarial method of calculation, using the Ogden Tables. *Wells* v *Wells* did not actually deal with the assessment of damages for a lost pension, but exactly the same principles apply. It will certainly be the correct method once s. 10 of the Civil Evidence Act 1995 is in force.

The multiplicand can be calculated as above — it is the difference between the annual pension the claimant would have received on retirement but for the injury and the annual pension that will now be received. The multiplier can be found from Ogden Tables 29–36. Choose the table according to the sex and retirement age of the claimant, and then read off the multiplier according to the claimant's age today and the appropriate rate of discount (2.5%). The tables take account not only of the element of accelerated receipt once the claimant reaches retirement age, but the further element of accelerated receipt, given that the claimant will receive a lump sum in respect of pension loss before reaching retirement age.

The multiplier will again need to be adjusted for contingencies other than mortality. The procedure is exactly the same as in multipliers for loss of future earnings — see **11.10.3.11**.

11.12.4 A SIMPLER METHOD OF ASSESSMENT

An alternative and simpler method of valuing a loss of pension rights, which can be agreed by parties negotiating a settlement, but which does not have the court's approval, is to obtain quotations from life assurance companies. If the claimant has had his or her pension right on retirement reduced from say £15,000 to £10,000 per year, find out the market price today of a £5,000 p.a. pension from age 65 for life, and take this as an appropriate sum.

11.13 Head 6: Future Expenses

11.13.1 SIMILARITY TO SPECIAL DAMAGES

These are likely to be the same items or the same sort of items as were included in the claim for special damages; but where the expenditure has not yet been incurred, or will continue into the future for a number of years or indefinitely, the loss is future loss and forms part of the award for general damages. Anything that was reasonably recoverable as special damages is also recoverable for the future.

11.13.2 'ONE OFF' ITEMS

Items of expenditure that are 'one off', such as the cost of home conversion or the purchase of special equipment, are quantified on a lump sum basis. If the court takes the present day value, the advantage of accelerated receipt is cancelled out by inflation.

11.13.3 RECURRING ITEMS

Recurring items, such as the cost of nursing care, the cost of a housekeeper, and the value of voluntary services, are quantified on a multiplier/multiplicand basis. The multiplicand is the annual cost or value of the service as at the date of trial. The multiplier, following *Wells* v *Wells*, will be selected from the Ogden Tables. If the item of expenditure will last only for a certain number of years, Table 38 will be appropriate; if the item of expenditure will last indefinitely, then the multiplier represents the claimant's life expectancy and Ogden Tables 19 and 20 will be used. The only contingency that is relevant is mortality, and so no further adjustment should be made to the multiplier found by reference to the tables. There may in occasional cases (but not as a general rule) be evidence that the claimant has a particularly low or high expectation of life, in which case the court may be persuaded to make an adjustment to the multiplier. This is likely to be done by assuming a different age for the claimant when reading the multiplier off the table. In the event that the claimant's injuries have substantially reduced life expectancy to a given number of years, then Table 38 will be the appropriate table.

There may frequently be several items of recurring expense, and each will need to be calculated with its own multiplicand and multiplier. Note that not all future expenditure will last indefinitely. For example, if the claimant is claiming for the cost of a gardener, when he or she used to do their own gardening, it is arguable that he or she should not recover this loss for life, because even if the claimant had not been injured he or she would probably have given up doing the gardening at some stage before death.

A claim for the cost of nursing care may well have to be calculated on a split basis, because as the claimant gets older, the cost will increase. In such cases the court will allow one multiplicand for, say, 10 years, and a higher multiplicand thereafter. The multiplier will be split in the way explained in **11.10.4**.

The cost of purchasing a new house is a recurring item: the multiplicand is 2.5% of the increased capital value (see **11.7.5**) and the multiplier represents the claimant's life expectancy.

Where the item of recurring expenditure is not an annual expense, the easiest way to calculate the loss is to spread the multiplicand over a number of years. For example, if the claimant will need a new wheelchair every five years for the rest of his or her life, at a cost of £1,000 at present day values, take a multiplicand of £200 and a multiplier from Ogden Table 19 or 20.

11.13.4 THE DOMESTIC ELEMENT IN THE COST OF CARE

Where there is a claim for the cost of future care of the claimant, as well as a claim for the claimant's lost earnings, care must be taken to avoid duplication or overlap of damages in the area of living expenses. It is quite likely that part of the cost of looking after the claimant in an institution will match what the claimant would have spent in looking after himself or herself (e.g., food, clothing). If no deduction were made, the claimant would therefore be compensated for some of the loss twice over. Rather than deducting living expenses from the award for loss of earnings, instead the 'domestic element' is deducted from the claim for the cost of care (*Lim Poh Choo* v *Camden and Islington Area Health Authority* [1980] AC 174). This involves an adjustment to the multiplicand, not the multiplier.

The domestic element is narrower than living expenses as defined by *Pickett* v *British Rail Engineering Ltd* [1980] AC 136: it is merely that portion of the living expenses that is replaced by the cost of care, and does not include any portion of the joint expenditure or what the claimant would have spent on pleasures. (It is irrelevant that the claimant can no longer enjoy those pleasures.)

11.14 Stage 3: Make any Necessary Deductions

11.14.1 INTRODUCTION

Following his or her injury, the claimant may have received benefits or made savings as well as suffered losses. On the compensatory principle, therefore, any gains made as a result of the injury should be deducted from any claim for losses suffered. However, the courts require a clear causative link between injury and benefit, and not all benefits received have to be deducted. There are various rules for different types of benefit. Some have been considered already: see **11.7.4.3, 11.7.4.4, 11.7.6, 11.10.7.2, 11.13.4**.

11.14.2 SOCIAL SECURITY BENEFITS

Social security benefits may well have been received by the claimant, but will be recovered by the state on payment of damages see: **11.17** below. Therefore they should be disregarded in the assessment of damages (i.e., no deduction should be made). This is expressly provided for in s. 17 of the Social Security (Recovery of Benefits) Act 1997.

11.14.3 CONTRACTUAL SICK PAY

Any sick pay received by the claimant from his or her employer under their contract of employment is equivalent to earnings and so must be deducted from any claim for lost earnings. For statutory sick pay see below in **11.17**.

11.14.4 INSURANCE

Where the claimant was insured against accidental injury and receives the benefits of that insurance policy, no deduction is to be made (*Bradburn* v *Great Western Railway* (1874) LR 10 Ex 1). The rule is the same even where the insurance premium was paid on the claimant's behalf by another (such as an employer). But where the claimant's employer runs a sick-pay scheme through an insurance policy, by which the claimant is contractually entitled to sick-pay under his or her contract of employment, such sick-pay is treated as part of his or her earnings and is to be deducted (*Hussain* v *New Taplow Paper Mills Ltd* [1988] 1 All ER 541).

11.14.5 PENSIONS

Where the claimant receives a pension as a result of his or her injuries, no deduction is to be made, whether the pension was payable as of right or was discretionary, whether it was contributory or non-contributory (*Parry* v *Cleaver* [1970] AC 1, re-affirmed by the House of Lords in *Smoker* v *London Fire and Civil Defence Authority* [1991] 2 AC 502). State retirement pensions are also not deductible (*Hewson* v *Downs* [1970] 1 QB 73; *Hopkins* v *Norcros plc* [1992] ICR 338).

However in *Longden* v *British Coal Corp.* [1998] 1 All ER 289 the House of Lords allowed a small exception to this rule. Where the claimant had received an incapacity pension consisting of a lump sum as well as an annual payment, the proportion of that lump sum that related to the period after the claimant would have retired was to be deducted from any claim for lost retirement pension.

11.14.6 REDUNDANCY PAYMENTS

Where the claimant has been made redundant and received a redundancy payment, this will not normally be deducted since the payment has nothing to do with the injury or incapacity to work (*Mills* v *Hassall* [1983] ICR 330). However, where the claimant has been made redundant or has been offered and accepted voluntary redundancy, but would not have been made redundant or would not have accepted redundancy but for the injury, then the redundancy payment is deductible (*Colledge* v *Bass Mitchells and Butlers Ltd* [1988] 1 All ER 536).

11.14.7 CHARITABLE DONATIONS

It sometimes happens, particularly following well-publicised disasters, that the claimant has benefited from a fund created by voluntary donations. Any such benefits are not deductible (*Redpath* v *Belfast and County Down Railway* [1947] NI 167).

Similarly, no account is to be taken of gifts from family or friends, or an ex gratia payment by the claimant's employer (*Cunningham* v *Harrison* [1973] QB 942). A voluntary payment by an employer may be deductible, however, where the employer is the liable defendant (*Hussain* v *New Taplow Paper Mills Ltd* [1988] 1 All ER 541) and particularly where the payment is expressed to be treated as an advance against any damages that may be awarded (*Williams* v *BOC Gases Ltd* [2000] ICR 1181). No deduction is made in respect of voluntary services provided by family and friends (see **11.4.1.2(m)** and **11.7.8**).

11.14.8 MAINTENANCE AT PUBLIC EXPENSE

If the claimant is being or has been maintained wholly or partly at public expense in a hospital, nursing home or other institution, any saving made must be deducted from any damages for lost earnings or earning capacity (AJA 1982, s. 5). This deduction is roughly equivalent to the deduction of the domestic element (see **11.13.4**).

11.14.9 FOREIGN REPAYABLE BENEFITS

If the claimant has received a foreign state benefit which he or she is by law obliged to repay if he or she recovers damages, then no deduction will be made from the damages to take account of this benefit, even if it would otherwise be deductible (*Berriello* v *Felixstowe Dock & Railway Co.* [1989] 1 WLR 695). To do so would penalise either the claimant or the provider of the benefit.

11.14.10 STATUTORY COMPENSATION

Where a claimant has received compensation payable under the Pneumoconiosis etc. (Workers' Compensation) Act 1979, and then recovers damages in respect of the same disease for which he or she received that compensation, those damages must be reduced by the full amount of the compensation received. By analogy, the same principle is likely to apply in respect of any other statutory compensation that may be payable for industrial injury or disease.

11.15 Stage 4: Contributory Negligence

11.15.1 INTRODUCTION

Damages may well have to be reduced to take account of the claimant's contributory negligence. The circumstances in which such a reduction is to be made are set out in **6.3.1**.

11.15.2 QUANTIFICATION

If there has been a finding of contributory negligence, the total sum of damages quantified so far must be reduced accordingly. If the finding is 25% contributory negligence, reduce the total award by 25%. If advising on quantum, form an opinion as to whether there is likely to be a finding of contributory negligence and, if so, reduce your estimate of damages accordingly.

11.15.3 REDUCTION FOR CONTRIBUTORY NEGLIGENCE IS MADE LAST

Note that any reduction for contributory negligence is made after taking account of any other deductions.

This sequence of deductions operates in the claimant's favour. To take an example:

Damages are assessed at £2,500. Contributory negligence is 50%. The amount to be deducted is £500.

If contributory negligence was taken account of first, the claimant would receive: £(2,500 × 50%) – £500 = £750.

In fact the other deductions are made first, and the claimant receives £(2,500 – 500) × 50% = £1,000.

11.16 Stage 5: Add Interest

11.16.1 INTRODUCTION

Interest will be awarded by the court under SCA 1981, s. 35A or CCA 1984, s. 69. By s. 35A(2) and s. 69(2), the award is prima facie mandatory, unless there are special reasons to the contrary. The sections give no guidelines as to interest rates or periods, which are in the court's discretion, but there are rules of practice.

11.16.2 INTEREST ON SPECIAL DAMAGES

Interest is awarded on special damages at half the 'appropriate rate' from the date of accident to the date of trial (*Jefford* v *Gee* [1970] 2 QB 130). The date of trial is the date of judgment on damages, not liability (*Thomas* v *Bunn* [1991] 1 AC 362).

The appropriate rate is the rate of interest allowed on the High Court Special Investment Account over the relevant period. This rate of interest is fixed from time to time by the Lord Chancellor, and can be found in Civil Procedure (the White book) at 7.0.15 and by checking the latest supplement. At the time of writing it is 7%.

11.16.3 INTEREST ON GENERAL DAMAGES

Interest is awarded on damages for pain and suffering and loss of amenity from the date of service of the writ to the date of trial (*Pickett* v *British Rail Engineering Ltd* [1980] AC 136). The rate was set at 2% a year by *Wright* v *British Railways Board* [1983] 2 All ER 698. It was thought that following *Wells* v *Wells*, the rate should be 3%, but this was ruled out in *Lawrence* v *Chief Constable of Staffordshire*, *The Times*, 25 July 2000. The rate therefore remains at 2%.

No interest is awarded on any damages for future loss.

11.17 Recovery of Benefits

11.17.1 INTRODUCTION

Since 1989 it has been government policy that when a claimant receives a compensation payment in respect of injuries, any social security benefits which he or she has received in the meantime should be repaid to the government. The scheme was first introduced by the Social Security Act 1989, amended a few times and consolidated into the Social Security Administration Act 1992. There were certain injustices in the scheme, notably that benefits could be recovered from a claimant's damages for pain, suffering and loss of amenity as well as loss of earnings, so that in some cases a claimant could be left with very little in the way of damages at all. A revised scheme was therefore introduced by the Social Security (Recovery of Benefits) Act 1997. A fundamental change is that benefits are no longer recovered from the claimant, but from the compensator.

11.17.2 HOW THE SCHEME WORKS

11.17.2.1 The basic outline

By ss. 1 and 6 of the Social Security (Recovery of Benefits) Act 1997, a person who makes a compensation payment (whether on his or her own behalf or not) to any other person in consequence of any accident, injury or disease, must pay an amount equal to the total amount of the recoverable benefits to the Secretary of State.

By s. 8 he or she may then deduct the amount paid to the Secretary of State from the compensation to be paid to the claimant under the appropriate head of damages, but not so as to reduce the amount payable to the claimant under that head below nil. So if the claimant has received more in benefits in respect of a particular type of loss than he or she is to receive by way of compensation, the claimant does not lose compensation under other heads to make up the difference.

On the other hand, the compensator must repay benefits in full to the Secretary of State, so if the benefits are greater than the compensation under the relevant head, he will pay more in total than would have been the case if there had been no recovery of benefits. However, by s. 22, if he was insured in respect of liability to the claimant, then he is also insured in respect of liability to the Secretary of State.

11.17.2.2 Recoverable benefits

The recoverable benefits are the listed benefits which have been or are likely to be paid to the claimant during the relevant period (s. 1(1) of the 1997 Act). The listed benefits are set out in sch. 2. The effect of s. 8 is that each benefit is recoverable from compensation in respect of a particular type of loss only. The table in sch. 2 is:

Head of compensation	*Benefit*
1. Compensaton for earnings lost during the relevant period	Disablement pension Incapacity benefit Income support Invalidity pension and allowance Jobseeker's allowance Reduced earnings allowance Severe disablement allowance Sickness benefit Statutory sick pay Unemployability supplement Unemployment benefit
2. Compensation for cost of care during the relevant period	Attendance allowance Care component of disability living allowance Disablement pension increase
3. Compensation for loss of mobility during the relevant period	Mobility allowance Mobility component of disability living allowance

By s. 24 of the 1997 Act the Secretary of State can amend sch. 2 by statutory regulation.

11.17.2.3 The relevant period

The relevant period is defined by s. 3 of the 1997 Act. In the case of accident or injury, it is five years from the date of the accident or injury. In the case of disease, it is five years from the date on which the claimant first claimed benefit in respect of that disease. In either case the relevant period comes to an end before the end of the five years when the defendant makes a compensation payment.

11.17.2.4 Certificates of recoverable benefits

How does the person making the compensation payment know how much to pay to the Secretary of State and how much to deduct from the compensation payment? He or she is given the necessary information by a certificate issued by the Compensation Recovery Unit. By s. 4 of the 1997 Act, before the compensator makes any compensation payment, he or she must apply for a certificate of recoverable benefits which informs the compensator how much he or she must pay to the Secretary of State if they make the compensation payment within a specified time. If the compensator does not make the payment within that time, he or she must apply for a new certificate.

11.17.3 COURT ORDERS

The scheme applies in exactly the same way whether the compensation is paid by a court order, by agreement or voluntarily. But where the court makes an order for the payment of damages (other than a consent order), then by s. 15 of the 1997 Act it must specify the amount awarded under each of the heads of compensation set out in sch. 2.

11.17.4 OTHER PROVISIONS

The above is only an abbreviated outline of the effect of the 1997 Act. There are other provisions dealing with reviews and appeals against the amounts of recoverable benefits, recovery of overpayments, payments by more than one person in respect of the same injury, and other matters. In particular, there is a power to make regulations exempting small payments (up to a specified sum) from the scheme, though no such exemption has been made.

11.17.5 CONTRIBUTORY NEGLIGENCE AND RECOVERY OF BENEFITS

Recovery bites into damages actually paid, after the assessment process is complete, so any reduction for contributory negligence will already have been made before the compensation payment is reduced to take account of the amount paid to the DSS.

11.17.6 INTEREST ON DAMAGES TO BE RECOVERED

A claimant is entitled to receive interest on all the special damages assessed, not just those damages which he or she will in fact be paid after the defendant has made a deduction in consequence of the recovery of benefits (*Wisely* v *John Fulton (Plumbers) Ltd* [2000] 2 All ER 545). However, the defendant can set off the benefits repaid to the DSS against both the damages and the interest on those damages (*Griffiths* v *British Coal Corporation* [2001] 1 WLR 1493).

11.18 Other Ways of Quantifying Damages

The methods of quantifying damages set out above have been developed over the years by judges, practitioners and Parliament. To a very large extent the rules are rules of practice rather than rules of law; nevertheless, judges are bound to follow guidelines laid down by the Court of Appeal and House of Lords, and it is in nobody's interest if a judge decides to take a maverick approach to the quantification of damages, arriving at a figure which could not have been predicted by either side. Accordingly, the methods set out above are universally used by courts, even though the quantum of damages is, strictly speaking, wholly within the judge's discretion, so long as his or her decision is just. Hence the need for legislation if any major changes are to be made (see **11.2.1**).

But parties negotiating a settlement are not bound to follow the conventional methods if they agree not to do so. They may agree to use actuarial calculations; they may agree to take full notice of inflation. In particular, unlike a judge, they are not obliged to agree to a once-and-for-all lump sum.

There is now also s. 2 of the Damages Act 1996 which provides:

> *(1) A court awarding damages in an action for personal injury may, with the consent of the parties, make an order under which damages are wholly or partly to take the form of periodical payments.*
> *(2) In this section 'damages' includes an interim payment which the court ... orders the defendant to make to the plaintiff ...*
> *(3) This section is without prejudice to any powers exercisable apart from this section.*

As an addition to its other powers, the court can now order damages to be paid by way of periodical payments. So, for example, rather than making a lump sum award of £100,000 for future medical expenses, the court could order the defendant to pay the claimant £10,000 per annum for life. However, this order could only be made with the consent of both parties, which will obviously not be forthcoming unless both will benefit from this method of payment.

In March 2002, the Lord Chancellor issued a consultation paper seeking views on whether the law should be changed to give the court power to order payment by way of periodical payments without needing the consent of the parties. Responses were invited by 7 June 2002.

11.19 Structured Settlements

11.19.1 WHAT IS A STRUCTURED SETTLEMENT?

A structured settlement is an agreement between the parties that damages will not be paid as a conventional lump sum, but rather in the form of future annual payments and future lump sums. It is not so much an alternative way of quantifying damages, as an alternative way of paying them.

A structured settlement is not something that can be imposed by a court, but must be agreed between the parties. It can then be approved by the court and incorporated into a Tomlin order if necessary. The first case in which a judge approved a structured settlement was reported in July 1989 (*Kelly* v *Dawes*, reported as a news item in *The Times*, 27 September 1990, but see *Kemp & Kemp*, para. 6A–075); since then there have been several hundred and there will be more and more every year as the idea takes hold.

The result of an effective structured settlement is likely to be that the claimant's needs are better provided for, that the claimant actually receives more money over his or her lifetime than they would with a conventional award, and that the defendant's insurer actually pays less.

11.19.2 WHEN IS A STRUCTURED SETTLEMENT APPROPRIATE?

The cases in which structured settlements have been agreed are all ones in which the claimant has suffered serious or very serious injuries, which have resulted in substantial ongoing future loss for the rest of the claimant's life. A structured settlement is of little use where there has been a complete recovery, or when the claimant's injuries are relatively minor, or where the bulk of damages are to compensate the claimant for past losses.

But where the future losses are high, because the claimant will need continued care or incur significant expense throughout his or her life, there is a real advantage to be gained in a structured settlement, provided the extra cash generated is not outweighed by the costs of setting up and administering the settlement. At present, this is likely to be where the sum to be paid by way of future instalments is more than about £100,000, though this threshold has already come down from £200,000 and is likely to fall further as the various professionals involved in the implementation of structured settlements gain more experience.

11.19.3 HOW DOES A STRUCTURED SETTLEMENT WORK?

11.19.3.1 Investment of a conventional lump sum

When a seriously injured claimant receives a conventional lump sum award, it is intended to compensate not only for the expense already incurred, but also to pay for all future needs. The claimant will therefore doubtless invest a proportion of it and use both capital and income to provide for himself or herself for the rest of their life.

The most effective way of ensuring that the money does not run out before death, the time of which may be very uncertain, is to purchase an index-linked annuity from a life office. The claimant will then receive an annual sum representing both capital and interest which will rise in line with inflation. But he or she will receive the annual sum net of income tax.

11.19.3.2 The structured settlement

The essence of a structured settlement is that the defendant's insurers will pay some of the damages as an immediate lump sum, to provide for the claimant's past and present needs, and will use the rest of the sum available to purchase an index-linked annuity for the claimant. The life office will pay the insurers the annual sum net of tax, but the insurers can recover that tax from the Inland Revenue, under an agreement made between the Inland Revenue and the Association of British Insurers in 1987, and will then pay the claimant the gross value of the annuity. The claimant thus receives more.

Because the claimant receives more a year than he or she would if they were to receive a conventional lump sum, it is possible for the defendant's insurers to negotiate a lower sum to be invested in the purchase of the annuity. Both sides therefore gain from the arrangement. If the parties focus on the claimant's annual needs, and then find out how much it would cost to purchase an index-linked annuity at that annual value for the claimant's life, they may well then be able to agree on that sum as the lump sum to be invested (after making allowance for costs). That sum is likely to be lower than the sum that would otherwise have been awarded.

11.19.4 HOW IS A STRUCTURED SETTLEMENT WORKED OUT?

The first step will be to work out or agree the value of the claimant's claim for damages on a conventional basis. Only if that sum is known can either side appreciate the benefits of a structured settlement, or whether those benefits will outweigh the costs.

There will then need to be a cooperative effort between a considerable number of people: the claimant's and the defendant's legal advisers, the defendant's insurers, a life assurance broker, an accountant with experience of structured settlements, a life office, and the Inland Revenue. If the claimant is a patient, the Court of Protection will also be involved, and if a claim has been commenced, the approval of the court is likely to be required.

Only if the scheme is in the correct form, will the Inland Revenue agree to treat the future instalments as payments of capital, and so refund the tax deducted by the life office.

The costs and professional fees are what make the setting up and administration of a structured settlement more expensive than a simple payment of damages. However, provided the sum to be invested is large enough these are likely to be offset by the tax savings and lower capital sums involved.

11.19.5 THE IMPORTANCE OF MAINTAINING FLEXIBILITY

Although the central ingredient of a structured settlement is the purchase of an annuity on the claimant's behalf by the defendant's insurers, there are many other ingredients that may be appropriate in individual cases. The claimant's situation, and likely future needs will be different in every case, and it is important that the settlement should be *structured* to cater for any possible or anticipated changes in the claimant's situation.

For example a structure which involves gradually increasing annual sums may be required if the claimant's condition is likely to deteriorate. Another way of dealing with this might be to purchase two annuities, one deferred. It may be wise to build in occasional future lump sums to enable the claimant to cope with specific anticipated events in the future.

The value of a structured settlement will be lost if it becomes an inflexible form of settlement revolving solely around the annuity.

11.19.6 RECOVERY OF BENEFITS

Structured settlements do not prevent recovery of benefits! Section 18 of the Social Security (Recovery of Benefits) Act 1997 enables regulations to be made setting out how benefits to be recovered will bite into sums paid by way of structured settlements and periodical payments ordered by the court under s. 2 of the Damages Act 1996. The Social Security (Recovery of Benefits) Regulations 1997 make the necessary provisions.

11.19.7 FURTHER READING

For further reading on structured settlements, see *Kemp & Kemp*, Chapter 6A, and *Butterworths PILS* Division XV–D.

TWELVE

QUANTUM OF DAMAGES FOR A FATAL ACCIDENT

12.1 Rights of Claim

12.1.1 INTRODUCTION

There are two rights of action that arise as a result of a fatal accident, both statutory. These are an action on behalf of the deceased's estate under the Law Reform (Miscellaneous Provisions) Act 1934 (LR(MP)A 1934); and a claim on behalf of the deceased's dependants under the Fatal Accidents Act 1976 (FAA 1976). These Acts were both amended by the Administration of Justice Act 1982 (ss. 3, 4), as a result of which (except in the case of deaths occurring before 1983) the two *rights* of action are entirely separate from each other and there is no overlap between them, though both will be founded on the same *cause* of action.

12.1.2 THE RIGHT OF CLAIM UNDER THE LR(MP)A 1934

12.1.2.1 Section 1 of the Act

Section 1 of the LR(MP)A 1934 provides:

> *(1) Subject to the provisions of this section, on the death of any person after the commencement of this Act all causes of claim subsisting against or vested in him shall survive against, or, as the case may be, for the benefit of, his estate. Provided that this subsection shall not apply to causes of claim for defamation.*
>
> *(1A) The right of a person to claim under section 1A of the Fatal Accidents Act 1976 (bereavement) shall not survive for the benefit of his estate on his death.*
>
> *(2) Where a cause of claim survives as aforesaid for the benefit of the estate of a deceased person, the damages recoverable for the benefit of the estate of that person—*
>
> *(a) shall not include—*
>
> *(i) any exemplary damages;*
>
> *(ii) any damages for loss of income in respect of any period after that person's death;*
>
> *(b) . . .*
>
> *(c) where the death of that person has been caused by the act or omission which gives rise to the cause of claim, shall be calculated without reference to any loss or gain to his estate consequent on his death, except that a sum in respect of funeral expenses may be included.*

12.1.2.2 The effect of the provision

The effect of this provision is that any cause of action which the deceased had at his or her death can still be pursued by his or her estate, so that if the deceased could have sued the defendant in negligence for damages for personal injury, his or her estate may step into his or her shoes and do so instead. The deceased's estate may claim damages in respect of any losses that had already accrued at the moment of death. So the estate will recover any damages that the deceased himself or herself could have recovered if he or she had instituted a claim for personal injury, pursued it, and obtained judgment, all in the instant before death; with the important exception of the damages the deceased could have recovered for loss of earnings in his or her lost years, which are not recoverable (s. 1(2)(a)(ii)), and the further exception of any claim for bereavement the deceased may have had (s. 1(1A)).

12.1.2.3 Dependants' losses not recoverable

The estate *cannot* recover damages in respect of any loss *resulting* from death, or which arises because of the death (s. 1(2)(c)). Such loss is not the deceased's own loss, but is his or her dependants' loss, and can be recovered by them under the FAA 1976. The single exception to this is funeral expenses, where the funeral was paid for out of the deceased's estate.

12.1.2.4 Damages form part of deceased's estate

The claimant(s) will be the deceased's personal representative(s) — the executor(s) or administrator of the estate. Damages recovered under the LR(MP)A 1934 form part of the estate and will be distributed in accordance with the terms of the deceased's will or the rules of intestacy.

12.1.3 THE RIGHT OF CLAIM UNDER THE FAA 1976

12.1.3.1 Sections 1 to 5 of the Act

Sections 1–5 of the FAA provide:

> ***Right of claim for wrongful act causing death***
> ***1.***—*(1) If death is caused by any wrongful act, neglect or default which is such as would (if death had not ensued) have entitled the person injured to maintain a claim and recover damages in respect thereof, the person who would have been liable if death had not ensued shall be liable to a claim for damages, notwithstanding the death of the person injured.*
> *(2) Subject to section 1A(2) below, every such claim shall be for the benefit of the dependants of the person (the deceased) whose death has been so caused.*
> *(3) In this Act 'dependant' means—*
> *(a) the wife or husband or former wife or husband of the deceased;*
> *(b) any person who—*
> *(i) was living with the deceased in the same household immediately before the date of the death; and*
> *(ii) had been living with the deceased in the same household for at least two years before that date; and*
> *(iii) was living during the whole of that period as the husband or wife of the deceased;*
> *(c) any parent or other ascendant of the deceased;*
> *(d) any person who was treated by the deceased as his parent;*
> *(e) any child or other descendant of the deceased;*
> *(f) any person (not being a child of the deceased) who, in the case of any marriage to which the deceased was at any time a party, was treated by the deceased as a child of the family in relation to that marriage;*
> *(g) any person who is, or is the issue of, a brother, sister, uncle or aunt of the deceased.*
> *(4) The reference to the former wife or husband of the deceased in subsection (3)(a) above includes a reference to a person whose marriage to the deceased has been annulled or declared void as well as a person whose marriage to the deceased has been dissolved.*
> *(5) In deducing any relationship for the purposes of subsection (3) above*
> *(a) any relationship by affinity shall be treated as a relationship by consanguinity, any relationship of the half blood as a relationship of the whole blood, and the stepchild of any person as his child, and*
> *(b) an illegitimate person shall be treated as the legitimate child of his mother and reputed father.*
> *(6) Any reference in this Act to injury includes any disease and any impairment of a person's physical or mental condition.*

Bereavement

***1A.**—(1) An claim under this Act may consist of or include a claim for damages for bereavement.*

(2) A claim for damages for bereavement shall only be for the benefit—

(a) of the wife or husband of the deceased; and

(b) where the deceased was a minor who was never married—

(i) of his parents, if he was legitimate; and

(ii) of his mother, if he was illegitimate.

(3) Subject to subsection (5) below, the sum to be awarded as damages under this section shall be [£10,000].

(4) Where there is a claim for damages under this section for the benefit of both the parents of the deceased, the sum awarded shall be divided equally between them (subject to any deduction falling to be made in respect of costs not recovered from the defendant).

(5) The Lord Chancellor may by order made by statutory instrument, subject to annulment in pursuance of a resolution of either House of Parliament amend this section varying the sum for the time being specified in subsection (3) above.

Persons entitled to bring the claim

***2.**—(1) The claim shall be brought by and in the name of the executor or administrator of the deceased.*

(2) If—

(a) there is no executor or administrator of the deceased, or

(b) no claim is brought within six months after the death by and in the name of an executor or administrator of the deceased, the claim may be brought by and in the name of all or any of the persons for whose benefit an executor or administrator could have brought it.

(3) Not more than one claim shall lie for and in respect of the same subject matter of complaint.

(4) The plaintiff in the claim shall be required to deliver to the defendant or his solicitor full particulars of the persons for whom and on whose behalf the claim is brought and of the nature of the claim in respect of which damages are sought to be recovered.

Assessment of damages

***3.**—(1) In the claim such damages, other than damages for bereavement, may be awarded as are proportioned to the injury resulting from the death to the dependants respectively.*

(2) After deducting the costs not recovered from the defendant any amount recovered otherwise than as damages for bereavement shall be divided among the dependants in such shares as may be directed.

(3) In a claim under this Act where there fall to be assessed damages payable to a widow in respect of the death of her husband there shall not be taken account the remarriage of the widow or her prospects of remarriage.

(4) In a claim under this Act where there fall to be assessed damages payable to a person who is a dependant by virtue of section 1(3)(b) above in respect of the death of the person with whom the dependant was living as husband or wife there shall be taken into account (together with any other matter that appears to the court to be relevant to the claim) the fact that the dependant had no enforceable right to financial support by the deceased as a result of their living together.

(5) If the dependants have incurred funeral expenses in respect of the deceased, damages may be awarded in respect of those expenses.

(6) Money paid into court in satisfclaim of a cause of claim under this Act may be in one sum without specifying any person's share.

Assessment of damages: disregard of benefits

***4.** In assessing damages in respect of a person's death in a claim under this Act, benefits which have accrued or will accrue to any person from his estate or otherwise as a result of his death shall be disregarded.*

Contributory negligence
5. *Where any person dies as the result partly of his own fault and partly of the fault of any other person or persons, and accordingly if a claim were brought for the benefit of the estate under the Law Reform (Miscellaneous Provisions) Act 1934 the damages recoverable would be reduced under section 1(1) of the Law Reform (Contributory Negligence) Act 1945, any damages recoverable in a claim under this Act shall be reduced to a proportionate extent.*

12.1.3.2 Basis of the right of action and recovery
The right of action under the FAA 1976 arises because of, and only because of, the deceased's death. It belongs to the dependants, who can recover damages in respect of the loss they have suffered as a result of his or her death. They can recover nothing of what the deceased himself or herself could have recovered: such damages belong to the estate and are recoverable under the LR(MP)A 1934. They can recover nothing in respect of losses they would have suffered even if the deceased had survived: such damages could either have been recovered by the deceased, or the dependants will have a separate right of action in their own name (e.g., in respect of their own personal injuries).

12.1.3.3 Who brings the claim?
Although the right of action belongs to the dependants, and damages will in the end be paid to them, the claim is prima facie brought by the executor or administrator of the estate (s. 2(1)). Not every de facto dependant has a right of action, only those brought within the Act by s. 1(3), (4) and (5).

12.1.3.4 Dependants must have a cause of action
The dependants must also have a cause of action. For the purposes of their claim they 'borrow' whatever cause of action the deceased had, the same cause of action which survives for the benefit of the estate under the LR(MP)A 1934. If the deceased had no cause of action, the dependants also have none.

12.1.4 THE RELATIONSHIP BETWEEN THE TWO CLAIMS

There will almost invariably be a claim under both Acts, with the same claimant and using the same cause of action to establish liability. Beyond that there is no longer any connection between the claims. Each is for different damages on behalf of different persons. The only exception to this is funeral expenses, which can be recovered under either Act, depending on who paid for the funeral (LR(MP)A 1934, s. 1(2)(c); FAA 1976, s. 3(5)).

Before 1983 there was a symbiotic relationship between the two claims: the estate could recover damages in respect of the deceased's earnings over the lost years, which could only be assessed by reference to the FAA award; and damages awarded to the estate under the LR(MP)A 1934 usually had to be taken into account in quantifying the FAA award. This relationship was, thankfully, effectively severed by the AJA 1982, which inserted s. 1(2)(a)(ii) into LR(MP)A 1934 and rewrote FAA 1976, s. 4, but you need to be aware of this history to understand reported cases.

12.1.5 WHERE THE DECEASED HAS COMMENCED A CLAIM FOR PERSONAL INJURY

It is not uncommon that an injured person commences a claim for personal injury, but dies before the claim is complete, or soon after damages are awarded. What is the position then of the estate and dependants?

12.1.5.1 Where the claim is still pending
In these circumstances, the estate have the right to continue the claim under the LR(MP)A 1934, but that will not be sufficient in itself because the estate cannot recover any damages in respect of the deceased's future loss of earnings (s. 1(2)(a)(ii)). It is these damages which would have provided for the dependants after the deceased's death and so the dependants will need to recover their loss by a separate claim under the FAA 1976.

12.1.5.2 Where the deceased had recovered damages in full

The dependants have no further claim under the FAA 1976. The damages awarded to the deceased were intended to restore him or her to the position he or she would have been in had he or she not been injured (including, if necessary, damages for lost earnings in the lost years), and so they cannot show that they have suffered any additional loss of dependency as a result of the death.

12.1.5.3 Where the deceased had recovered provisional damages

The position is now governed by s. 3 of the Damages Act 1996 which provides:

> *(1) This section applies where a person—*
> *(a) is awarded provisional damages; and*
> *(b) subsequently dies as a result of the act or omission which gave rise to the cause of claim for which the damages were awarded.*
> *(2) The award of the provisional damages shall not operate as a bar to a claim in respect of that person's death under the Fatal Accidents Act 1976.*
> *(3) Such part (if any) of—*
> *(a) the provisional damages; and*
> *(b) any further damages awarded to the person in question before his death, as was intended to compensate him for pecuniary loss in a period which in the event falls after his death shall be taken into account in assessing the amount of any loss of support suffered by the person or persons for whose benefit the claim under the Fatal Accidents Act 1976 is brought.*
> *(4) No award of further damages made in respect of that person after his death shall include any amount for loss of income in respect of any period after his death.*
> *(5) In this section 'provisional damages' means damages awarded by virtue of subsection (2)(a) of section 32A of the Supreme Court Act 1981 or section 51 of the County Courts Act 1984 and 'further damages' means damages awarded by virtue of subsection (2)(b) of either of those sections.*
> *(6) Subsection (2) above applies whether the award of provisional damages was before or after the coming into force of that subsection; and subsections (3) and (4) apply to any award of damages under the 1976 Act or, as the case may be, further damages after the coming into force of those subsections.*
> *(7) ...*

Section 3 sorts out a problem that existed when a claimant commenced a claim for personal injury, and was awarded provisional damages, but then died. In such a case the dependants were precluded from suing for their lost dependency under the FAA 1976 and it was unclear whether the estate, under the LR(MP)A 1934, could continue the personal injury claim and seek a further award under s. 32A of the Supreme Court Act 1981, including damages for lost earnings in the 'lost years'.

Section 3 adopts the sensible solution. In such cases, a barrier is brought down on the personal injury claim — the estate can only seek a further award under s. 32A in respect of the deceased's losses up to the date of death. Instead, the dependants can bring a claim under the FAA 1976 for their lost dependency, but account must be taken of any damages the deceased received as compensation for losses in the period after death and which the dependants may have inherited.

12.2 Quantification of Damages under the LR(MP)A 1934

12.2.1 GENERAL PRINCIPLES

Since the claim is basically a claim by the deceased for damages for personal injury, damages will be quantified upon the same principles and in the same stages as a personal injury claim. The total sum, however, is likely to be relatively small, since there is no claim for any future loss. It is only likely to be substantial if there was a significant delay between accident and death.

12.2.2 SPECIAL DAMAGES

Special damages are likely to be small, unless they include, for example, damage to a motor vehicle, lost earnings between accident and death, or funeral expenses. On the other hand, there will usually be some special damages sufficient to justify a claim under the LR(MP)A 1934, even if nothing else is recoverable under this Act.

12.2.3 GENERAL DAMAGES

The only head of general damages recoverable is pain and suffering and loss of amenity, and then only if there was a significant period of time between the accident and death. If death was instantaneous or nearly instantaneous, nothing is recoverable, since any pain and suffering is in reality part of the death (*Hicks* v *Chief Constable of South Yorkshire* [1992] 1 All ER 690). If the deceased was unconscious between the accident and death, damages for loss of amenity only are recoverable. The longer the deceased survived after the accident, the greater the award will be, but it is still going to be small compared to what would be given to an injured claimant with a life-time's pain, suffering and loss of amenity ahead of him or her.

12.2.4 DEDUCTIONS

The award will be subject to any deductions that would have been made in a personal injury claim (see **11.14**).

12.2.5 CONTRIBUTORY NEGLIGENCE

The award will be subject to reduction for the deceased's contributory negligence (see **11.15**).

12.2.6 INTEREST

Interest will be added as in personal injury claims (see **11.16**).

12.2.7 RECOVERY OF BENEFITS

The compensator will be liable to repay benefits under the Social Security (Recovery of Benefits) Act 1997, but will be able to reduce the damages paid to the deceased's estate in the usual way (see **11.17**).

12.3 Quantification of Damages under the FAA 1976

12.3.1 THE SOLE HEAD OF DAMAGES

With the single and simple exception of damages for bereavement (s. 1A), the loss recoverable under the FAA 1976 is wholly financial loss, and what is being assessed is the value of the 'dependency', which is the only head of damages. The dependency consists of:

(a) the amount the deceased would have applied to the benefit of his or her dependants;

(b) any additional expense the dependants have been put to as a result of his or her death; and

(c) any additional losses the dependants have suffered as a result of his or her death;

over the period for which they would have remained dependent.

If the dependants have suffered loss of income, it does not matter what the source of that income was. So, for example, if the deceased's only source of income was State benefits, and as a result of his or her death those benefits are no longer payable, the dependants can recover their loss to the extent that the lost benefits were applied to their support (*Cox* v *Hockenhull* [1999] 3 All ER 577).

12.3.2 THE SEVEN-STAGE PROCESS

The quantification of damages is a seven-stage process:

Stage 1: Calculate the pre-trial loss.

Stage 2: Assess the future loss.

Stage 3: Add lump sums.

Stage 4: Add bereavement.

Stage 5: Contributory negligence.

Stage 6: Add interest.

Stage 7: Apportion between dependants.

12.4 Stage 1: Calculate the Pre-Trial Loss

12.4.1 WHAT IS THE PRE-TRIAL LOSS?

The pre-trial loss is the total value of the dependency so far, that is from the date of death to the date of trial (or the date of settlement or the date on which you are advising as to quantum). It is roughly equivalent to the special damages in a personal injury claim.

Like special damages it is, in theory at least, precisely ascertainable: in reality a great deal of estimation may be required, but it should still be quantified as accurately as possible.

12.4.2 THE APPROACHES THAT MAY BE ADOPTED

The basic principle of assessment is exactly the same in every case: the court is trying to put a value on each of the three aspects of the dependency (see **12.3.1**). However, the items that will be included within the dependency vary according to the relationship between the dependants and the deceased, and so the court's approach to the assessment tends to vary as well. There are three main approaches that may be adopted:

(a) The item by item approach — where each item of loss and expenditure is added up one by one.

(b) The earnings minus living expenses approach — where the court looks at what the deceased earned, takes away personal living expenses, and assumes whatever is left to be the dependency.

(c) The conventional percentage approach — where the court assesses the likely dependency as x% of the deceased's earnings.

These three approaches are not mutually exclusive: the court may use a little of each. Where the claim is for the death of a husband/father, however, the modern practice is to use the conventional percentage approach almost exclusively.

Whether an item is to be included or not is simply a matter of evidence. What approach the court adopts to assessment will also depend on the evidence, or the lack of it, and convenience. It is easiest to look at the assessment process according to certain, well established types of claim, but there is no rule that any item of dependency can only be recovered in certain types of claim; it is recoverable wherever it exists. Do not therefore be misled into generalisation: every case depends on its own facts.

12.4.3 CLAIMS FOR THE DEATH OF A HUSBAND/FATHER

12.4.3.1 The item by item approach

This approach is only likely to be possible, but will be the most reliable, where there exist detailed household accounts. It is, however, difficult to persuade a judge to use this approach, rather than the quick and simple conventional percentage approach.

Where the husband was the breadwinner, and the dependants are his wife and children, or just his wife, the items likely to form a part of the dependency are:

(a) Housekeeping money.

(b) Rent, mortgage instalments.

(c) Council tax.

(d) Repairs, maintenance, decoration, cleaning.

(e) Fuel bills.

(f) Telephone.

(g) Clothing.

(h) School fees.

(i) Costs of running a car, travel and transport.

(j) Holidays and outings.

(k) Gifts, entertainments, sports and leisure, pets.

(l) Pocket money.

(m) Insurance.

(n) TV rental.

(o) One-off purchases, e.g., furniture, luxury goods.

12.4.3.2 Deductions

From each of these any element of the deceased's own living expenses must be deducted (housekeeping money, for example, is likely to include an element of his food and keep). Expenditure which is joint, i.e., where there is no saving as a result of death (e.g., rent, fuel bills), does not have to be reduced. (Note the difference between this rule and the rule for living expenses in a lost years claim: see **11.10.7.2**.)

12.4.3.3 Other losses

To this add any other losses. For example, the widow may as a result of her husband's death have had to give up work for a while and so have lost earnings; the family may have lost other free perks from the deceased's employers. Also add any loss of benefits in kind, or additional expenditure the dependants have been put to. Common examples are:

(a) The value of D-I-Y work around the home, where the deceased used to carry out repairs and improvements, which can have considerable annual value. Take care to include only the value of the work, not the cost of materials.

(b) The value of fruit and vegetables grown by the husband in the garden or allotment.

(c) The loss of use of a company car for private purposes.

(d) The loss of other employer's perks: e.g., health insurance; free goods or services; school fees.

12.4.3.4 Total the loss

If the evidence of the family's expenditure is on a weekly basis, calculate the amount per week and multiply by the number of weeks between death and trial. Similarly if the accounts are monthly. Some benefits in kind are more easily valued on an annual basis, in which case bring them in at that stage.

12.4.3.5 The 'earnings minus living expenses' approach

Where the evidence is not complete enough for the item by item approach, the court may use the quicker and easier earnings minus living expenses approach. Take the deceased's net earnings (weekly or monthly) and deduct his personal living expenses. His living expenses under the FAA 1976 include all that he spent exclusively on himself, both needs and pleasures, but *not* a portion of any expenditure for the joint benefit of himself and his dependants. What is left will be the prima facie value of the dependency, to which can be added any additional losses or benefits in kind. This approach is now almost entirely obsolete.

12.4.3.6 The conventional percentage approach

These days the court is likely to save time and trouble by going directly to a conventional percentage figure. This is 75% where the dependants are widow and child(ren), or 67% where the widow is the sole dependant; i.e., the court assesses the dependency as 75% or 67% of the deceased's net earnings (see *Harris* v *Empress Motors Ltd* [1984] 1 WLR 212).

12.4.3.7 Arriving at a percentage

Whatever approach has been used, it is usually helpful to express the dependency as a percentage of the deceased's net earnings. This makes it easier to take account of any likely increases in pay over the pre-trial period.

12.4.3.8 Changes in the value of the dependency between death and trial

These must be taken into account — both actual changes and changes that would have occurred but for the husband's death. The most obvious example of an actual change is a child who becomes financially independent at some point during the pre-trial period. His or her dependency obviously comes to an end, or at least is very substantially reduced from that time.

But there is usually likely to be some evidence of changes that would have occurred as well. The deceased's earnings might well have increased during the pre-trial period through pay rises, promotion, career moves, building up a business etc. If this is the case the question arises, would the dependency have increased as well? If there would have been no increase, simply value the dependency as at the date of death and multiply by the appropriate number of weeks or months. If the increase in the dependency would have been in proportion to the increased earnings, the percentage approach is helpful. The dependency continues to be the same fixed percentage of the increased net pay. But if there would have been an increase proportionally greater or smaller than the increase in earnings, then an adjustment will have to be made to the percentage. Similar considerations apply if the deceased's earnings would have fallen during the pre-trial period, for example as a result of retirement. In the absence of evidence to the contrary, assume that the dependency would have increased or decreased in line with the change in income, applying the fixed percentage.

12.4.3.9 Deceased's savings

If the deceased saved regularly, the money may or may not be part of the dependency, according to how he would eventually have spent it. If some of it would eventually have been applied to his dependants' benefit and he saved regularly, then a suitable portion of the savings can be added to the weekly or monthly dependency. If savings were irregular, it may be more appropriate to add a lump sum at Stage 3.

12.4.3.10 Widow's remarriage or prospects of remarriage

These are not to be taken into account in assessing her dependency (FAA 1976, s. 3(3)). However, if the claim is for the death of a breadwinner wife, the husband's remarriage or prospects must be taken into account.

12.4.3.11 Widow's earnings or earning capacity

Where a widow has lost earnings as a result of the death, this loss forms part of the dependency. Where a widow was a working woman both before and after the death clearly her earnings are irrelevant to her claim under the FAA 1976. A non-working widow's earning capacity can usually be ignored (*Howitt* v *Heads* [1973] QB 64). If she goes out to work after her husband's death her earnings should probably be ignored even if she would not have worked but for her husband's death: the earnings are simply a realisation of her earning capacity, not a gain resulting from the death.

12.4.3.12 Family living beyond its means

It may be that the amount the deceased was spending on himself and his dependants was more than he was earning. If this was being paid for out of his capital, then the dependency can be valued at its actual rate but account must be taken of how long the capital would have lasted. If it was being subsidised by a loan, the value of the dependency will be reduced to take account of the amount the deceased would have had to repay.

12.4.4 CLAIMS FOR THE DEATH OF A WIFE/MOTHER

12.4.4.1 The items forming the dependency

Where the wife was working, the value of her contribution to the family expenses can be quantified in much the same way as for a husband (see **12.4.3**). But whether the wife was working or not, the main item in the dependency is likely to be the value of her services as a wife and mother. There may also be a claim for lost benefits in kind — where the wife did D-I-Y work, or made clothes for her husband and children, for example.

12.4.4.2 Assessing the value of a wife's services

The value of a wife's services is not easily quantified, and is very much in the court's discretion. At the very least it is likely to be assessed as the cost of employing a home-help and/or a housekeeper. Nevertheless, there is a good argument for looking at a wife's services more broadly and valuing each service she performed for the family, not just those that a housekeeper can perform (*Regan* v *Williamson* [1976] 1 WLR 305). Where the wife was in full-time employment, the amount of time she had available to care for the family is less than it would have been if she were a full-time housewife, and so the value of her services is proportionally less (see e.g., *Cresswell* v *Eaton* [1991] 1 All ER 484). Where the wife was a poor mother, the value of her services will be lower (see *Stanley* v *Saddique* [1992] QB 1).

If the husband has reasonably given up his work in order to stay at home and look after the home and children, then the dependency may be assessed on the basis of the husband's lost earnings (*Mehmet* v *Perry* [1977] 2 All ER 529). Similarly if a relative has given up full-time work in order to be able to do so, the dependency may be based on that relative's loss of earnings. But if the relative's full-time care replaces only part-time care by the mother a discount will need to be made (*Cresswell* v *Eaton*).

Where a father is the defendant being sued in respect of his wife's death, and he has given up work to look after their children, the value of the services he is providing should be set off against the value of the mother's services lost, so as to reduce the children's claim (*Hayden* v *Hayden* [1992] 4 All ER 681).

12.4.5 CLAIMS FOR THE DEATH OF A PARENT

Where the dependants claiming are simply the children, either because both parents were killed simultaneously, or the family was a one-parent family, or because the surviving parent has no claim since he or she is the defendant being sued, some special considerations apply.

To the extent that the children's claim is for the death of their father who provided financial support, it can be quantified as in **12.4.3**. To the extent that the children's claim is for the death of their mother, it cannot be quantified simply on the basis of the cost of employing a housekeeper, for they have lost more than this. It may be appropriate to assess the cost of providing a full-time nanny for the children, if they are young, and this loss is recoverable even if no nanny in fact needs to be employed because the children are being looked after by a relative (*Hay* v *Hughes* [1975] QB 790). Alternatively, particularly when the children are older, it may be more appropriate to assess their loss on the basis of the cost of providing a foster home; at the very least some account must be taken of the fact that they will not need a nanny throughout the period of their dependency (*Spittle* v *Bunney* [1988] 3 All ER 1031).

If the children have been legally adopted since the death of their parents, their dependency from the date of adoption will be limited to any difference between the value of the dependency provided by their father (assuming he was the breadwinner) and that provided by their adoptive father. The care provided by the adoptive mother replaces that provided by the natural mother and so a claim for the value of their mother's services comes to an end on adoption (see *Watson* v *Willmott* [1991] 1 QB 140).

12.4.6 CLAIMS FOR THE DEATH OF A CHILD

Where the claim is made by parents in respect of the death of their child, the dependency is likely to be assessed item by item and to be fairly small. If the child was adult, and was in fact supporting his or her parents at the date of death, account must be taken of the likelihood that this support would have diminished or ceased if he or she left home or got married. In the case of a minor child the parents have lost little more than the chance that they might have received some support in the future, plus the occasional gifts.

12.4.7 CLAIMS BY OTHER DEPENDANTS

A claim by a cohabitee can be assessed in the same way as a claim by a husband or wife; claims by grandchildren or grandparents, if appropriate, in the same way as claims by children and parents. In the case of other relatives, the claim is likely to be very small and can be quantified item by item.

12.4.8 FUNERAL EXPENSES

Having calculated all the rest of the pre-trial loss, add funeral expenses if they were incurred by the dependants.

12.5 Stage 2: Assess the Future Loss

The future loss to the dependants consists of (a) the loss of dependency over the remainder of the deceased's working life, and (b) the loss of dependency flowing from the deceased's pension, where the dependants would have received any benefit from it. A widow cannot however recover in respect of her husband's retirement pension if she has instead received a widow's pension under the same scheme from her husband's employers (*Auty* v *National Coal Board* [1985] 1 All ER 930).

12.5.1 THE MULTIPLICAND

The multiplicand is the annual value of the dependency as at the date of trial. It takes account of all the items dealt with under Stage 1, and includes the three aspects of the dependency (see **12.3.1**). It also takes account of any likely changes in the value of the dependency that would have occurred between the date of death and the date of trial. Everything that has been said in **12.4** with regard to the dependency applies equally to the future loss. The multiplicand is the answer to the question 'What is the annual loss as at today's date?'

Although a widow's earning capacity can usually be ignored, it may need to be taken into account where, for example, a widow has lost her job because of her husband's death, but can reasonably be expected to resume work soon (*Cookson* v *Knowles* [1977] QB 913). A widow's future earnings or earning capacity may also be taken into account in assessing the value of the children's dependency where they are claiming for the death of their father (*Dodds* v *Dodds* [1978] QB 543).

As with personal injury claims, there is likely to be a growing tendency to make split awards in the future. Where there is evidence that the deceased's earnings would have increased at some point after death, the court will achieve the most accurate assessment of the dependency by taking separate multiplicands for separate periods, and apportioning the multiplier. There may be a single multiplicand for the whole of the period of dependency (the deceased's and the dependants' joint lives), or the period may be divided into the years before retirement, and the pension years, with the first multiplicand being based on the deceased's net earnings and the second based on the annual value to the dependants of the deceased's pension.

12.5.2 THE MULTIPLIER

12.5.2.1 Introduction

As in personal injury cases, the multiplier is not a real number of years, but is discounted to take account of accelerated receipt and contingencies. It represents the number of years for which the dependency would have lasted. This is prima facie the deceased's and dependants' joint lives. In the case of a deceased husband and widow, the dependency would have lasted until the first of them died.

Following the decision in *Wells* v *Wells* [1998] 3 All ER 481, it would seem incongruous not to take an actuarial approach to the quantification of damages. The conventional approach was even more intuitive and unscientific in fatal accident claims than it was in personal injury claims. But *Wells* v *Wells* was concerned only with personal injury claims, and no more modern approach has yet been approved by the Court of Appeal or House of Lords. A new Section D to the explanatory notes to the Ogden Tables explains how the tables can be used to quantify damages in fatal accident cases with reasonable accuracy. However this approach results in a much more complicated calculation than that in personal injury cases. It cannot at present be stated with any confidence, therefore, that this is the correct approach to use.

12.5.2.2 The conventional approach

Before *Wells* v *Wells* the multiplier was selected in a manner very similar to that used in personal injury cases (see **11.10.3.2**). The period being measured was the period from the deceased's date of death (*not* the date of trial as in personal injury claims) and the end of the period of dependency. This had to be estimated taking into account the deceased's age, the age(s) of the dependant(s), the deceased's likely retirement age, the deceased's and dependants' life expectancy, and a large number of other variables such as job security, promotion prospects, health, etc. A fairly substantial discount was made for contingencies and uncertainties, and a discount for accelerated receipt based on a notional rate of return on investment of 4–5%. Tables in *Kemp & Kemp* enabled comparisons with previous cases to be made, and the final result was usually a rough and ready approximation.

12.5.2.3 The conventional approach today

Even without an approved new method of calculation, it seems that the conventional approach is too out of date to use. At the very least a discount rate of 2.5% should surely be used, which renders tables of multipliers in pre-*Wells* cases useless, and necessitates some reference to the Ogden Tables. This would suggest that the following method might be appropriate.

First decide whether to assess the dependencies for the pre-retirement years and the pension years together or separately. If they are to be taken together, then use Ogden Tables 19 and 20, looking under the 2.5% column. In the case of a husband and wife, look up the multiplier for a male of the age the deceased was at the date of his death, and the multiplier for a female of the age the widow was at that date: whichever is the smaller figure will be the correct multiplier to take as a starting point.

Alternatively, the working years and retirement years may be calculated separately. Use tables 21–28 to find the multiplier for the dependency up to the deceased's retirement, and tables 29–36 for the pension loss after that date. A widow is entitled to recover a sum in respect of her husband's retirement pension, where she would have derived benefit from it.

12.5.2.4 Discount for contingencies

The multiplier found by the above method must then be discounted to take account of contingencies other than mortality, as in personal injury cases. There is no easy guide as to how this should be done. It is necessary to take account of contingencies relating not only to the deceased, but also to all of the dependants. The result in the past was a rather bigger discount than might have been made in a personal injury case. This ought logically to continue to be the case. In the absence of anything better, since this is still a less than accurate method of selecting the multiplier, it is likely that the courts will continue to make the conventional discount of 10%, at least, making further adjustments as necessary.

12.5.2.5 Other contingencies

There are a large number of other contingencies which may have a specific effect, and cause the multiplier to be adjusted upwards or downwards:

(a) Evidence of the deceased's actual life expectancy. If this can be shown to be plainly lower or greater than average for a person of the deceased's age, an adjustment may need to be made.

(b) The possibility of divorce. The fact that at the deceased's death the marriage was showing signs of collapse does not mean that the dependency is automatically reduced: a dependant's right to financial support continues even after divorce, and so the dependency might well have been unaffected. However, the possibility also exists that after divorce the deceased would have remarried, which might have resulted in a diminished level of support for the first spouse, so the risk of divorce may be a relevant factor (*Martin* v *Owen*, *The Times*, 21 May 1992).

(c) Children's ages and marriage prospects. The court should be aware of how long any children would have remained dependent on the deceased. The actual dependency of young children is obviously longer than that of adult or nearly-adult children, and may be a factor affecting the multiplier. Similarly the age at which the children will cease full-time education and become financially independent is material. These matters will certainly make a difference when the children alone are the dependants. However they will not normally do so when there is also a dependent spouse. When children cease to be dependent, the usual expectation is that the dependency of the spouse simply increases proportionately, so no adjustment needs to be made.

(d) The fact that a cohabitee had no enforceable right to financial support by the deceased (FAA 1976, s. 3(4)). This must result in some reduction in the multiplier, since the cohabitee's dependency was less secure than a spouse's.

12.5.2.6 Factors which do not affect the multiplier

The following factors do not affect the choice of multiplier to be used in assessing future loss:

(a) A widow's remarriage or prospects of remarriage. This is expressly excluded from consideration by FAA 1976, s. 3(3).

(b) The likelihood of future inflation (*Cookson* v *Knowles* [1979] AC 556). This is the same principle as for personal injury (see **11.10.3.10**). The decision in *Hodgson* v *Trapp* (see **11.10.3.6**) must by implication apply also to claims under the FAA 1976.

12.5.2.7 A single multiplier

Although there may be several dependants, nevertheless in the vast majority of cases the dependency has conventionally been assessed as a single sum, there being just one multiplier to take account of all the dependants' claims. This is because, if the deceased had a certain amount of money available to support any dependants, that sum would have been spread among them in some way or other, but would not have been affected overall by their individual needs. However, in a minority of cases, where it seems that the circumstances of the case demand it, the court has assessed the multiplier and multiplicand for each dependant separately, and it may be that after *Wells* v *Wells* it will do so more frequently.

12.5.2.8 Deduct the pre-trial period

The multiplier chosen by the above method runs from the date of death. Since the dependency for the pre-trial period has already been calculated separately, the actual multiplier to be applied to the annual future loss is therefore what is left after deducting the pre-trial period (*Graham* v *Dodds* [1983] 2 All ER 953). So if, for example, the multiplier selected is 16, and the period from death to trial is 3 years 9 months, the multiplier applied to the future loss is 12.25. (Distinguish the rule in personal injury claims (see **11.10.3.10**).) But where the pre-trial period has virtually swallowed up the multiplier, the court may take this into account and adjust the multiplier upwards to permit some future loss — see *Corbett* v *Barking, Havering and Brentwood Health Authority* [1991] 2 QB 408 (true dependency 18 years, multiplier prima facie 12, but pre-trial period 11½ years, so multiplier increased to 15, allowing 3½ years future loss).

12.5.3 SPLIT AWARDS

As suggested above, it may become increasingly common for the court to make split awards when calculating the future dependency. It may value different periods of the dependency with a different multiplicand, it may take the working years separately from the pension years, it may take the dependency of each dependant separately. The manner of calculation will be as explained in **11.10.4**.

12.5.4 TAKING STAGES 1 AND 2 TOGETHER

When advising on the quantum of damage, if there is no evidence as to how the dependency would have increased after death, then there is little point in assessing the pre-trial loss and the future loss separately. Simply value the dependency as at the date of death and apply a suitable multiplier without deducting the pre-trial period.

12.5.5 THE OGDEN APPROACH TO FUTURE LOSS

As mentioned above, Sir Michael Ogden in his explanatory notes to the Tables proposes a more actuarial approach to the calculation of future loss. This has not yet had the approval of any higher court, and it is arguably in contradiction with the House of Lords decision in *Cookson* v *Knowles* [1979] AC 556 (though Ogden argues that it is not). It involves changing the rule that the multiplier runs from the date of death, and it involves calculating the dependency in three separate amounts: the pre-trial period, the pre-retirement period and the pension period. It also involves calculating the dependency of each dependant separately. It is fully explained in Section D of the Explanatory Notes, to which you should refer if you wish to use this method. Although it is lengthy, it is clearly explained and it is not any more difficult than the method of selecting and refining the multiplier in personal injury cases.

12.6 Stage 3: Add Lump Sums

There can be added to the total sum arrived at so far any lump sums which it can be shown that the dependants would have benefited from in the future — for example, the deceased's savings or capital.

12.7 Stage 4: Add Bereavement

The spouse of the deceased or the parents of an unmarried minor (but no other dependants) can recover damages for bereavement, quantified as a fixed lump sum (FAA 1976, s. 1A). The sum can be specified from time to time by the Lord Chancellor and is currently £10,000 (or £7,500 for causes of action accruing before 1 April 2002). The parents of an unmarried child cannot recover damages for bereavement where he or she was under 18 at the date of injury but over 18 on the date of death (*Doleman* v *Deakin, The Times,* 30 January 1990).

12.8 Stage 5: Contributory Negligence

The total sum quantified so far must be reduced if there has been a finding of contributory negligence by the deceased. Take off the appropriate percentage.

Contributory negligence by a dependant must also be taken into account, but only as regards that dependant's share of the dependency (an example of a situation where the dependency for each dependant *will* have to be assessed separately).

12.9 Stage 6: Add Interest

Interest will be awarded by the court under SCA 1981, s. 35A. By s. 35A(2) the award is prima facie mandatory, unless there are special reasons for the contrary. The guidelines for the award of interest were laid down by *Cookson* v *Knowles* [1979] AC 556.

(a) Interest is awarded on the pre-trial loss from the date of death to the date of trial at half the 'appropriate rate'. For the meaning of 'appropriate rate' see **11.16.2**.

(b) Interest is awarded on damages for bereavement at the full appropriate rate from the date of death to the date of trial (*Prior* v *Hastie* [1987] CLY 1219).

(c) No interest is awarded on damages for future loss.

When advising on the quantum of damages it is not usual to make any attempt to calculate interest.

12.10 Stage 7: Apportion between Dependants

Although there is usually only one multiplier and damages are awarded as a single lump sum, the court must indicate how that sum is to be divided up between the dependants (FAA 1976, s. 3(2)). The apportionment must bear some relationship to the comparative value of each dependant's dependency, but does not have to be exact.

The only difficulties arise when apportioning between a widow and child(ren). The widow always gets the larger share, which will include the joint dependency of the family as a whole. The children, on the other hand, get all that is truly their share of the dependency, not just 'pocket money' (*Benson* v *Biggs Wall & Co. Ltd* [1982] 3 All ER 300). The greater the number of children, the younger the children are, the larger their share. A table in *Kemp & Kemp* (para. 23–050) shows the children's share ranging between about a twentieth and a half of the total damages.

Damages for bereavement are not, of course, apportioned.

12.11 Deductions

You might have expected Stage 5 to be 'make any necessary deductions' but it is not, because there are no deductions. This is the effect of FAA 1976, s. 4, which provides that any benefits which have accrued, or will accrue, to the dependants as a result of the deceased's death are to be disregarded. No deduction needs to be made, therefore, in respect of sums inherited from the estate, damages recovered under the LR(MP)A 1934, widow's pension, widow's benefit, insurance money, charitable donations, or anything else, even where the result is that the dependants are better off than they would have been but for the death (see e.g., *Pidduck* v *Eastern Scottish Omnibuses Ltd* [1990] 2 All ER 69). Nor can any deduction be made for the value of benefits in money's worth: for example where a father's second wife is providing a higher standard of motherly services than the children's deceased mother ever did (*Stanley* v *Saddique* [1992] QB 1). However, s. 4 does not prevent the value of a father's services being set off against the value of the deceased mother's services (*Hayden* v *Hayden* [1992] 4 All ER 681).

12.12 No Recovery of Benefits

A person making a compensation payment under the FAA 1976 is not liable to repay benefits under the Social Security (Recovery of Benefits) Act 1997 (Social Security (Recovery of Benefits) Regulations 1997 (SI 1997/2237), r. 2(2)(a)).

THIRTEEN

OTHER EQUITABLE REMEDIES

This can only be a brief outline of some of the other important equitable remedies. For further discussion see Goff and Jones, *Law of Restitution* and *Snell on Equity*.

13.1 Personal and Proprietary Claims

Remedies such as suing for damages for tort or breach of contract are personal remedies which means that if the person sued is insolvent the client is unlikely to recover any money (subject to any security taken as part of a contractual arrangement).

A few remedies, most notably trust remedies and tracing, give rights '*in rem*', which means that the remedy is strictly against the property rather than the wrongdoer, so it is unaffected by the insolvency of the wrongdoer. Provided the claim is made out, and the property can be identified, it belongs to the person seeking the remedy and no other creditor can make claims to it.

13.2 Tracing

Tracing is available where property is taken and dealt with contrary to a person's fiduciary duties. It is mainly used in the context of breaches of trust but it is not confined to these. A tracing order can be made to recover the property itself or the proceeds of sale if they can be sufficiently identified.

13.2.1 MIXED FUNDS

Where proceeds have been paid into a mixed fund, the basic rule is that the first payment in is related to the earliest payment out (*Devaynes* v *Noble, Clayton's Case* (1816) 1 Mer 572). However, where the money is paid into a bank account, the trustee will be deemed to spend his or her own money before spending a beneficiary's money (*Re Hallett's Estate* (1880) 13 ChD 696).

A beneficiary may be able to claim a charge on property bought from a mixed fund (*Re Hallett's Estate* (above)). It may also be possible for a beneficiary to claim a proportion of any profit made from a mixed fund (*Re Tilley's Will Trusts* [1967] Ch 1179).

13.2.2 LIMITS TO THE RIGHT TO TRACE

There are limits to the right to trace. A trustee or someone in a fiduciary capacity must admit the claim of a beneficiary, giving priority to it, as must a volunteer. An innocent person will share property equally with a beneficiary who claims a right to trace. Once property has passed to a purchaser for value without notice, a right to trace will be extinguished.

13.3 Constructive Trusts

On the facts of a particular case, a constructive trust may arise in equity to provide an additional or alternative remedy. There has been much academic debate as to whether a constructive trust can strictly speaking be regarded as a 'remedy', rather than simply as an operation of substantive law. It is clearly so regarded in the United States, but while there is some authority for regarding it as a remedy in the United Kingdom (see especially Lord Denning MR in *Hussey* v *Palmer* [1972] 1 WLR 1286), there is no agreement on the matter. The technical distinction has little relevance so long as the facts justify the finding of a constructive trust.

In general terms, a constructive trust can arise wherever there is a fiduciary relationship; it does not require the existence of a formal trust (*English* v *Dedham Vale Properties Ltd* [1978] 1 WLR 93). The broad basis for finding a constructive trust is to prevent unjust enrichment (*Carl Zeiss Stiftung* v *Herbert Smith & Co. (No. 2)* [1969] 2 Ch 276; *James* v *Williams* [2000] Ch 1 (CA)).

A constructive trust has been held to arise in the following circumstances:

(a) Where a person in a fiduciary position gains any unauthorised personal benefit or profit from that position (see *Keech* v *Sandford* (1726) Sel Cast King 61).

(b) Where particular property is subject to a fiduciary duty (see *Tito* v *Waddell (No. 2)* [1977] Ch 106).

(c) Where property has been acquired as a result of information obtained by someone acting as a fiduciary (see *Boardman* v *Phipps* [1967] 2 AC 46, but see *Sabnam Investments* v *Dunlop Heywood* [1999] 3 All ER 652).

(d) Where a stranger to a trust has actual or constructive knowledge of a trust and knowingly receives trust property. There is a very large number of reported cases dealing with the degree of knowledge required and whether there was sufficient proof of knowledge on the facts. If dealing with this issue it is especially important to check recent case-law. An interesting example is *Bank of Credit and Commerce International (Overseas) Ltd (in liquidation)* v *Akindele* [2000] 4 All ER 221.

(e) A person who dishonestly procures or assists in a breach of trust is liable to make good any resulting loss (see *Belmont Finance Corp Ltd* v *Williams Furniture Ltd* [1979] Ch 250 and *Royal Brunei Airlines Sdn Bhd* v *Tan* [1995] 3 WLR 64).

(f) An agent acting for a trust can become a constructive trustee if he or she:

   (i) becomes chargeable with some part of the trust property; or

   (ii) knowingly assists in a dishonest or fraudulent design on the part of the trustee; or

   (iii) acts without proper instructions.

(See *Blyth* v *Fladgate* [1892] 1 Ch 337.)

However, an agent such as a solicitor will not become a constructive trustee simply by acting as an agent (see *Barnes* v *Addy* (1874) LR 9 Ch App 224, *Mara* v *Browne* [1896] 1 Ch 199 and *Williams-Ashman* v *Price and Williams* [1942] Ch 219).

13.4 Subrogation

Subrogation involves a person being able to take over the rights or assets of another party to avoid a third party benefiting unjustly from a benefit conferred on them by the first person. The right of subrogation is well established in insurance law. So, for example, where an insurer has paid an employee insurance money in respect of injuries suffered at work, the insurer can take over any rights the insured employee may have had against his or her employer (or third parties). See further Goff and Jones, p. 523 *et seq.*

13.5 Quasi-contract

The main quasi-contract remedies are *quantum meruit* and *quantum valebat*. For these remedies there may have been a contract and a dispute over whether there was a breach. Even if the issues are decided in favour of one party, the court may order that party to pay the other a 'reasonable' amount for any benefit conferred or asset transferred if it would be unjust to allow the person to retain that benefit without compensation.

13.6 Benefits Conferred in an Emergency

Similar principles of avoidance of unjust enrichment underlie the cases where a person has been allowed to claim remuneration for goods provided in an emergency to a person under a legal incapacity or services rendered in an attempt to save life or prevent injury (*Williams* v *Wentworth* (1842) 5 Beav 325; *Great Northern Railway Co.* v *Swaffield* (1874) LR 9 Ex 132).

13.7 Rights to Contribution and Recoupment

There are various situations where a person has a common law or statutory right to recover some or all of the money he or she has paid out in satisfying a claim by a third party from someone else whom that third party could have claimed against, or who was somehow involved in the situation which gave rise to the third party's claim. The most important statutory remedy is under the Civil Liability (Contribution) Act 1978. Common law examples arise with joint tenants, partners and joint contractors.

13.8 Benefits Conferred through Mistake, Duress or Undue Influence

This is a complex and rapidly changing area. Basically, if the claim succeeds, a person may be able to rescind a contract, mortgage, trust or other obligation and recover money or property notwithstanding that there appeared to be, in form at least, a valid contract or gift or other transfer. In dealing with any of these areas it is necessary to establish whether the claim falls within one of the recognised categories which give rise to relief, whether it can be argued it would only involve a small extension of one of those categories or whether you will need to try to rely on a general principle of prevention of unjust enrichment, unconscionable bargains etc. If the latter is the case it is obviously going to be more difficult to convince a court that the remedy is obtainable.

Two recent cases extend and clarify the scope of remedies in cases of payments made under mistakes of law: *Kleinwort Benson Ltd* v *Lincoln City Council (No. 2)* [1998] 3 WLR 1095 (HL), *Nurdin and Peacock plc* v *D.B. Ramsden & Co. Ltd* [1999] 1 All ER 941. Restitutionary remedies in the case of benefits conferred under contracts which later were held to be void have been considered extensively in the 'interest rate swap transaction' cases which followed the decision that local authorities had no power to enter into such transactions. Key decisions in this area include *Hazell* v *Hammersmith & Fulham London BC* [1991] 1 All ER 545, *Kleinwort Benson Ltd* v *Sandwell BC* [1994] 4 All ER 890, *Westdeutshe Landesbank Girozentrale* v *Islington London BC* [1996] AC 669, *Guiness Mahon & Co. Ltd* v *Kensington & Chelsea Royal London Borough Council* [1998] 2 All ER 272.

13.9 Benefits Conferred as a Result of Fraud or Criminal Conduct

Irrespective of whether the law recognises general principles of prevention of unjust enrichment, a person has always been able to seek a remedy to prevent someone from benefiting from their fraudulent conduct or other criminal conduct. The remedy could be rescission or return of property.

13.10 Fraudulent Preferences and Avoidance of Voluntary Transfers

Where a person becomes insolvent, the creditors may be able to call in property voluntarily transferred by that person to others or used to 'fraudulently' pay off one creditor at the expense of others. Any property called in would form part of the debtor's estate and would be distributed to creditors in accordance with the normal rules of priority of creditors and equal treatment for creditors of equal ranking. See further Insolvency Act 1986, ss. 238 to 241.

FOURTEEN

JUDICIAL REVIEW

The judicial review of administrative claim is an increasingly important area of law. The number of cases involving judicial review increases every year. However, there are clear limits to the scope of judicial review.

14.1 Scope of Judicial Review

There are a number of restrictions on the availability of judicial review. In summary, those restrictions are:

(a) Judicial review is only available in 'public law' cases.

(b) Usually, judicial review may only be used as the remedy of last resort.

(c) The applicant must have 'sufficient interest'.

(d) The applicant must act promptly.

Each of these restrictions is considered in the sections which follow.

14.2 Public Law Cases Only

Judicial review procedure is governed by CPR, Part 54 (which replaces RSC O. 53). CPR, r. 54.1(2)(a) defines a claim for judicial review as meaning a claim to review the lawfulness of (i) an enactment, or (ii) a decision, action or failure to act in relation to the exercise of a public function. It is therefore only 'public law' claims which can be made by way of judicial review. It follows that judicial review is only available against:

(a) public bodies exercising public functions; and

(b) 'inferior' courts.

14.2.1 PUBLIC BODIES

The term 'public body' includes bodies set up by statute, along with government departments and non-statutory bodies which exercise public functions. See *R* v *Panel on Take-overs and Mergers, ex parte Datafin plc* [1987] QB 815 (where a non-statutory body regulating certain business dealings in the City of London was held to be susceptible to judicial review) and *R* v *Advertising Standards Authority Ltd, ex parte Insurance Services plc* (1990) 2 Admin LR 77 (where the Advertising Standards Authority, another non-statutory body, was held to be susceptible to judicial review).

Judicial review may thus be claimed against decisions of such diverse public bodies or authorities as: borough councils, government ministers, the British Broadcasting Corporation, boards of prison visitors.

Where a body derives its functions and authority from contract, judicial review is not available. See *Law* v *National Greyhound Racing Club* [1983] 1 WLR 1302 (where the Greyhound Racing Club was held not to be susceptible to judicial review) and *R* v *Disciplinary Committee of the Jockey Club, ex parte Aga Khan* [1993] 1 WLR 909 (where the same decision was reached in the case of the Jockey Club). This is because in such cases the applicant can pursue a remedy for breach of contract.

Similarly, in *R* v *Muntham House School, ex parte R, The Times*, 26 January 2000, a pupil at the school was excluded and judicial review of that decision was sought. Most of the fees were in practice paid by a local educational authority, but the school was not a publicly-funded school in the sense of receiving grants or other direct funding from the public sector. The local authority entered into a purely contractual relationship with the school to place a child there. Therefore, it was held that the decision by the school to exclude a pupil did not have a sufficient public law chracter to make it amenable to judicial review.

Where the public body is a charity, it may be preferable to pursue a remedy under charity legislation. For example, in *Scott* v *National Trust* [1998] 2 All ER 705, it was held that the National Trust, being a charity of exceptional importance to the nation and being subject to special statutory provisions, constitutes a public body. However, because it is a charity, a challenge should be brought under the special procedure set out in s. 33 of the Charities Act 1993; the availability of this alternative remedy meant that judicial review would not normally be granted.

Even if the body is a public body against which judicial review may be sought, judicial review is only available to challenge decisions made by such bodies when they are acting in a public law (rather than private law) capacity. If there is a 'private law' remedy (for example, for breach of contract), the applicant should bring a claim based on that private law claim, and should not seek judicial review. See *O'Reilly* v *Mackman* [1983] 2 AC 237; *Cocks* v *Thanet District Council* [1983] 2 AC 286; *Davy* v *Spelthorne Borough Council* [1984] AC 262 and *Roy* v *Kensington and Chelsea and Westminster Family Practitioner Committee* [1992] 1 AC 624. So, for example, a person who claims to have been unfairly dismissed from the employment of a public body cannot challenge that decision by way of judicial review.

14.2.2 INFERIOR COURTS

Although judicial review is normally thought of as a means of challenging the decisions of public bodies, it is also a means by which the decisions of certain courts may be challenged. Decisions of magistrates' courts may be challenged in this way. However, decisions of the Crown Court may only be challenged by judicial review if the decision does not relate to a trial on indictment, since the Supreme Court Act 1981, s. 29(3), excludes from the scope of judicial review 'matters relating to trial on indictment'. In *Director of Public Prosecutions* v *Manchester Crown Court and Ashton* [1993] 2 All ER 663, the House of Lords held that a decision to stay proceedings as an abuse of process came within this exception. The House of Lords confirmed that s. 29(3) applies to matters which affect the conduct of a Crown Court trial (covering orders made before the trial) and matters which are an integral part of the trial process (which covers orders made during, or even at the very end of the trial, together with some pre-trial orders).

Despite the breadth of this definition, the question of what matters relate to trial on indictment has continued to generate case law. For example *R* v *Harrow Crown Court, ex parte Perkins*; *R* v *Cardiff Crown Court, ex parte M* (1998) 162 JP 527. In the first case, the applicant sought judicial review of the decision of a Crown Court judge not to order the prosecution to pay his costs when they decided to offer no evidence against him. It was held that the exercise of the judge's discretion on the question of costs is an integral part of the trial process (even if the case concludes without the empanelment of a jury) and so judicial review is excluded by s. 29(3) of the Supreme Court Act 1981. In the second case, a Crown Court judge refused to make an order to protect the identity of a juvenile defendant under s. 39(1) of the Children and Young Persons Act

1933 and it was held that the power to make an order under s. 39, which can be exercised in respect of a juvenile defendant, complainant or witness, is collateral to the trial on indictment and so is amenable to judicial review. In *R* v *Manchester Crown Court, ex parte H* [2000] 1 WLR 760, the Divisional Court confirmed that it has jurisdiction to entertain an application for judicial review of an order lifting reporting restrictions under s. 39 of the 1933 Act (and declined to follow *R* v *Winchester Crown Court, ex parte B* [1999] 1 WLR 788, where the court had reached the opposite conclusion).

Where there has been a final determination of a case in a magistrates' court (that is, the accused has either been acquitted or else has been convicted and sentenced), appeal to the Divisional Court by way of case stated is generally more appropriate. See the Magistrates' Courts Act 1980, s. 111, and *R* v *Ipswich Crown Court, ex parte Baldwin* [1981] 1 All ER 596; *R* v *Oldbury Justices, ex parte Smith* (1994) 159 JP 316. Further, it was held in *R* v *Gloucester Crown Court, ex parte Chester* [1998] COD 365, that where a person is convicted by a magistrates' court and appeals to the Crown Court, further appeal against conviction to the High Court on a point of law should be by way of case stated, not judicial review.

Challenging decisions of magistrates' courts and of the Crown Court is dealt with more fully in the ***Criminal Litigation and Sentencing Manual***.

Theoretically, judicial review could be used to challenge decisions of a county court, but a decision should not be challenged in this way if it is possible to challenge the decision by appeal to the Court of Appeal.

Decisions of coroners' courts are also susceptible to challenge by way of judicial review (see, for example, *R* v *Her Majesty's Coroner for Inner West London, ex parte Dallaglio* [1995] COD 20 (a case arising out of the sinking of the *Marchioness*) as are decisions of election courts established under the Representation of the People Act 1949.

Because the scope of judicial review is limited to the review of 'inferior' courts, it does not extend to decisions of the High Court, the Court of Appeal, or the House of Lords.

14.2.3 JUDICIAL REVIEW v PRIVATE LAW REMEDIES

In *The Trustees of Dennis Rye Pension Fund* v *Sheffield City Council* [1997] 4 All ER 747, the Court of Appeal gave guidance for those cases on the borderline between private law and public law. Lord Woolf MR made the following observations:

(a) If it is not clear whether judicial review or a private law claim is the most appropriate way to proceed, it is safer to make an application for judicial review.

(b) If a case is brought by way of an ordinary claim (seeking a private law remedy) and the defendant applies to strike the claim out on the ground that it should have been brought by way of judicial review, the court should ask itself whether it is clear that permission would have been granted had the claimant sought to bring judicial review proceedings.

(c) If the claimant brings an ordinary (private law) claim and it is equally, or more, appropriate than an application for judicial review, and the defendant tries to strike the claim out on the basis that it should have been a judicial review claim, the claim should not be struck out.

(d) In cases where the claimant brings an ordinary claim but it is unclear whether proceedings should have been brought by way of judicial review instead, it should be borne in mind that the court can order the transfer of the case to the Crown Office List instead of striking the claim out.

(e) The choice made by the claimant as regards the type of claim will not normally be regarded as an abuse of process where that choice has no significant disadvantages for the parties, the public or the court.

In *Clark* v *University of Lincolnshire & Humberside* [2000] 3 All ER 752, the Court of Appeal had to consider, in the context of a higher education institution, the competing claims of contract, applications to the visitor, and judicial review. It was held that, although the arrangement between a fee-paying student and a higher education corporation is a contract, disputes suitable for adjudication under the contract's dispute resolution procedures might be unsuitable for adjudication in the courts: where issues of academic or pastoral judgement arise, a university is properly equipped to deal with those issues, whereas a court is not. So, for example, cases where the question is what mark or class ought to be awarded, or whether an aegrotat was justified, are not justiciable in the courts. The Court went on to hold that where a university is subject to the supervisory jurisdiction of a visitor, that procedure should be used rather than litigation in the courts. However, where there is no such provision and the matter is not one of academic or pastoral judgement, the court can adjudicate on allegations of breach of contractual obligations. The Court held that a contractual claim should not be struck out merely because judicial review would be the more appropriate remedy. If, however, it is clear that the claimant is bringing the case in contract to take improper advantage of the six-year limitation period (as against the three-month time limit for judicial review), the court can strike out the claim if satisfied that the court's processes are being misused or, because of the lapse of time or other circumstances, no worthwhile remedy can be expected.

14.3 Availability of Alternative Remedies

Judicial review is often regarded as a remedy of last resort. It follows that other forms of redress must be sought first (see, for example, *R* v *Inland Revenue Commissioners, ex parte Preston* [1985] AC 835 at p. 852, per Lord Scarman and *R* v *Chief Constable of Merseyside Police, ex parte Calveley* [1986] QB 424 at p. 433, per Lord Donaldson of Lymington MR). If there is a mechanism for appealing against the decision complained of, the mechanism must be used; if the result is unfavourable, it may well be possible to challenge the appellate decision by means of judicial review.

However, this is not a hard-and-fast rule; there are many cases where judicial review has been granted despite the existence of an alternative remedy. See, for example, *R* v *Huntingdon District Council, ex parte Cowan* [1984] 1 WLR 501; *R* v *Devon County Council, ex parte Baker* [1993] COD 253 and *R* v *Leeds City Council, ex parte Hendry, The Times*, 20 January 1994. In the last of those cases, the existence of a statutory appeal to a magistrates' court against a decision to withhold a hackney carriage licence was held not to be a bar to the claim for judicial review.

In *Harley Development Inc.* v *Commissioners of Inland Revenue* [1996] 1 WLR 727, the Privy Council said that where a comprehensive statutory appeals procedure exists but was not used by the applicant, an application for judicial review would be entertained only in exceptional circumstances. The same approach was adopted in *R* v *Commissioners of Customs and Excise, ex parte Bosworth Beverages Ltd, The Times*, 24 April 2000. Similarly, in *R* v *Secretary of State for the Home Department, ex parte Capti-Mehmet* [1997] COD 61, Laws J reiterated the principle that an applicant for judicial review will usually be required to exhaust all alternative remedies before the court will grant leave to apply for judicial review and that this rule applies unless there are exceptional circumstances justifying departure from it. His Lordship went on to say that a failure to exhaust alternative remedies brought about by the error or incompetence of the applicant's legal representatives will not of itself constitute an exceptional circumstance; however, such failures do not weigh as heavily against the applicant as a deliberate decision not to exhaust alternative remedies. Exceptional circumstances may arise from a combination of factors which individually are insufficient. Relevant factors include whether the applicant gave an early intimation of an intention to challenge the decision. Strong legal merits, such that the court is satisfied that the applicant was denied 'substantial justice' before the inferior court, body or tribunal, will weigh powerfully in favour of finding that exceptional circumstances exist.

In *R* v *Lambeth LBC, ex parte Ogunmuyiwa, The Times*, 17 April 1997, the applicant had been led to believe that her case would be reviewed by the local authority; however, the local authority failed to carry out that review. Popplewell J held that this case was an exception to the rule that the applicant should have exhausted all other remedies before seeking judicial review. Again, in *R* v *Wiltshire County Council, ex parte Lazard Brothers & Co. Ltd, The Times*, 13 January 1998, a statutory appeal was available to the applicant. However, the statutory appeal (under the Wildlife and Countryside Act 1981) took the form of a public enquiry. Despite the existence of a statutory remedy which the applicant had not exercised, Dyson J quashed the decision of the council; he held that the council had made a plain error of law and that it would be unfair to require the applicant to go through the costly and time consuming appeal procedure.

A similar approach was taken in *R* v *Falmouth & Truro Health Authority, ex parte South West Water Ltd* [2000] 3 All ER 306 (CA). This case was mainly concerned with the abatement of a statutory nuisance (Public Health Act 1936, s. 259(1)(a)). However, Simon Brown LJ (at p. 332) made some general comments on cases where there is an alternative to judicial review, such as a statutory appeal: 'If the applicant has a statutory right of appeal, permission [for judicial review] should only exceptionally be given'. The judge considering the application for permission should, however, have regard to all relevant circumstances, including the 'comparative speed, expense and finality of the alternative process, the need and scope for fact-finding, the desirability of an authoritative ruling on any point of law arising, and (perhaps) the apparent strength of the applicant's substantive challenge'.

14.4 Sufficient Interest

In order to seek judicial review, the applicant must have sufficient interest in the matter to which the application relates, sometimes known as *locus standi* ('standing'). This means that the applicant must be able to show a legitimate expectation of being heard. This generally requires that the applicant must be directly affected by the decision which is being challenged. In *Council of Civil Service Unions* v *Minister for the Civil Service* [1985] AC 374, Lord Diplock (at pp. 408–9) said that to have a legitimate expectation in respect of a decision, the applicant must be affected by the decision, in that the decision has the effect of:

(a) altering rights or obligations of that person which are enforceable by or against him in private law, or

(b) depriving him of some benefit or advantage which either:

  (i) he has in the past been permitted by the decision-maker to enjoy and which he can legitimately expect to be permitted to continue to do until there has been communicated to him some rational ground for withdrawing it on which he has been given an opportunity to comment, or

  (ii) he has received assurance from the decision-maker that it will not be withdrawn without giving him first an opportunity for advancing reasons for contending that they should not be withdrawn.

Such expectation may be based on an express promise by the decision-maker (as in *R* v *Liverpool Corporation, ex parte Liverpool Taxi Fleet Operators' Association* [1972] 2 QB 299) or on the practice adopted in the past by the decision-maker (e.g., *R* v *Secretary of State for the Home Department, ex parte Ruddock* [1987] 1 WLR 1482).

It should be noted that even if the applicant is granted permission to seek judicial review (on the basis that he or she has 'sufficient interest') it is open to the court which hears the substantive application for judicial review to decide that the applicant does not in fact have sufficient interest. See *IRC* v *National Federation of Self-Employed and Small Businesses Ltd* [1982] AC 617 at p. 642 per Lord Diplock.

14.5 The Need to Act Promptly

Section 31(6) of the Supreme Court Act 1981 provides:

> *where the High Court considers that there has been undue delay in making an application for judicial review, the court may refuse to grant—*
> *(a) leave for the making of the application; or*
> *(b) any relief sought on the application,*
> *if it considers that the granting of the relief sought would be likely to cause substantial hardship to, or substantially prejudice the rights of, any person or would be detrimental to good administration.*

CPR, r. 54.5(1), says that the claim form seeking judicial review must be filed 'promptly and in any event not later than three months after the grounds to make the claim first arose'. It follows from the wording of this provision that a claim may fail for delay even if it is brought within the three-month period. PD 54, para. 4.1 says that where the claim is for a quashing order in respect of a judgment, order or conviction, the date when the grounds to make the claim first arose is the date of the judgment, order or conviction.

If the three-month period has already expired, the court may grant an extension of time, but only if there is 'good reason' for doing so. Even if the court considers that there is good reason for extending the period, the court may still refuse permission (or, where permission has been granted, refuse to grant the remedy sought) if it takes the view that the granting of the remedy would cause hardship or prejudice or be detrimental to good administration.

In *Caswell* v *Dairy Produce Quota Tribunal for England and Wales* [1990] 2 AC 738, Lord Goff thought it appropriate that permission to apply for judicial review out of time should be granted where the judge finds that there is a good reason for extending time; the question of whether the remedy should be withheld on the ground of prejudice or hardship or detriment to good administration should be dealt with at the substantive hearing.

Where there has been delay, any explanation for that delay should be given in the application for permission to seek judicial review.

In *R* v *Secretary of State for the Home Department, ex parte Ruddock* [1987] 1 WLR 1482, a delay in the grant of legal aid was said to be a 'good reason' for delay in making the application for permission to seek judicial review. However, in *Phillips* v *Derbyshire County Council* [1997] COD 130 the applicant missed the relevant deadline by four days. Her expert adviser had failed to send papers to her solicitor, and the solicitor had failed to chase the papers. Sedley J held that the series of derelictions of duty by the applicant's advisers did not provide material upon which the court could exercise its discretion to extend time.

In *R* v *Criminal Injuries Compensation Board, ex parte A* [1997] 3 All ER 745, the Court of Appeal made the point that 'the better the prospects of success, the readier will the court be to extend time even where the delay is unjustifiable, i.e., the merits themselves can contribute to or even supply the "good reason"' (per Simon Brown LJ at p. 759). When this case went to the House of Lords (*R* v *Criminal Injuries Compensation Board, ex parte A* [1999] 2 WLR 974), it was held that where permission to apply for judicial review has been given without notice, an application to set permission aside might be made, although such applications are not to be encouraged. Unless permission is set aside, the question of permission cannot be reopened at the substantive hearing on the basis that there were no grounds for extending time under RSC O. 53, r. 4(1). What the court can do under s. 31(6) of the Supreme Court Act 1981 is to refuse to grant relief on the basis of the applicant's delay. It was also pointed out that where the application for permission has been adjourned to the substantive hearing, the questions under both RSC O. 53, r. 4(1) and s. 31(6) of the 1981 Act might both have to be determined.

In *R* v *Newbury District Council, ex parte Chievely Parish Council, The Times*, 10 September 1998, it was noted by the Court of Appeal that important decisions can be taken by public and private bodies, and by individuals, on the strength of some decisions, such as the granting of planning permission. It is therefore in the interests of good administration that any challenge should be made quickly. The Court held that this was so even if there is no evidence of actual hardship or prejudice to the rights of third parties.

14.6 Procedure for Seeking Judicial Review

The procedure for seeking judicial review is contained in CPR, Part 54 and PD 54. An application for judicial review has two stages: an application for permission to seek judicial review and then (if permission is granted) the substantive application for judicial review.

14.6.1 PRE-ACTION PROTOCOL

There is now a pre-action protocol for judicial review claims, which basically requires a letter before claim and a response, or a failure to respond within the time allowed, before the claim is filed. However, it is recognised that the protocol will not be appropriate in every case, for example where the defendant does not have the legal power to change the decision being challenged, or where the matter is urgent. In such cases there will be no sanction for failing to comply with the protocol. The claim form must state that the protocol has been complied with, or give reasons for non-compliance.

14.6.2 SEEKING PERMISSION TO APPLY FOR JUDICIAL REVIEW

Part 54 claims for judicial review are dealt with in the Administrative Court. Documents have to be filed at the Administrative Court Office, the Royal Courts of Justice, Strand, London, WC2A 2LL.

Under the *Practice Direction (Administrative Court: Establishment)* [2000] 1 WLR 1654, the parties to an application for judicial review are described in the proceedings as being: 'The Queen on the application of [name of applicant], claimant v [the name of the public body against whom the proceedings are brought], defendant'.

Under CPR, r. 54.4, the court's permission to proceed is required in order to bring a claim for judicial review.

14.6.3 THE PAPERWORK

The first step in a claim for judicial review is to file a claim form. As well as the matters that normally have to appear in a claim form (see CPR, r. 8.2), r. 54.6 provides that the claimant has to state:

(a) the name and address of any person he or she considers to be an interested party (defined in r. 54.1(2)(f) as any person, other than the claimant and defendant, who is directly affected by the claim;

(b) that he or she is requesting permission to proceed with a claim for judicial review;

(c) any remedy (including any interim remedy) he or she is claiming.

The claim form has to be accompanied by the documents required by PD 54. PD 54, para. 5.6 provides that the claim form must include or be accompanied by:

(a) a detailed statement of the claimant's grounds for bringing the claim for judicial review;

(b) a statement of the facts relied on;

(c) any application to extend the time limit for filing the claim form;

(d) any application for directions;

(e) a time estimate for the hearing.

PD 54, para. 5.7 provides that the claim form must also be accompanied by:

(a) any written evidence in support of the claim or the application to extend time;

(b) a copy of any order that the claimant seeks to have quashed;

(c) where the claim for judicial review relates to a decision of a court or tribunal, an approved copy of the reasons for reaching that decision;

(d) copies of any documents on which the claimant proposes to rely;

(e) copies of any relevant statutory material;

(f) a list of essential documents for reading in advance by the court (with page references to the passages relied on).

The claim form must be served on the defendant, and (unless the court otherwise directs) on any person the claimant considers to be an interested party, within seven days after the date of issue.

Where the claim for judicial review relates to proceedings in a court or tribunal, any other parties to those proceedings must be named in the claim form as interested parties (PD 54, para. 5.1). It follows that where a defendant in a criminal case seeks judicial review of a decision of a magistrates' court or the Crown Court, the prosecution must always be named as an interested party (para. 5.2).

A person served with the claim form who wishes to take part in the judicial review must file an acknowledgement of service not more than 21 days after the service of the claim form. The acknowledgement of service must be served on the claimant, and on any other person named in the claim form, not later than seven days after it is filed. The acknowledgement of service must (if the person filing it intends to contest the claim) set out a summary of the grounds for contesting the claim (and must state the name and address of anyone whom the person filing it considers to be an interested party)

CPR, r. 54.9 says that a person who fails to file an acknowledgement of service may not (unless allowed by the court) take part in any hearing to decide whether permission to proceed should be given. However, if that person complies with any direction of the court regarding the filing and service of detailed grounds for contesting the claim (or supporting it on additional grounds), together with any written evidence, he or she may take part in the substantive hearing of the claim for judicial review.

14.6.4 DETERMINING THE APPLICATION FOR PERMISSION

PD 54, para. 8.4 provides that the court will generally, in the first instance, consider the question of permission without a hearing.

Where there is a hearing, neither the defendant nor any other interested party need attend the hearing unless the court directs otherwise (para. 8.5). Where the defendant or any interested party does attend a hearing, the court will not generally make an order for costs against the claimant (para. 8.6).

If the applicant has sufficient standing to bring the claim for judicial review and there has not been undue delay, the judge will go on to consider the merits of the application.

The test applied by the single judge is whether the claimant's application for judicial review discloses an arguable case.

In *R* v *Secretary of State for the Home Department, ex parte Doorga* [1990] Imm AR 98 and in *R* v *Secretary of State for the Home Department, ex parte Begum* [1990] Imm AR 1, Lord Donaldson MR said that if the judge is satisfied that there is no arguable case, the application for permission should be refused. If the judge is satisfied that there is an arguable case, permission should be given. If the judge is uncertain whether or not there is an arguable case, the application for permission should be adjourned to enable a hearing to take place so that oral arguments from both the claimant and the defendant (and other interested parties) may be heard.

14.6.5 REFUSAL OF PERMISSION

CPR, r. 54.12 provides that if the court, without a hearing, refuses permission to proceed or gives permission that is subject to conditions or on certain grounds only, the court will serve its reasons for making the order along with the order itself.

Under CPR. r. 54.12, 'the claimant may not appeal but may request the decision to be reconsidered at a hearing' (and must file a request for such a hearing within seven days of the service of the court's reasons for the decision refusing permission).

CPR, r. 54.13 states that neither the defendant, nor anyone else served with the claim form, may apply to set aside an order giving the claimant permission to proceed.

In *R* v *Secretary of State for Trade & Industry, ex parte Eastaway* [2000] 1 WLR 222, the House of Lords held that, under CPR, Part 52, permission (from the lower court or the Court of Appeal) is required to appeal to the Court of Appeal against refusal by a judge to grant permission to apply for judicial review. No further appeal lies to the House of Lords.

Where the claimant seeks to rely on grounds other than those for which the court gave permission to proceed, he or she must first obtain the court's permission (CPR, r. 54.15). Where the claimant intends to rely on additional grounds at the hearing of the claim for judicial review, he or she must give notice to the court and to any person served with the claim form no later than seven clear days before the hearing.

In *R* v *Staffordshire County Council Education Appeals Committee, ex parte Ashworth* [1997] COD 132, the claimant had two main grounds for seeking judicial review. The judge granted permission on one ground but expressly refused permission on the other ground. At the substantive hearing, the claimant sought to rely on both grounds. Turner J held that where permission has been granted on one ground but not expressly refused on another, the claimant may rely on both grounds at the substantive hearing, provided that notice is given to the defendant that the claimant intends to do so. However, where permission is expressly refused on a particular ground, it is open to the court which hears the substantive application not to permit the claimant to rely on that ground, since the attempt to do so may well amount to an abuse of process.

14.6.6 PROCEDURE IF PERMISSION IS GIVEN

Under CPR, r. 54.14, once the claimant has been given permission to proceed, the defendant (and anyone else served with the claim form who wishes to contest the claim or to support it on additional grounds) must, within 35 days after service of the order giving permission, serve:

(a) detailed grounds for contesting the claim (or supporting it on additional grounds; and

(b) any written evidence.

Where the party filing the detailed grounds intends to rely on documents not already filed, he or she must file a paginated bundle of those documents when filing the detailed grounds (PD 54, para. 10.1).

Any person may apply for permission to file evidence or to make representations at the judicial review hearing.

Where all the parties agree, the court may decide the claim for judicial review without a hearing (CPR, r. 54.18).

Otherwise the claimant must file and serve a skeleton argument not less than 21 working days before the date of the hearing of the judicial review claim (PD 54, para. 15.1). The defendant (and any other party wishing to make representations at the hearing) must file and serve a skeleton argument not less than 14 working days before the date of the hearing (para. 15.2). The skeleton arguments must contain:

(a) a list of issues;

(b) a list of the legal points to be taken (together with any relevant authorities, with page references to the passages relied on);

(c) a chronology of events (with page references to the bundle of documents);

(d) a list of essential documents for advance reading by the court;

(e) a list of persons referred to.

14.6.7 EXPEDITED HEARING

The sheer weight of cases where judicial review is sought means that claims can take a long time to be dealt with. In urgent cases, an expedited hearing may be sought. In such a case, the claim form must contain a request for an expedited hearing and must set out the reasons why such a hearing is sought. See also *Practice Direction (Crown Office List)* [1987] 1 WLR 232.

14.6.8 HEARING AN APPLICATION FOR JUDICIAL REVIEW

Criminal cases are heard by a Divisional Court (normally two High Court judges, although in complex cases there may be three); civil cases are heard by a single judge sitting in public (unless the judge who gives permission for the application to proceed directs that the case be heard by a divisional court).

The hearing takes the form of legal argument based on the contents of the claim form and the written evidence. Since the evidence is in written form, no witnesses are usually called. In rare cases, however, witnesses can be cross-examined on their evidence. This will only be so where there is a genuine dispute of fact which has to be resolved and which cannot properly be resolved simply on the basis of the written evidence or where the court considers that a party's evidence might be misleading or, in a material respect, incomplete (*R* v *Arts Council of England, ex parte Women's Playhouse Trust, The Times*, 20 August 1997).

Counsel for the claimant speaks first, followed by counsel for the defendant; counsel for the claimant has the right to reply.

14.7 Grounds for Seeking Judicial Review

In *Council of Civil Service Unions* v *Minister for the Civil Service* [1985] AC 374, Lord Diplock (at p. 410) identified three heads under which judicial review might be sought: illegality, irrationality and procedural impropriety.

14.7.1 ILLEGALITY

Lord Diplock defined illegality in this context by saying that 'the decision-maker must understand correctly the law that regulates his decision-making power and must give effect to it' (*Council of Civil Service Unions* v *Minister for the Civil Service* [1985] AC 374 at p. 410). In other words, the decision must be within the decision-maker's jurisdiction. An act is outside jurisdiction (*ultra vires*) where the decision-maker purports to exercise a power which he or she does not possess, or else uses a power for a purpose other than the purpose for which the power was granted. For example, where there is a statutory power to order the destruction of food which is unfit for human consumption, an order to destroy food which is not unfit for human consumption is illegal (see *R* v *Thames Magistrates' Court, ex parte Clapton Cash & Carry* [1989] COD 518).

Where a discretionary power is being exercised, the decision-maker must not adhere to a fixed policy without having regard to the circumstances of the particular case under consideration. See *R* v *Secretary of State for the Home Department, ex parte Findlay* [1985] AC 318 (a challenge to the Home Secretary's parole policy). The point is that there is no objection to a decision-maker having a policy, provided consideration is given to each individual case to see if there is any reason why the policy should not apply to that case (see *R* v *Port of London Authority, ex parte Kynoch Ltd* [1919] 1 KB 176).

14.7.2 IRRATIONALITY

Another word for irrationality is 'unreasonableness'. The classic definition of unreasonableness was set out by Lord Greene MR in *Associated Provincial Picture Houses Ltd* v *Wednesbury Corporation* [1948] 1 KB 223 at p. 234: a decision may only be quashed if it is 'so unreasonable that no reasonable [decision-maker] could ever have come to it'.

In many cases, the basis for claiming that the decision is an unreasonable one will be that the decision is flawed by irrelevance. In *Associated Provincial Picture Houses Ltd* v *Wednesbury Corporation* at pp. 233–4, Lord Greene MR said that the court is entitled to investigate whether a decision-making body 'has taken into account matters which it ought not to take into account, or conversely, has refused to take into account matters which it ought to take into account'.

For example, in *R* v *Lewisham London Borough Council, ex parte Shell (UK) Ltd* [1988] 1 All ER 938, a local authority boycotted Shell's products because that company had connections in South Africa (which was then subject to a system of racial apartheid); this boycott was declared unlawful, because the decision was motivated by irrelevant considerations. In *R* v *Somerset County Council, ex parte Fewings* [1995] 1 WLR 1037 a ban on stag hunting on the council's land, based on moral and ethical objections, was declared unlawful since s. 122 of the Local Government Act 1972 did not enable such considerations to be taken into account.

Although the courts remain reluctant to usurp the function of the original decision-maker, there is a discernible (albeit tentative) start towards a move away from the traditional *Wednesbury* approach in cases involving human rights. For example, in *R* v *Secretary of State for the Home Department, ex parte Javed, The Times*, 9 February 2001 (QBD), Turner J was considering an asylum case. His Lordship said that, although the courts have historically been reluctant to evaluate evidence when reviewing decisions of the executive, under the Human Rights Act 1998 the court has a positive duty to give effect to the European Convention on Human Rights and to ensure that there is an effective remedy in cases of suspected breach of the Convention rights. It follows that where an executive decision needs to be reviewed on the facts, the court is competent to carry out that exercise once the relevant material has been placed before it. An appeal to the Court of Appeal ([2002] QB 129) was dismissed.

However, in *R (on the application of Isiko and others)* v *Secretary of State for the Home Department* [2001] 1 FLR 930 (another immigration case) the Court of Appeal said that, in reviewing a decision of the executive to see if it complies with the Human Rights Act 1998, the court will not substitute its decision for that of the executive, but will decide whether the decision-maker has exceeded the discretion given to him. The executive's discretion has to be exceeded before a decision can be categorised as unlawful. In the area of immigration and deportation, for example, difficult choices have to be made between the rights of the individual and the needs of society and it is appropriate for the courts to recognise that there is an area of judgment within which the judiciary will defer, on democratic grounds, to the considered opinion of the elected body or person whose decision was said to be incompatible with an individual's Convention rights. Nonetheless, where a fundamental right is engaged, the court will insist that that fact is recognised by the decision-maker, who is therefore required to demonstrate that his proposed action does not interfere with the individual's right, or if it does, that there exist considerations which amount to substantial objective justification for the interference. The graver the impact of the decision in question upon the individuals affected by it, the more substantial the justification that is required. Within that framework, the court would give due deference to the primary decision-maker.

In *R* v *Secretary of State for the Home Department, ex parte Daly* [2001] 2 AC 532, Lord Steyn pointed out that differences in approach between the traditional *Wednesbury* ground of review and the approach of proportionality (the approach adopted by the European Court of Human Rights) may sometimes yield different results. The doctrine of proportionality might require the reviewing court to assess the balance which the decision-maker had struck, not merely whether it was within the range of rational or reasonable decisions; the proportionality test might go further than the traditional grounds of review in as much as it might require attention to be directed to the relative weight accorded to interests and considerations; even the heightened scrutiny test is not necessarily appropriate to the protection of human rights. This does not, said Lord Steyn, mean that there has been a shift to merits review: the respective roles of judges and administrators are fundamentally different and will remain so. Even in cases involving Convention rights, the intensity of review in a public law case will depend on the subject matter in hand.

In *R (on the application of Samaroo)* v *Secretary of State for the Home Department* [2001] UKHRR 1150, the applicants were challenging deportation decisions. The Court of Appeal held that in deciding what proportionality requires in any particular case, the issue will usually have to be considered in two separate stages. At the first stage, the question is: Can the objective of the measure be achieved by means which are less interfering with an individual's rights? The essential purpose of this stage of the inquiry is to see whether the legitimate aim can be achieved by means that do not interfere, or interfere so much, with a person's rights under the European Convention on Human Rights. That inquiry must be undertaken by the decision-maker in the first place. At the second stage, it is assumed that the means employed to achieve the legitimate aim are necessary, in the sense that they are the least intrusive of Convention rights that can be devised in order to achieve the aim. The question at this stage of the consideration is: Does the measure have an excessive or disproportionate effect on the interests of affected persons? Where the legitimate aim cannot be achieved by alternative means less interfering with a Convention right, the task for the decision-maker, when deciding whether to interfere with the right, is to strike a fair balance between the legitimate aim on the one hand, and the affected person's Convention rights on the other. How much weight he gives to each factor will be the subject of careful scrutiny by the court. The court will interfere with the weight accorded by the decision-maker if, despite an allowance for the appropriate margin of discretion, it concludes that the weight accorded was unfair and unreasonable. In this respect, the level of scrutiny is undoubtedly more intense than it is when a decision is subject to review on traditional *Wednesbury* grounds, where the court usually refuses to examine the weight accorded by the decision-maker to the various relevant factors.

14.7.3 PROCEDURAL IMPROPRIETY

Most claims of procedural impropriety involve alleged breaches of the rules of natural justice. There are two fundamental rules of natural justice:

(a) The rule against bias (sometimes described by the Latin phrase *nemo judex in re sua* or *nemo judex in causa sua*, which mean that no one should be a judge in his or her own cause). The point is that the decision-maker should not have an interest in the outcome of the case under consideration. There must be a 'real danger of bias on the part of the relevant member of the tribunal in question, in the sense that he might unfairly regard (or have unfairly regarded) with favour, or disfavour, the case of a party to the issue under consideration by him' (*R* v *Gough* [1993] AC 646 at p. 670 per Lord Goff of Chieveley).

The question of bias was also considered by the Privy Council in *Roylance* v *General Medical Council (No. 2)* [1999] 3 WLR 541. The appellant had made an allegation of bias on the part of the chairman of the GMC's Professional Conduct Committee and sought to admit written evidence relating to the private discussions of the PCC. The Privy Council pointed out that an essential element in a fair hearing is that the decision-maker should be impartial. That calls for a state of mind which is free from any influences extraneous to the merits of the particular case, which is capable of a dispassionate inquiry and an objective judgment, and which is not turned aside by any motivation to favour one side as against the other. The decision-maker might be influenced quite unconsciously in one direction or the other by extraneous considerations in ways evident to or suspected by others but of which he or she is unaware. However, in the present case, the appellant had failed to establish a case of bias. In particular, the questions asked by the chairman of witnesses did not disclose a biased approach. The Privy Council went on to consider the admissibility of the evidence relating to the private discussions of the PCC. It was held that in the context of the making of any corporate judicial decision, the detail of discussion and the manner by which the decision was reached ought normally to remain confidential and only in quite exceptional circumstances, if ever, could any inquiry be permitted into such discussions held in private. The appellant's application was contrary to that general principle of confidentiality. The written evidence did not present a criticism of such gravity as to justify the extraordinary step of inquiring into the working of the PCC in the course of their deliberations into the case.

(b) The right to a fair hearing (sometimes described by the Latin phrase *audi alteram partem* which means 'hear the other side'). In *Ridge* v *Baldwin* [1964] AC 40 a chief constable was dismissed from office without receiving any notice of his proposed dismissal and without being given any opportunity to argue against his dismissal. The House of Lords held it to be essential to a fair decision-making process that the person who is the subject of the decision should:

(i) have notice of the allegations which he or she has to meet (for example, in *R* v *Huntingdon District Council, ex parte Cowan* [1984] 1 WLR 501 the refusal of an entertainment licence was quashed on the ground that the applicant had not been informed of the objections which the police had made to the grant of the licence); and

(ii) have an adequate opportunity to meet those allegations by making representations (whether orally or in writing) and, in appropriate cases, by calling evidence in support of those representations (see, for example, *R* v *Deputy Industrial Injuries Commissioner, ex parte Moore* [1965] 1 QB 456). Another example is to be found in *R* v *Birmingham City Council, ex parte M, The Times*, 13 October 1998. The Court of Appeal said that where an appeal is made to an education committee concerning the allocation of a child to a particular school, and the committee is minded to disbelieve the case advanced by the appellant, the committee should give the appellant the chance to deal with the specific points troubling the committee. Similarly, in *R* v *Secretary of State for the Home Department, ex parte Harry* [1998] 3 All ER 360, it was held that where the Home Secretary decides not to accept the recommendation of a Mental Health Review Tribunal that a patient should be transferred to a less secure hospital, the Home Secretary is entitled to seek advice from other sources, such as the Advisory Board on Restricted Patients. However, the patient should be told the gist of any new information; he or she should be given the opportunity to make written representations to the Board; he or she should be told what advice the Board gives; and he or she should have the opportunity to make written representations about the advice to the Home Secretary.

However, in *R* v *Governor of Swaleside Prison, ex parte Wynter, The Times*, 2 June 1998, it was held that a prisoner appearing before a prison disciplinary tribunal following a positive drug test under s. 16A of the Prisons Act 1952 is not generally entitled to cross-examine the laboratory scientist who tested the specimen provided by the prisoner. However, the prisoner should be told what checks were carried out to ensure the accuracy of the test result.

In all judicial review applications it must be remembered that it is not the merits of the decision which are at issue: the sole issue is whether the decision was a lawful decision reached by the correct procedure.

14.7.4 THE GIVING OF REASONS

In *R* v *Secretary of State for the Home Department, ex parte Doody* [1994] 1 AC 531, the House of Lords held that even though there is no general duty to give reasons for a decision, in many cases the reasons for the decision will have to be revealed 'as an effective means of detecting the kind of error which would entitle the court to intervene' (per Lord Mustill). In *R* v *Harrow Crown Court, ex parte Dave* [1994] 1 WLR 98, for example, it was held that when it dismisses an appeal under s. 108 of the Magistrates' Courts Act 1980 against summary conviction by a magistrates' court, the Crown Court should give sufficient reasons to demonstrate that it had identified the main contentious issues in the case and how it had resolved them.

In *R* v *Ministry of Defence, ex parte Murray* [1998] COD 134, it was held that where a statute confers the power to make decisions affecting individuals but does not contain an express requirement that the decision-maker must give reasons for the decision, the court will imply such a requirement if, but only if, the interests of fairness so require.

14.8 Remedies

The remedies which may be granted following an application for judicial review are set out in CPR, r. 54.2. The principal 'public law' remedies which may be granted are:

(a) A 'quashing order' (formerly known as '*certiorari*'): this has the effect of quashing the decision being challenged.

(b) A 'mandatory order' (formerly known as '*mandamus*'): this is a peremptory order which has the effect of requiring the defendant to carry out a particular public duty; most commonly, the effect is to compel a decision-maker to reconsider his decision.

(c) A 'prohibiting order' (formerly known as 'prohibition'): the effect of this remedy is similar to that of an injunction, in that it prevents a public body from acting or continuing to act in a way which is unlawful.

CPR, r. 54.19, provides that where the court makes a quashing order, it may remit the matter to the decision-maker and direct the decision-maker to reconsider the matter and reach a decision in accordance with the judgment of the court. On the other hand, where the court considers that there is no purpose to be served in remitting the matter to the decision-maker, the court may (subject to any statutory provision) take the decision itself.

Additionally, under r. 54.3, the court has the power to grant what would normally be regarded as 'private law' remedies, namely:

(a) *Declaration.* The effect of a declaration is to state the law on a particular point. So, if a decision is quashed because the decision-maker misunderstood the law, the court can grant a declaration setting out the correct interpretation of the law (e.g., *R* v *West London Coroner's Court, ex parte Gray* [1988] QB 467).

(b) *Injunction.* This has the same effect as prohibition with one difference, which is that an injunction may be an interim remedy (i.e., pending the full hearing) whereas prohibition may not be granted as an interim remedy.

A claim for judicial review may include a claim for damages but cannot be used to claim damages only (r. 54.3(2)).

More than one remedy may be sought in the same application.

The grant of a remedy is discretionary. Reasons for refusing to grant the remedy sought include such matters as:

(a) The conduct of the applicant, so that the applicant does not deserve assistance (e.g., *Dorot Properties Ltd* v *Brent London Borough Council* [1990] COD 378).

(b) Adverse consequences to the public as a whole (e.g., *R* v *Secretary of State for Social Services, ex parte Cotton, The Times*, 14 December 1985), or the impact on third parties (e.g., *R* v *Panel on Take-Overs and Mergers, ex parte Guinness plc* [1990] 1 QB 146).

(c) If no harm has been done, in that the following of the proper procedure by the decision-maker would have made no difference (for example *R* v *Secretary of State for the Environment, ex parte Walters, The Times*, 2 September 1997, where the Court of Appeal held that even if a decision-maker fails to comply with a statutory consultation process, the court is entitled to refuse to grant relief in judicial review proceedings).

14.9 Interim Remedy

There is a power to grant an interim remedy in judicial review proceedings. In *R* v *Ministry of Agriculture, Fisheries & Food, ex parte Monsanto* [1998] QB 1161, it was held that the court should apply the principles which govern the grant of an interim injunction (see *American Cyanamid* v *Ethicon* [1975] AC 396) to the question of whether to grant an interim remedy in judicial review proceedings.

14.10 Further Reading

There are a number of textbooks on judicial review, including:

Aldous and Alder, *Applications for Judicial Review*, 2nd edn, Butterworths, 1993.
Clayton and Tomlinson, *Judicial Review Procedure*, Hart Publishing, 1999.
Clyde and Edwards, *Judicial Review*, W. Green & Son Publications, 1999.
De Smith, Woolf and Jowell, *Judicial Review of Administrative Action*, 6th edn, Sweet & Maxwell, 2001.
Emery and Smythe, *Judicial Review*, Sweet & Maxwell, 1986.
Fordham, *Judicial Review Handbook*, 2nd edn, Hart Publishing, 1997.
Fulford, *A Criminal Practitioner's Guide to Judicial Review and Case Stated*, Jordans, 1999.
Gordon, *Judicial Review Deskbook*, Chancery Wiley Law Publications, 1998.
Gordon, *Judicial Review: Practice and Procedure*, 2nd edn, Sweet & Maxwell, 1995.
Hadfield (ed.), *Judicial Review*, Gill and Macmillan.

Manning, *Judicial Review Proceedings*, 2nd edn, Legal Action Group, 2000.
Sedley et al., *Judicial Review and Crown Office Practice*, Sweet & Maxwell, 1998.
Supperstone and Goudie, *Judicial Review*, 2nd edn, Butterworths, 1997.

14.11 Exercises

14.11.1 EXERCISE 1 SARAH-JANE LOVEJOY

Problem
The applicant (Sarah-Jane Lovejoy) wishes to challenge a decision to remove her from the Housing Committee of Westwold Borough Council. She wants the decision quashed and to be reinstated to membership of the Housing Committee

The borough council is a public body and so is susceptible to judicial review. The decision is a public law one (there being no private law remedy). The decision was taken on 2 October 2002 and her application is dated 30 October 2002 (so Mrs Lovejoy is within the three-month time limit and has acted promptly). The decision affects her directly and so she plainly has sufficient interest to bring her claim.

Action/solution
Draft grounds for inclusion on the Claim Form and draft a witness statement which (with relevant exhibits) sets out the claimant's claim — example provided.

Claim Form (extract)

IN THE HIGH COURT OF JUSTICE

QUEEN'S BENCH DIVISION: ADMINISTRATIVE COURT

RELIEF SOUGHT

A quahing order to quash the decision of the Westwold Borough Council taken on 2 October 2002 to remove the claimant from its Housing Committee and a mandatory order directed to the Westwold Borough Council requiring it to restore the claimant to membership of its Housing Committee.

GROUNDS ON WHICH RELIEF IS SOUGHT

(1) The decision to expel the claimant from her membership of the Housing Committee of Westwold Borough Council was taken for improper motives;

(2) The decision was taken in breach of the rules of natural justice in that the claimant was not given any or any adequate opportunity to show why she should not be expelled from the committee;

(3) Accordingly, the decision was one which no reasonable Council could have taken.

Written evidence in support of application

Filed on behalf of the Claimant
Deponent: S-J Lovejoy
1st Affidavit of Deponent
Date of Swearing: 30 October 2002

IN THE HIGH COURT OF JUSTICE No.:

QUEEN'S BENCH DIVISION: ADMINISTRATIVE COURT

IN THE MATTER of an application by Sarah-Jane Lovejoy for permission to apply for Judicial Review.

BETWEEN

THE QUEEN, on the application of SARAH-JANE LOVEJOY — Claimant

and

WESTWOLD BOROUGH COUNCIL — Defendant

WRITTEN EVIDENCE OF SARAH-JANE LOVEJOY

I, Sarah-Jane Lovejoy, of 17 Acacia Grove, Ferrenby, Grimeshire, school teacher, make oath and say as follows:

1. I make this written evidence in support of my application for permission to seek judicial review of the decision of the Housing Committee of the Westwold Borough Council, taken on 2 October 2002, to remove me from that Committee. The matters to which I depose below are true to the best of my knowledge and belief, and are within my personal knowledge unless stated otherwise.

2. In May 2001 I was one of three Councillors elected to represent the town of Ferrenby at the Westwold Borough Council. I was elected as an Independent and not as a representative of any political party.

3. The rules relating to appointment of committees are contained in the Council's Standing Order A.12. This provides:

   (a) The Council shall, at its Annual Meeting, appoint the Standing Committees set out in Appendix A to these Standing Orders.

   (b) The Council may, at the Annual Meeting, appoint such additional Committee or Committees as it may think desirable.

   (c) The Council may, at any other time, appoint such Committee or Committees as may be necessary to carry out the work of the Council.

   (d) The Council may at any time dissolve a Committee or alter its membership.

4. Standing Order A.13 provides as follows:

   (a) Where a Committee is appointed pursuant to Standing Order A.12(a), the membership and functions of such Committee shall be those set out in Appendix A to these Standing Orders.

(b) Where a Committee is appointed pursuant to Standing Order A.12(b) or A.12(c), the membership and functions of such Committee shall be as determined by the Council when such Committee is appointed.

5. The list of Standing Committees shown in Appendix A to Standing Order A.12 includes the following:

(4) The Housing Committee

Number of members: 20

Functions:

(a) To keep under constant review the housing needs of the Borough.

(b) To formulate proposals to secure appropriate improvements in housing provision within the Borough.

(c) To implement the housing policy for the time being of the Council.

(d) To manage all land and properties for the time being within the ownership or control of the Council.

(e) To exercise the powers and duties of the Council created or conferred by statute with regard to:

(i) the provision of public housing;

(ii) the housing of homeless persons;

(iii) ensuring the fitness of public housing and of houses in multiple occupation.

6. The annual meeting of the Council takes place in May of each year and it is at that meeting that individual councillors are appointed to the various committees. Because Committees are appointed at each annual meeting, a councillor can only be appointed to serve on a committee for one year at a time.

7. At the annual meeting of the Council in May 2002, I was appointed to the Housing Committee. In the normal course of events I would have expected to serve on that Committee until May 2003.

8. After the annual meeting in May 2002 the Housing Committee comprised 11 Labour members, 6 Conservative members, 2 Liberal Democrat members and myself, an Independent. The political composition of the Housing Committee was approximately the same as the political composition of the Council as a whole. The Committee was chaired by Benjamin MacDonald, a Labour member.

9. The Council owns a derelict site about a mile from Westwold. One of the issues on which I had campaigned during the election at which I was elected was the need for the Council to do more to house the homeless. It seemed to me that it was ridiculous for the Council to own a piece of waste ground which could so easily have accommodation built on it to house the homeless.

10. I therefore proposed that hostel accommodation be built on the waste ground. The proposal was considered by the Housing Committee in July 2002. My proposal was lost by 11 votes to 9.

11. My proposal had been vigorously opposed by the Chairman of the Committee. He argued that by providing hostel accommodation, we would be encouraging homeless people to come to Westwold and that our limited resources should be targeted on people who were already in the Borough but without permanent homes. He said that

this was best done by the Council working in partnership with a number of local Housing Associations to produce permanent accommodation at comparatively low rents.

12. A few days after the meeting, I realised that the waste ground in question is within the area represented by Mr MacDonald and that he himself lives close to the site. I spoke to him on the telephone and he admitted to me that he had been lobbied by local residents who were opposed to my idea because of the effect it might have on property prices and that he himself was concerned that the presence of a hostel for the homeless would 'change the character of the neighbourhood and probably increase the crime rate'.

13. I was so furious at what Mr MacDonald had said to me that I proposed a motion of no confidence in his Chairmanship at the next meeting of the Housing Committee, in September 2002. I was unable even to get anyone to second my motion and so it was not put to a vote.

14. The day after the meeting I went to the office of the local newspaper, the Westwold Messenger. The Editor agreed to publish a letter for me about my proposal for creating hostel accommodation. There is now produced and shown to me marked Exhibit S-JL1 a true copy of the letter as published that week by the Messenger. In the letter I accused the Chairman of the Housing Committee of putting concern for property prices before concern for people and suggesting that he should resign from his Chairmanship of the Housing Committee and from his membership of the Labour Party.

15. On 20 September 2002 I received a letter dated 18 September 2002 from Mr MacDonald saying that a meeting of the Housing Committee had been convened in my absence and that the Committee had decided to recommend that I should be removed from its membership. I refer to Exhibit S-JL2, which is a true copy of that letter.

16. A meeting of the full Council was due to take place on 2 October 2002, before the next scheduled meeting of the Housing Committee. The Council meeting was attended by 55 councillors and was chaired by the Leader of the Council, Margaret Jowett. At the meeting, Mr MacDonald accused me of bringing the Council into disrepute by making a public statement casting doubt on the integrity of the Chairman of one of its Committees. I was asked if I had anything to say. I then tried to explain the arguments in favour of my proposal for housing homeless people. However, Mrs Jowett said that the merits of my proposal were not the issue and that no further comments from me would be entertained.

17. I tried to make the point that councillors are elected by the public and so the public have the right to know if decisions are taken for questionable reasons, but the Leader would not allow me to say anything further.

18. At the end of the discussion, a resolution accepting the recommendation that I should be removed from the Housing Committee was passed by 38 votes to 17.

19. I am advised by my Solicitor, Paula Stephenson of Wright & Co., that the procedure by which I was removed from the membership of the Housing Committee was flawed in that I was not given an adequate opportunity to state my case and that the decision to remove me from the Housing Committee merely for criticising its Chairman was a decision which no reasonable Council could have taken.

20. Accordingly, I ask the Court for permission to seek judicial review of the decision of the Council to remove me from membership of the Housing Committee.

Sworn this 30th day of October 2002
before me

[*Signed: Sarah-Jane Lovejoy*]

[*Signed: Roger Stoughton*]
Solicitor

Exhibit S-JL1

[From the Westwold Messenger, 12 September 2002]

Dear Sir,

When I was elected as a councillor on Westwold Borough Council, one of the issues on which I campaigned was the need to provide housing for homeless people within the borough. A golden opportunity to provide such housing comes from the waste ground on the Boxton Road, about a mile from Westwold town centre.

As a member of the Housing Committee, I put forward a proposal that this land should be used for purpose-built accommodation for homeless people. My proposal was rejected.

I believe that the people who elected me have a right to know why my proposal was killed off and why people will be sleeping rough unnecessarily in this borough.

The Housing Committee is chaired by Benjamin MacDonald. He thinks that housing homeless people on the waste ground will lower property prices in the area. Yes, he lives nearby. Yes, some narrow-minded residents said 'Not in our back yard'. Their reasons? That homeless people are a bunch of criminals and will lower the tone of the neighbourhood.

Mr MacDonald was willing to put concern for property prices before concern for people.

A man with this lack of principle should not be the Chairman of the Housing Committee. He should also have the decency to resign from the Labour Party, to whom he is a disgrace.

Yours faithfuly,

Sarah-Jane Lovejoy (Cllr)

Exhibit S-JL2

WESTWOLD BOROUGH COUNCIL
The Town Hall
Westwold
Grimeshire
IR16 4LJ

18 September 2002

Dear Councillor Lovejoy,

I am writing to inform you that the Housing Committee has recently met to consider the scurrilous comments you made about me in your letter to the Westwold Messenger. The Committee has decided to recommend to the Council that you should be removed from your membership of the Housing Committee. You are plainly unfit to serve on it.

Yours sincerely,

Benjamin MacDonald
Chairman, Housing Committee

14.11.2 EXERCISE 2 PAUL WEBB

Problem
Grimwold Borough Council maintain a market which is held in Grimwold on Thursdays. Several years ago, the Borough Council made a by-law which included the following provisions:

(1) A person may only be a stall-holder at the Grimwold Market provided that he is the holder of a current stall-holder licence issued by the Council and a stall-holder may only sell goods of the type specified in his stall-holder licence.

(2) A licence granted under this by-law shall state:

  (i) the name and permanent address of the stall-holder;

  (ii) the date of expiry of the licence; and

  (iii) the goods which the stall-holder is permitted to sell under the licence.

(3) Each stall-holder licence granted under this by-law shall be for a period not exceeding three years and shall be renewable for periods of up to three years thereafter.

(4) A stall-holder licence may be revoked by the Council if, in the opinion of the Council, the stall-holder sells goods other than those specified in his stall-holder licence or is otherwise guilty of misconduct in his use of the market.

In 1999, Paul Webb applied for and was granted a licence to sell 'pet food and other requisites for pet-owners'. In 2001 this licence was renewed by the Borough Council. In a letter dated 2 October 2002, the Council wrote to Mr Webb telling him that his stall-holder licence was being revoked. The reason given in the letter was that he had 'been seen by a market inspector employed by the Council to sell goods other than those of a type permitted under his stall-holder licence'.

Mr Webb feels aggrieved because he was not given a chance to explain to the Council that the sale of angling tackle was on a temporary basis. He also believes that the real reason for the revocation of his licence is that a pet food shop opened up in Grimwold a few months ago and it is not doing very well. It is owned by a David Morgan, whose sister-in-law is Ellen Green, one of the councillors who sits on the subcommittee of the Council which deals with the market. It is now 30 October 2002.

Action
Advise Mr Webb whether he is able to seek judicial review of the decision to revoke his licence and, if so, on what grounds. If a judicial review application is appropriate, draft the relevant documents which will be needed to make the application.

FIFTEEN

REAL PROPERTY LAW

15.1 Repossession

15.1.1 THE PRIMARY REMEDY

The primary remedy available as of right to the owner of land is repossession by means of an action for recovery of land.

The applicant must prove title as the owner of the land in question and establish an intention to repossess. The onus is then on the occupier to show that he or she has a right either under a licence, tenancy or otherwise to remain in possession. The procedure is governed by Part 55 of the Civil Procedure Rules 1998.

15.1.2 POSSESSION CLAIMS AGAINST TRESPASSERS

CPR, Part 55, provides the landowner with a rapid remedy against anyone who occupies the land without her or his consent. The landowner need only issue a claim form claiming possession. Five clear days, or two clear days in case of non-residential premises, after service of the claim form the Court may make an order for possession. Where the occupier entered as a trespasser the Court has no power to suspend the order. The order will be effective even though the landowner cannot discover the names of the occupiers. This procedure is used most commonly against squatters although it is also available against ex-licensees. The Court has power under the Housing Act 1980, s. 89, to suspend an order against certain ex-licensees (e.g., an occupier under a restricted contract or secure tenancy) for 14 days or up to six weeks in case of exceptional hardship.

15.1.3 INTERIM POSSESSION ORDERS

Rules 8–15 of CCR O. 24 enable a landowner to obtain a possession order without a court hearing against occupiers who entered the land as trespassers. The landowner applies by a claim form, supported by affidavit and various undertakings, e.g., as to paying damages, for an interim possession order, which the court may make not less than three days after the date of issue of the application. The order commands the occupier to vacate the premises within 24 hours of service and informs the occupier of the date for a hearing in the presence of both parties not less than seven days later. Under the Criminal Justice and Public Order Act 1994, s. 76, it is a criminal offence for such an occupier to remain in the premises after this 24-hour period has elapsed and the occupier may be arrested by a uniformed constable without warrant. The Act also imposes criminal liability on a landowner who obtains an interim possession order by knowingly or recklessly making false or misleading statements (s. 75). Guidance is given to local authorities in the use of such proceedings against unauthorised campers by Department of Environment circular (for its effect on proceedings see *R* v *Brighton & Hove Council, ex parte Marmont* [1998] 2 PLR 48. For the use of s. 113 by a licensee, see *Manchester Airport plc* v *Duttan*, *The Times*, 5 March 1999, CA.

15.1.4 DAMAGES FOR TRESPASS

A landowner may claim damages against a trespasser for trespass. Such a claim will include compensation for the use and occupation of the land which is normally awarded on the basis of the current letting value of the property. Where the occupier is a former tenant and holds over as a tenant at will/on sufferance this part of the claim is generally known as a claim for 'mesne profits' becoming damages for trespass when the owner terminates the tenancy at will/on sufferance, e.g., by demanding possession.

15.1.5 LANDLORD AND TENANT — ADDITIONAL REMEDIES

As between landlord and tenant various additional remedies are available.

15.1.5.1 Damages for breach of covenant

This is an ordinary contractual remedy.

15.1.5.2 Forfeiture

This is only available where the lease expressly provides for forfeiture for breach of covenant or where there is a breach of a condition. Procedures vary according to the type of covenant breached:

(a) *Rent.* The landlord must make a formal demand for rent unless either the lease permitting forfeiture contains a provision dispensing with this requirement — every well-drafted lease will contain such a provision — or, in some circumstances, when there is more than six months' rent in arrear.

(b) *Other covenants.* In most cases the Law of Property Act 1925 (LPA 1925), s. 146 requires a notice to be served which:

  (i) specifies the breach complained of;

  (ii) if the breach is remediable, requires the tenant to remedy it;

  (iii) where the landlord wants financial compensation, calls on the tenant to pay it.

See also Leasehold Property (Repairs) Act 1938, s. 1 and Housing Act 1996, ss. 81 and 82, for additional requirements of a valid s. 146 notice imposed in the case of forfeiture for breach of repairing covenant and for failure to pay service charges, respectively.

Forfeiture will be invalid if the breach has been waived, e.g., by the landlord accepting rent with knowledge of the breach unless the breach is a continuing one, e.g., of a repairing covenant.

Even if the forfeiture is valid a tenant may still apply to the court for relief from forfeiture. This will be granted more readily in the case of forfeiture for non-payment of rent than where the forfeiture is for breach of some other covenant.

15.1.5.3 Action to enforce payment and distress

A landlord may enforce payment of rent either by an action for the money or by distress (seizing the tenants' goods). A landlord should beware. Distress is an intricate remedy.

If the distress is illegal, excessive or irregular, the landlord may be liable for damages for wrongful distress.

15.1.5.4 Statutory protection of residential occupiers

Generally when a landlord is dealing with a tenant or a licensee of a dwelling house, regard should be had to the provisions of the Protection from Eviction Act 1977 (as amended by the Housing Act 1988) which:

(a) impose criminal penalties for the unlawful eviction and harassment of residential occupiers;

(b) require a notice to quit served in respect of a tenancy to be of four weeks' duration and to contain prescribed information;

(c) require the service of a four week notice containing prescribed information to terminate most periodic licences;

(d) require a landlord to effect forfeiture through court proceedings rather than by a physical re-entry onto the land;

(e) in the case of residential tenants and licensees not entitled to the statutory protection given by the Acts mentioned in the next paragraph, restrict the owner to recovering possession through court proceedings;

(f) provide a civil claim for damages against a landlord who unlawfully evicts a residential occupier in breach of these requirements.

Further, in the case of tenants entitled to statutory protection under the Rent Act 1977 (protected tenants), the Housing Act 1985 (secure tenants), or the Housing Act 1988 (assured tenants), the landlord is restricted in the exercise of his or her common law rights to possession on, e.g., service of a notice to quit and will normally have to prove the existence of statutory grounds for possession. Note, however, that most assured tenancies granted after 28 February 1997 will take effect as assured shorthold tenancies and as such will be subject to an easily satisfied mandatory ground for possession (Housing Act 1988, s. 19A added by Housing Act 1996, s. 96).

15.2 Mortgagee's Remedies

There are a number of options open to a mortgagee when mortgagors fail to keep up with instalment payments under a mortgage.

15.2.1 ACTION FOR MONEY DUE

The mortgagee can sue for the money due once the date for repayment has arrived. This is unlikely to be the best remedy for the mortgagee unless perhaps the mortgagor has substantial other assets and the value of the property mortgaged has fallen below the amount owed. More often the mortgagee will use other powers to enforce a sale and then, if there is a shortfall, sue the mortgagor for the difference.

15.2.2 FORECLOSURE

A mortgagee can apply for an order for foreclosure when the mortgagor is in breach of obligations under the mortgage which provide that the principal sum secured under the mortgage becomes due. If a foreclosure order is granted and made absolute, the legal title to the mortgaged property is automatically transferred to the mortgagee and the mortgagor loses all rights in the property. So in a subsequent sale of the property any proceeds above the amount owed under the mortgage can be retained by the mortgagee.

Because of the potential unfairness to the mortgagor, foreclosure is a procedurally cumbersome remedy and there is uncertainty for the mortgagee. An order can be set aside even after it has been made absolute (*Campbell* v *Holyland* (1877) 7 ChD 166). Also the mortgagor can apply for, and the court readily grants, an order substituting an order for sale for the foreclosure (LPA 1925, s. 91(2)). This means that the mortgagor receives any proceeds of sale left after discharging the debt, costs and expenses of sale in the same way as if the mortgagee had exercised its powers of possession and sale in the first place. For these reasons foreclosure is rarely used by institutional lenders.

15.2.3 POSSESSION

Most institutional lenders' standard mortgage conditions give the mortgagee a right to possession of the property without there being any breaches of the mortgagor's obligations. It is very rare that a mortgagee will enforce the right to possession without there being arrears of repayment instalments and without having obtained an order for possession. The right to possession is usually exercised only as a preliminary step to exercising the power of sale. However in a potentially far reaching decision *Ropaigealach* v *Barclays Bank plc* [1999] 3 WLR 17, the Court of Appeal reasserted the view that as mortgagees were entitled to possession they could use their common law right to re-enter the property peacefully and take possession and that s. 36 of the Administration of Justice Act 1970 had not extinguished this right nor did s. 6 of the Criminal Law Act 1977 apply.

If there are arrears outstanding the mortgagee will usually be granted an order for possession unless (rarely) the mortgagor successfully applies to have the mortgage set aside for, for example, undue influence, or (much more commonly) the mortgagor can claim the benefit of one of the statutory regimes which provide some protection (Administration of Justice Act 1970, s. 36, for residential occupiers of 'dwelling houses' or alternatively Consumer Credit Act 1974, s. 129, for commercial or residential 'regulated agreements'). Under s. 36, possession will be suspended if the mortgagor can satisfy the court that the arrears on the instalments due (not the principal sum secured) are likely to be paid within a 'reasonable time'.

15.2.4 SALE

A power to sell is implied into every mortgage made by deed (see LPA 1925, s. 101).

The exercise of that power is conditional upon any *one* of the following requirements being satisfied:

(a) that a notice requiring payment of the mortgage money has been served on the mortgagor and there has been a default in the payment of part of it or all of it;

(b) the interest payments must be two or more months in arrears; or

(c) there must be a breach of some provision of the Act or the mortgage deed.

One advantage of a sale over foreclosure is that the power to sell is generally exercisable without a court order.

Once possession is obtained, it is usually not necessary to obtain a court order to sell the mortgaged property.

The mortgagee in possession owes the mortgagor a duty of care in relation to the property while in possession and in relation to carrying out the sale (as does an estate agent who has conduct of the negotiations for sale) although the extent of the duties is not entirely clear (*Parker-Tweedale* v *Dunbar Bank plc* [1991] Ch 12; *Cuckmere Brick Co. Ltd* v *Mutual Finance Ltd* [1971] Ch 949; *Garland* v *Ralph Pay & Ransom* (1984) 271 EG 106; *Morgan* v *Lloyds Bank plc* [1998] 3 Lloyd's Rep 73).

Conduct of the sale can be given to the mortgagor (*Cheltenham and Gloucester plc* v *Booker* (1997) 29 HLR 634).

15.2.5 APPOINTMENT OF A RECEIVER

There is a power to appoint a receiver in the case of all mortgages made by deed (see LPA 1925, s. 101). In the absence of a deed a mortgagee may still apply, in appropriate cases, for a receiver to be appointed. Obviously one disadvantage here is that extra costs will be incurred by such an application.

15.3 Order for Sale under the Trusts of Land and Appointment of Trustees Act 1996

If the trustees under a trust of land refuse to sell or exercise powers of management or if any requisite consent cannot be obtained, any person interested may apply to the court for a vesting or other order for giving effect to the proposed transaction under the Trusts of Land and Appointment of Trustees Act 1996.

Unlike under trusts for sale, the new trusts of land make no distinction between the powers of sale and postponement of sale — they are of equal weight. The factors that the 1996 Act require the court to take into account in deciding whether to order a sale are based on the case law which developed interpreting the old s. 30 of the LPA 1925. It is unlikely that there will be a great difference in the way the courts deal with those applications. The main concerns will still be what was the purpose of the trust and whether that purpose still subsists. It is also likely that the courts will remain reluctant to refuse an order for sale where the application is brought by the trustee in bankruptcy of one co-owner (*TSB Bank plc* v *Marshall* [1998] 3 EGLR 100).

15.4 Easement

Where there is an infringement of an easement, a claim for an injunction and/or damages may be brought. The claimant may also ask for a declaration as to the extent or scope of an easement (*Lomax* v *Wood* [2001] 1 All ER 80). In extreme cases the remedy of abatement may be used (see *Lagan Navigation Co.* v *Lambeg Bleaching, Dyeing & Finishing Co.* [1927] AC 226). This is a self-help remedy usually consisting of removing the obstacle complained of.

15.5 Registered Land

The usual remedy for people who claim they have suffered loss as a result of an omission of their interests in the records at the Land Registry is to apply for financial compensation from the Land Registry itself (Land Registration Act 1925). If the loss is as a result of failure to register, rather than a mistake at the Registry, there may be a professional negligence claim against those who handled any dealings with the interest.

An application can be made to rectify the register to ensure that for the future it includes the interest claimed (LPA 1925, s. 82). This remedy is at the discretion of the Chief Registrar. Claims for rectification can be made by consent as a result of negotiations to avoid litigation or after a court decision. It can also be used where a person is claiming to be the new legal owner of a piece of land by virtue of adverse possession. It is rare for rectification to be granted where the result would adversely affect the title of the proprietor unless the proprietor has caused or contributed to the error by fraud or negligence or there are other special circumstances which make it unjust not to rectify (see *Emmet on Title*, para. 20.022 *et seq.*). For a recent example, see *N. Allee & Co.* v *David Hodson & Co.* [2001] All ER (D) 141.

15.6 Exercise

Problem

Mr and Mrs Bowler had a joint mortgage with the Great and Good Building Society. They were two months in arrears in their instalment payments after they both had lost their jobs. At a hearing at the Kingswood County Court they argued that they would be able to pay off the arrears within four years. The district judge rejected their defence and granted possession. The Bowlers moved in with relatives. The building society did not get an order for sale but put the property for sale straightaway. It has been on the market for about six months. The building society has just informed the Bowlers it has had an offer of £45,000 for the property which it is likely to accept. The Bowlers paid £47,000 for the property in 1991. The mortgage was for £44,000. The Bowlers have just sought legal advice. They say they have been told by a friend who is an estate agent that the firm the building society is using have done very little to market the property and that if the property had been well marketed and looked after over the last six months it should fetch over £48,000.

Solution
The Bowlers are out of time to lodge an appeal against the granting of the order for possession (14 days from the order being made: CCR O. 37) and it does not appear in any case that they would be able to show that no reasonable judge would have granted the order.

The building society did not need to get an order to allow it to sell as it could rely on its statutory power or a power granted in the mortgage.

The building society as mortgagee in possession does owe the Bowlers a duty of care. It is clear that it will be in breach if it does not take reasonable steps to protect the property from, for example, vandalism, but it does not have to repair, redecorate etc. to make the property more attractive to potential buyers. The Bowlers may be able to argue that the building society should have rented the property out for the six months and so the property would have been better kept and rental income would have been received (*Brandon* v *Brandon* (1862) 10 WR 287). However, the building society might well be able to defend such a claim by saying that it was not 'wilful default' not to rent out the property because it might have made it more difficult to sell.

There is a common law duty, and, in the case of a building society, a statutory duty to take 'reasonable care' to obtain the best price for the property (Building Societies Act 1986, sch. 4, para 1(1)(a), *Cuckmere Brick Co. Ltd* v *Mutual Finance Ltd* [1971] Ch 949). On the facts known at present it is unlikely that the Bowlers could obtain an injunction to prevent sale as there is no clear breach of these duties. They could sue the building society for damages but they would have difficulty both in establishing a breach and showing the measure of loss. The sale was put in the hands of an estate agent. Provided some efforts were made to market the property which were within the broad range of acceptable marketing strategies, it would be hard to show a breach of the duty of care by either the building society or the estate agent. The cases tend to support the view that the lender is not obliged to wait for the market to improve or take special steps to sell the property (*Predeth* v *Castle Philips Finance Co. Ltd* [1986] 2 EGLR 144).

If, which appears unlikely on present information, a claim succeeded, the damage the Bowlers would receive would be based on what they should have received from the sale if there had been no breach. As this is speculative, the court is traditionally conservative in estimating what price would have been achieved. They would have received the price less the costs of sale (which might have been higher) and the sums owed to the lender as well as the lender's costs. It is likely that if the proposed sale goes ahead the Bowlers will still owe the building society some money. This shortfall would be taken into account in calculating damages.

If there is a shortfall if the sale goes ahead, the building society can sue the Bowlers for that amount notwithstanding the sale. If they have no means, the building society may not think it worth pursuing the claim, at least in the short term.

SIXTEEN

REMEDIES IN THE LAW OF TRUSTS

16.1 Introduction

Students should note that the following outline is purely for general guidance, not least in that many academic courses emphasise basic principle rather than trust remedies. Such brief notes involve generalisations, and any remedy that appears appropriate must be fully researched for application to a particular case. This section is intended to provide a guide to approach and thought processes rather than a comprehensive answer.

16.2 Identifying Precisely What Issues Require to be Resolved

In trying to decide which remedy is appropriate in a particular case, certain issues require to be resolved.

16.2.1 WHAT IS THE PROBLEM?

(a) There is some doubt about whether a trust has arisen or the terms of a trust (see **16.3**).

(b) There is a trust and the terms are clear, but there is doubt as to whether a particular action can be carried out (see **16.4**).

(c) There is a trust with clear terms, but something has been done which does not appear to be within the terms of the trust (see **16.5**).

16.2.2 BE CLEAR AS TO THE VIEWPOINT FROM WHICH YOU APPROACH THE PROBLEM

(a) From the position of the settlor.

(b) From the position of a trustee.

(c) From the position of a beneficiary.

Do note that for any of these you might be making or defending a claim.

16.2.3 WHICH COURT HAS JURISDICTION?

(a) Trust matters are assigned to the Chancery Division.

(b) County courts have jurisdiction in certain trust matters.

16.3 Doubts about the Validity of the Trust

Any difficulty as to whether a trust has arisen and, if so, what its terms are, is primarily a matter of substantive law. Consider the relevant substantive law to see if, on the facts of the case, a valid trust has or has not arisen, and if so, what its terms are.

If advising the settlor, your aim will be to avoid the need for recourse to any remedies by clarifying or altering any doubtful provisions. If the trust has been set up and is operating, the settlor may be able to make alterations if the trust instrument provides for this; otherwise it is no longer the settlor's concern.

The trustees are at risk from future claims by beneficiaries, or potential beneficiaries, if they apply the trust funds in ways which, when challenged later, prove to be incorrect because a provision was invalid. In advising the trustees you need to balance the benefit of protection for the trustees from such possible claims against the need not to waste trust funds on unnecessary applications to court.

If, after careful consideration of the substantive law, you consider that there is no real doubt, then an application should not be made to court and the trustees will be able to resist a charge that they acted in 'wilful default' by showing that they relied on legal advice. If there is any serious doubt about the meaning, but, under whatever interpretation is proved correct, the beneficiaries and all potential beneficiaries are *sui juris*, then they can give their consent to the trustees' interpretation. Otherwise it is necessary for the trustees to apply to the court to construe the trust document or testamentary disposition by means of a Part 8 claim. All those whose interests may be affected by the outcome should be made defendants. The remedy sought is directions as to the answers to particular questions relating to the meaning of provisions in the document. Other consequential remedies can be sought such as drawing up accounts and directions for application of property *cy près* where there is a failed charitable disposition (see also the ***Drafting Manual***).

It is rare, although not impossible, for a beneficiary or someone claiming to be a beneficiary to bring a construction claim. Usually they are defendants and can argue their point of view in that capacity. If the trustees do not apply for a construction claim, a disappointed potential beneficiary would have to consider bringing a claim for breach of trust (see below).

16.4 Doubts about Powers

Although a trust may be clearly valid, there may be doubts about whether a particular transaction can or cannot properly be carried out within its terms. Answers here are again largely a matter of specific legal principle, and the following notes merely make some general suggestions. The starting point must always be to identify precisely what the terms of the trust are, and to seek to interpret them.

The settlor can alter the setlement to give the trustees new powers only if the trust deed permits. If it does not, the problem is for the trustees alone.

The trustees have to consider whether they consider it is necessary or advisable to have a particular power. The beneficiaries can give their views but the trustees must make the decisions and they are under no obligation to consult or follow the wishes of the beneficiaries (unless the trust deed says they must consult).

If it is considered by the trustees that the power is necessary, and the beneficiaries are *sui juris*, their consent can be obtained to waive their rights to sue in the future in relation to what would amount to a breach of trust. In the case of a charitable trust, the Charity Commissioners can authorise certain transactions which are not expressly permitted in the trust deed.

In all other circumstances it will be necessary for the trustees to apply to court.

The general power to help in such a case is provided by the TA 1925, s. 57, which provides that where some transaction is required in the management or administration of any property vested in trustees, which is in the opinion of the court expedient, but which cannot be carried out because no power to carry it out has been given to the trustees, then the court may confer the necessary power on the trustees, subject to such conditions as the court thinks fit. This power is wide and flexible (see, for example, *Mason* v *Fairbrother* [1983] 2 All ER 1078).

An alternative, which may be of assistance in appropriate circumstances where the terms of the existing trust are causing difficulty, is an application under the Variation of Trusts Act 1958.

16.5 Possible Breach of Trust

If the existence and terms of a trust are clear, but some action has been performed or not performed and a beneficiary objects to its performance or non-performance, there may have been a breach of trust. What actions and omissions amount to a breach are beyond the scope of these notes, which only outline how to approach a case, but where there is a breach, a range of remedies may be available (see **16.6**).

16.5.1 IDENTIFYING A POTENTIAL BREACH

Beneficiaries (whether with a fixed or future interest or just a right to be considered under a discretionary trust) can bring a claim for breach of trust if it appears that the trustees have failed in their duties in any way. This could be by positive actions or by failing to control other trustees or agents.

The main difficulty in advising beneficiaries is that they often have very little information on the administration of the trust and so it is difficult to decide what sort of breaches may have occurred. The beneficiaries have a right to see the trust documents and accounts, and, if they do not have these, the first step is to demand them (*Re Londonderry's Settlement* [1965] Ch 918).

16.5.2 ANALYSING THE POTENTIAL BREACH

First it is necessary to identify specifically:

(a) What exactly is alleged to be a breach.

(b) Whether there is more than one potential breach.

(c) When each possible breach was committed.

Then the person(s) who may have committed the breach must be identified. For example:

(a) One or more of the trustees.

(b) Anyone else, e.g., an agent acting for the trustees.

(c) Any beneficiary who might be liable for instigating a breach.

Next it must be decided which of the potential defendants should actually be sued:

(a) Who is likely to have sufficient assets to indemnify the beneficiary?

(b) Is the case against a possible defendant legally or factually weak?

(c) Are there any reasons for not suing a potential beneficiary, such as family reasons?

Lastly, what has been lost from the trust as a result of the alleged breach must be identified as precisely as possible:

(a) In terms of capital.

(b) In terms of income.

(c) In terms of specific assets.

It is only in the light of a proper and accurate analysis of the above areas that the lawyer can review the range of possible and/or appropriate remedies.

16.5.3 LIABILITY

While a trustee is prima facie liable only for his or her own acts, he or she will also be liable for the acts of a co-trustee where he or she:

(a) has stood by while a breach of trust was committed;

(b) leaves trust administration in the hands of a co-trustee without inquiry;

(c) leaves the trust funds in the sole control of a co-trustee;

(d) fails to take appropriate steps on becoming aware of a breach of trust.

Where on the facts more than one trustee is responsible for a breach, liability will be joint and several (see *Bahin* v *Hughes* (1886) 31 ChD 390). Execution can be levied by a successful claimant beneficiary against any trustee held liable. As between trustees, however, liability is shared equally, so if one trustee pays more than his or her appropriate share for a breach, he or she can claim a contribution from any other trustees found liable.

The court has a power to exempt a person from liability to make a contribution, and therefore potentially to make another trustee solely liable. This can be done where:

(a) One trustee alone received or misappropriated trust funds, or otherwise benefited from the breach.

(b) One trustee was a solicitor who advised on the breach.

(c) One trustee is also a beneficiary, making that trustee liable to the extent of his on her beneficial interest (*Chillingworth* v *Chambers* [1896] 1 Ch 685).

A solicitor trustee's partners cannot be held vicariously liable for a fraudulent breach of trust (*Walker* v *Stones* [2000] 4 All ER 412). For a consideration of when it is appropriate to relieve a trustee of a small estate of liability to account, see *Re Evans (deceased)* [1999] 2 All ER 777.

For guidance on a drafting Particulars of Claim in a breach of trust action, see **Chapter 28** in the ***Drafting Manual***.

16.6 The Range of Remedies

16.6.1 FINANCIAL COMPENSATION

The measure of compensation varies with the type of breach committed, but basically it is always based on a liability to make good the loss caused to the trust.

Note that normally capital loss will be compensated from the date of loss with interest. So long as the interest on capital represents the loss of capital growth, a claim for lost income will also lie; but take care to avoid double recovery where interest represents lost income.

It should be appreciated that in most cases money claimed will be repaid to the trust for proper administration, rather than paid directly to a claimant beneficiary.

The following categories give some guide to the measure applied in particular circumstances.

16.6.1.1 Payment of trust funds to wrong person

Liability is to make good to the trust the amount wrongly paid out, with interest.

16.6.1.2 Improper sale of authorised investments

Liability, at the option of the beneficiary, is:

(a) To make good the value at which the authorised investment was sold, less any proceeds of sale of any improper investment purchased with the proceeds.

(b) Or to repurchase the authorised investment, again, with credit for the proceeds of sale of any improper investment purchased.

(c) Or to place the beneficiaries in the position they would have been in if the authorised investment had not been sold (*Re Massingberd* (1890) 63 LT 296).

In any event, the trustee can claim no credit if the authorised investment has also fallen in value.

16.6.1.3 Unauthorised investment

If the unauthorised investment results in a loss, liability is to sell it and make good any loss with interest. If the unauthorised investment results in a loss of interest, liability is to make up the difference between the interest that was received and the interest that might have been received from an authorised investment.

If the unauthorised investment results in a profit, liability is that the profit can be claimed for the trust. Alternatively, if all beneficiaries are of age and *sui juris*, they can adopt the unauthorised investment (*Re Lake* [1903] 1 KB 439).

If unauthorised activity results in no loss to the trust, and the resulting assets are held for the beneficiaries, there is no loss to be compensated, e.g., a building is built on trust land without authority (*Vyse* v *Foster* (1872) LR 8 Ch App 309).

16.6.1.4 Improper retention of unauthorised investment

Liability is the difference between the price for which the investment is finally sold, and what it would have fetched if sold at the correct time.

16.6.1.5 Non-investment

Money can be held in a bank account while an investment is being sought (TA 1925, s. 11), but should not be left uninvested for an unreasonable time.

Liability for non-investment is to make good any interest lost due to failure to invest. If there is a failure to invest in a specified investment, liability is to purchase as much of that investment as could have been purchased at the time the duty to purchase arose (*Nestlé* v *National Westminster Bank plc* [1993] 1 WLR 1260).

16.6.1.6 Use of trust funds for private purposes

If the trustee makes private use of the trust funds, liability is:

(a) To make good any capital loss, with interest (at a higher rate and compound if the money has been used in the trustee's business; see *Attorney-General* v *Alford* (1855) 4 De G M & G 843).

(b) Alternatively, to pay over to the trust any actual profit received (or, if funds have been mixed, an appropriate part of any profit).

In an interesting recent example the House of Lords held that beneficiaries had a right to choose between a lien and a proportionate share of an asset irrespective of whether there had been a mixing of funds (*Foskett* v *McKeown* [2000] 3 All ER 97).

16.6.1.7 Fraud

If a trustee acts fraudulently, liability is not only to make up any capital loss, but to pay compound interest.

16.6.1.8 Interest on financial compensation

Interest will normally be awarded on capital ordered to be repaid to the trust. Interest is normally at a basic flat rate (formerly 4%, but now based on the Special Investment Account rate), but a higher rate may be granted in cases of fraud, where a higher rate of interest ought to have been received by the trust, or where the trustee has personally benefited from a higher rate of return. Simple interest will normally be awarded, compound interest in limited cases.

16.6.1.9 Taxation of financial compensation

No deduction will be made to take account of tax that might have had to be paid on the assets but for the breach (*Re Bell's Indenture* [1980] 1 WLR 1217; *Bartlett* v *Barclays Bank Trust Co. Ltd (No. 2)* [1980] 2 All ER 92).

16.6.2 TAKING AN ACCOUNT

The claim for an account has a long history, first in common law, and then as a remedy available in a Chancery Court to support a legal or equitable right. An account can usefully be claimed by a beneficiary against a trustee or an executor, as well as in partnership, agency, and real property cases. For rules regarding the taking of an account see CPR, Part 40, and for a summary order for an account, CPR, Part 25. Note that it is normally appropriate in a breach of trust action to seek the taking of an account and the payment of sums found due, rather than seeking damages.

16.6.2.1 Nature of an account

An account consists of a schedule of all sums due from one side to the other, setting off sums due the other way, to reach a figure due to compensate the applicant. It can take into consideration any relevant payments, e.g., rent received.

An application for an account should be accompanied by an application for an order that any sum found due be paid over to the trust.

An account can be ordered only where a breach has been proved, not merely to see if there has been a breach (*Re Wrightson* [1908] 1 Ch 789).

16.6.2.2 Obligation to replace assets

An account is appropriate to a trust claim rather than a claim for damages as the obligation is to replace assets. Rules of assessment of damages such as remoteness have no place in assessing trust loss.

An account can be ordered with regard to the whole of the trust property, or to the part with regard to which a breach has been proved (*Re Tebbs* [1976] 1 WLR 924).

16.6.2.3 Accounts and wilful default

Where there is an omission to act rather than an active breach, an account is taken on the basis of wilful default, i.e., on the basis of what would have been received but for the wilful default (this does not necessarily imply a conscious failure to act so long as the failure involves a breach of trust). At least one act of wilful default must be referred to in the statement of case and proved to get an account on this basis.

16.6.2.4 Defence to the claim

It is a defence to a claim for an account that the parties have already stated in writing sums due between them, arriving at a balance figure. This will not succeed, however, if there has been any mistake or fraud to vitiate the account.

16.6.3 TRACING AND CONSTRUCTIVE TRUSTS

Tracing is a right *in rem* against a particular item of property, rather than against a trustee. Such a remedy will be particularly useful where a beneficiary has a good reason for wishing to recover a particular item of property, either because of what the item is, or because the trustee is unlikely to have sufficient assets to satisfy a claim personally (see *Re Diplock* [1948] Ch 465).

Although tracing was available at common law, it is now subject to equitable principles, and will therefore not be granted if it would be inequitable to do so.

Where a trustee has obtained other property which was not the subject of the trust but as a result of his or her position as a trustee, it is likely to be imposed with a constructive trust and the trustee is obliged to bring it into the trust.

These remedies are considered further in **Chapter 13**.

16.7 Exercise

Problem

Juliet, who is 16 years old, is a beneficiary under a trust set up by her grandfather, Colin Lewis. She has not seen the terms of the trust but knows that her three cousins are also beneficiaries; she has received varying amounts of money and since she was 11 her school fees have been paid from the trust.

At the beginning of term Juliet's father, Steve, was informed by her school that the fees had not been paid by the trustees despite a number of reminders. Steve was unable to contact the trustees, who are his uncle Joe and an accountant friend of his father, Fred Treece. Steve eventually spoke to Joe's wife. She was very evasive but said that Joe was having a bit of trouble with Fred and that he had discovered a few problems with Joe's handling of the finances. She said Joe had gone to Fred's house in Cumbria to try to sort things out. Steve paid the school fees himself to avoid Juliet having any disruption to her schooling.

Steve is now very concerned about the trust. He has seen some accounts, although they are not very recent. He showed them to an accountant friend who said that the bulk of the trust fund seemed to be in investments which are very safe but produce very low income and that there were a number of odd-looking withdrawals from the fund.

Solution

There appears to be enough evidence to commence a breach of trust claim. The claim can be brought by Juliet (acting through her father as next friend). The other beneficiaries do not have to be involved as the remedy sought is not damages for loss but reconstitution of the trust fund. She does not have to show she has personally lost financially, only that the trustees have breached their duties. The trustees would have to make up the loss to the fund and account for any profits they had made in breach of their duties.

Steve does not have a direct claim against the trustees for the school fees as he is not a beneficiary and (presumably) there is no contract between him and the trustees.

Up-to-date accounts and a copy of the trust deed should be formally requested from the trustees as Juliet has a right to copies (*Re Londonderry's Settlement* [1965] Ch 918).

Juliet can choose whether to proceed against Fred and Joe or just one of them at this stage and wait to commence proceedings against the other. If it is discovered that the trustees, in breach of their duties, have transferred trust assets to other people then tracing remedies against that property can be considered.

Juliet will have personal claims against the trustees as well as being able to trace any trust property in their hands and any profits they have made.

Joe will be liable for any fraudulent losses caused by Fred if Joe has not supervised and checked up on him properly.

Depending on the precise wording of the trust document, there is no obvious breach of trust in leaving the fund in safe investments. There is no duty to speculate! However, there may well be a breach if they have not diversified the funds, kept a balance between investment production and capital growth and kept the investments under review. If it was found that the trustees breached these duties, there would have to be an inquiry into what the funds would have been worth if properly invested. The courts are likely to go for a very conservative estimate (*Nestlé* v *National Westminster Bank plc* [1993] 1 WLR 1260).

The situation needs to be kept under careful watch. If more evidence comes to light, injunctive relief to protect the funds may be expedient. Juliet could also consider applying to have the trustees replaced or an additional trustee appointed. This can be done in the breach of trust application or, if urgent, by an interim application.

SEVENTEEN

REMEDIES FOR THOSE SUFFERING UNLAWFUL DISCRIMINATION

17.1 Introduction

17.1.1 LEGAL FRAMEWORK

This area of law is governed by legislation:

(a) The Race Relations Act 1976 (RRA 1976).

(b) The Sex Discrimination Act 1975 (SDA 1975).

(c) The Equal Pay Act 1970 (as amended).

(d) The Sex Discrimination Act 1986.

(e) The Disability Discrimination Act 1995 (DDA 1995).

(f) The Human Rights Act 1998.

(g) Part Time Workers (Prevention of Less Favourable Treatment) Regulations (PTW Regulations) 2000 (SI 2000/1551).

(h) And, in relation to the United Kingdom's international obligations, by the Treaty of Rome and by the European Convention on Human Rights (see **Chapter 19**).

17.1.2 WHAT TYPES OF DISCRIMINATION ARE MADE UNLAWFUL?

Three different kinds of discrimination are made unlawful by the RRA 1976 and SDA 1975: namely, direct and indirect discrimination, and victimisation.

The DDA 1995 prohibits direct discrimination and victimisation, but not indirect discrimination. The definition of direct discrimination differs from that in the RRA 1976 and the SDA 1975. Unlike in those Acts, employers have a defence of justification against a claim of direct discrimination.

The PTW Regulations 2000 provide a remedy for direct discrimination on grounds of being a part-time worker.

The Human Rights Act 1998 prohibits discrimination on wider grounds than earlier legislation, but only in respect of rights guaranteed by the Act itself.

17.1.3 WHEN IS DISCRIMINATION ACTIONABLE?

It is not every discrimination which is actionable, *but only* those acts which occur in the fields of employment, education and goods, facilities, services and premises.

The ***Employment Law in Practice Manual*** can be referred to if amplification is needed of the points in this chapter.

17.2 Discrimination Explained

17.2.1 WHAT IS DIRECT DISCRIMINATION?

This is less favourable treatment on racial or sexual grounds, because of marital status or disability, or because of being a part-time worker, and includes racial segregation (RRA 1976, s. 1(1)(a); SDA 1975, ss. 1(1)(a), (2) and 3(1)(a)), and victimisation (RRA 1976, s. 2, SDA 1975, s. 4 and DDA 1995, s. 55). Segregation on grounds of sex is not unlawful discrimination. Discrimination is a question of fact and the burden of proof rests upon the applicant.

Direct discrimination is based on the failure to treat equally those who are, in all other respects, equal. Trivial differences are ignored on the *de minimis non curat lex* principle.

17.2.1.1 On racial grounds
Racial grounds are described as those relating to: colour, race, nationality or ethnic or national origins (RRA 1976, s. 3(1)). The meaning of 'ethnic origins' was considered in the case of *Mandla* v *Dowell Lee* [1983] 2 AC 548.

It is legitimate to draw an inference of race discrimination in circumstances where the applicant has demonstrated that he or she is a member of a minority racial group and that he or she has been less favourably treated than others have been treated (*King* v *Great Britain China Centre* [1991] IRLR 513). There is an onus on the employer to provide an explanation for the treatment and failing such explanation the tribunal can draw an inference of racial discrimination. However, unfair treatment does not become discrimination merely because the person affected is from an ethnic minority (*Zafar* v *Glasgow City Council* [1998] IRLR 36).

17.2.1.2 On grounds of sex
This includes the unequal treatment of men, unless this relates to 'special treatment afforded to women in connection with pregnancy or childbirth' (SDA 1975, s. 2).

17.2.1.3 Is harassment included in the meaning of direct discrimination?
Sexual and/or racial harassment have been held to amount to direct discrimination (see Code/Recommendation published by EC in 1991). The Code of Conduct is annexed to the Recommendation.

Sexual harassment is defined in the TUC Guide 'Sexual Harassment at Work,' as

> repeated and unwanted verbal or sexual advances sexually explicit derogatory statements or sexually discriminatory remarks. . . which are offensive (and). . . which cause the (victim) to feel threatened, humiliated, patronised or harassed. . . or which create a threatening or intimidating environment.

See *Strathclyde Regional Council* v *Porcelli* [1986] IRLR 134.

The new rules governing procedure in tribunals enable a tribunal, where a case involves allegations of sexual misconduct, to make an Order restricting reporting.

17.2.1.4 How is pregnancy dealt with?
In *Webb* v *Emo Air Cargo (UK) Ltd* (C–32/93) [1994] QB 718, the European Court of Justice makes it clear that dismissal on grounds of pregnancy where an employee is recruited for an unlimited term is discrimination and that a pregnant female employee can not be compared with the position of a man similarly incapacitated for medical or other reasons. Pregnancy is not comparable with pathological conditions or other conditions which might justify dismissal without discriminating on grounds of sex.

Note that the Trade Union Reform and Employment Rights Act 1993, based on the EC Directive (92/85) on pregnancy and maternity protection, abolished in October 1994 all threshold provisions related to dismissals because of pregnancy.

The House of Lords has subsequently interpreted the SDA 1975 consistently with the Directive (*Webb* v *Emo Air Cargo (UK) Ltd* [1995] IRLR 645). Per Lord Keith:

> ... in a case where a woman is engaged for an indefinite period, the fact that the reason why she will be temporarily unavailable for work at a time when to her knowledge her services will be particularly required is pregnancy is a circumstance relevant to her case, being a circumstance which could not be present in the case of a hypothetical man.

Where the action complained of is dismissal, the Employment Rights Act 1996, s. 99 provides that dismissal is automatically unfair if connected with pregnancy or giving birth. However, where the less favourable treatment results in, e.g., a loss of promotion or training opportunity, their Lordships' interpretation in *Webb* seems likely to provide a remedy. The higher award available in SDA cases means that SDA claims may also be appropriate in dismissal cases.

17.2.1.5 On grounds of disability

DDA 1995 prohibits direct discrimination (but not indirect discrimination) in a variety of areas. It is, however, in the area of employment law where issues are likely to arise most frequently. Under s. 5 of the 1995 Act, an employer discriminates against a disabled person if, for a reason relating to the person's disability it treats him or her less favourably than it treats, or would treat others to whom that reason does not apply and it cannot show that that treatment is justified.

A justification must be both 'material' and 'substantial' and the test is an objective one for the tribunal, not the employer, to establish (*Morse* v *Wiltshire County Council* [1998] IRLR 352, EAT).

To establish liability for discrimination on the grounds of disability it must be shown that the employer was aware of the disability (*O'Neill* v *Symm & Co.* [1998] IRLR 233, EAT). The same is true in respect of the duty under s. 6 to make 'reasonable adjustments'. These include alterations to the premises, hours of work or re-training if the workplace or work arrangements place a disabled applicant at a 'substantial disadvantage' compared with those who are not disabled. A failure to make such reasonable adjustments may constitute direct discrimination under the 1995 Act. For guidance as to how a tribunal should approach such claims, see *Morse*.

Disabled applicants are protected from victimisation under provisions similar to the SDA 1975 and RRA 1976.

17.2.2 WHAT IS INDIRECT DISCRIMINATION?

Indirect discrimination (only available in SDA and RRA cases) is often called 'covert discrimination' and involves the imposition of a requirement or condition which may not in itself be discriminatory (racially or on grounds of sex) but which has a disproportionately adverse impact on a racial group or groups, or on groups of women or men. So, for example, if admission to the Bar were denied to all those with brown eyes, this would have a disproportionately adverse impact on black Africans, or black people from the Caribbean and, prima facie, would be an indirect (or covert) act of discrimination. (See RRA 1976, s. 1(1)(b) and SDA 1975, s. 1(1)(b).)

In *R* v *Secretary of State for Employment, ex parte Equal Opportunities Commission* [1995] 1 AC 1, the threshold provisions of the Employment Protection (Consolidation) Act 1978 (16 hours' weekly work) were held to be incompatible with European Union law, in particular because the great majority of part-time workers being women were excluded from the protection afforded by the Sex Discrimination Act 1975.

'Requirement or condition' has been strictly construed to involve an absolute bar (see *Perera* v *Civil Service Commission* [1983] IRLR 166). However, in sex discrimination cases involving employment, a broader concept — 'provision, criterion or practice' — has been substituted following the implementation of Directive 97/80/EC. This will be an easier test for applicants to meet.

Recent cases have considered the issue of women and the responsibilities of child care arrangements. In *London Underground Ltd* v *Edwards (No. 2)* [1997] IRLR 157, the employee had worked for several years as a train operator on a shift which accommodated her child care arrangements. To improve efficiency the employer altered the shift patterns, which made it impossible for the employee to continue working and look after her child. She accepted a voluntary severance and claimed that the new shifts imposed constituted indirect discrimination. The employer failed to justify the new requirements and the tribunal concluded that the proportion of female employees who could comply with the new arrangements was 'considerably smaller' than the proportion of men who could do so and was thus discriminatory.

17.2.2.1 How is disproportionate impact proved?

Statistical evidence can be presented to help prove disproportionate impact, although some concern has been expressed at the possible use of elaborate statistical evidence (see *Perera* v *Civil Service Commission* [1983] IRLR 166).

17.2.2.2 Detriment must be caused

The particular applicant must show that she or he cannot comply with the particular condition and has thereby suffered disadvantage, i.e., that the imposition of the condition directly causes detriment.

17.2.2.3 The respondent has a defence of justification

The burden of establishing that the indirect discrimination was justified and therefore not unlawful rests with the respondent, who must show objectively sound and tolerable reasons, or good and adequate reasons that the condition corresponds to a real need as opposed to being merely convenient. Justification is a question of fact for the court or tribunal.

17.2.3 WHEN ARE AFFIRMATIVE ACTION PROGRAMMES LAWFUL?

The legislation is based on an equal opportunities approach *and not* a fair shares approach, therefore reverse discrimination within the fields specified in the legislation (see **17.1.3**) is unlawful.

There are, however, some limited opportunities for lawful affirmative action programmes (see RRA 1976, ss. 35–38 and SDA 1975, ss. 47 and 48).

17.3 Discrimination in Employment

The statutory provisions governing this field of discrimination can be found in RRA 1976, ss. 4–15, SDA 1975, ss. 6–21, DDA 1995, ss. 4–18 and the PTW Regulations 2000. It is wise to consult the legislation to see whether a particular discrimination is exempted. It should be noted that discrimination may be lawful where it relates to a genuine occupational qualification (RRA 1976, s. 5; SDA 1975, s. 7) — for example, where only those of Chinese origin are employed to wait on tables in a Chinese restaurant.

Particular provisions deal with the employment of partners by partnerships, gaining membership of a trade union, gaining qualifications, the provision of vocational training and the operation of employment agencies, etc.

17.3.1 THE INDIVIDUAL'S REMEDIES FOR DISCRIMINATION IN EMPLOYMENT CASES

17.3.1.1 Jurisdiction and limitation period

Employment tribunals have jurisdiction to deal with these claims. See RRA 1976, s. 54, SDA 1975, s. 63 and DDA 1995, s. 8. The general rule is that claims must be presented within three months of the discriminatory act complained of (unless the act complained of is a continuing one) but note that where a right provided for by a Directive is asserted, time only begins to run when that Directive is fully brought into effect in the UK.

17.3.1.2 What orders can the tribunal make?

The employment tribunal can make the following orders:

(a) An order declaring each party's right (SDA 1975, s. 65(1)(a), RRA 1976, s. 56(1)(a)) or a declaration to the same effect (DDA 1995, s. 8(2)(a)).

(b) An award of compensation including compensation for injury to feelings (SDA 1975, s. 65(1)(b), RRA 1976, s. 56(1)(b), Race Relations (Remedies) Act 1994, DDA 1995, s. 8(2)(b)).

(c) A recommendation of action to be taken within a specified time, in default of which an additional sum of compensation can be ordered to be paid (RRA 1976, s. 56(1)(c); SDA 1975, s. 65(1)(c). DDA 1995, s. 8(2)(c)).

(d) Exemplary damages are not available (*Deane* v *Ealing London Borough Council* [1993] ICR 329).

The DDA 1995 provides for a criminal sanction (penalty up to £5,000) in respect of those who knowingly or recklessly give false assurances that, because of some provision in the legislation, an unlawful act is not, in fact, unlawful.

17.3.2 PROCEDURE

The procedure for making a claim is set out in RRA 1976, s. 54, SDA 1975, s. 63 and DDA 1995. See also *King* v *Great Britain China Centre* [1991] IRLR 513. See also the Employment Tribunal (Construction and Rules of Procedure) Regulations 1993 (SI 1993/2687).

17.3.2.1 Using the questionnaire procedure

This procedure entitles the applicant to seek answers to a series of questions from the respondent (see RRA 1976, s. 65, SDA 1975, s. 74 and DDA 1995, s. 56). The applicant can ask questions which are designed to gather the information necessary to decide whether to pursue the application and help prove the case. A failure on the part of the respondent to reply timeously to such a questionnaire, and replies which are evasive or equivocal, entitle the court or tribunal to draw such inferences as are considered appropriate. Also tribunals can require written answers to questions which it believes may clarify issues and thereby assist the hearing.

17.3.2.2 The role of ACAS

Whenever there appears to be a reasonable prospect of settlement, ACAS (Advisory, Conciliation and Arbitration Service) has a duty to promote a settlement of the dispute. It can also act when requested to do so by both parties.

17.3.2.3 Pre-hearing review

Either party to the case, with the agreement of the tribunal, or the tribunal itself, can request a pre-hearing review. The purpose of this hearing is to establish whether either the application or defence has any merit. If the tribunal takes the view that there is no merit in one party's case, then that party will be warned that, if unsuccessful, costs may be awarded against them, or require a party to pay a deposit of up to £150 as a condition precedent to bringing or continuing the action.

17.3.2.4 Appeals

These can be made to the Employment Appeal Tribunal on a point of law within 42 days from the date the tribunal sent extended written reasons for its decision to the parties.

17.4 Discrimination in Other Fields

17.4.1 EDUCATION

Discrimination in education is covered by RRA 1976, ss. 17–19, SDA 1975, ss. 22–28 and DDA 1995, ss. 29–31. Such discrimination will be actionable in the following situations:

(a) In terms of admission.

(b) By not accepting an application.

(c) In access to benefits, etc.

(d) By excluding or causing other detriment.

See *R* v *Bradford Metropolitan Borough Council, ex parte Sikander Ali*, *The Times*, 21 October 1993.

There are statutory exemptions which apply to single-sex establishments and further education courses in physical training.

17.4.1.1 Who is responsible for discriminatory acts?
RRA 1976, s. 17 and SDA 1975, s. 22 provide tables, specifying those who are deemed responsible for acts of discrimination.

17.4.1.2 What action can be taken?
No application can be made unless notice has been given to the Secretary of State, and until either the Secretary has not responded within two months of that notice, or does not wish to consider the matter (RRA 1976, s. 7; SDA 1975, s. 66).

17.4.2 GOODS, FACILITIES, SERVICES AND PREMISES

Discrimination in the field of goods, facilities, services and premises is covered by RRA 1976, ss. 20–27, SDA 1975, ss. 29–36 and DDA 1995, ss. 19–28. Discrimination in this field will be actionable by denial of the goods, facilities or services concerned, or by denial of equal quality or terms.

17.4.2.1 What facilities and services are covered?
Section 21(2) of the RRA 1976, SDA 1975, s. 29(2) and DDA 1995, s. 19(3) give a list of examples (not exhaustive):

(a) Access to and use of any place which members of the public or a section of the public are permitted to enter.

(b) Accommodation in a hotel, boarding house or other similar establishment.

(c) Facilities by way of banking or insurance or for grants, loans, credit or finance.

(d) Facilities for education.

(e) Facilities for entertainment, recreation or refreshment.

(f) Facilities for transport or travel.

(g) The services of any profession or trade, or any local or other public authority.

Voluntary bodies are excepted from the sex discrimination legislation, as are certain other situations — for example, single-sex toilets (SDA 1975, ss. 34, 35), and associations of whatever size set up to be enjoyed by persons of a particular racial group (not defined by colour), and associations with less than 25 members (RRA 1976, ss. 25, 26).

17.4.2.2 When will discrimination in the provision of housing or in the disposal of premises be actionable?
A claim will lie if discrimination is shown in the following instances:

(a) In offering or refusing housing, etc.

(b) In the operation of any waiting list.

(c) In access to any benefits, etc.

(d) By denying access to any benefits, etc.

(e) By eviction or causing other detriment.

17.4.3 THE INDIVIDUAL'S REMEDIES FOR DISCRIMINATION IN EDUCATION AND IN THE PROVISION OF GOODS AND FACILITIES, ETC

For procedure, see CCR, O. 49, r. 17 (preserved in CPR, sch. 2). Notice must be given to the Commission for Racial Equality or the Equal Opportunities Commission, who can support the claim by giving assistance and can recoup their costs from any damages ordered to be paid to the applicant by the court.

17.4.3.1 Jurisdiction and limitation period
In cases brought under the RRA 1976, application is made to a designated county court; in cases made under the SDA 1975 and DDA 1995, application is made to a county court. In either case the appropriate court is one in the district in which the respondent resides or carries on business, or where the acts in respect of which the proceedings are brought took place.

A claim must be brought within six months of the act complained of. This period is extended to eight months in cases where discrimination occurs in the field of education and notice has been given to the Secretary of State, who does not wish to consider the matter further, or where a period of two months has elapsed since referral to the Secretary of State (RRA 1976, s. 57; SDA 1975, s. 66).

17.4.3.2 Who hears the case?
In RRA 1976 cases, the case will be heard by a judge and two assessors, unless the parties agree to dispense with them.

In SDA 1975 cases, either party or the judge can summon an assessor whose costs will be met out of public funds.

17.4.3.3 What are the powers of the court?
The court may make any orders which it could make on a successful claim in the law of tort, i.e.:

(a) A declaration of rights.

(b) An order for damages (at large), including an order for damages for injury to feelings.

(c) An injunction to prohibit or mandate certain acts.

17.4.3.4 How is evidence obtained?
Note that the questionnaire procedure applies here (see ***Employment Law in Practice Manual***).

The court has discretion to order disclosure provided that it is necessary in order to dispose fairly of the proceedings or to save costs.

17.5 Damages

17.5.1 IS THERE ANY LIMITATION ON THE RIGHT OF THE INDIVIDUAL TO CLAIM DAMAGES IN THE COUNTY COURT?

In race discrimination cases no compensation will be awarded where a claim of indirect discrimination is substantiated, but the respondent proves that the action complained of was unintentionally discriminatory (RRA 1976, s. 57) (but see *J. H. Walker* v *Hussain* [1996] IRLR 11 for a restrictive interpretation of this provision). A similar restriction on compensation in cases of unintentional indirect discrimination has been removed by SDA 1975, s. 65(1B).

17.5.2 WHAT FIGURE IS LIKELY TO BE AWARDED FOR INJURY TO FEELINGS?

Substantial awards can be made, and in *Noone* v *North West Thames Regional Health Authority* [1988] IRLR 195, a figure of £3,000 was awarded by the Court of Appeal. For guidance on the proper level of these awards, see *Chief Constable of West Yorkshire* v *Khan* [2000] IRLR 324. Exemplary damages are not available (see *AB* v *South West Water Services* [1993] 1 All ER 609, CA; *Deane* v *Ealing London Borough Council* [1993] IRLR 209). Injury to feelings is so fundamental to a claim of sex discrimination that it is almost inevitable (see *Murray* v *Powertech (Scotland) Ltd* [1992] IRLR 257, EAT).

The tribunal has the discretion to make an award against the employer as well as other employees as in *Armitage, Marsden and H.M. Prison Service* v *Johnson* [1997] IRLR 162 where a prison officer who had suffered a sustained campaign of racial discrimination by fellow officers was awarded a total of £21,000 for injury to feelings against the Prison Service and the guilty officers involved.

17.6 Liability for Putting Pressure on Others to Discriminate

It is unlawful to aid, attempt, or to instruct or induce someone else to contravene the provisions aimed at preventing discrimination in employment and in other fields. Liability will be imposed vicariously on an employer/principal who instructs or induces an employee/agent to do so.

It is important to note that employers are liable for offences under the RRA 1976 by their employees regardless of the common law principles of vicarious liability. Section 32(1) which places a liability on the employer for acts done by an employee 'in the course of employment' whether or not it was done with the employer's knowledge is to be given a wide interpretation. Unless an employer can demonstrate that all reasonable steps have been taken to prevent the discrimination, an employer will not be permitted to escape liability by seeking to apply principles drawn from a separate area of law. See *Jones* v *Tower Boot Co. Ltd* [1997] IRLR 168.

17.7 Case Preparation

See the checklists in **Table 17.1**.

Table 17.1 Discrimination Checklists — How to Prepare a Case

CHECKLIST: APPLICATION BY AN INDIVIDUAL

(1) *At first sight, was there direct or indirect discrimination?*

- (a) Does the discriminatory act relate to a field covered by the legislation?
- (b) Is it an act which gives an individual a right of claim?
- (c) When did the act occur?
- (d) When do the time limits run out?

(2) *How is the discrimination to be proved?*

- (a) What evidence is there provided in the papers?
- (b) What does the lay client say happened?
- (c) Consider having a conference to establish the lay client's side of the case.
- (d) What further evidence will be needed to prove the case?
- (e) Where can that evidence be obtained?

  - (i) Has a questionnaire been sent?
    - (aa) If so, have the replies been received? Are they clear and unequivocal?
    - (bb) If they are not, what inferences could/should the court/tribunal draw?
  - (ii) If a questionnaire has not been sent, consider sending one.
    - (aa) Should it be in the standard form?
    - (bb) Consider carefully the questions which need to be asked if discrimination stands a chance of being proved.
  - (iii) Is the Code applicable and has it been broken?

- (f) What has happened to the applicant since the discriminatory act complained of?

  - (i) What financial loss has the applicant suffered?
  - (ii) To what extent have the applicant's feelings been injured?

CHECKLIST: RESPONDENT

(1) *What allegations of discrimination have been made?*

Ascertain the allegations exactly.

(2) *Is the application within time limits?*

Can it be pursued in law?

(3) *If the allegation is of direct discrimination does the respondent admit the allegation?*

(a) If not, with what facts does the respondent disagree?
What evidence supports the respondent's view of the facts?
How is that evidence to be proved?
What interpretation of the law might avoid a finding of discrimination?

(b) If the respondent admits discrimination, identify:

- (i) What the respondent is willing to do for the applicant.
- (ii) What would be the result of action?
- (iii) Negotiate a settlement — is a calculation agreement necessary?

(4) *If the allegation is of indirect discrimination*

- (a) Was a requirement or condition (or in SDA 1975 employment cases a provision, criterion or practice) applied?
- (b) Is it right that it has a disproportionately adverse impact on the applicant's racial group or on women or men?
- (c) What statistical evidence might undermine the allegation of disproportionate impact?
- (d) Did the applicant suffer any detriment as a result? What evidence is there of detriment?
- (e) Was the requirement or condition justified? If, so, why? How is justification to be proved?

(5) *Is the whole application one in which the principle of* de minimis non curat lex *could be argued to apply?*

(6) *What submissions could be made to reduce any damages which might be ordered?*

(7) *What submissions could be made to avoid or agree recommended action for the future?*

17.8 Enforcing the Law

17.8.1 CLAIM BY THE EQUAL OPPORTUNITIES COMMISSION OR COMMISSION FOR RACIAL EQUALITY

The Equal Opportunities Commission (EOC), the Commission for Racial Equality (CRE) or the Disability Rights Commission (DRC) can conduct a formal investigation. This is intended to deal with discrimination which occurs on a larger scale, for example, practices which are believed to be discriminatory and which exist throughout an industry or local authority etc. See **Figure 17.1**.

The CRE, EOC or DRC can institute an investigation on their own initiative, provided they believe that there has been an unlawful discriminatory act, and must investigate if required to do so by the Secretary of State.

Individuals who suffer acts of discrimination can inform the CRE, EOC or DRC of their experience, and it is on knowledge obtained in this way that a decision to mount a formal investigation may be made (RRA 1976, s. 48; SDA 1975, s. 57, Disability Rights Commission Act 1999, s. 3).

Figure 17.1 Powers of the CRE, EOC and DRC to enforce the law

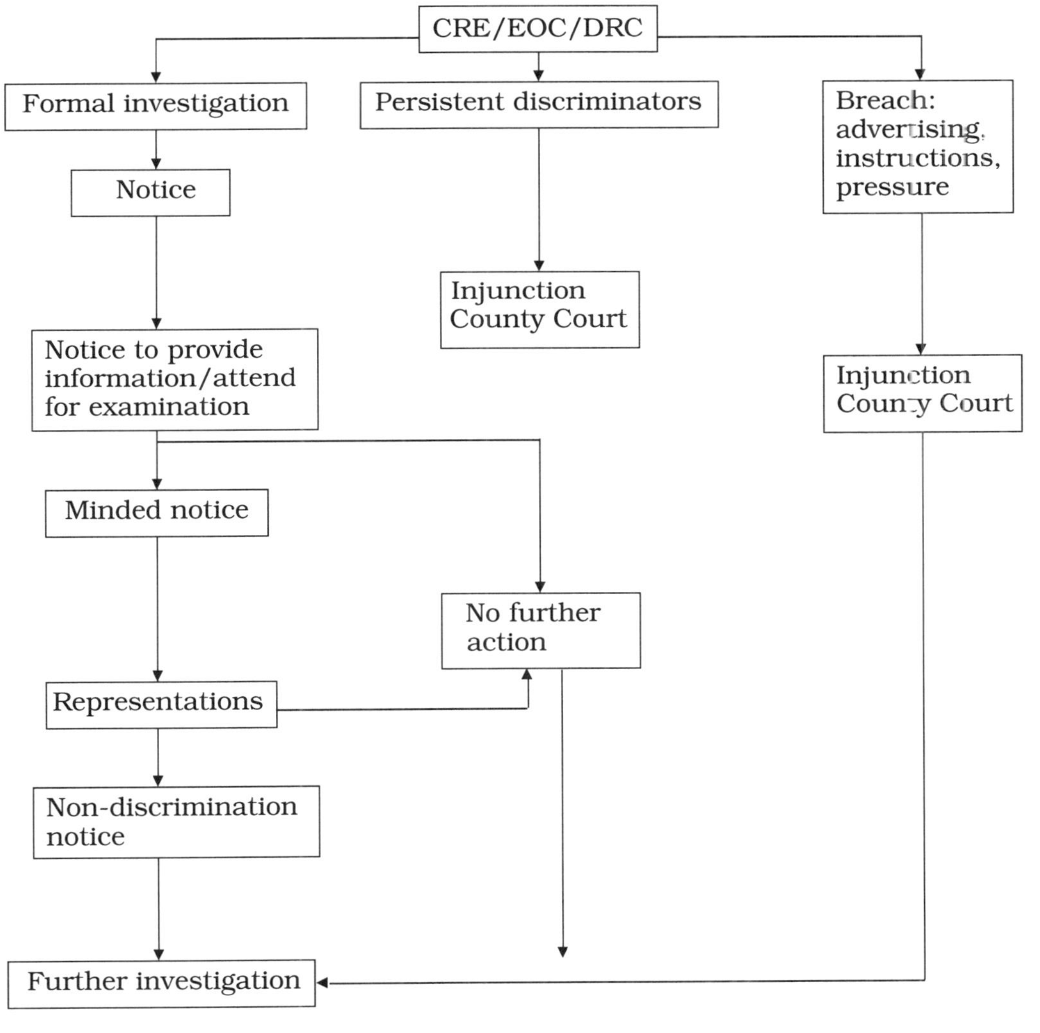

17.8.1.1 What procedural requirements apply when a formal investigation is mounted?
Terms of reference must be drawn up by the relevant Commission, and these should state that the persons named are believed to have done or be doing specified acts which are unlawful. If required to investigate by the Secretary of State, notice must be given to all parties named of the investigation.

By notice the CRE, EOC or DRC can require a person who:

(a) is believed to be committing unlawful discriminatory acts; or

(b) applies a requirement or condition which results in an unlawful act of indirect discrimination or victimisation whether or not there is a specific victim (CRE and EOC only); or

(c) advertises in a discriminatory way; or

(d) gives instructions to others to discriminate; or

(e) induces others to discriminate; or

(f) where such notice is ordered by the Secretary of State

to provide specific written information or to attend for oral examination and produce such documents as may be required which are in that person's possession or control, subject to the rules of evidence governing the production of documents in the High Court. An order can be obtained from the county court if a failure to comply with such a notice occurs or is reasonably believed to be likely. Information acquired in this way is confidential subject to RRA 1976, s. 52 and SDA 1975, s. 61. (See *R* v *Commission for Racial Equality, ex parte Hillingdon London Borough Council* [1982] AC 779.)

17.8.1.2 What are the possible results of a formal investigation?
Following a formal investigation the EOC, CRE or DRC may:

(a) Recommend future action.

(b) Recommend a change in the law.

(c) Deliver the report to the Secretary of State (when that investigation was requested by the Secretary of State), who must publish it.

(d) Publish the report or make it available for inspection (subject to a fee, if required).

(e) Serve a non-discrimination notice (NDN) on the person formally investigated, having first served a notice stating that the Commission is minded to serve an NDN. The minded notice must specify the grounds on which the NDN is contemplated, and give an opportunity for representations to be made either orally or in writing within 28 days. The Commission must take account of any such representations before issuing an NDN.

17.8.1.3 What is a non-discrimination notice?
A non-discrimination notice is a notice that requires the person served to commit no further such acts of discrimination. Where the notice requires a change of practice, then the relevant Commission must be informed that the change in practice has been made. It may also require the person served to provide the Commission with further information and specify the time and manner in which that information is to be provided, which must be no later than five years from the date of the notice.

An appeal against an NDN must be made within six weeks of the NDN being served. Appeals in relation to employment matters will be heard in the employment tribunal, and in relation to the other fields of discrimination will be heard in the county court for the district in which the acts to which the requirements relate were done (and in the RRA 1976 cases, this must be a designated county court).

The NDN should be accompanied by a statement of the findings of fact. The notice of appeal should specify each finding of fact that is challenged, each allegation of fact which it is intended to prove, and any other grounds on which it is alleged that the requirements contained in the NDN are unreasonable.

Appeals are governed by CPR, Part 52.

17.8.1.4 What are the powers of the tribunal/court on appeal?

If the requirement contained in the NDN is considered unreasonable because it is based on an incorrect finding of fact or for any other reason, the court or tribunal must quash the requirement. The court or tribunal can direct that a requirement be substituted for the quashed requirement. It is possible to challenge all or any of the findings of fact on which the requirements contained in the notice were based.

17.8.2 CLAIM AGAINST THE PERSISTENT DISCRIMINATOR

The Commission can apply to a county court for an injunction restraining a person, who within five years of a finding of discrimination made in an employment tribunal or county court, or within five years of the issue of an NDN, discriminates or who continues to apply a condition or requirement which is discriminatory but which has no specific victim, from continuing to act unlawfully.

17.8.3 DISCRIMINATORY ADVERTS, INSTRUCTIONS TO DISCRIMINATE AND PRESSURE TO DISCRIMINATE

Only the Commission has power to enforce compliance with these aspects of the legislation. Application can be made to an employment tribunal (employment matters) or to a county court (other fields) for a decision as to whether the allegation of discrimination can be made out, or to a county court for an injunction where the Commission believes that a breach of this part of the legislation has occurred and that further breaches are likely unless restrained by order.

In any case in which an application is made to the county court for an injunction restraining further acts of discrimination, the Commission can apply to an employment tribunal for a declaration that a discriminatory act in relation to employment has occurred and, if just and equitable, the court can make a declaration and an order recommending action, as though a complaint had been successfully made by the person discriminated against.

17.9 Other Remedies

17.9.1 THE EQUAL PAY ACT 1970

The Equal Pay Act 1970 (as amended by the Sex Discrimination Act 1986) provides for the enforcement, as a breach of contract, of the clause implied into all contracts preventing less favourable treatment on grounds of sex. The application is made to an employment tribunal. Equal terms and conditions of employment are required where the work undertaken is the same as that of another employee of the opposite sex, or where the work concerned has been rated as that equivalent in a job evaluation study, or where it can be established that the work concerned is of equal value to that of another employee of the opposite sex, unless the difference in pay is because of matters other than sex.

The remedy is to seek a new set of terms and conditions which provide for equality, and damages to offset past losses arising from the breach of contract. See the chapter 'Equal Pay' in the ***Employment Law in Practice Manual***.

17.9.2 EUROPEAN LAW

17.9.2.1 The Treaty of Rome

Article 141 (ex 119) of the Treaty of Rome, which provides for equal pay for equal work between men and women, has been held to be directly enforceable by an individual.

17.9.2.2 European Directives

Directives from the Council may sometimes have direct effect when relied upon by an individual against a member State or its public authority (*Marshall* v *Southampton and South West Hampshire Area Health Authority (Teaching)* (152/84) [1986] QB 401; in subsequent proceedings the national limit on the amount of damages available was struck down as failing to allow the damage suffered to be made good: *Marshall* v *Southampton and South West Hampshire Health Authority (Teaching) (No. 2)* (C–271/91) [1994] QB 126).

Relevant Directives include:

(a) The Equal Pay Directive 75/117/EEC of 10 February 1975.

(b) The Equal Treatment Directive 76/207/EEC of 9 February 1976. This covers the equal treatment of women and men in respect of access to employment, (including) promotion and vocational training and working conditions.

(c) Framework Directive on Equal Treatment in Employment 2000/78/EC, which requires the prohibition of discrimination on grounds of religion or belief, disability, age or sexual orientation.

Judicial review is available for the purposes of securing a declaration that UK primary legislation is incompatible with European law. See *R* v *Secretary of State for Transport, ex parte Factortame Ltd (No. 3)* [1992] QB 680 and *R* v *Secretary of State for Employment, ex parte Equal Opportunities Commission* [1995] 1 AC 1.

For further details on European law, see **Chapter 18**.

17.10 Exercises

17.10.1 EXERCISE 1

Problem

The ABC Building Society is unwilling to advance money for the improvement of terraced houses without front gardens in an area where members of ethnic minority groups live. Your instructing solicitors have presented you with a copy of a report which states that 86% of ethnic minority families living in that area live in terraced houses without front gardens, and that 46% of white families living there live in terraced houses without front gardens.

Please advise in the following situations on appropriate procedure and remedies, treating each as independent of the other:

(a) A, who owns a terraced house without a front garden in this area, and is a member of an ethnic minority group, believes she has been indirectly discriminated against. The ABC Building Society has refused to advance money on a mortgage for improvements to her home as a result of this policy.

(b) The local Community Relations Council has received a number of complaints from residents in the same situation as A, but who are unwilling to take action themselves as they fear that they will be seen as troublemakers and be denied any chance of a mortgage if they were to do so.

Solution

(a) This concerns facilities by way of banking or loans for finance which is a field in which racial discrimination is illegal. See RRA 1976, s. 21(2); SDA 1975, s. 29(2). As 14% of ethnic minority families can comply with the condition (86% cannot), and 54% of white families can comply (46% cannot), the proportions suggest that this meets the requirement that a considerably smaller proportion of A's racial group can comply with the condition compared with the proportion of people not in A's racial group who can comply.

A's remedy is to file a claim under the RRA 1976 in the county court where the ABC Building Society carries on business or in the district where the act took place (perhaps the relevant branch of the society). ABC will have a defence if it can justify the condition irrespective of race; a financial motive for the condition will not be sufficient reason to constitute justifiction.

There is no need for A to prove that ABC had an intention to discriminate. However, if ABC can show that the effect of the condition was unintentional, then no damges will be awarded to A. Generally A will be able to recover injury to feelings plus other losses subject to proof of causation. It is unlikely that A would obtain an injunction against ABC and the likely remedy would be a declaratory order and a recommendation as to action to avoid further discrimination.

(b) The Community Relations Council should make a complaint to the Commission for Racial Equality. RRA 1976, s. 43, gives the CRE power to investigate allegations of discriminatory behaviour. The CRE may issue a recommendation to the ABC and investigate whether this has been complied with. If not, it may issue an NDN, which ABC may appeal in the county court. Failure to comply with an NDN entitles the CRE to file an action in the county court. A possible action exists in the European Court of Human Rights, although both routes require a long period of time and A and others needing immediate protection may not see the benefit.

17.10.2 EXERCISE 2

Problem

Mrs Smith has been sexually harassed at work by her section supervisor, Mr James. Her complaints, which have now been verified by her employers consisted of: Mr James asking her out, touching her and pressing against her whenever he had cause to come into her office, and telling others in the company that she was free with sexual favours and that when he had finished with her he would pass her on.

Mr James has been dismissed, and Mrs Smith has decided to continue to work for her employers. You are asked to advise her as to her remedies (if any), the best forum in which to pursue them, and the amount of damages which she is likely to receive.

EIGHTEEN

EUROPEAN COMMUNITY LAW REMEDIES

18.1 Introduction

European Community law (Community law) enables private individuals and legal persons to obtain remedies in the national courts of Member States, the European Court of Justice (ECJ) and the Court of First Instance (CFI).

The ***European Competition Law in Practice Manual*** deals with the ability of parties to use Community law in national courts, and is not repeated here. However, questions may arise in national courts as to the interpretation or validity of EC laws and such questions may be referred to the ECJ. See **18.2**. This chapter considers preliminary references (Article 234 (ex 177) EC), judicial review (Arts 230 and 232 (ex 173 and 175)), claims for damages (Article 288 (ex 215)), the plea of illegality (Article 241 (ex 184)) and infringement proceedings under Article 226 (ex 169).

18.2 Preliminary Rulings

18.2.1 WHAT IS A PRELIMINARY RULING?

A preliminary ruling is given by the ECJ on a Community law point, either on interpretation or validity of Community law. Such a ruling will have been requested by a national court during proceedings before that court in which the Community point has arisen. Provision for this is made in Article 234 (ex 177) of the EC Treaty. It is an indirect action before the ECJ, with the ECJ intervening in national litigation. The CFI cannot hear preliminary references; see Article 225 (ex 168a).

English rules for preliminary references are in the Civil Procedure Rules; Criminal Appeal (References to the European Court) Rules 1972 (SI 1972/1786). The procedure has three stages:

(a) The national court makes the reference.

(b) The national proceedings are suspended.

(c) The national court applies the ECJ ruling to the case and continues to judgment.

18.2.2 IN WHAT AREAS OF COMMUNITY LAW DOES THE ECJ HAVE JURISDICTION TO GIVE RULINGS?

The ECJ can give rulings on the interpretation of Community law (Article 234(1)(a), (b), (c) EC). This includes, for example, the EC Treaty, treaties amending or supplementing it, acts of the Community institutions and international treaties entered into by the Community. These rulings may include decisions as to whether a particular provision has direct effect.

The ECJ also gives rulings on the validity and interpretation of acts of the Community institutions (i.e., Community secondary legislation) (Article 234(1)(b) EC) and on the interpretation of the statutes of any body established by an act of the Council if the statutes so provide.

The ECJ cannot rule on the facts of the case before the national court, nor on the validity of national law and its incompatibility with Community law. The national court alone has jurisdiction in these matters, although the effect of a preliminary reference is often to determine the outcome of a case in a particular way. The national court should not ask questions on these matters. If it does, the ECJ may reformulate the question so that it can be answered in a more abstract manner or may refuse to answer the question. However, the questions are likely to be closely related to the facts of the particular case.

The ECJ cannot tell the national court what to refer or how to exercise its discretion to refer. These are matters for the national court.

The national court may not interpret Community law if there is doubt about its meaning. It should refer any questions to the ECJ for interpretation. Equally it cannot rule on the validity of a Community provision (*Foto-Frost* v *Hauptzollamt Lübeck-Ost* (314/85) [1987] ECR 4199).

18.2.3 WHO CAN REFER A QUESTION TO THE ECJ?

Questions can be referred only by national courts or tribunals. An individual cannot ask the ECJ directly for a preliminary ruling, but a party to a claim before the national court may apply to the national court for a reference to be made. The national court alone has the discretion to decide to refer.

18.2.3.1 Courts which must refer

A national court against which there is no judicial remedy in national law is obliged to refer to the ECJ when a Community question arises (Article 234(3)). There are two views about which court that might be: it can be the highest court in the particular case (predominant view) or the highest court in the land (i.e., House of Lords in the United Kingdom).

A court against which there is no judicial remedy is not obliged to refer if:

(a) The question has already been decided by the ECJ (although a further reference can be made).

(b) The meaning of the Community provision in question is clear, obvious and the court is free from doubt as to meaning. In this case, however, the national court must also be convinced that the meaning is equally clear to the courts of other Member States and to the ECJ (*CILFIT* v *Ministry of Health* (283/81) [1982] ECR 3415). This criterion should not be easy to satisfy. However, see the Queen's Bench Divisional Court ruling in *R* v *Manchester Crown Court, ex parte DPP* (cited below at **18.2.4**).

18.2.3.2 Courts that may refer

Any court or tribunal may refer a question to the ECJ if a preliminary ruling is *necessary to enable the court to give judgment* (Article 234(2)). This applies to all courts which are not the court of last resort.

Regardless of the nomenclature given to a court or tribunal in a Member State, the court must first be considered a genuine court by the ECJ in order to be able to use Article 234. The ECJ will not accept a reference from a body that it does not consider to be a court. The ECJ has a broad view of what constitutes a court — see *Pretore di Salo* (14/86) [1987] ECR 2545, where a public prosecutor/examining magistrate was held to be a 'court'.

The ECJ has a similarly broad view of what constitutes a court or tribunal *of a Member State*: a court in French Polynesia was stated to be such a court and entitled to make use of Article 234 in *Leplat* v *French Polynesia* (C–260/90) [1992] 2 CMLR 512.

18.2.4 AT WHAT STAGE IN LITIGATION CAN A NATIONAL COURT MAKE A REFERENCE?

A national court has power to refer:

(a) if a Community question is raised in the case before it; and

(b) a preliminary ruling on the question is necessary to enable the national court to give judgment.

The national court alone can decide how to exercise its discretion to refer. The following are considerations which the national court may take into account in exercising this discretion:

(a) Are the facts of the case decided? If these are decided first, the relevant issues in the case are clarified. Although a magistrates' court may refer a question, it is preferable that a reference is made at a later stage after all the evidence has been adduced and there is no question of the respondent being acquitted on the facts (*R* v *Plymouth Justices, ex parte Rogers* [1982] QB 863). However, magistrates' courts have referred questions — e.g., about Sunday trading (*Torfaen Borough Council* v *B & Q plc* (145/88) [1990] 2 QB 19).

(b) Are the relevant issues clarified?

(c) Are questions of national law settled?

(d) Is the Community point potentially decisive of the case?

(e) Is there a consistent line of ECJ case law on the Community point, and should it be followed?

(f) Is the Community point unclear?

Other considerations *might* include:

(a) The difficulty of the Community point.

(b) Delay. (Could take up to two years, with national proceedings suspended until the ECJ remits the reference.)

(c) Costs.

(d) Views of the parties. A reference is more likely if both parties agree it is necessary.

(e) Workload of the ECJ.

See the judgment of Lord Denning MR in *H.P. Bulmer Ltd* v *J. Bollinger SA* [1974] Ch 401 and the many later cases that have considered *Bulmer*.

Delay played a large part in the refusal of the Divisional Court to refer an issue to the ECJ in *R* v *Manchester Crown Court, ex parte DPP* [1992] 3 CMLR 329.

The stage in the case when the reference should be made is for the national court to decide (*Pretore di Salo* v *Persons Unknown* (14/86) [1987] ECR 2545). In theory a reference can be made at any stage, but it is preferable if the facts have been decided and legal issues clarified first.

National courts may make references in interlocutory proceedings. There is no obligation on courts from which there is no judicial remedy to make a reference in interlocutory proceedings, provided the decision is subject to review in subsequent proceedings, which may be started or requested by either party (*Hoffman-La Roche AG* v *Centrafarm Vertriebsgesellschaft Pharmazeutischer Erzeugnisse mbH* (107/76) [1977] ECR 957).

For the procedure on making an application for a preliminary reference, see the ***Advocacy Manual*, Chapter 33**. See also the *Practice Direction (ECJ References: Procedure)* [1999] 1 WLR 260.

18.2.5 WHAT IS THE EFFECT OF A PRELIMINARY RULING ON THE CASE?

A preliminary ruling on interpretation or validity is binding on the national court in the case in which the ruling is sought. If the Community provision thus ruled upon is decisive to the judgment, the court has to decide the case according to the ruling.

18.2.5.1 Does a preliminary ruling have retrospective application?

A preliminary ruling on interpretation and validity is deemed to declare what the law has always been. It usually has retrospective effect. However, the ECJ may impose temporal restrictions on the effect of a ruling in exceptional cases if retroactivity of the ruling would cause serious repercussions (usually economic) or uncertainty in the law. The limitations apply only to the actual case in which the ruling is sought. See, e.g., *Defrenne* v *Sabena (No. 2)* (43/75) [1976] ECR 455.

The ECJ may also limit the effect of the ruling in other ways, e.g., only vertical (not horizontal) direct effect for directives; direct effect only for overt (not covert) sex discrimination. These limitations are not restricted to the actual case in which the ruling is sought.

18.2.5.2 What happens if the English courts do not comply with previous preliminary rulings?

If the English courts fail to follow previous preliminary rulings on validity or interpretation, the Commission may be able to bring an enforcement claim against the UK (see Article 226 EC at **18.7**).

18.3 Claims for Annulment using Article 230 EC

18.3.1 INTRODUCTION

Article 230 (ex 173) provides a direct claim in the European Court of Justice, to annul the acts of Community institutions. To bring a successful claim under Article 230, there are three jurisdictional barriers to overcome.

18.3.1.1 Nature of the act

The following acts may be reviewed:

(a) acts adopted jointly by the European Parliament and the Council;

(b) acts of the Council;

(c) acts of the Commission;

(d) acts of the European Central Bank;

(e) acts of the European Parliament, if intended to produce legal effects *vis-à-vis* third parties.

If the act is not within (a)–(e) above, one cannot use Article 230 to seek its annulment. Does the act have legal effect? Only such acts may be challenged under Article 230.

So, an act which is merely advisory and thus produces no legal changes is immune from attack. An example would be an opinion from the Commission. In order to minimise those acts which may not be challenged, the ECJ has used a broad interpretation of acts which produce legal effects — see e.g., the *ERTA* case, *Commission* v *Council* (22/70) [1971] ECR 263. However, there are limits to the category. In *Nederlandse Associatie van de Farmaceutische Industrie* v *Commission* (T-113/89) [1990] ECR II-797, the applicants sought to annul letters sent to themselves and the appropriate Dutch government ministry. The letters stated that certain agreements concerning the Dutch pharmaceuticals market fell within Article 85 (now 81) EC but should be exempted if two specific conditions were met. The CFI upheld a Commission objection to the admissibility of the action — the letters were purely factual in nature and could not have any influence over the applicants' legal position.

18.3.1.2 Parties

(a) Does the applicant have *locus standi*? This divides into two categories, the privileged and the non-privileged applicants.

(i) The privileged applicants are the Council, the Commission and the Member States (Article 230(2)). These parties have an absolute right to seek annulment of any act, so long as it was intended to have legal effect. Under the original Treaty provision, the European Parliament had no standing to apply. In 1990, the ECJ discovered a 'common law right of action' allowing the Parliament to seek annulment. Subsequently, the Treaty was amended so that it expressly permitted such applications by the Parliament, also by the Court of Auditors and the European Central Bank. (The two latter institutions have now been removed by the Treaty of Nice 2001.) Applications by privileged applicants are heard by the Court of Justice.

(ii) The non-privileged applicants are natural or legal persons (Article 230(4)). Applications by non-privileged applicants are heard by the CFI. In order to use Article 230, parties in this category must demonstrate an interest in the (challenged) act. This can be done in any one of three ways:

(aa) The act is a decision, addressed to the applicant.

(bb) The act is a decision addressed to another but is of direct and individual concern to the applicant.

(cc) The act is in substance a decision, although in the form of a regulation, and is of direct and individual concern to the applicant.

(*Note*: Decisions are individual measures, e.g., 'Bloggs Plc has broken the Community competition laws'. Regulations are normative measures, intended to affect everyone, e.g., 'all cars produced in the Community from 1990 onwards must be capable of using lead-free petrol'.)

(b) If (and only if) the act and the applicant fall within the preceding criteria, can that applicant challenge that act.

18.3.1.3 Limitation period

The claim must be started within a limitation period of two months. The period starts from the date the act was published, or when it was communicated to the applicant by the institution or when the applicant found out about the act. There are also grace periods set out in the rules of procedure of the Court of Justice. The safest, and simplest, course is to start proceedings as soon as is practicable after learning of the act.

18.3.2 GROUNDS ON WHICH AN ACT MAY BE ANNULLED

(a) Once the jurisdictional barriers are overcome, one of the four grounds of illegality must be established. These are:

(i) Lack of competence. This is similar to *ultra vires*. This ground will be satisfied if either an EC institution acts in a field not covered by the Treaty, or if one institution acts in a field expressly reserved for another.

(ii) Infringement of an essential procedural requirement. This is a difficult category to define since many of the judgments of the Court interpreting it seem to have been made on an *ad hoc* basis. Not every procedural requirement will be regarded as 'essential'; not all of the 'essential procedural requirements' are laid down in the rules of procedure. An example of an essential procedural requirement is the obligation to give reasons for promulgating all legally-binding acts (Article 253 (ex 190) EC). The institution must make it clear, usually within the act itself, why and how the act has been created.

(iii) Infringement of the EC Treaty or of a rule of law relating to its application. Since the powers of the institutions derive from the Treaty, almost any error by an EC institution could be regarded as an infringement of the Treaty. This ground of illegality is frequently used by applicants and the European Court. The 'rules of law' are those which the European Court regards as underpinning the Treaty. Examples include international treaties and general principles of law (equality, legitimate expectations, proportionality).

(iv) Misuse of power. This is rarely used, probably because it is difficult to establish. The motives of the institution or official responsible for the act must be examined.

(b) If the applicant can prove that at least one of the grounds of illegality applies, the act will be annulled. The European Court seems not to be too concerned with maintaining rigid divisions between the four grounds of illegality — it is sufficient if at least one is clearly applicable; the Court may not even refer to it specifically in its judgment. In practice, ground (iii) covers most successful applications for annulment.

For detailed analysis of the interpretation and application of Article 230, reference should be made to standard textbooks on EC law (e.g., Hartley, *Foundations of EC Law*; Steiner, *Textbook on EC Law*). As an aid to following your way through the Article, a flowchart is included (see **Figure 18.1**). Actions under Article 230 brought by natural/legal persons concerned with the 'competition' rules (Articles 81 and 82 (ex 85 and 86) EC) should be brought in the Court of First Instance.

18.3.3 THE EFFECT OF A SUCCESSFUL CLAIM UNDER ART. 230

The challenged act is annulled and void. No further action based on the act is permitted; all acts done pursuant to the annulled act must usually be undone (see Article 231 (ex 174) EC). The Court cannot amend the act nor substitute a new act. It is possible, though, to preserve some of the challenged act if the parts which require annulment can be severed from the whole.

For reasons of legal certainty and continuity, acts which are possibly invalid (voidable) are presumed to have legal effect unless and until they are successfully challenged in court. There is only one exception to this presumption that these defective acts continue to have legal effect until either annulled or withdrawn — this occurs when the act is regarded as legally non-existent. For the act to be legally non-existent, it must be tainted by an irregularity whose gravity is so obvious that it cannot be tolerated by the Community legal order — such a finding is reserved for quite extreme situations (see, for example, *Commission* v *BASF AG* (C–137/92 P) [1994] ECR I–2555). In most situations, therefore, one must challenge acts pursuant to Article 230 (ex 173) EC and do so within the limitation period. Once that period has elapsed, the only way to attack the legality of such acts is to raise a plea of illegality under Article 241 (ex 184) EC (see **18.6**).

18.4 Claim under Article 232 EC for a Failure to Act

18.4.1 INTRODUCTION

Article 232 (ex 175) is, to a large extent, the mirror image of Article 230 (ex 173). Whereas Article 230 is used to annul existing acts of the EC institutions, Article 232 is used to complain about the absence of an act.

18.4.2 THE BASIS OF A CLAIM USING ART. 232

The legal basis is that there has been inaction on the part of a Community institution (the Council, Commission or European Parliament). This inactivity must constitute an infringement of the EC Treaty; for it to do so, the institution must be under a duty to act. This duty can be imposed either by the EC Treaty itself or by secondary legislation, enacted pursuant to the Treaty.

The Court of Justice has indicated that if the Treaty requires an institution to enact a measure by a certain date and that institution fails to do so, there may be a potential claim under Article 232. Whether or not a claim can be pursued will depend upon the discretion, if any, which is given to the institution. If it has a choice as to the aims of the enactment, then a failure to legislate will only give rise to an Article 232 claim; if it has a choice only as to the means to be employed to get a specific result, then there is an obligation to act and an omission will justify a claim under Article 232.

18.4.3 WHO CAN USE ART. 232?

(a) Privileged applicants. These are the Member States and the institutions of the Community. They may complain to the Court of Justice about any failure to act in breach of an obligation; there is no need to prove a special interest in the case.

(b) Non-privileged applicants. Any natural or legal person can complain that a Community institution has failed to address an act to it (i.e., take a measure of individual application). This applies to any act except recommendations and opinions (i.e., acts which are not legally binding). In practice, this means that people or businesses can complain about a failure to pass a decision which will affect their legal position, either as the putative addressee of such a decision or because it will be of individual and direct concern to them (see further Article 230 at **18.3.1.1**).

18.4.4 THE PROCEDURE FOR A CLAIM USING ART. 232

Before one begins proceedings alleging a failure to act, the institution concerned must be given an opportunity to act. A written communication is sent to the institution, setting out specifically what measures it is suggested that the institution should take. The document must also warn that a failure to take these measures will be followed by a claim under Article 232. The institution then has two months in which to act.

Such a claim by the institution need only be a 'definition of its position'. It seems that almost any communication from the institution within the two months will suffice to define its position, even if it is a simple refusal to act. If this communication is susceptible of review under Article 230, its annulment may be sought, thus putting the onus back on the institution to act. But the communication is not always reviewable, and the other party may then be left without a remedy — unable to force the institution to act and with no act of which complaint can be made.

18.4.5 GOING TO COURT

If the institution does not define its position within the two-month period, it is then possible to bring a claim in the CFI (or Court of Justice, for privileged applicants). The applicant has a further two months within which the claim must be brought. If the institution is found guilty of failure to act, it will be required to take all the measures necessary to comply with the judgment of the Court (see Article 233 (ex 176) EC) although no specific steps will be ordered by the Court of Justice.

18.4.6 USING ARTS. 230 AND 232 TOGETHER

It is not always clear (to an applicant who wants to use the Article 232 procedure) whether the EC institution has failed to define its position within the two months or not. This is likely to be the case where the institution does not take the desired steps but does send a letter, refusing to act as required. In such circumstances, the applicant may be unsure whether the letter is a definition of position.

One way to deal with this is to start proceedings under both Articles 230 and 232, alleging that the letter is not a definition of position (and thus Article 232 is the basis of the claim) but that, if the Court finds it is a proper definition, then it should be annulled (thus proceeding under Article 230 EC).

Figure 18.1 An Action for annulment under Art. 230 EC

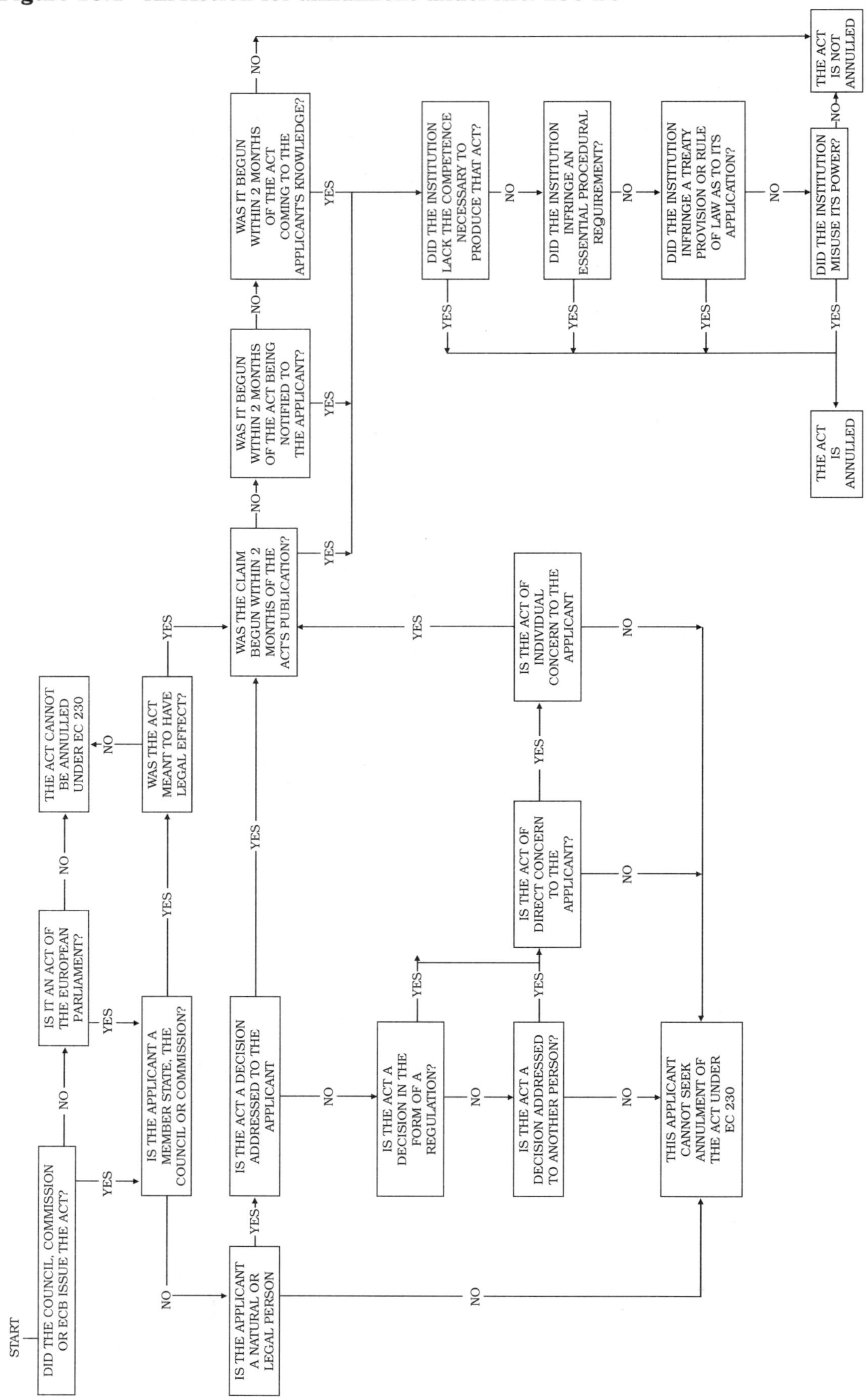

18.5 Non-contractual Liability of the EC under Article 288(2)

18.5.1 INTRODUCTION

Article 288(2) (ex 215(2)) states that '... the Community shall, in accordance with the general principles common to the laws of the member States, make good any damage caused by its institutions or by its servants in the performance of their duties'.

Article 235 (ex 178) EC gives exclusive jurisdiction to the European Court to deal with claims under Article 288(2).

18.5.2 WHAT MUST BE SHOWN IN A CLAIM UNDER ART. 288(2)?

From the express terms of the Article, a number of elements can be seen:

(a) Damage must have been suffered (usually by the applicant, although it seems that the right to sue can be assigned).

(b) A Community institution or its servants must have acted or omitted to act in the performance of its duties.

(c) Both the damage and the act (or omission) are causally linked.

A fourth element has been read into Article 288(2) by the European Court. This is the notion that there must be a wrongful act or omission, sometimes referred to as '*fault*'. This has been justified by reference to the general principles of law common to the Member States. This fourfold test was reaffirmed by the court in *Campagnia Italiana Alcool SAS Di Mario Mariano & Co.* v *Commission* (C-358/90) [1992] 2 CMLR 876.

18.5.2.1 Damage

The applicant must allege clearly those injuries which have actually been sustained and on what basis he or she says that the Community should make good. The European Court will demand proof of the damage, although when determining liability it may not look at the exact amount involved. Sometimes, if satisfied that some damage has occurred, the Court will give a ruling on liability only and postpone its assessment of damages to a later date. Under Article 288(2) the Court may declare the Community liable for imminent damage (so long as it is foreseeable with sufficient certainty). It does not matter that the damage cannot be precisely quantified yet. When one establishes the cause of damage, one may have to act swiftly in order to forestall even greater damage.

Interest can be claimed by an applicant. It is usually awarded from the date of judgment.

The Court sometimes awards compensation for non-pecuniary loss (see *Adams* v *EC Commission* (145/83) [1985] ECR 3539). The Commission was found to be liable to Mr Adams for a breach of confidentiality. It was ordered to pay him £100,000 for his mental anguish. More usually, an applicant seeks compensation for pecuniary loss. Such pecuniary loss should not be based on speculation, e.g., the profit that was expected on a contract which in fact was never made because of the Community's wrongful act.

18.5.2.2 An act or omission of an institution or its servant

The acts or omissions of the servants of the EC have rarely been the express basis of an action under Article 288(2). On an occasion when the issue of Community liability for its servants arose, the Court held that the Community is only liable for those acts of its servants which are 'the necessary extension of the tasks entrusted to the institution'. The Court seems to regard this as a difficult test to satisfy.

18.5.2.3 Causation

This is required by Article 288(2) and is always acknowledged by the Court as a necessary condition for liability. Nevertheless, the Court gives little overt consideration to it in the reported cases. A quite relaxed interpretation seems to be applied.

18.5.2.4 Fault

The Court has not gone so far as to declare the Community liable under Article 288(2) in the absence of fault, even though the idea of strict liability for the acts of public bodies exists in some Member States. The court requires proof of a wrongful act or omission. An act may be wrong either in its purpose or its procedure; a wrongful omission occurs when there is a duty to act which has not been performed.

18.5.3 RELATIONSHIP BETWEEN ART. 288(2) AND ARTS 230 AND 232

An overlap can be seen between these three Articles. The limitation period for claims under Article 288(2) is five years from the date of injury. Hence, if a party wanted to sue on the basis of an act or omission which could have been challenged under Arts 230 or 232 but was not, the limitation period for claims for review could be greatly extended.

The Court has stated that a claim for compensation under Article 288(2) is an independent form of claim. The fact that to award damages under this Article might have the same effect as a claim for review should not render it inadmissible. The practical result is that the time limits within which one may challenge acts which could have been reviewed under Arts 230 or 232 are extended by Article 288(2).

18.5.4 LEGISLATIVE ACTS OF THE COMMUNITY

The Court has ruled very restrictively on the admissibility of claims under Article 288(2) for damage caused by *legislative acts* (i.e., those acts which a non-privileged applicant could not challenge under Article 230 — usually Regulations).

Where a party sues because of damage caused by a legislative act *and* that act involved choices of economic policy, then there is no liability under Article 288(2) unless:

(a) A superior rule of law has been broken.

(b) The breach is sufficiently serious.

(c) The rule of law is one designed to protect the individual.

(d) The basic elements of Article 288(2) are satisfied.

Superior rules of law are the same as those rules which are applied by the Court in claims under Article 230 EC. A sufficiently serious breach has been interpreted as demanding proof of a manifest and grave disregard of the limits on the exercise of the Community's powers. 'A rule of law intended to protect the individual' requires the rule to protect clearly the interests of a class or classes, and if it does so, then an individual within such class may sue.

The leading case is *Aktien-Zuckerfabrik Schöppenstedt* v *Council* (5/71) [1971] ECR 975, which sets out principles (a) to (d). The ECJ has noted that a finding that a legislative measure is invalid does not, of itself, mean that the Community has incurred non-contractual liability for damage caused to individuals. For such liability to exist, an applicant must go on to prove that a sufficiently serious breach of a superior rule of law for the protection of the individual had occurred: *Industrie-en Handelsondernem-ing Vreugdenhil BV* v *Commission* (C-282/90) [1992] ECR I-1937.

18.5.5 SHARED RESPONSIBILITY

Sometimes a Community measure empowers a Member State to act on its behalf. An example is a Community act which imposes a levy on specific imported goods. The act may put the tasks of ascertaining the amount due in each case and its collection into the hands of the Member State. If following the annulment of the Community act, reimbursement of such a levy is sought, from whom should it be claimed? From the Community or the Member State?

The Court has held that where a legislative act of the Community has been implemented by national authorities, then an individual who alleges that he or she has suffered a loss by virtue of such implementation may challenge the validity of the act in national courts, suing the national authorities. The national court will be able to refer the question of the validity of the Community act to the ECJ under Article 234 (ex 177). But the existence of this method of redress will effectively protect the individual only if it can result in the alleged damage being made good. It follows that a claim by an individual for damages under Article 288(2) in the European Court will be admissible, notwithstanding that the individual has not used legal remedies available in national law, so long as it is not disputed that those remedies were incapable of guaranteeing him or her effective protection.

18.6 Plea of Illegality under Article 241 EC

18.6.1 INTRODUCTION

Article 241 (ex 184) applies only to regulations. It provides protection for those against whom it is sought to apply an illegal regulation.

18.6.2 THE GROUNDS FOR MAKING THE PLEA

The grounds for making the plea of illegality are precisely the same as those used in a claim under Article 230. The claim is that, although the measure has not been annulled under Article 230, nevertheless it is invalid and should not be relied on in the current proceedings.

18.6.3 WHEN MAY THIS PROTECTION BE CLAIMED?

Article 241 provides only for an indirect challenge to the validity of an EC regulation, i.e., one made in the course of other proceedings in the European Court. It gives no direct right of claim in the European Court, nor does it allow an indirect attack to be made in the course of litigation in a national court (this is the function of Article 234(b) EC).

Article 241 can be relied on in the following situations:

(a) In a claim under Article 230. If the legality of a measure which is apparently legal is challenged, an earlier measure, which is the legal foundation of the later one, might be attacked.

(b) In a claim under Article 232. If the refusal of the EC institution to act is apparently valid, being based on an existing law, that law might be challenged using Article 241.

(c) In a claim under Article 226. If a Member State is accused of acting in violation of Community law and the Commission brings a claim under Article 226, it seems that the Member State could rely on the plea of illegality as a defence. It would argue that the law it has violated is illegal.

(*Note*: This would not be possible if the Member State was the 'person' to whom the original law was addressed.)

18.6.4 WHO CAN USE ART. 241?

Article 241 may be invoked by 'any party' to proceedings, in which a regulation is in issue.

(a) A Member State may be able to challenge any legislative act, regardless of the fact that it could have used Article 230 (see *Italy* v *Council* (32/65) [1966] ECR 389; *Commission* v *Belgium* (156/77) [1978] ECR 1881).

(b) A natural or legal person may use Article 241 to challenge any *legislative* measure (it cannot use Article 230 because it has insufficient interest or 'standing').

(c) A natural or legal person may use Article 241 to challenge an individual measure if it was not the addressee of the measure. Although an Article 230 claim may have been possible in such circumstances, this may not have been realised within the three-month time limit for an Article 230 claim. The European Court has taken a generous attitude here.

(d) The addressee of an individual measure cannot use Article 241 — the measure should have been challenged under Article 230.

18.6.5 EFFECT OF THE PLEA OF ILLEGALITY

If the illegality of the measure can be established in what is, essentially, a collateral argument, then the legal basis for the main legislation will usually have been lost. Article 241 provides a parasitic line of attack on validity of EC measures, it does not create a separate claim.

18.7 Enforcement Claims against Member States under Article 226 EC

18.7.1 INTRODUCTION

Article 226 (ex 169) is used (and only used) by the European Commission in order to ensure that Member States comply with their obligations under the EC Treaty. The Commission will give the Member State concerned an opportunity to discharge its obligations before proceeding further, but if this opportunity is not taken, the Commission can then bring the matter before the European Court. Only the Commission brings claims under Article 226. Private or legal persons cannot initiate such a claim, although they can complain to the Commission about an infringement. The Commission has no duty to pursue the complaint, although it often does.

The Commission will not start an enforcement claim in every instance of non-compliance that comes to its attention. It may not be expedient to publicise an incident of non-compliance. The Commission will be in contact with the Member State informally to see whether or not it is in breach of Community law and, if so, to persuade the State to rectify its position. The Commission has a discretion whether or not to bring proceedings under Article 226.

18.7.2 WHAT SORT OF OMISSIONS LEAD TO AN ENFORCEMENT CLAIM?

The non-compliance of the Member State may exist because of either action or inaction on its part. To act in contravention of an EC law may result in an enforcement claim; similarly, a failure to act when required to do so by EC law exposes the State to the same risk. Examples include the failure of a Member State to implement a directive within the allotted time, either properly or at all, and passing national laws which infringe Treaty Articles.

The mere existence of a national law which is inconsistent with an EC law can expose a State to an enforcement claim. This is so even if the Member State disavows any intention to use the national law. The continued existence of such a law creates uncertainty for those who might wish to rely on Community law.

Failure to implement a directive into national law, within the allotted time, may also expose a Member State to a claim in its own courts. Such claims may be brought by individuals or companies who allege that they have suffered loss as a result of the Member State's failure. See, e.g., *Francovich* v *Italy* (C6/90, 9/90) [1991] ECR I–5357.

18.7.3 PROCEDURE UNDER ART. 226

18.7.3.1 The invitation to submit counter arguments

If the Commission considers that a Member State has failed to fulfil a Treaty obligtion, it will invite the Member State to submit its arguments about the issue. The invitation will be written, indicating what specific allegations the Commission is interested in and why. If no reply is received, the Commission may renew its invitation. The Commission must take care when issuing the invitation since the contents of the letter will form the basis of any subsequent enforcement claim in the Court of Justice.

If the Commission concludes that the Member State has not discharged an obligation which Community law has imposed on the State (and the situation has not been rectified by the Member State following the Commission's formal invitation to submit observations), then the Commission will deliver a reasoned opinion.

18.7.3.2 The reasoned opinion

The reasoned opinion serves two purposes. First, it is a statement of the facts and law which establish a violation of the Treaty. The detail of the opinion must be adhered to by the Commission: if it subsequently takes the matter to the Court it may not raise any new violations. Secondly, it should indicate what steps must be taken by the State to end the violation, and set a time limit for those steps to be taken.

18.7.3.3 Still no compliance? Go to court

Once the Commission has issued its reasoned opinion and the time limit has expired without remedial steps being taken by the defaulting State, the Commission may take the matter to the European Court. No time limit is imposed on the Commission within which an enforcement claim must be brought before the Court. The Commission has freedom as to when (as well as if) an enforcement matter should be raised with the Court.

The Court will consider the issue of non-compliance, together with any defence which the Member State may raise, and then deliver judgment. An example of such a defence is that the Commission itself has violated the Treaty in its investigation or reasoned opinion. Whilst these procedural arguments have succeeded in the Court on occasion, generally States are unsuccessful in defending enforcement claims.

18.7.4 CONSEQUENCE OF CONTINUED DEFAULT

If the Court finds against the Member State, the State must take the necessary measures to comply with the judgment.

If the defaulting State fails to take the 'necessary measures', under Article 228, the Commission may pursue it for a second time to the European Court, seeking a financial penalty for non-compliance.

18.7.5 INTERIM RELIEF IN URGENT CASES

In cases of urgency, the Commission can apply to the European Court for interim measures to be taken, pursuant to Article 243 EC. For example, see *Commission* v *United Kingdom* (31/77 R and 53/77 R) [1977] ECR 921, where the UK was ordered to terminate certain financial aid to pig producers forthwith.

NINETEEN

EUROPEAN CONVENTION ON HUMAN RIGHTS AND FUNDAMENTAL FREEDOMS

19.1 Introduction

Sometimes, recourse to the European Convention on Human Rights and Fundamental Freedoms ('the Convention') is the last avenue open to one's client. Perhaps other, national, remedies have been sought unsuccessfully; or access to those remedies has been denied; or no appropriate remedies exist. In such circumstances, the responsible lawyer must be able to consider the possibility of advising his or her client to pursue a claim under the Convention. With the Human Rights Act 1998 in force (see **19.3**), those rights are enforced in national courts, although the right of appeal to Strasbourg is maintained (see **19.4**).

19.1.1 SUPERVISION AND COMPLIANCE WITH THE CONVENTION

The European Commission and Court of Human Rights in Strasbourg were established to ensure that the Contracting Parties complied with their obligations under the Convention. In November 1998 Protocol 11 of the Convention came into force creating a single full-time Court of Human Rights replacing the Commission and previous courts. In addition, the Committee of Ministers (composed of the Ministers for Foreign Affairs of the 43 Member States of the Council of Europe or their Deputies) has a power to make decisions when the case has not been brought before the Court and has authority to supervise the execution of the Court's judgment. These institutions, all based in Strasbourg, are creations of the Council of Europe and should not be confused with similarly named bodies established by the 15 Member States of the European Union.

19.1.2 SIGNATURES AND RATIFICATION

The Convention came into force on 3 September 1953. Of the 43 Member States of the Council of Europe, most have now ratified the Convention. The Member States are: Albania, Andorra, Armenia, Austria, Azerbaijan, Belgium, Bulgaria, Croatia, Cyprus, Czech Republic, Denmark, Estonia, Finland, France, Georgia, Germany, Greece, Hungary, Iceland, Ireland, Italy, Latvia, Liechtenstein, Lithuania, Luxembourg, Malta, Moldova, Netherlands, Norway, Poland, Portugal, Romania, Russia, San Marino, Slovakia, Slovenia, Spain, Sweden, Switzerland, 'The Former Yugoslav Republic of Macedonia', Turkey, Ukraine, United Kingdom.

There have been several Protocols to the Convention. Not all participating countries have ratified these Protocols.

19.1.3 PLACE OF THE CONVENTION IN EUROPEAN COMMUNITY LAW

The European Community is not a signatory of the Convention, so the Convention cannot be relied on directly as a source of Community law by individuals.

The question of the accession of the Community to the European Human Rights Convention was considered by the full court and all Advocates General of the European Court of Justice in Opinion 2/94 on 28 March 1996. The Court noted that human rights were referred to and emphasised in the Single European Act and Treaty on European Union. In addition, fundamental rights already formed an integral part of the general principles of law it applied to cases. The Court concluded that accession was not possible in the present Community system and such substantial constitutional change would require amendment to the Treaty.

However, an important aspect of the general principles of Community law is respect for fundamental rights. Articles 12 and 13 (ex 6 and 6a) of the EC Treaty set out specific non-discrimination provisions.

19.2 Rights and Freedoms under the Convention

19.2.1 PURPOSE OF THE CONVENTION

Article 1 of the Convention states that contracting parties 'shall secure to everyone within their jurisdiction the rights and freedoms defined in Section 1 of the Convention'. Thus, countries must ensure that their laws are compatible with the rights and freedoms enshrined in the Convention and must remedy any infringement whenever it occurs.

An important point to note is that Article 1 extends the protection of the Convention to all individuals who find themselves within the territory of a contracting country whether they are nationals of that country or not. Furthermore, an individual need not be a national of any country adhering to the Convention in order to be accorded respect for their human rights by contracting parties. (In *D* v *UK* [1997] 24 EHRR 423, an application was declared admissible from a citizen of St. Kitts who complained that his deportation from the UK to St. Kitts would put him at risk of a reduced life expectancy and of inhuman and degrading treatment since he was suffering from AIDS and would be exposed to a lack of adequate medical treatment and living conditions.)

The Convention guarantees basic political and civil rights but is not concerned with economic rights or freedoms. So, for example, the right not to undergo forced labour is protected but there is no right to work. The protected rights are set out in Articles 2–14 of the Convention. These rights have been enlarged by some of the subsequent Protocols of the Convention (Nos. 1, 4, 6 and 7).

For a basic checklist of the rights and freedoms protected by the Convention, see **Table 19.1**. Note that many of the rights are subject to exceptions or exclusions — some of these restrictions are specific to a right, while others are of more general application.

19.2.2 RESTRICTIONS ON THE RIGHTS AND FREEDOMS

Many of the rights set out in the Convention have permissible exceptions to their scope. Some rights are absolute in their terms (e.g., Article 3); some have a limitation on their scope (e.g., the definition of forced labour in Article 4); while others have quite specific exceptions (e.g., in Article 5 to prevent the commission of an offence).

The most frequent form of exception involves quite broad references to the need to protect: public morals (Articles 6, 8, 9, 10, 11); the interests of other individuals, including reputation (Articles 6, 8, 9, 10, 11); national security (Articles 6, 8, 10, 11); public health (Articles 8, 9, 10, 11); public safety (Articles 8, 9, 10, 11); public order (Articles 6, 9); the interests of justice (Article 6); the economic well-being of the country (Article 8); territorial integrity (Article 10); the authority and impartiality of the judiciary (Article 10); and to prevent disorder and crime (Articles 8, 10, 11) and disclosure of confidential information (Article 10).

These broad exceptions are often limited by the twin requirements that they must be prescribed by law, and necessary in a democratic society (Articles 8, 9, 10 and 11).

As these provisions all permit exceptions to the basic rights and freedoms guaranteed by the Convention, it is usual for the Commission and Court to interpret them quite restrictively.

19.2.3 HUMAN RIGHTS IN THE CONVENTION

19.2.3.1 Article 2: right to life

> 1. *Everyone's right to life shall be protected by law. No one shall be deprived of his life intentionally save in the execution of a sentence of a court following his conviction of a crime for which this penalty is provided by law.*
> 2. *Deprivation of life shall not be regarded as inflicted in contravention of this article when it results from the use of force which is no more than absolutely necessary:*
>   *(a) in defence of any person from unlawful violence;*
>   *(b) in order to effect a lawful arrest or to prevent the escape of a person lawfully detained;*
>   *(c) in action lawfully taken for the purpose of quelling a riot or insurrection.*

This is an absolute right which cannot be derogated from even in time of war. The only exceptions allowed are those set out in the Article. The Article allows judicial death sentences to continue although the death penalty was eventually declared to be abolished by the 6th Protocol. That protocol was finally ratified by the United Kingdom after the abolition of the death penalty for all offences by the Crime and Disorder Act 1998. Other exceptions include, to the extent that use of force is absolutely necessary, defence of oneself or others against unlawful violence (see *McCann, Farrell and Savage* v *UK* (1996) 21 EHRR 97, concerning the Gibraltar shooting of three IRA members).

In *Osman* v *UK* (2000) 29 EHRR 245, the applicants, mother and son, brought a claim alleging a failure by the police to protect them from the second applicant's teacher. The teacher, following a series of threats and incidents, had shot and wounded the second applicant and another teacher, shot and killed the second applicant's father and the other teacher's son. The Court did not find a violation of Article 2 in this case. The Court accepted that in certain circumstances Article 2 implied a positive obligation on the authorities to take preventive operational measures to protect an individual whose life was at risk from the criminal acts of another. However, the Court also took into account the difficulties in policing modern societies, the unpredictability of human conduct and operational choices which needed to be made in terms of priorities and resources and concluded that the positive obligation had to be interpreted in a way that did not impose an impossible and disproportionate burden on the authorities. (See also under Article 6.)

In *Jordan* v *UK* (2001) 11 BHRC 1, the Court held that there was a violation of Article 2 where an unarmed man was shot by a police officer, and in *Edwards* v *UK*, 14 March 2002, (46477/99), the Court held that there were violations of Articles 2 and 13 for the manslaughter of a mentally disordered prisoner by his cellmate.

'Everyone' covers all people who are affected by a threat to their life whether directly or indirectly. Doubt exists whether 'everyone' includes the unborn child; this can be important when considering termination of pregnancy (see *Paton* v *UK* (1980) 3 EHRR 408). Other issues under this Article include dumping of radioactive waste, sterilisation and euthanasia.

The protection afforded by the Article is quite broad, so that in addition to the injunction against taking life, countries should seek to safeguard life. In *Pretty* v *UK*, 29 April 2002, (0002346/02), the applicant suffered from motor neurone disease and was paralysed from the neck down. Her life expectancy was short, she was fed by a tube and her speech was very unclear. Her intellect and capacity to make decisions were, however, unimpaired. She wished her husband to assist in her suicide and requested the Director of Public Prosecutions to undertake not to prosecute him. The Director refused to provide such an undertaking and the applicant claimed that there had been violations of Articles 2, 3, 8, 9 and 14. The Court held that there had been no violation of Article 2, which did not impose on States a positive obligation to protect a 'right to die', and that the applicant's rights under Articles 3, 8 and 9 taken together with Article 14 had not been breached.

19.2.3.2 Article 3: prohibition of torture

No one shall be subjected to torture or to inhuman or degrading treatment or punishment.

No one is to be subjected to any conduct which could come within this prohibition; this is an absolute prohibition. The Article applies to any act for which a participating country is responsible, regardless of the rank of the perpetrator of the act. The three types of treatment form a sliding scale of severity. Torture is seen as an aggravated form of inhuman treatment. It is said to be deliberate inhuman treatment causing serious and cruel suffering. In *The Greek Case* (1969) 132 Yearbook of ECHR 196, the Commission said:

> ... all torture must be inhuman and degrading treatment, and inhuman treatment also degrading. The notion of inhuman treatment covers at least such treatment as deliberately causes severe suffering, mental or physical which, in the particular situation is unjustifiable. The word 'torture' is often used to describe inhuman treatment, which has a purpose, such as the obtaining of information or confessions, or the infliction of punishment and it is generally an aggravated form of inhuman treatment. Treatment or punishment of an individual may be said to be degrading if it grossly humiliates him before others or drives him to act against his conscience.

The test set by the Court, of conduct which falls within this Article, is a high one. The majority of cases involve physical ill-treatment but psychological ill-treatment may also be considered. As well as considering the nature and circumstances of the act, the Court may also consider factors personal to the applicant such as age and health.

The Court has acknowledged that the classification of conduct as torture or inhuman treatment may change over time as a reflection of the fact that the Convention is a living instrument and that there is increasingly greater awareness and higher standards expected in the protection of human rights.

When adjudicating on the interrogation methods used by UK security forces in Northern Ireland, the Court declared that the techniques used had involved inhuman and degrading treatment, but were not of such an intensity and cruelty as to become torture (*Ireland* v *UK* (1978) 2 EHRR 25). The techniques included subjecting to continuous loud noise, sleep deprivation, food and water restriction, standing for long periods.

In 1993 the Court found that the treatment suffered by Mr Tomasi, consisting of being slapped, kicked, punched, made to stand for long periods, spat on, made to stand naked, deprived of food and threatened with a firearm amounted to inhuman and degrading treatment (*Tomasi* v *France* (1993) 15 EHRR 1). In an important and recent case the Court further developed the definition of torture. The applicant in *Selmouni* v *France* (2000) 29 EHRR 403, was held in police custody for three days in relation to a drug trafficking investigation. During that time he was ill-treated by the police who beat him with a baseball bat, urinated on him and lit blowlamps under his feet. The Court was satisfied that the treatment he received was serious, cruel and amounted to torture.

Ill treatment in prison is very likely to be held to amount to inhuman or degrading treatment. In *Keenan* v *UK* (2001) 33 EHRR 39, the Court held that there were violations of Articles 3 and 13 in respect of a mentally disordered prisoner who had committed suicide after having been held in the segregation unit following an adjudication in the prison. In *Price* v *UK* (2001) 11 BHRC 401, it was held to be degrading treatment where a disabled woman was held in custody in a police station and in a prison where she was cold, was at risk of developing sores, was required to sleep on a bed which was too hard or unreachable, and was unable to go to the toilet or keep clean without the greatest of difficulty.

Judicial corporal punishment has been found to be degrading treatment contrary to Article 3 (*Tyrer* v *UK* (1978) 2 EHRR 1). In *A* v *UK* [1999] 27 EHRR 61 the Court found that the law providing that the prosecution had to prove an assault went beyond reasonable chastisement did not provide adequate protection to the applicant. The applicant's father had been charged with assault after hitting him with a garden cane. His defence was reasonable chastisement which was accepted by the jury who acquitted him of actual bodily harm. Both the Commission and the Court found that the treatment of the father amounted to behaviour prohibited by Article 3. The Court's finding that the criminal law did not provide adequate protection to A, the victim, may place an additional burden on judges and prosecutors in future to consider carefully whether a victim's rights have been adequately protected.

Racial discrimination has been found to be capable of amounting to degrading treatment (decision of the Commission in *East African Asians* v *UK* (1981) 3 EHRR 76, where British nationals were denied entry to the United Kingdom on the grounds of their colour and racial origin).

Other cases under this Article have occurred in the area of immigration and extradition (see *D* v *UK* at **19.2.1**, *Soering* v *UK* (1989) 11 EHRR 439 where the Court held that it would be contrary to Article 3 to extradite a German national to the United States to face murder charges which carried the death penalty and *Hilal* v *UK* (2001) 33 EHRR 31, where there was held to be a violation where a decision was made to deport an overstayer to Tanzania).

19.2.3.3 Article 4: prohibition of slavery, servitude and forced labour

1. No one shall be held in slavery or servitude.
2. No one shall be required to perform forced labour or compulsory labour.
3. For the purpose of this Article the term 'forced or compulsory labour' shall not include:
(a) any work required to be done in the ordinary course of detention imposed according to the provisions of Article 5 of this Convention or during conditional release from such detention;
(b) any service of a military character or, in case of conscientious objectors in countries where they are recognised, service exacted instead of compulsory military service;
(c) any service exacted in case of an emergency or calamity threatening the life or well-being of the community;
(d) any work or service which forms part of normal civic obligations.

No one is to be held in slavery or servitude, nor required to perform forced or compulsory labour. This does not prevent the State demanding the performance of military service (or a substitute for conscientious objectors); nor does it mean that lawfully detained prisoners cannot be required to work; nor would a requirement to undertake pro bono work in pupillage be considered a breach of this Article (*Van der Mussele* v *Belgium* (1984) 6 EHRR 163)! Forced labour involves two elements: the work is performed against the will of the worker; the requirement to do the work is unjust or oppressive (or the work involves avoidable hardship). See further the report of the Commission in *Iversen* v *Norway* (1468/62) 6 Yearbook of ECHR 278.

19.2.3.4 Article 5: right to liberty and security of the person

1. Everyone has the right to liberty and security of person. No one shall be deprived of his liberty save in the following cases and in accordance with a procedure prescribed by law:

(a) the lawful detention of a person after conviction by a competent court;
(b) the lawful arrest or detention of a person for non-compliance with the lawful order of a court or in order to secure the fulfilment of any obligation prescribed by law;
(c) the lawful arrest or detention of a person effected for the purpose of bringing him before the competent legal authority on reasonable suspicion of having committed an offence or when it is reasonably considered necessary to prevent his committing an offence or fleeing after having done so;
(d) the detention of a minor by lawful order for the purpose of educational supervision or his lawful detention for the purpose of bringing him before the competent legal authority;
(e) the lawful detention of persons for the prevention of the spreading of infectious diseases, of persons of unsound mind, alcoholics or drug addicts or vagrants;
(f) the lawful arrest or detention of a person to prevent his effecting an unauthorised entry into the country or of a person against whom action is being taken with a view to deportation or extradition.
2. Everyone who is arrested shall be informed promptly, in a language which he understands, of the reasons for his arrest and of any charge against him.
3. Everyone arrested or detained in accordance with the provisions of paragraph 1(c) of this Article shall be brought promptly before a judge or other officer authorised by law to exercise judicial power and shall be entitled to trial within a reasonable time or to release pending trial. Release may be conditioned by guarantees to appear for trial.
4. Everyone who is deprived of his liberty by arrest or detention shall be entitled to take proceedings by which the lawfulness of his detention shall be decided speedily by a court and his release ordered if the detention is not lawful.
5. Everyone who has been the victim of arrest or detention in contravention of the provisions of this Article shall have an enforceable right to compensation.

No one is to be deprived of their liberty except in a manner prescribed by law and in certain specified situations, e.g.. by order of a court after conviction. A requirement that aliens possess a valid passport does not conflict with Article 5. The UK infringed Article 5 when holding detainees under the Prevention of Terrorism (Temporary Provisions) Act 1984, by not bringing them before a court or releasing them promptly after arrest (*Brogan* v *UK* (1989) 11 EHRR 117). However, this right must be applied in a manner appropriate to the circumstances. The Court observed (*Murray* v *UK* (1994) 19 EHRR 193) that due account had to be taken of the special nature of terrorist crime, the threat it posed to democratic society and the exigencies of dealing with it.

In *O'Hara* v *UK* (37555/97), *The Times*, 13 November 2001, the applicant was released without charge after being held for six days and thirteen hours during which he was interrogated as a terrorist suspect. The Court held that the detention period was in breach of the requirement in Article 5(3) for an arrested person to be brought promptly before an appropriate judicial officer.

In *Caballero* v *UK* (2000) 30 EHRR 643, the Court accepted the government's concession of a violation of Article 5(3) and (5) in the application of s. 25 of the Criminal Justice and Public Order Act 1994. That section denied bail to those who were charged with murder, manslaughter or rape (or their attempts) who had previously been convicted of such offences. As a consequence the section was amended by s. 56 of the Crime and Disorder Act 1998 which allows bail to be granted to those convicted of one of the above offences if the court is satisfied that there are exceptional circumstances.

There have been a number of cases involving the use of bind overs referred to the Court. In *Steel and Others* v *UK* (1999) 28 EHRR 603, the Court found various breaches of Article 5 of the Convention in respect of various applicants who had been bound over following complaints of breach of the peace. In *Hashman and Harrup* v *UK* (2000) 30 EHRR 241, a case involving hunt saboteurs who had disrupted a hunt by blowing hunting horns and shouting and faced breach of the peace proceedings, the Court found that there had been a violation of their Article 10 rights to freedom of expression

19.2.3.5 Article 6: right to a fair trial

> *1. In the determination of his civil rights and obligations or of any criminal charge against him, everyone is entitled to a fair and public hearing within a reasonable time by an independent and impartial tribunal established by law. Judgment shall be pronounced publicly but the press and public may be excluded from all or part of the trial in the interest of morals, public order or national security in a democratic society where the interests of juveniles or the protection of the private life of the parties so require, or to the extent strictly necessary in the opinion of the court in special circumstances where publicity would prejudice the interests of justice.*
>
> *2. Everyone charged with a criminal offence shall be presumed innocent until proved guilty according to law.*
>
> *3. Everyone charged with a criminal offence has the following minimum rights:*
>
> *(a) to be informed promptly, in a language which he understands and in detail of the nature and cause of the accusation against him;*
>
> *(b) to have adequate time and facilities for the preparation of his defence;*
>
> *(c) to defend himself in person or through legal assistance of his own choosing or, if he has not sufficient means to pay for legal assistance, to be given it free when the interests of justice so require;*
>
> *(d) to examine or have examined witnesses against him and to obtain the attendance and examination of witnesses on his behalf under the same conditions as witnesses against him;*
>
> *(e) to have the free assistance of an interpreter if he cannot understand or speak the language used in court.*

It is important as a first step to determine the application of Article 6 to ensure protection. The Article applies only to cases involving the determination of civil rights and obligations and criminal charges. The Court has developed criteria for determining whether proceedings are civil or criminal and will have regard to national classification, the nature of the offence and the severity of the penalty, but these factors are not always necessarily determinative. Regulatory contraventions which are not classified as criminal (e.g., parking offences) may nonetheless be criminal for the purposes of Article 6 because they often carry a sanction of a punitive deterrent kind. Disciplinary proceedings do not attract the protection of Article 6. The Article covers pending proceedings as well as access to court (Golder v *UK* (1975) 1 EHRR 524); time limits on cases have been found to be acceptable in the interest of administration of justice (see *Stubbings* v *UK* (1997) 23 EHRR 213). However other defences and immunities may prevent access to court, e.g., *Tinnelly and McElduff* v *UK* (1999) 27 EHRR 249, concerning public interest immunity certificates and *Osman* v *UK*, concerning public policy immunity from suit in negligence against the police investigating or preventing crime. Questions of admissibility of evidence have generally been considered to be matters for national law and national courts have been given a fairly wide discretion in governing their proceedings.

Access to legal representation is of paramount importance and denial of access to legal advice is incompatible with Article 6: *Murray* v *UK* (1996) 22 EHRR 29, *Magee* v *UK* (2001) 31 EHRR 822 and *Averill* v *UK* (2001) 31 EHRR 839. In *Brennan* v *UK*, 16 October 2001, (39846/98), the applicant was a man of low intelligence who was interviewed for a total of 35 hours in police detention. A police officer remained present within earshot of the applicant's first consultation with his solicitor and the Court held that this infringed his right to effective exercise of his defence rights in accordance with Article 6(3)(c) read in conjunction with Article 6(1).

Absence of legal aid to pursue a claim through the courts may infringe Article 6 (*Airey* v *Ireland* (1979) 2 EHRR 305) and constitute denial of access to courts. It has also been found that a requirement to pay security for costs may be denial of access to the courts (*X* v *Sweden* (7973/77) 17 Decisions and Reports 74). The denial of legal aid when pursuing an appeal against a criminal conviction may infringe Article 6 (*Boner* v *UK* (1994) 19 EHRR 246; *Maxwell* v *UK* (1994) 19 EHRR 97). In *Robins* v *UK* (1998) 26 EHRR 563, the Court held there had been a violation of Article 6 in that costs proceedings following litigation had not been determined within a reasonable time.

Fair trial is undefined but case law has added specific rights; the proceedings as a whole have to be considered. Aspects of fair trial guarantees have included the opportunity to receive and respond to submissions, the opportunity to give evidence, equality of arms (that parties should have reasonable opportunity to put their case in conditions which do not put them at a substantial disadvantage vis-à-vis their opponent).

Impartiality and independence of the tribunal are also aspects of fair trial guarantees. Many Court Martial cases have raised the question of impartiality because of the role of the convening officer (see *Findlay* v *UK* (1997) 24 EHRR 221, *Coyne* v *UK*, *The Times*, 24 October 1997, *Smith, Ford and Others* v *UK*, 27 September 1999, unreported). There have also been cases involving the apparent bias of jurors (*Pullar* (1996) 22 EHRR 391, *Gregory* v *UK* (1997) 25 EHRR 577 and *Sander* v *UK* (2001) 31 EHRR 1003). In *Gregory*, the defendant was black and a note was received from the jury stating 'jury showing racial overtones one member to be excused'. The judge consulted counsel and reminded the jury of their duty to decide the case on the evidence without prejudice. The Court found that the firmly worded direction by the judge was enough to dispel any doubts about impartiality. In *Sander*, a British national of Asian origin was on trial during which a juror had reported that at least two members of the jury had made racist remarks and jokes, which one juror had admitted. The judge's direction to the jury was considered by the Court to have been insufficient to dispel the reasonable impression of a lack of impartiality and there was therefore a violation of Article 6(1).

For cases involving points of evidence, see generally the ***Evidence Manual***.

19.2.3.6 Article 7: prohibition of retrospective criminal liability

> *1. No one shall be held guilty of any criminal offence on account of any act or omission which did not constitute a criminal offence under national or international law at the time when it was committed. Nor shall a heavier penalty be imposed than the one that was applicable at the time the criminal offence was committed.*
> *2. This Article shall not prejudice the trial and punishment of any person for any act or omission which, at the time when it was committed, was criminal according to the general principles of law recognised by civilised nations.*

In *S.W. and C.R.* v *UK* (1995) 21 EHRR 363, involving marital rape, the Court found that the change in the law (criminalisation of marital rape) was reasonably foreseeable and therefore there was no violation of Article 7. However in *Welch* v *UK* (1995) 20 EHRR 247, a case involving the retrospective imposition of confiscation orders on defendants convicted of drug offences, the Court considered that this involved the imposition of a penalty and having regard, inter alia, to the punitive nature of the measure, found that there had been a violation of Article 7.

Other cases raised under this Article have involved applicants sentenced for sexual offences who after their release found themselves subject to registration on a sex offenders register (see, for example, *Ibbotson* v *UK* (1999) 27 EHRR CD 332, *Adamson* v *UK* (1999) 28 EHRR CD 209, both of which were unsuccessful). It was said that the registration was not a penalty. In addition, the provision of information to the police (the defendants had to give all their names and aliases, dates of birth and notify any change of name or address within 14 days) was an interference with private life (Article 8) but the measure pursued a legitimate aim taking into account the gravity of the harm that may have been caused to victims and the State's duty to provide protection. The requirement to provide the information could not, therefore, be deemed to be disproportionate.

19.2.3.7 Article 8: right to respect for private and family life, home and correspondence

> *1. Everyone has the right to respect for his private life, his home and his correspondence.*
> *2. There shall be no interference by a public authority with the exercise of this right except such as is in accordance with the law and is necessary in democratic society*

in the interests of national security, public safety or the economic well-being of the country, for the prevention of disorder or crime, for the protection of health or morals, or for the protection of the rights and freedoms of others.

These are not absolute rights. They may be restricted by a public authority, acting lawfully and only doing what is 'necessary in a democratic society'. Article 8 allows such restriction only to achieve certain aims, e.g, protection of morals, public safety. The Court held in *Laskey, Jaggard and Brown* v *UK* (1997) 24 EHRR 39, that the prosecution and conviction of the applicants for sado-masochistic practices was an interference in their private life which was 'necessary in a democratic society' and so held that there had been no violation of Article 8.

There have been many cases under Article 8, forcing the Commission and Court to define its terms. Private life has a wide definition and includes personal identification, name (*Guillot* v *France* (1996) ECHR Series A No. 687), dress (*Kara* v *UK* [1999] EHRLR 232, sexual identity (*Cossey* v *UK* (1990) 13 EHRR 622) and family life (which may include artificial and non-conventional family life) (*X, Y, Z* v *UK* (1997) 24 EHRR 143). Home has also been extended to offices (*Niemietz* v *Germany* (1993) 16 EHRR 97). In the case of *Smith and Grady* v *UK* (2000) 29 EHRR 493 and *Lustig-Prean and Beckett* v *UK* (2000) 29 EHRR 548, the Court found a violation of Articles 8 and 13 in the cases of homosexuals who were excluded from the armed forces because of the policy of the Ministry of Defence. Many cases have involved prisoners' rights concerning visits, interference with mail and compulsory and random drug tests. Private life may also include personal and private space (see, for example, *Govell* v *UK* [1998] EHRLR 438, a covert surveillance case). Personal and private space may extend to include environmental cases. In *Rayner* v *UK* (1986) 47 DR 5 the Commission accepted the applicant's argument that aircraft noise interfered with his Article 8 rights and in *Hatton and Others* v *UK* (2001) 11 BHRC 634 the Court held that there were violations of Articles 8 and 13 due to the level of noise caused at the applicants' homes by aircraft using London Heathrow Airport at night. In *Guerra* v *Italy* (1998) 26 EHRR 357 the State's failure to inform the applicant of the risks and hazards associated with living near a chemicals factory was a violation of Article 8.

Private life does not include the right to keep a dog or a gun; respect for a woman's private life is not interfered with by making rules governing when a pregnancy may be lawfully terminated.

When interference may be justified, the authorities must still act within the law. If there are no laws regulating the interference, these must be created. See e.g., *Malone* v *UK* (1984) 7 EHRR 14 on telephone tapping, which led eventually to the UK enacting the Interception of Communications Act 1985, and *Khan* v *UK* (2001) 31 EHRR 1016. In *PG and JH* v *UK*, 25 September 2001, (44787/98), the Court held that the use of a covert listening device at the applicant's flat and at the police station were in violation of Articles 8 and 13.

19.2.3.8 Article 9: freedom of thought, conscience and religion

1. *Everyone has the right to freedom of thought, conscience and religion; this right includes freedom to change his religion or belief and freedom, either alone or in community with others and in public or private, to manifest his religion or belief, in worship, teaching, practice and observance.*
2. *Freedom to manifest one's religion or beliefs shall be subject only to such limitations as are prescribed by law and are necessary in a democratic society in the interests of public safety, for the protection of public order, health or morals, or for the protection of the rights and freedoms of others.*

Again, this right is subject to lawful interference when necessary in a democratic society and in order, for example, to protect the rights and freedoms of others.

Pacifism has been held to fall within Article 9 (see *Arrowsmith* v *UK* (1978) 19 Decisions and Reports 5) but freedom of belief was not manifested by distributing leaflets to British soldiers urging them to avoid service in Northern Ireland.

In *Gay News Ltd and Lemon* v *UK* (1982) 5 EHRR 123 the Commission, rejecting the applicant's claim, found that the blasphemy laws were an acceptable way of protecting offended Christian feelings. However, in *Choudhury* v *UK* (17439/90) (1991) 12 HRLJ 172, the Commission rejected the applicant's claim that the failure to prosecute the blasphemous attacks on the Muslim faith (in Salman Rushdie's *Satanic Verses*) was contrary to this Article.

19.2.3.9 Article 10: freedom of expression

> *1. Everyone has the right to freedom of expression. This right shall include freedom to hold opinions and to receive and impart information and ideas without interference by public authorities and regardless of frontiers. This Article shall not prevent States from requiring the licensing of broadcasting, television or cinema enterprises.*
>
> *2. The exercise of these freedoms, since it carries with it duties and responsibilities, may be subject to such formalities, conditions, restrictions or penalties as are prescribed by law and are necessary in a democratic society, in the interests of national security, territorial integrity or public safety, for the prevention of disorder or crime, for the protection of health or morals, for the protection of the reputation or rights of others, for preventing the disclosure of information received in confidence, or for maintaining the authority and impartiality of the judiciary.*

This includes the right to hold an opinion and to receive and impart information and ideas without interference. The freedom is subject to exceptions: any derogation must be prescribed by law and only be such as is necessary in a democratic society. When examining the necessity of a derogation, the Commission will allow a certain discretion to the State concerned, known as its 'margin of appreciation', on the understanding that the State's authorities are better informed about what is necessary in that country at that time than is the Commission. See, e.g., the case on the 'Little Red School Book'. *Handyside* v *UK* (1976) 1 EHRR 737; prosecution under the UK obscene publication legislation was challenged, the book having been previously published in Denmark and other countries. The Court decided that the decision whether to prosecute was within the UK's area of discretion.

Expression includes not only words but also gestures, pictures, images, actions and dress (see *Hashman and Harrup* v *UK* (2000) 30 EHRR 241, under Article 5 above *Stevens* v *UK* (1986) 46 DR 245). Means of expression could include radio, television film and electronic information systems.

Cases brought under this Article have included *Sunday Times* v *UK* (1979) 2 EHRR 245 (the Thalidomide drug case) in which the Court found that an injunction was not necessary; the newspaper had a duty in providing information and the public had a right to receive it and *Goodwin* v *UK* (1996) 22 EHRR 123 (refusal to reveal journalistic source) where the Court found that the fine for contempt of court was a disproportionate restriction on the applicant's freedom of expression.

19.2.3.10 Article 11: freedom of assembly and association

> *1. Everyone has the right to freedom of peaceful assembly and to freedom of association with others including the right to form and to join trade unions for the protection of his interests.*
>
> *2. No restrictions shall be placed on the exercise of these rights other than such as are prescribed by law and are necessary in a democratic society, in the interests of national security or public safety, for the prevention of disorder or crime for the protection of health or morals or for the protection of the rights and freedoms of others. This Article shall not prevent the imposition of lawful restriction on the exercise of these rights by members of the armed forces, of the police or of the administration of the State.*

Article 11 covers the right to assemble peacefully and to associate with others, including the right to join a trade union. These rights are subject to similar limitations as in Articles 8 and 10.

The existence of a 'closed shop' agreement between British Rail and the 'rail trade unions' was the subject of a complaint by BR employees — see *Young* v *UK* (1981) 4 EHRR 38. They successfully challenged the threat of dismissal, although the Court was reluctant to decide that the freedom to join a union implied a similar right not to do so. Note the fact that this complaint related to an agreement between BR and the unions. The United Kingdom was not a party to the agreement. However, as the closed shop agreement was lawful under UK employment laws, the UK could be the subject of a complaint because it was not securing the rights and freedoms of the Convention (Article 1).

This Article was also invoked, unsuccessfully, in the GCHQ case (*Council of Civil Service Unions* v *UK* (11603/85) (1987) 50 DR 228) after the UK government had removed the right of civil servants to form and join in a trade union although one had existed there for decades.

19.2.3.11 Article 12: right to marry

> *Men and women of marriageable age have the right to marry and to found a family, according to the national laws governing the exercise of this right.*

These acts are subject to any relevant national laws governing their exercise. An example of a complaint frequently made involves transsexuals claiming the right to marry. Often they are stopped from doing so by their original birth certificate's declaration of gender. Complaints have been made about the refusal of the authorities to amend birth certificates. The Commission has held that such refusal is an infringement of the right to marry (see *Van Oosterwijka* v *Belgium* (7654/76) 11 Decisions and Reports 194) but a UK transsexual, Caroline Cossey, failed in a similar (widely reported) complaint (*Cossey* v *UK* (1990) 13 EHRR 622).

19.2.3.12 Articles 13 and 14: ancillary rights

> *Article 13 Effective remedy*
> *Everyone whose rights and freedoms as set forth in this Convention are violated shall have an effective remedy before a national authority notwithstanding that the violation has been committed by persons acting in an official capacity.*
>
> *Article 14 Prohibition of discrimination*
> *The enjoyment of the rights and freedoms set forth in this Convention shall be secured without discrimination on any ground such as sex, race, colour, language, religion, political or other opinion, natinoal or social origin, association with a national minority, property, birth or other status.*

Article 13 states that the victim of a violation of the Convention must have access to an effective remedy in the offending country.

Article 14 requires that the rights and freedoms covered by the Convention are to be available to all, without discrimination on any ground. It seems that Article 14 should not be understood as creating a general prohibition against discrimination.

19.2.3.13 Article 15: derogation from the Convention

> *1. In time of war or other public emergency threatening the life of the nation any High Contracting Party may take measures derogating from its obligations under this Convention to the extent strictly required by the exigencies of the situation, provided that such measures are not inconsistent with its other obligations under international law.*
> *2. No derogation from Article 2, except in respect of deaths resulting from lawful acts of war, or from Articles 3, 4 (paragraph 1) and 7 shall be made under this provision.*
> *3. Any High Contracting Party availing itself of this right of derogation shall keep the Secretary General of the Council of Europe fully informed of the measures which*

it has taken and the reasons therefor. It shall also inform the Secretary-General of the Council of Europe when such measures have ceased to operate and the provisions of the Convention are again being fully executed.

For most Convention rights, Article 15 permits a country to derogate from its obligations in times of war or other serious public emergency. Such derogation is narrowly interpreted being permitted only to the 'extent required by the exigencies of the situation'. In circumstances other than war, Article 15 requires either a crisis situation or an exceptional and imminent danger which '. . . affects the whole population and constitutes a threat to the organised life of the community of which the State is composed' (*Lawless* v *Ireland (No. 3)* (1961) 4 Yearbook of the ECHR 438 at pp. 472–3). The United Kingdom sought to derogate from the Convention by way of its response to the judgment in *Brogan* v *UK* (1989) 11 EHRR 117 (see **19.2.3.4**) on periods of detention under the prevention of terrorism legislation. Rather than amend the legislation to comply with the Convention, the United Kingdom chose to derogate from Article 5(3) in 1988. This derogation was considered by the Court in *Brannigan* v *UK* (1993) Series A, No. 258-B. The derogation was limited, applying only to 'terrorism connected with the affairs of Northern Ireland'. The Court referred to the context of the derogation (i.e., 'the nature of the terrorist threat in Northern Ireland') and held that in the circumstances the UK had not exceeded its margin of appreciation.

Even when such derogation is permitted, some Articles must still be observed; thus respect for life (other than deaths in lawful acts of war) and the prohibition of torture and maltreatment must be maintained (additionally Articles 4(1) and 7 must continue to be respected).

The Government derogated from the Convention when it enacted the Anti-Terrorism, Crime and Security Act 2001 in the wake of the 11 September terrorist incidents in the USA and the military action in Afghanistan.

Furthermore, a participating country may denounce the Convention; in effect, resign from participation, There is a minimum 'stay' required; no denouncement is allowed until the expiry of five years' membership. Six months' notice is required. Existing violations at the time of withdrawal are still within the jurisdiction of the Convention.

19.2.3.14 Articles 16, 17 and 18: additional restrictions and rights

Article 16 Restrictions on political activity of aliens
Nothing in Articles 10, 11 and 14 shall be regarded as preventing the High Contracting Parties from imposing restrictions on the political activity of aliens.

Article 17 Prohibition of abuse of rights
Nothing in this Convention may be interpreted as implying for any State, group or person any right to engage in any activity or perform any act aimed at the destruction of any of the rights and freedoms set forth herein or at their limitation to a greater extent than is provided for in the Convention.

Article 18 Limitation on use of restrictions on rights
The restrictions permitted under this Convention to the said rights and freedoms shall not be applied for any purpose other than those for which they have been prescribed.

19.2.4 PROTOCOLS

Since 1950 a number of protocols have come into force, some adding further rights and liberties and others of a more administrative nature. Protocol 1, in force for the States which ratified it, since May 1954, added the rights of property, education and free elections. Protocol 2, in force since 1970, conferred on the Court of Human Rights competence to give advisory opinions. Protocol 3 modified the procedure of the Commission by abolishing the system of sub-commissions. Protocol 4, in force since May 1988, added the rights of freedom from imprisonment for debt, freedom of movement, freedom from exile and prohibition of compulsory expulsion of aliens.

Protocol 5, in force since December 1971, concerns the procedure for election of members of the Commission and Court. Protocol 6, in force since March 1985, concerns the abolition of the death penalty. Protocol 7, in force since November 1988, added the rights of no expulsion without due process of law, right to appeal in criminal cases, right to compensation for miscarriages of justice, immunity from prosecution or sentence when already acquitted or convicted for the same offence and equality of rights between spouses. Protocol 8, in force since January 1990, deals with the procedure allowing the Commission to sit in chambers and to set up committees. Protocol 9, in force since October 1994, concerns the rights of direct access of individuals to the Court of Human Rights. Protocol 10, which has not yet entered into force, provides for decisions of the Committee of Ministers to be taken by simple majority instead of the two-thirds majority presently required. Protocol 11, which was opened for signature on 11 May 1994, brought about the establishment of a single Human Rights Court replacing the Commission in October 1998. Protocol 12, of 4 November 2000, provides for a general prohibition of discrimination 'on any ground such as sex, race, colour, language, religion, political or other opinion, national or social origin, association with a national minority, property, birth or other status'.

19.2.5 INTERPRETATION

The emphasis is on a teleological approach, that is one that seeks to realise its objects and effects. Reliance is also placed on the principle of proportionality and the doctrine of the margin of appreciation. The doctrine recognises that when a State takes legislative or judicial action on a Convention right, it must be given a certain amount of discretion. Criticism may arise when the doctrine is applied so widely that it appears that the State is being allowed to engage in the questionable practice.

Table 19.1 Rights and freedoms protected by the Convention and its Protocols and restrictions

Right or freedom	Provision
The right to life	Article 2
Prohibition of torture, inhuman or degrading treatment or punishment	Article 3
Prohibition of slavery, servitude or forced labour	Article 4
The right to liberty and security of person	Article 5
Right to a fair trial	Article 6
Prohibition on criminal laws that are retroactive	Article 7
Right to respect for private and family life, home and correspondence	Article 8
Freedom of thought, conscience and religion	Article 9
Freedom of expression	Article 10
Freedom of peaceful assembly and association, including the right to join a trade union	Article 11
Right to marry and found a family	Article 12
Everyone whose rights and freedoms are violated shall have an effective remedy before a national court	Article 13
Prohibition of discrimination in the enjoyment of rights and freedoms guaranteed by the Convention	Article 14
Derogation in time of war or public emergency	Article 15
Restrictions on political activity of aliens	Article 16
Prohibition of abuse of rights	Article 17
Limitations on the restrictions on rights	Article 18
Protection of property, right to education, right to free elections	First Protocol, Articles 1–3
Prohibition on deprivation of liberty on ground of inability to fulfil a contractual obligation, liberty of movement and freedom to choose residence, prohibition of expulsion of nationals	Fourth Protocol, Articles 1–3
Prohibition of death penalty	Sixth Protocol, Article 1
Prohibition on expulsion of lawfully resident aliens, right of appeal, rights of autrefois acquit and convict, equality of rights and responsibility of spouses in marriage	Seventh Protocol, Articles 1–5
General prohibition of discrimination	Twelth Protocol, Articles 1–2

Note that the UK has ratified Protocols 1 and 6 and signed but not ratified Protocol 4. Protocol 7 has been neither signed nor ratified by the UK.

19.3 The Human Rights Act 1998

In the White Paper which accompanied the Human Rights Bill the government set out its aim as enabling people to enforce their Convention rights against the State in the British courts rather than having to incur the delays and expense involved in taking a case to Strasbourg. The Act came into force on 2 October 2000.

19.3.1 SCOPE OF THE ACT

The Human Rights Act 1998 gives effect to the rights and freedoms in Articles 2 to 12 and 14 of the Convention, Articles 1 to 3 of the First Protocol and Articles 1 and 2 of the Sixth Protocol which should be read with Articles 16 to 18.

19.3.2 MAIN PROVISIONS

Section 2 of the Human Rights Act 1998 states that courts and tribunals determining questions under the Act must take into account judgments, decisions, declarations and opinions of the Commission and the Court. Section 3 states that legislation should be read and given effect in a way which is compatible with Convention rights. When taking into account these matters and trying to give effect to Convention rights, it is important to remember that prior to Protocol 11 coming into force in October 1998 there was a two-tier system of Commission and Court at Strasbourg and decisions of the Court were more authoritative than those of the Commission. Neither the decisions of the Commission nor those of the Court have been or will be binding on our courts. In addition, it is important to remember that the Convention is a 'living instrument'; attitudes and culture change and legislation reflects those changes (for example, changes in the attitudes towards criminalisation of homosexuality (*Dudgeon* (1982) 4 EHRR 149) and lowering of age of consent for male homosexual conduct (*Sutherland*, 1 July 1997, unreported); definition of torture, see **19.2.3.2** above, *Ireland* v *UK* (1978) 2 EHRR 25 and *Selmouni* v *France* (2000) 29 EHRR 403). It is also important to remember in taking into account the judgments of the Court that in many cases the margin of appreciation has been applied.

Some cases in which the courts interpreted legislation in a way which was compatible with Convention rights were *R* v *A* [2001] 2 WLR 1546; *R* v *Lambert* [2001] 3 WLR 206 and *R* v *Offen & Others* [2001] 1 WLR 253.

There is a requirement on public authorities to act in a way which is compatible with the Convention (s. 6). The definition of public authorities is wide and includes courts and tribunals and persons whose functions are those of a public nature but does not include either the House of Parliament or persons exercising functions in connection with proceedings in Parliament. Section 6(2) limits the duty on public authorities to the extent that they could not have acted differently or that the statute could not be read or given effect to in a way which was compatible with Convention rights.

A person aggrieved by an act or omission on the part of the public authority which is incompatible with the Convention right, and who is a victim of that act, is able to challenge that act or omission in the courts or tribunals (s. 7). The question of who is a victim may create argument. In judicial review cases the test is a wide one of 'sufficient interest'. Under the Convention a victim has been defined as someone who is the victim of the violation (Article 34). The latter definition could potentially exclude public interest groups such as Age Concern or the Joint Council for the Welfare of Immigrants. Proceedings may be brought by way of appeal against the decision or on application for judicial review (s. 9). Damages or other relief will be awarded for any act of a public authority which the court finds unlawful (s. 8).

19.3.3 DECLARATIONS OF INCOMPATIBILITY

The Higher Courts (House of Lords, Privy Council, Courts-Martial Appeal Court, Court of Appeal or High Court) are given power to make declarations of incompatibility where a provision is incompatible with one of the Convention rights (s. 4). That declaration will have the effect of prompting the government to change the law. Declarations of incompatibility were made in *R (on the application of H)* v *Mental Health Review Tribunal & SOS for Health* [2001] 3 WLR 512 and in *Wilson* v *First County Trust* [2001] 3 WLR 42. Section 10 deals with the power of a Minister of the Crown to take remedial action when legislation has been declared incompatible with a Convention rights. (Compare that with the European Communities Act 1972 under which European law which has direct effect takes precedence over domestic law. The difference between EU law and ECHR is that it is a requirement of membership of the EU that member States give priority to directly effective EC law in their own legal systems; there is no such requirement in the Convention.) New legislation is stamped with a statement of compatibility with the Human Rights Act 1998 in accordance with s. 19.

19.4 Enforcing the Convention before the Court of Human Rights

Protocol 11 established a new single full-time Court to which all applicants have access (see **19.4.2**); the Commission was therefore abolished.

Transitional arrangements regulate cases submitted under the old system (Articles 4 and 5 of the Protocol) and the remaining cases before the Commission.

19.4.1 ORGANISATION

The Court consists of the number of judges equal to that of Contracting parties. There is a national from each State except San Marino and Liechenstein which have appointed an Italian and Swiss judge respectively. Judges are appointed for six years; the Court has a registry and judges may be assisted by law clerks. When deciding on cases the Court sits in committees consisting of three judges, Chambers of seven judges or a Grand Chamber of seventeen judges. The Court can appoint substitute members for cases.

19.4.2 THE BASIC PROCESS

Under the new system, individual (Article 34) and State (Article 33) applications come before the Court. The Registry of the Court establishes contact with the parties. A three-judge committee, or in certain cases a larger seven-judge Chamber, considers questions of admissibility (Articles 29 and 35). If the application is declared admissible, the Chamber may make itself available to the parties with a view to securing a friendly settlement. If no friendly settlement is reached the Chamber will deliver its judgment (Articles 29 and 44) which is final. In cases where a question of principle is involved or questions regarding interpretation or application or where the Chamber does not intend to follow the Court's previous case law, the Chamber may refer the case to the Grand Chamber of 17 judges (Article 43).

The Court gives a reasoned judgment. There may be dissenting speeches. The Court's judgment is final and the defendant countries which are found to be in contravention must abide by the judgment.

The Committee of Ministers supervises the execution of the Court's judgment.

19.4.2.1 Compensation

If a victim can show financial loss arising from a violation, he should be compensated. Normally this will happen via the national legal system of the contravening country. If the system does not provide for compensation in such situations as that of the complainant, or such compensation as is available is inadequate, the complainant may seek an award of 'just satisfaction' from the Court (Article 41 (ex 50)). In meritorious cases, the Court fixes a sum for the contravening country to pay the complainant.

19.4.3 WHO CAN COMPLAIN?

Two avenues of complaint exist, either by a country or by individuals.

Inter-State applications Under Article 33, any participating country may complain about alleged breaches by another such country. There is no requirement that the complainant country show an especial interest in the alleged violations (e.g., Denmark, Sweden and Norway complained about the activities of the Greek State during the regime of the 'colonels').

Individuals Under Article 34, one or more individuals may complain of a violation, so long as two criteria are satisfied. First, the complainant must be the victim of a violation; secondly, the respondent State must have declared that it recognises the right of individuals to petition the Court. This last point is of great importance as without such a declaration, complaints against that country by individuals will be impossible.

19.4.4 HOW TO COMPLAIN

The Court provides an application form with an explanatory note. However, applications may simply be made by letter to The Registrar, European Court of Human Rights, Council of Europe, F-67075 Strasbourg, Cedex, France. The application should contain a brief outline of the complaint, an indication of the right(s) and/or freedoms alleged to have been violated, a list of remedies which have been tried in the State concerned and a list of the official decisions with the date and name of court or authority making the decision. The official languages are French and English and applicants are asked to indicate which they prefer to use. The Registrar will reply to all correspondence and keep the applicant informed about the progress of the case. The Registrar may ask for additional information, or indicate if there is an obvious difficulty with admission or may indicate how the Commission and/or Court has dealt with previous cases of a similar nature.

Legal aid is available for complaints to the Commission. It is granted on conditions similar to those current in Member States which run such schemes.

19.4.5 IS THE COMPLAINT ADMISSIBLE?

The test of admissibility is a preliminary hurdle which is encountered by would-be complainants. The secretariat applied various requirements to each complaint it received, and the intention is to continue the practice based on the Commission's Rules of Procedure.

The requirements that must be met for a complaint to be admissible are:

(a) The applicant must be a victim of a violation of the Convention; he or she must be able to show that a right or freedom protected by the Convention has been violated. Also, the complainant must show that he or she is either the actual victim or is interested in some significant way, perhaps by being a parent or guardian of the actual victim.

(b) All domestic remedies for the violation must have been exhausted. To the extent that effective remedies are available under national law, they must be pursued and exhausted **before** a complaint can be made to the Court. It is immaterial whether the remedy is judicial or administrative in nature, although a remedy that exists purely as an act of grace is not included (e.g., seeking a royal pardon).

(c) The complaint must be lodged with the Registry within six months of the final decision in the matter. 'Final decision' here refers to the pursuit by the victim of an effective domestic remedy. The six-month period may be interrupted or suspended by special circumstances.

(d) The petition must not be anonymous.

(e) The petition must not be substantially the same as one previously examined by the Court or Commission (unless it contains relevant new information).

(f) The complaint must not be 'manifestly ill-founded' or incompatible with the Convention or an abuse of the right of petition. These hurdles are not strictly defined by the Court but were frequently used by the Commission to reject complaints. Obvious examples of incompatibility are complaints of the violation of rights which are not protected by the Convention, or violation by a country which is not participating in the Convention. 'Manifestly ill-founded' is a reason based on the lack of a *prima facie* case of violation of a Convention right.

If the case is admissible, a friendly settlement is negotiated. If unsuccessful, the case goes before the Court for a full hearing.

19.5 Reports and Further Reading

19.5.1 COURT REPORTS

The official publication of judgments of the European Court of Human Rights is published in two series: Series A (Judgments and Decisions) and Series B (Pleadings, Oral Arguments and Documents). The publication appears in English and French.

The European Human Rights Reports ('EHRR') are published in English by Sweet & Maxwell. They contain judgments of the Court and certain Commission reports and decisions.

The Court's website is at: www.echr.coe.int.

19.5.2 TEXTBOOK AND PERIODICALS

Baker (editor), *Human Rights Act 1998: A Practitioner's Guide*, Sweet & Maxwell, 1999.
Clayton & Tomlinson, *The Law of Human Rights*, Oxford University Press, 2001.
Clements, *European Human Rights*, Sweet & Maxwell, 1994.
European Human Rights Law Review, Sweet & Maxwell.
European Law Review, Sweet & Maxwell.
Farran, *UK Before the European Court of Human Rights, Case Law and Commentary*, Blackstone Press (OUP), 1996.
Grosz, Beatson and Duffy, *The 1998 Act and the European Convention*, Sweet & Maxwell, 2000.
Harris, O'Boyle and Warbrick, *European Convention on Human Rights*, Butterworths, 1994.
Jacob and White, *The European Convention on Human Rights*, Clarendon Press, 1996.
Leach, *Taking a Case to the European Court of Human Rights*, Blackstone Press (OUP), 2001.
Lester and Pannick (eds), *Human Rights Law and Practice*, Butterworths, 1999.
Mensah, *European Human Rights Case Locator 1960–2000*, Cavendish, 2000.
Simor & Emmerson, *Human Rights Practice*, Sweet & Maxwell, looseleaf.
Starmer, *European Human Rights Law: The Human Rights Act 1998 and the European Convention on Human Rights*, Legal Action Group, 1999.
Starmer, Strange & Whitaker, *Criminal Justice, Police Powers & Human Rights*, Blackstone Press (OUP), 2001.
Wadham and Mountfield, *Blackstone's Guide to the Human Rights Act 1998*, Blackstone Press (OUP), 2000.

PART II

FINANCIAL IMPLICATIONS OF SEEKING REMEDIAL RELIEF

TWENTY

UNDERSTANDING TAX AND REVENUE LAW

20.1 The Importance of Revenue Law for Barristers

20.1.1 WHY THE BARRISTER NEEDS A KNOWLEDGE OF REVENUE LAW

It is very important for all barristers to have a basic understanding of the revenue law system for a variety of reasons:

(a) Tax can be an integral part of calculating what a client is entitled to, and therefore part of giving a client full advice on available remedies. Tax can be directly relevant when calculating damages in a tort or contract case, or when calculating a maintenance claim.

(b) Even if tax will not form part of the detailed arithmetic in a case, advising generally on tax implications may form part of providing full and practical advice for a client. This may be because an asset at stake in a case may be liable to tax, or because of implications for the client's personal tax position.

(c) Barristers are self-employed and therefore need to provide annual accounts for the Inland Revenue, and, if appropriate, regular returns for VAT.

Any belief that a barrister can get by without at least an adequate working knowledge of the tax system is therefore out of date and also somewhat naive. It is not that the individual barrister will necessarily be expected to give detailed advice about tax to every client, but any barrister seeking to provide a good quality of service for a client should be capable of seeing where tax may be relevant to a case. There must be a risk that a barrister who does not spot where tax may be relevant to the assessment of damages could be open to a claim for negligence, or may at least risk criticism from a client or instructing solicitor. If a client has a claim for £100,000 but is likely to have to pay tax at 40% this must be made clear!

It may well be that, having spotted that tax is relevant, the appropriate step is to call in an accountant to assist or at least advise the client to talk to an accountant, but the barrister should at least appreciate the need to take steps like this. It is, however, not realistic to assume that if an accountant is called in, the barrister will have no further involvement in the tax side of the case. The barrister will still need to be sufficiently familiar with the relevant tax provisions to talk to the accountant intelligently, and the barrister may well still need to be able to understand the tax implications in the case sufficiently to present them in court or deal with them as part of a negotiation.

These materials are not intended to provide a detailed understanding of tax law, they are simply intended to offer a sufficient basic understanding to fulfil the following aims:

(a) To familiarise students with the basic principles of revenue law.

(b) To approach the tax system from the point of view of the barrister and to put most emphasis on areas the barrister is most likely to encounter.

(c) To illustrate ways in which tax issues may arise in a case.

(d) To provide a basis for further research.

Inevitably, an attempt to reduce a complex area to basic principles will result in some omissions and generalisations, and students are warned that they should always check points and ensure that their knowledge of this area is up to date. These materials do not deal with relatively specialist areas such as the taxation of trusts. The Inland Revenue website is an excellent source of information at www.inlandrevenue.gov.uk.

20.1.1.1 Cases where tax may be relevant

Tax may be relevant in providing advice or considering remedies in any of the following circumstances:

(a) Drafting a contract, or dealing with a breach of contract.

(b) Drafting a will or settlement, or dealing with a problem with either.

(c) Almost any commercial case.

(d) Dealing with a real property or landlord and tenant case.

(e) Assessing compensation or damages in any case.

(f) Financial provision on divorce.

20.1.1.2 When the barrister may need to advise on tax

The points at which a barrister may need to deal with tax matters include:

(a) In analysing the facts and figures of the case.

(b) In advising a client in conference or in an opinion on the possible effects of tax on damages or compensation.

(c) In presenting tax issues at trial, both in dealing with evidence and in making submissions.

(d) In being able to talk to expert witnesses such as accountants.

20.1.1.3 Dealing with a problem

It is easy to overlook tax aspects in concentrating on complex substantive law issues, but the really effective barrister will never do so. They may not be complex — it may simply be a matter of advising a claimant that a figure for damages will have to go into business accounts to be taxed — but wherever there are figures in a case there will almost always be something to say about tax.

It is not easy to provide a simple checklist for identifying and dealing with tax issues that will apply in every case. There will be many variables in the type of case and the parties. However, the following general points should prove valuable:

(a) In looking at the financial side of any case always consider whether there are tax aspects. It may help to consider whether there is a taxable source or context in the case, e.g., a business or employment.

(b) Do not make simple judgments about the whole case — different aspects of the case may have different tax implications.

(c) Consider whether a figure in a case is capital or income (or partly one and partly the other).

(i) If the figure is capital, consider the rules of capital gains tax and of inheritance tax.

(ii) If the figure is income, consider whether it fits within one of the schedules.

(d) Bear in mind the point of view from which you wish to consider tax, e.g., are you for a claimant who may want more because he will have to pay tax, or for a defendant who may wish to deduct damages paid?

(e) Bear in mind at what stage in the case you are considering tax, e.g., do you need further information, are you preparing for a negotiation, or are you preparing arguments for a judge.

20.2 Brief Outline of the Tax System

20.2.1 INCOME OR CAPITAL

There is a fundamental distinction between capital and income, with separate rules and separate taxes for each. This distinction is a matter of fact, and also largely a matter of common sense. Cases use the analogies of trees (capital) and fruit (income) or of lakes (capital) and streams (income) (*Pool* v *Guardian Investment Co. Ltd* (1921) 8 TC 167). The capital is the larger, long-term asset and income the regular, smaller-scale, product. Generally capital is not relevant for income tax purposes and vice versa, though there are a few specific exceptions, see *Tucker* v *Granada Motorway Services Ltd* [1979] 1 WLR 683, HL.

20.2.2 SOURCES OF TAX LAW

(a) Statutes: The basis of all tax law (no common law principles): Income and Corporation Taxes Act 1988 (ICTA 1988); Provisional Collection of Taxes Act 1968 and annual Finance Acts; Taxation of Chargeable Gains Act 1992 (TCGA 1992); and Inheritance Tax Act 1984 (ITA 1984).

(b) Cases.

(c) Statements of Practice: Issued by the Inland Revenue (also press releases and extra-statutory concessions).

A budget is announced in the autumn (at the same time as public expenditure announcements) leading to a Finance Act the following spring. Note that there is no common law in revenue law, and no equitable principles.

Tax statutes are construed strictly. To be taxable, an event must fall precisely within the wording of a statute. Tax avoidance, that is organising one's affairs in a legal way to pay as little tax as possible, is permissible, but tax evasion is not. It is vital to appreciate this distinction so as to act ethically in advising a client.

A taxpayer is entitled to organise his affairs in a way which is legal, even if the result is to decrease his tax liability (*IRC* v *Duke of Westminster* [1936] AC 1, HL) but a transaction which is a pure sham and which is carried out solely to avoid tax can be ignored (*W. T. Ramsay Ltd* v *IRC* [1982] AC 300, HL). A scheme may, however, be effective if it is not a total sham that was entirely preplanned (*Craven* v *White* [1989] AC 398).

20.2.3 FOREIGN ELEMENT OF TAXATION

Tax liability where there is a foreign element depends primarily on three basic concepts: domicile (see e.g., *Plummer* v *IRC* [1988] 1 WLR 292); residence; ordinary residence. Double taxation relief may be available where there is a foreign context. The foreign element of taxation is complex and is not dealt with here.

20.3 Basic Outline of Income Tax

20.3.1 THE SCHEDULAR SYSTEM

Income will be taxable if it falls within one of the following schedules, depending on the rules for that schedule: ICTA 1988, ss. 1, 15–20. Once you have decided a figure is income, the next stage is to decide which schedule applies.

Schedule A Profits or gains from land in the UK.
Schedule B Woodlands (abolished from 1988–89: FA 1988, s. 65).
Schedule C Profits from public revenue dividends payable in the UK.
Schedule D Case I: Profits or gains from any trade.
Case II: Profits or gains of a profession or vocation.
Case III: Interest, annuities and other annual payments.
Case IV: Profits or gains from securities outside the UK.
Case V: Profits or gains from possessions outside the UK.
Case VI: Profits not within any other case or schedule.
Schedule E Emoluments from an office or employment.
Schedule F Distributions from companies resident in the UK.

The right schedule must be used for each separate item of income. Deductions are exclusively set against income of the same schedule, see *Mitchell and Edon* v *Ross* [1962] AC 814, HL. One schedule may be more beneficial than another for the taxpayer. A loss under one schedule cannot automatically be set against income under another schedule.

20.3.2 THE ASSESSMENT OF INCOME TAX

The basic rate of tax for 2002–2003 is 22%. There is a lower rate of 10% on the first £1,880 of taxable income. Higher rate tax of 40% is charged on all income in excess of £29,400. These rates were set in the Finance Act 2002.

The income tax year runs from 6 April in one year to 5 April in the following year, the current year being 2002–2003.

Basic stages of assessing income tax

(a) Income is calculated under each separate schedule, including any taxable benefits.

(b) Any allowable deductions are made directly against the income under each schedule.

(c) The net figures under each schedule are added together to give total income for tax purposes.

(d) Personal reliefs and allowances are deducted: ICTA 1988, ss. 256–278. The personal allowance for a single person for 2002–2003 is £4,535.

(e) Tax is charged at the appropriate rates.

Administration of the tax system

(a) The tax return is completed by the individual. (The Inland Revenue also have wide powers to get information from employers etc.)

(b) An assessment of tax due is then made. A system of self-assessment has been introduced. If the individual chooses not to assess his own tax then the assessment is made by a tax inspector.

(c) An appeal against the assessment can be made within 30 days: TMA 1970, ss. 31, 44–56.

(d) The appeal is heard by the General Commissioners or the Special Commissioners.

(e) From here either side can appeal to the High Court and beyond on a case stated.

Once the tax assessment is made, tax must be paid within the time specified by statute and in the assessment or fines will be imposed. However, some tax is collected at source, for example under the Pay As You Earn system for employees.

20.4 Basic Outline of Capital Gains Tax and Other Taxes

20.4.1 CAPITAL GAINS TAX

This tax is payable on a capital gain made when a capital asset is disposed of, but only on the *gain*, not on the full value, and normally only on the gain accruing since March 1982.

There is an annual allowance of gains of £7,500 before tax is payable. Tax is paid on gains at a rate equal to the individual's marginal rate of income tax therefore at 22% or 40%.

20.4.2 INHERITANCE TAX

This tax is payable when the capital value of an individual's estate is reduced as the result of a transfer. The taxable figure is the amount of the reduction.

As a gift during life is potentially exempt, and will escape tax if the donor survives for seven years, the tax is payable primarily on death. There is an annual allowance of transfer up to £3,000 in the year. Tax liability is based on the total transferred over a seven-year cumulation period. There is a nil rate of tax until the cumulative total over that period exceeds £234,000, above which tax is payable at 20% during life, or at 40% on death or within three years of death.

20.4.3 CORPORATION TAX

This tax is paid by companies and unincorporated associations on the net income plus the capital gains of the body at the rate of 30% or 20% for a small company. There is a starting rate of 10% for companies with taxable profits of less than £10,000.

20.4.4 STAMP DUTY

This is payable on certain types of transfers.

20.5 Basic Outline of Value Added Tax

Value Added Tax (VAT) was introduced into the United Kingdom on 1 January 1973, as a result of joining the EEC. Because it is an EEC tax, EEC directives on the administration of the tax can apply directly. See Value Added Tax Act 1994; Value Added Tax Regulations 1995.

Liability to the tax is on the supply for consideration of goods or services: 1994 Act, ss. 4–9, sch. 4 and sch. 5. Tax liability arises at the time of the supply. The taxable person is the person making the supply in the course of their business. A person who is liable for the tax should be registered, subject to specified limits: 1994 Act, s. 3, sch. 1.

Compulsory registration applies when the value of taxable supplies in a year exceeds £54,000, including cases where it is foreseen that the value is likely to succeed such figure etc. Voluntary registration below this figure is possible. Ignorance of the need to register is no excuse for not registering. HM Customs and Excise provide a very informative website at www.hmce.gov.uk.

20.5.1 THE CHARGE

Output tax is charged at the time of supply at a standard rate of 17½%: 1994 Act, s. 2. An invoice should be issued within 30 days of a supply, though there are exceptions and special schemes for retail businesses. Tax is charged on the value of goods, which is generally the price paid or the market value.

Input tax gives credit for VAT paid by a person registered for VAT (to prevent VAT being charged several times over in the course of an item going to an ultimate consumer): 1994 Act, s. 25.

20.5.2 ACCOUNTING AND PAYMENT

VAT liability is self-assessed by the registered person, the cost of such assessment thus falling on the taxpayer. Accounts must be rendered every three months in the prescribed form. Tax must be paid within 30 days of the submission of an account.

Because of potential abuse of self-assessment there are wide powers for tax authorities to inspect documents, enter premises etc.

20.5.3 EXEMPTIONS AND ZERO RATING

Exemption is available for many groups of transactions, such as insurance, education, health services etc.: 1994 Act, s. 31, sch. 9.

Zero rating is also available for groups of transactions, including food, books, fuel, transport, clothing and charities: 1994 Act, s. 30, sch. 8. This is a matter of government policy.

20.6 The Tax Position of Someone who is Employed

20.6.1 INTRODUCTION

The barrister might need a knowledge of the tax considerations relevant to employed people in connection with:

(a) Drawing up a contract of employment, from the point of view of an employer or an employee.

(b) Advising on any dispute involving a contract of employment.

(c) Advising whenever an employer or an employee is a party in a case.

(d) The termination of a contract of employment, especially if an employee is dismissed in breach of the contract and claims damages.

(e) Taking full or part-time employment personally.

Schedule E taxes those who work under agreed terms for a regular salary, from a shop assistant to a managing director: ICTA 1988, ss. 19, 131–207.

The basic issues with regard to an employed person might be:

(a) Does the individual concerned hold an office or employment?

(b) What taxable income does the individual have? What fringe benefits are taxable? On what basis is each benefit taxed? Is the individual a higher paid person or director?

(c) What deductions can be made from taxable income?

(d) How and when will tax be payable?

(e) In the case of loss of employment: Does the contract provide for compensation? If not, will the compensation be taxed by statute?

20.6.2 OFFICE OR EMPLOYMENT DEFINED

Schedule E applies where an individual holds an 'office' or 'employment'.

(a) An office is a position which has an existence independent of any individual person who fills it, see *Great Western Railway Co.* v *Baxter* [1920] 3 KB 266. Under this definition a judge holds an office.

(b) An employment exists where a person works under an agreement with detailed terms for the performance of their work for regular payment.

It is important to contrast a series of agreements for work which are part of a profession (and therefore not subject to Sch. E) with a long-term, full-time agreement to work for one employer (which would be subject to Sch. E): see *Davies* v *Braithwaite* [1931] 2 KB 628 and *Fall* v *Hitchin* [1973] 1 All ER 368. It has been held that a barrister's clerk is not an employee and is therefore not taxable under Sch. E: *McMenamin* v *Diggles* [1991] 4 All ER 370.

20.6.3 INCOME OR EMOLUMENTS

If an individual holds an office or employment, his or her income under Sch. E will generally include all money (salary, commission etc.) and most fringe benefits derived from the office or employment, ICTA 1988, s. 131. Any sum that is paid in respect of services past, present or future is liable to tax and any payment that is related to the terms of work will generally be liable to tax: *Hamblett* v *Godfrey* [1987] 1 All ER 916, HL, and *Holland* v *Geoghegan* [1972] 3 All ER 333.

20.6.3.1 Rules for all employees

Virtually all income and fringe benefits will be taxable, and there has been an increasing move in this direction over recent years. However, some benefits are taxed on a more favourable basis than others, and many are attractive despite being taxable.

Money payments from an employer All money payments from the employer related to work will be taxable, unless it can be shown that they do not come from the employment itself. This will, for example, include a Christmas allowance or bonus: *Laidler* v *Perry* [1966] AC 16, HL. Any kind of commission, or expense allowances will normally be taxable, such as a mileage allowance (*Perrons* v *Spackman* [1981] 1 WLR 1411) or a living allowance.

The payment may escape tax if:

(a) It is a gift. For example, a personal payment made for passing an examination or for some other special achievement like winning a prize may escape tax: *Moore* v *Griffiths* [1972] 3 All ER 399.

(b) It does not come from the contract of employment. For example, the proceeds of a benefit season for a cricketer may escape tax (*Seymour* v *Reed* [1972] AC 544, HL) (but contrast *Moorhouse* v *Dooland* [1955] Ch 284).

(c) It is compensation for something other than work done. For example, a payment that is made for giving up private practice on taking up employment rather than for work done may escape tax (*Pritchard* v *Arundale* [1972] Ch 229) (but contrast *Glantree Engineering Ltd* v *Goodhand* [1983] 1 All ER 542).

Money payments from third parties These are taxable if they are made in relation to work done. For example, tips given to a taxi driver are taxable (*Calvert* v *Wainwright* [1947] KB 526).

Indirect payments Such payments will be taxed if they are really related to work, or if an employer is discharging an obligation of an employee. If, for example, an employer pays electricity bills and telephone bills for an employee, the cost will be taxable: *Nicol* v *Austin* (1935) TC 531.

Vouchers and credit cards If these are supplied or paid for by the employer they will basically be taxed on use, except where used for tax deductible purposes, and with other limited exceptions: ICTA 1988, ss. 141–144; FA 1988, ss. 47–48.

Fringe benefits Benefits other than money are subject to the 'convertibility test' — if they could be converted into money, they are taxed on the amount of money they would raise. If, for example, an employee could have a car or a higher salary, he can be taxed on the higher salary available, as that could be gained by not having the car: *Heaton* v *Bell* [1970] AC 728, HL. If an employer buys a suit for an employee, it could be sold at second-hand value, and so can be taxable on that value (*Wilkins* v *Rogerson* [1961] Ch 133) but if a clothes allowance is given rather than a suit the full amount of the allowance will be taxable: *Fergusson* v *Noble* 1919 SC 534.

If a benefit cannot be turned into money it will escape tax unless a specific statutory rule makes it taxable. If, for example, an employee is given a flat which he has to live in and which he is unable to let out it has no market value: *Tennant* v *Smith* [1892] AC 250, HL.

Living accommodation If accommodation is provided by reason of the employment, by statute there will be a charge to tax on the annual value of the property, unless an exception applies: ICTA 1988, ss. 145, 146. The exceptions are:

(a) that it is necessary for the proper performance of the employee's duties that he should reside in the accommodation, or

(b) that the accommodation is provided for the better performance of the duties of the employment, and it is an employment in which it is customary for an employer to provide living accommodation for an employee, or

(c) where there is a special threat to the security of the employee and he resides in the accommodation as part of special security arrangements.

Thus if a director of a farming company lives in a house owned by the company, he can be liable for tax: *Stones* v *Hall* [1989] STC 138. There is an additional charge where the cost of providing the accommodation exceeds £75,000.

Special statutory provisions Sick pay, maternity pay, income support etc. taxable under Sch. E by statute: ICTA 1988, ss. 148–152. Other sums are also specifically made taxable by statute. For example, any sum paid in respect of a restrictive covenant related to employment is taxable: ICTA 1988, s. 313; FA 1988, s. 73.

Exceptions to charge
Profit-related pay Tax relief is available on profit-related pay up to £4,000 per year provided an approved scheme has been set up: ICTA 1988, ss. 169–184, sch. 8.

Payroll deduction schemes A sum of up to £1,200 per annum will not be taxed if it is paid from an employee's salary to a charity under a recognised payroll deductions scheme: ICTA 1988, s. 202.

Training courses The cost of a course of training is not taxable if it is specifically related to the job done (Extra Statutory Concession A63) nor is the cost of a retraining course: ICTA 1988, ss. 588–589. The cost of certain vocational training courses is also tax deductible: FA 1991, ss. 32–33.

Entertainment The provision of entertainment is not taxed if it is not provided by the employer or a person connected with the employer and is not for particular services: FA 1988, ss. 47–48.

20.6.3.2 Additional rules for employees earning £8,500 a year or more and directors

All employees who earn more than £8,500 a year or a director (with certain exceptions) is subject to special rules in addition to the ordinary principles outlined above. Essentially anything provided to the employee or his family by reason of his employment will be taxable, tax being paid on the cost to the employer of providing the benefit: ICTA 1988, ss. 153–168, sch. 7. The figure of £8,500 has not been raised for many years, so these rules now apply to virtually all employees.

Expense allowances These are taxable, however provided, less sums spent for deductible purposes: ICTA 1988, s. 153.

Benefits in kind These are taxable, including accommodation other than living accommodation, entertainment, domestic or other services, and any other benefits and facilities of whatsoever nature: ICTA 1988, ss. 154, 155, 156. Note that tax is on the cost of providing the benefit, which will often be less than the market value of the benefit. In *Pepper* v *Hart* [1993] AC 593 it was held by the House of Lords that where a teacher at a fee paying school was offered a place for his own child, tax should be charged on the marginal cost of providing the place, not on the fee another child would pay.

Living accommodation This is subject to the above rules (**20.6.3.1**), but ancillary services of heating, lighting, repairs etc. are also charged to tax, subject to a limit if the employee falls within an exception to charge for the accommodation: see ICTA 1988, s. 163.

Cars Tax is paid on 35 per cent of the list price of the car: ICTA 1988, ss. 157–159; FA 1993, s. 70. A car available from a 'pool' is not charged to tax. The amount charged to tax may be modified depending on the number of miles driven for business purposes in a year. There is a separate charge for petrol, charged on a cash equivalent, or for the provision of a chauffeur. Parking spaces provided near work are not taxed: FA 1988, ss. 45, 46.

School fees Educational fees are taxable if paid by the employer for a member of the family or household of an employee, with limited exceptions: ICTA 1988, s. 165. This statutory section overrides a previous decision that paying school fees escaped tax: *Wicks* v *Firth* [1983] 1 All ER 151, HL.

Beneficial loans These are taxed on the difference between any interest paid and a set official rate of interest where the total loan exceeds £5,000: ICTA 1988, ss. 160, 161.

Share purchase schemes If shares are made available at less than full value by reason of employment, there is a charge to tax: ICTA 1988, s. 162. Note that there are special statutory provisions for share option schemes (ICTA 1988, ss. 135–140, 185–187) and for employee share ownership schemes: FA 1989, ss. 67–74.

Basis of taxation While the above rules tax many fringe benefits, the result is not necessarily bad:

(a) The employee is only taxed on the cost of provision, and the employer may well be able to get goods or services at a favourable cost.

(b) The fact that a benefit is taxable means that the value is added to taxable income, but the employee only pays the appropriate tax (20%, 23% or 40%), not the full cost of the benefit.

(c) The charge to tax on a benefit such as a car remains less than the cost of buying and running one.

(d) Some benefits are not taxable: the provision of supplies or services on the employer's premises used solely in performing the employment (ICTA 1988, s. 155); the provision of meals in a canteen where meals are provided for staff generally (ICTA 1988, s. 155); the provision of entertainment is not taxed if it is not provided by the employer or a person connected with him, and it is not a reward for specific work (FA 1988, s. 49).

20.6.3.3 Expenses — deductions

The employee may deduct any sums which he or she spends wholly, exclusively and necessarily in the performance of the duties of the employment: ICTA 1988, ss. 198, 199–202. This test is notoriously strict.

Travelling expenses These must be necessary to do the job, and must be incurred in performing the job. For example, it has been held that a barrister could not deduct the cost of travelling to Portsmouth to be Recorder as the travel was not part of his duties: *Ricketts* v *Colquhoun* [1926] AC 1, HL. The cost of going from home to work is not deductible. The cost of travelling to a conference is only deductible if attendance is necessary for the individual's job: *Owen* v *Burden* [1972] 1 All ER 886.

It is not possible to deduct more than it is necessary to spend on the travel: *Marsden* v *IRC* [1965] 2 All ER 364. The cost of travel involved in itinerant employment or where there is more than one place of employment is deductible. For example, a doctor on call can deduct the cost of driving to hospital as he starts work giving advice from home on the telephone: *Pook* v *Owen* [1970] AC 244, HL.

Other expenses

(a) The money must be spent in the performance of the duties of the job. For example, it is not possible to deduct the cost of a meal eaten when the employee has to stay at work late as it is not part of the job to eat: *Sanderson* v *Durbridge* [1955] 1 WLR 1087. For a similar reason the cost of childcare while the work is done is not deductible: *Halstead* v *Condon* (1970) 46 TC 289. To illustrate how strictly this test is applied, in *Smith* v *Abbott* [1994] 1 All ER 673, HL, it was held that although journalists read other newspapers 'to allow their duties to be performed' they did not read them 'in the performance of their duties', so the cost of subscriptions was not deductible. Qualifying for a job is not part of performing it, so it has been held that an articled clerk could not deduct the cost of the Law Society examinations: *Lupton* v *Potts* [1969] 3 All ER 1083.

(b) The expenditure must be necessary for the work. It may, for example, be useful for a bank manager to join a golf club to do his job fully, but it is not strictly necessary, so it will not be deductible: *Brown* v *Bullock* [1961] 3 All ER 123.

(c) The expenditure must be wholly and exclusively for the work. A personal element to the expenditure will usually be fatal. For example, it has been held that a vicar could not deduct the cost of a slide projector for use in his sermons as it could be used for other purposes: *White* v *Higginbottom* [1983] 1 WLR 416.

Entertainment expenses These are deductible only in limited circumstances: ICTA 1988, s. 577.

20.6.3.4 Basis of assessment of tax

Tax is charged on the total taxable income of the employee in the tax year, less all allowable deductions: ICTA 1988, ss. 203–207.

20.7 The Tax Position of Someone who is Self-employed or Runs a Small Business

20.7.1 INTRODUCTION

The barrister might need a knowledge of the tax considerations relevant to self-employment or running a small business in the following circumstances:

(a) If someone who runs a business is the claimant or defendant in any case being conducted, including any contract or tort action.

(b) If a business is involved in any legal transaction, for example any contract, deed or settlement.

(c) If the financial position of a business is relevant to a case, e.g., to a maintenance application.

(d) Personally, in that barristers are self-employed.

Income from a trade, profession or vocation is taxed under Schedule D, Cases I and II: ICTA 1988, ss. 18, 53–130.

The basic issues that might need consideration in this area are:

(a) Is the individual concerned carrying on a trade, or profession or vocation?

(b) If so, what taxable income do they have? (This must include notional payments, valuation of stock etc.)

(c) What deductions can be made against this income?

(d) How is tax payable assessed?

20.7.2 TRADE, PROFESSION OR VOCATION DEFINED

20.7.2.1 Trade: Case I: ICTA 1988, ss. 18, 53–55, 832, sch. 5

A trade is basically an exchange of goods or services for money with a view to making a profit. However, it may not be easy to distinguish trading from capital transactions, or from a hobby: see *Ransom* v *Higgs* [1974] 3 All ER 949, HL. Whether someone is trading is a matter of fact to be decided in an individual case. However, a decision will normally be based on the 'badges of trade' which were set down by a Royal Commission in 1954, and which are still relevant: *Marson* v *Morton* [1986] STC 563.

The 'badges of trade' are:

(a) Subject matter: If what is being dealt with is of a type or quantity which would not be needed for personal use, a trade is probably being carried on. For example, dealing with 1,000,000 toilet rolls is a trade: *Rutledge* v *IRC* (1929) 14 TC 490.

(b) Period of ownership: If something is held while it has personal use there is probably not a trade when it is disposed of. However, if it is held while it is commercially useful there may be a trade: see *IRC* v *Reinhold* (1953) 34 TC 389 and *Mitchell Bros* v *Tomlinson* (1957) 37 TC 224.

(c) Frequency of transactions: If something is done once or twice there is probably not a trade. If it is done frequently, there may well be a trade: see *Leach* v *Pogson* (1962) 40 TC 585.

(d) Supplementary work: There may well be a trade where supplementary work is carried out on quite a large scale to make something more saleable (*Cape Brandy Syndicate* v *IRC* [1921] 2 KB 403) or where an office is set up to deal with something: *Martin* v *Lowry* [1927] AC 312, HL.

(e) Reason for realisation: A personal reason for sale would probably exclude trading, while a commercial reason for sale would indicate a trade.

(f) Motive: Intentionally dealing in a commodity to make a profit is probably trading: *Wisdom* v *Chamberlain* [1969] 1 All ER 332. However, simply taking reasonable steps to enhance the value of an asset does not necessarily involve trading (*Taylor* v *Good* [1974] 1 All ER 1137) and simply making personal investments will not necessarily involve trading: *Simmons* v *IRC* [1980] 2 All ER 798, HL.

Note also the principle of mutuality. A group carrying out an activity solely for mutual benefit and not dealing with outsiders will not normally be held to be trading: see *Fletcher* v *IRC* [1972] AC 414.

An element of illegality will not prevent a finding that there is a trade, though total illegality might. For example, it has been held that a prostitute is liable to pay tax on her earnings: *IRC* v *Aken* [1988] STC 69.

20.7.2.2 Profession or vocation: Case II

A profession is defined as an occupation involving intellectual skill (see *IRC* v *Maxse* [1919] 1 KB 647), for example, working as a barrister. A vocation is a calling or a way of spending one's life, for example, being a jockey.

20.7.3 INCOME — PROFITS OR GAINS

All income derived from the carrying on of a trade, profession or vocation must be entered in annual accounts and is liable for tax: ICTA 1988, s. 18.

20.7.3.1 Money payments

A money payment will always be taxable if it relates to work done, even if it is described as something else, such as an 'interest relief grant': *Ryan* v *Crabtree Denims Ltd* [1987] STC 402. A payment will normally be taxed when it is paid or legally payable, unless it is returnable: *Elson* v *Price's Tailors Ltd* [1963] 1 All ER 231

A payment that is *ex gratia* rather than paid as of right may escape tax (*Murray* v *Goodhews* [1978] 2 All ER 40) and payments which are capital other than income will not be liable to income tax.

20.7.3.2 Compensation payments

Any compensation for the loss of income for trade or profession, or for the loss of ability to earn income will be taxed: see *McGowan* v *Brown and Cousins* [1977] 3 All ER 844. For example, an EC grant for restricting milk production is taxable: *White* v *G & M Davies* [1979] STC 415.

However, compensation will not be taxed if it relates to the capital structure of a business rather than to income (*Van den Berghs Ltd* v *Clark* [1935] AC 431, HL) or possibly if it substantially restricts the conduct of the business for a period: *Higgs* v *Olivier* [1952] Ch 311. A purely *ex gratia* payment will not be taxed: *Simpson* v *John Reynolds & Co. (Insurance) Ltd* [1975] 2 All ER 88.

20.7.3.3 Notional receipts

A notional receipt may need to be entered into the accounts, even if no money is actually paid, to avoid any improper benefit to the trader from dealing with trade assets for personal reasons. This is the equivalent of taxing fringe benefits for Schedule E. The rule is that if a trader deals with trading stock in a personal or non-commercial way, he or she should put into the trading accounts as theoretical income the market value for which he could have sold the item. If, for example, a grocer takes a tin of beans from his shop for a meal, he must enter the same figure as income as he would have done if he had sold the beans. The rule was established in the case of *Sharkey* v *Wernher* [1956] AC 58, HL, where five horses were taken from a stud farm business for private stable and it was held that the owner must enter in the accounts of the stud farm what she could have sold the horses for, not just the costs of breeding them.

This rule is open to objection in that it taxes a theoretical figure, and there may sometimes be problems in assessing market value, but the rule does balance the deductibility of the cost of acquiring the trading stock. The rule does not apply where there is a proper commercial transaction, albeit at an undervalue: *Jacguilden (Western Hall) Ltd* v *Castle* [1971] Ch 408. It seems that it also does not apply to a profession rather than a trade: *Mason* v *Innes* [1967] Ch 1079.

20.7.3.4 Trading stock or work in progress

This needs to be valued each year and included in accounts as an asset of the trade, following accepted accountancy practice: *Pearce* v *Woodall-Duckham Ltd* [1978] 2 All ER 793. An intangible such as 'know-how' can be part of trading stock: *Rolls Royce Ltd* v *Jeffrey* [1962] 1 All ER 801, HL.

20.7.4 EXPENSES — DEDUCTIONS

The fact that tax is charged on 'profits' implies that deductions can be made: ICTA 1988, ss. 18, 74–91. A list of things that cannot be deducted is provided by ICTA 1988, s. 74. Normal accountancy principles apply for deductions as well as for income. In practice anything that is thought to be deductible can be entered into the accounts, but it may then be challenged when the accounts are submitted to the Inland Revenue.

20.7.4.1 Income not capital

To be deductible a sum spent must be income not capital: ICTA 1988, s. 74(f), (g). For example, a sum paid to renegotiate a lease may be capital rather than income: *Tucker* v *Granada Motorway Services Ltd* [1979] 1 WLR 683, HL.

20.7.4.2 Purpose

To be deductible, money must be spent for the purposes of the trade, profession or vocation: ICTA 1988, s. 74(a), (e). A payment to get rid of an unsatisfactory employee may be deductible as that is for the benefit of the business: *Mitchell* v *B. W. Noble Ltd* [1927] 1 KB 719. However, it has been held that the cost for a farmer of going to Australia to see if he might move there was not deductible as it was not for his existing business: *Sargeant* v *Eayrs* [1973] 1 All ER 277. It is only possible to deduct actual expenditure, not anticipated expenditure: *RTZ Oil and Gas Ltd* v *Ellis* [1987] 1 WLR 1422. It may not be possible to deduct the cost of large-scale theft as this will not be part of the trade: *Bamford* v *ATA Advertising Ltd* [1972] 3 All ER 535.

20.7.4.3 Wholly and exclusively

The money must be spent wholly and exclusively for the trade, profession or vocation: ICTA 1988, s. 74(a), (b), (c). For example, it has been held that a female barrister could not deduct the cost of black clothing because her personal need for clothing was fatal to the claim: *Mallalieu* v *Drummond* [1983] 2 All ER 1095, HL. Similarly it has been held that a firm of solicitors could not deduct the cost of weekly lunches as they had to eat anyway (though they could deduct the cost of an annual conference): *Watkis* v *Ashford, Sparkes & Harward* [1985] 2 All ER 916. It is not normally possible to apportion a cost — a personal element will be fatal: see *Murgatroyd* v *Evans-Jackson* [1967] 1 WLR 423.

20.7.4.4 Types of payment

To employees Any payment made to or for the benefit of employees will normally be deductible as being an expense of running the business, even if the payment is indirect: *Heather* v *P. E. Consulting Group Ltd* [1973] Ch 189.

Travelling expenses Travelling costs incurred in the course of carrying out the trade or profession will normally be deductible. This might include the cost of travel from home if a business is carried on from the home: *Horton* v *Young* [1972] Ch 157. The cost of regular travel from home to work is not otherwise deductible: *Newsom* v *Robertson* [1953] Ch 7. Travel to a conference that includes taking a holiday will not be deductible (*Bowden* v *Russell and Russell* [1965] 2 All ER 258) unless any tourism involved is minimal: *Edwards* v *Warmsley, Henshall & Co.* [1968] 1 All ER 1089.

Renovation and repair The capital costs of renovation are not deductible (see *IRC* v *Scottish & Newcastle Breweries Ltd* [1982] 2 All ER 244) (although they may attract a capital allowance). However, repair costs will be deductible: ICTA 1988, s. 74(d). It is important to make this distinction between capital and income as both may be involved in a single case: *Law Shipping Co. Ltd* v *IRC* (1924) 12 TC 621.

Management expenses The expenses of managing a trade, running an office, advertising etc. are deductible: ICTA 1988, ss. 74(i)–(m), 577, 79. For example, the cost of a publicity campaign will be deductible: *Morgan* v *Tate & Lyle Ltd* [1955] AC 21.

Entertainment expenses Entertainment expenses, including gifts, are generally not deductible. For example, journalists cannot deduct the cost of providing drinks for informers: *Associated Newspapers Ltd* v *Fleming* [1973] AC 628, HL. However, there are a few statutory exceptions, such as provision for bona fide members of staff, provision of small items with conspicuous advertisements, and provision of something which it is the normal course of the trade to provide with the object of advertising to the public: ICTA 1988, s. 577; FA 1988, s. 72.

Pensions Provision for a pension will normally be tax deductible, up to maximum limits (ICTA 1988, ss. 618–629) and so long as a personal pension scheme complies with specified rules: ICTA 1988, ss. 630–655.

20.7.5 CAPITAL ALLOWANCES

Where a capital sum has been spent for a purpose within statutory categories, a capital allowance may be available to set against the income of a trade: Capital Allowances Act 2001 (CAA). Note that allowances are only available in limited categories, not for any capital expenditure. The Capital Allowances Act 2001 largely codified previous law.

20.7.5.1 General principles

Money spent must be capital not income to attract an allowance. If expenditure is of income the question is whether it is deductible. The allowance may take the form of a first-year allowance of part of the cost, and/or a writing down allowance over a period of years. If the item on which an allowance has been made is disposed of before the full allowance is made, a balancing charge or allowance may arise.

20.7.5.2 Types of allowance

Industrial buildings An allowance may be available for constructing an industrial building or structure within a limited definition: CAA 2001, ss. 21–38. There will be a writing down allowance of 1/25th of the original costs of the building every year. A building such as a football stand which is not within the specified categories will not attract an allowance: *Brown* v *Burnley Football Co. Ltd* [1980] 3 All ER 244.

Plant and machinery An allowance may be available for fixed or movable items which are purchased for long-term use in a trade: CAA 2001, ss. 11–14. There will be a writing down allowance of 25% of the expenditure each year on a decreasing balance basis. Assets of a trade will normally be pooled to calculate the allowance. There are special rules for short-life assets. The type of things which might attract an allowance of this kind are a library of books (*Munby* v *Furlong* [1977] 2 All ER 953); shop fittings (*Leeds Permanent Building Society* v *Proctor* [1982] 3 All ER 925); and new decorative concepts that are not purely maintenance: *IRC* v *Scottish & Newcastle Breweries Ltd* [1982] 3 All ER 322.

20.7.6 ASSESSMENT OF TAX

20.7.6.1 Preparing accounts

Accounts must be drawn up annually, including all income, deductions etc., and following accepted accountancy practice: ICTA 1988, ss. 60-63. Note that it is not necessary to use the tax year, just a period of 12 months. An inspector can assess tax on the basis of the income required to support the tax payer's standard of living if his or her accounts are inadequate: *Coy* v *Kime* [1987] STC 114. Actual rather than theoretical amounts must be put into accounts: *Willingale* v *International Commercial Bank Ltd* [1978] AC 834.

Earnings basis Under this basis a sum is entered into the accounts when it is legally earned: *Johnson* v *W. S. Try Ltd* [1946] 1 All ER 532; and is deducted when the legal liability to pay it out arises: *Southern Railway of Peru Ltd* v *Owen* [1957] AC 334, HL.

Cash basis Under this basis, sums are only put into the accounts when they are actually received or actually paid out. This basis is only allowed where it can be justified.

There can be change of basis so long as it is justified in accountancy practice. A change of basis should not result in any sum escaping taxation: ICTA 1988, ss. 104–106.

20.7.6.2 Assessment

Tax was formerly assessed on the preceding year's income: ICTA 1988, s. 60. That is, tax was assessed on the profit shown in the set of accounts drawn up in the course of the tax year preceding the tax year for which the assessment was made. However, from 1997–98 tax is charged on a current year basis, that is, on the profit shown by the set of accounts drawn up in the current tax year: FA 1994, ss. 200–218.

20.7.6.3 Commencement of business

It is a matter of fact when a business starts. Expenditure incurred within seven years before the start of a business can be deducted when the business starts, so long as it otherwise qualifies for deduction: ICTA 1988, s. 401.

20.7.6.4 Discontinuance of business

It is a matter of fact when a business ends. For example, a complete change of the nature of a business can be treated as a discontinuance: see *Ingram & Son Ltd* v *Callaghan* [1969] 1 WLR 456. There are special rules where there is a change of ownership of a trade: ICTA 1988, ss. 103, 104, 105, 108.

20.7.6.5 Basis of assessment

The current-year basis of assessment applies, that is, the business is taxed on the basis of the set of accounts drawn up during the tax year. Thus if the annual accounts are normally drawn up on 31 December, tax for the tax year 2002–2003 will be charged on the basis of the accounts drawn up on 31 December 2002.

This causes practical difficulties, as the accounts are not drawn up until near the end of the tax year, and may not in fact be finalised until the end of the tax year, or possibly later. To deal with this, two payments of tax on account for the tax year 2002–2003 will be required in January and July 2003, with any adjustment in the actual amount of tax due being made at the latest date for which the tax return for 2002–2003 can be returned, which is 31 January 2004. Normally the payment on account will be half of the amount of tax paid in the previous year.

Self-assessment of tax has now come into operation. For this a new-style tax form is used. It remains possible for taxpayers simply to complete this form and return it to the Inland Revenue to have their tax calculated for them. If they wish to take this option they must return the form by September in the relevant year. Any individual who wishes to calculate the tax due personally does not have to return the form until January of the following year.

All taxpayers are obliged to keep records relevant to their income and capital gains, and to keep them until at least 22 months after the end of the tax year to which they relate. Those who are self-employed will have to keep these records until five years after the last date on which the relevant tax return could be filed. Relevant records will include things like invoices, receipts and bank statements.

Prior to 1994–95, trades and professions were assessed on a preceding-year basis, meaning that their tax was assessed on the basis of the set of accounts that they drew up in the year preceding the year of assessment. Businesses that were assessed on that basis have now been brought within the new rules for the current-year basis of assessment (with transitional provisions). The preceding-year basis meant that it was not necessary to have payments of tax on account and there could in some cases be quite a long period between the time when money was earned and the time when tax was paid on it. However, it did mean that there had to be complex rules for commencing or ending a business.

20.7.7 RELIEF FOR LOSSES

Relief for any loss does not come about automatically, but must be claimed in writing under the appropriate statutory provison: ICTA 1988, ss. 380-392.

(a) Relief can be claimed against other income in the same tax year, or the following tax year: ICTA 1988, ss. 380, 382.

(b) Relief can be claimed against future profit of the same trade or profession: ICTA 1988, s. 385.

(c) Commencement losses: If a loss is sustained in the first three years of a trade or profession, it can be rolled backwards up to three years: ICTA 1988, s. 381.

(d) Terminal losses: A loss sustained in the final year of a trade or profession can be rolled backwards up to three years: ICTA 1988, ss. 388, 389.

20.7.8 PARTNERSHIPS

Basically trading partnerships are also subject to Schedule D, Case I, but there are some special rules: ICTA 1988, ss. 112–118.

Individuals carrying on business together with a view to making a profit form a partnership: Partnership Act 1890, s. 1. Whether a partnership exists is a question of fact.

Partnership profit is computed in one account, then divided between the partners according to their shares. To be deductible a sum must be spent for the benefit of the whole partnership: *Mackinlay* v *Arthur Young McLelland* [1990] 1 All ER 45, HL. Any loss is shared in the same way as a profit: *Reed* v *Young* [1986] 1 WLR 649, HL.

Any change of partners is treated as a discontinuance of trade unless all elect otherwise: ICTA 1988, s. 113.

There are other special rules, for example, payments to provide benefits for former partners are deductible: ICTA 1988, ss. 683, 628.

20.8 The Tax Position of a Company

20.8.1 INTRODUCTION

The barrister may need some knowledge of how corporation tax is charged whenever the client is incorporated. Such knowledge may also be relevant if a client has a major shareholding or other interest in a company. A company is liable to pay corporation tax on its profits rather than income tax or capital gains tax: ICTA 1988, ss. 208–255.

20.8.2 COMPANY DEFINED

Companies and unincorporated associations are liable for corporation tax: ICTA 1988, ss. 6, 832. It has been held that rugby clubs and Rotary clubs are unincorporated associations for this purpose (*Frampton* v *Worthing Rugby Football Club* [1987] STC 273) but not the Conservative Central Office (*Conservative and Unionist Central Office* v *Burrell* [1982] 1 WLR 522).

20.8.3 COMPUTATION OF PROFITS

20.8.3.1 Income
Income is calculated under Schedule D, Case I rules: ICTA 1988, ss. 9, 337, 208.

20.8.3.2 Chargeable gains
Gains are calculated under CGT principles: ICTA 1988, ss. 337–347.

20.8.3.3 Deductions

(a) Income expenses may be deducted under Schedule D, Case I rules.

(b) Capital allowances are available.

(c) Interest payments are only deductible if specifically allowed: ICTA 1988, s. 337

(d) Charges on income are deductible from profits after other reliefs: ICTA 1988, ss. 338, 339.

(e) Management expenses are usually deductible: ICTA 1988, s. 75.

(f) Payments to charity are deductible if made in a tax deductible way: ICTA 1988, s. 339.

20.8.3.4 Losses
A loss can be set against other income in the same year, set against profits of a later year, or set against profits of the previous three years. There are limits on transferring a loss: ICTA 1988, ss. 393–396, 768.

20.8.4 ASSESSMENT OF TAX

20.8.4.1 Accounting periods
Accounts should be drawn up for 12-month periods: ICTA 1988, s. 12. This does not need to be a tax year, but can be any regular 12-month period.

20.8.4.2 Tax years
The corporation tax year runs from 1 April to 31 March. If a company uses a different accounting period, its accounts will have to be apportioned: ICTA 1988, s. 12.

For example A plc has an accounting period of 1 July–30 June. In 2001–2002 it has a profit of £1,000,000, and in 2002–2003 a profit of £1,200,000. For the financial year 2002 the taxable profit is:

$$\frac{3}{12} \times £1{,}000{,}000 + \frac{9}{12} \times £1{,}200{,}000$$
$$= £250{,}000 + £900{,}000 = £1{,}150{,}000$$

20.8.4.3 Assessment of tax
Corporation tax is currently charged at 30%: ICTA 1988, ss. 8, 10. For small companies, with profits less than £300,000 at 20%: ICTA 1988, s. 13. There is marginal relief for profits up to £1,500,000.

20.8.5 THE DISTRIBUTION OF PROFITS

Up to 1999, a company making a dividend payment had to pay advance corporation tax on it at a rate equivalent to basic tax. This was to ease the collection of tax, and the amount paid could then be deducted from mainstream corporation tax. Although simple in principle, this system became over complex, and it has been abolished save to the extent that companies can continue to pay relief for advance corporation tax already paid.

The fact that advance corporation tax had been paid also provided a tax credit for the recipient of the distribution. Since 6 April 1999 this has been modified. To take into account the fact that corporation tax will have been paid on profits, dividends received by individuals are only taxed at a rate of 10% or 32.5% for a higher rate tax payer.

20.8.6 GROUPS AND CONSORTIA

Each company is taxed separately under normal rules, but some special rules apply to give benefits to the group by passing figures from one company to another. Group dividends: ICTA 1988, s. 247. Charges on income: ICTA 1988, s. 247. Surrender of ACT: ICTA 1988, s. 240. Group relief: ICTA 1988, ss. 402–413. Intra-group transfers. Demergers: ICTA 1988, ss. 213–218.

20.8.7 CLOSE COMPANIES

There are special rules for close companies, in addition to the above rules: ICTA 1988, ss. 414–430. A close company is one controlled by five or less participators or by its directors. Special rules include:

(a) Widened definition of distribution, so ACT payable on benefits.

(b) Loans to participators may be subject to ACT.

(c) Apportionment of income. Rules now abolished: FA 1989, ss. 103–107. Special rules for close investment holding companies: FA 1989, sch. 12.

(d) A close company may be liable to inheritance tax: ITA 1984, ss. 94–102.

20.9 The Tax Position Regarding Capital Assets

The tax considerations relevant to a case may depend on the type of asset that is at stake. It is impossible to deal comprehensively with every type of asset that might be at stake in limited space, but, in general terms, tax considerations are most likely to be relevant where a relatively valuable capital asset is at stake. This could include real property, personal property or intangible property such as a substantial shareholding.

The following sections cover the main principles of the two taxes that are most likely to be relevant regarding a capital asset: capital gains tax (**20.10**) and inheritance tax (**20.11**). There are also some outline comments on the taxation of real property in **20.12**.

The barrister is likely to need a knowledge of these taxes when a case relates to or may result in the transfer of a capital asset because the ownership of such an asset is in dispute, because someone has died, or because a divorce is taking place. Capital gains tax can also be relevant when a substantial sum of money changes hands, and it can therefore be relevant to an award of damages in any case.

20.10 Capital Gains Tax

20.10.1 INTRODUCTION

Capital gains tax is governed by the Taxation of Chargeable Gains Act 1992 (TCGA 1992) and all references are to that Act unless otherwise stated.

The basic issues for capital gains tax purposes are:

(a) Is a capital asset involved?

(b) Has that asset been disposed of?

(c) Can any exemption or relief be claimed? (Consider all possibilities.)

(d) If not, what is the gain accruing on the disposal?

(e) What can be deducted in assessing that gain?

Some quite fundamental changes to the tax are being introduced to encourage longer term investment and remove the complexity of the indexation system (FA 1998).

20.10.2 TAXABLE ASSETS

All forms of property are assets for the purposes of CGT, including incorporeal property: TCGA 1992, s. 20. Any property that is capable of being owned can be liable for CGT (*Kirby* v *Thorn EMI* [1988] 1 WLR 445), including contractual rights (*O'Brien* v *Benson's Hosiery (Holdings) Ltd* [1980] AC 562, HL).

20.10.3 EXEMPTIONS AND RELIEFS

It is important to be fully aware of the range of exemptions available for the benefit of the client.

(a) The first £7,500 of gains in year of assessment is not taxed: s. 3.

(b) Sterling is not liable to CGT, though other currencies are potentially liable: s. 20.

(c) Chattels disposed of for a consideration less than £6,000 are exempt from CGT: s. 262. There is marginal relief where consideration is just over £6,000.

(d) The main private residence of an individual is exempt: ss. 222–226.

A house can consist of more than one building (*Batey* v *Wakefield* [1982] 1 All ER 61). Part of a house can be exempt (*Green* v *IRC* [1982] STC 485). A caravan may be a dwelling house (*Makins* v *Elson* [1977] 1 All ER 572).

Note that a house is only totally exempt if it is the main private residence throughout ownership, or where periods are treated as being exempt. Periods at the beginning and end of ownership, and while the owner lives elsewhere due to employment may be treated as being exempt in certain circumstances.

Otherwise only a proportion of the gain is exempt, being:

$$\text{amount of gain} \times \frac{\text{period qualifying for exemption}}{\text{total period of ownership}}$$

e.g., house bought for £60,000 and sold for £80,000, gain is £20,000. If house was owned for five years but only exempt for three of them then £20,000 $\times \frac{3}{5}$ = £12,000 is exempt, £8,000 is taxable.

(e) Cars are exempt, but not goods vehicles: s. 263.

(f) Wasting assets are exempt, that is assets with a predictable life not exceeding 50 years: ss. 44–47.

(g) Gambling winnings, including lotteries and games with prizes are exempt: s. 51.

(h) Savings certificates are exempt; also government securities: ss. 120.

(i) Medals and awards are exempt, unless they were acquired for money or money's worth: s. 268.

(j) A debt disposed of by the original creditor is not liable to CGT, but a debt on a security may be: ss. 251–255. (This is to limit the possibilities for claiming a loss on a debt.) See *Marren* v *Inglis* [1980] 3 All ER 95 and *Aberdeen Construction Group Ltd* v *IRC* [1978] 1 All ER 962, HL.

(k) Insurance and assurance: s. 23. The rights of an insurer are not liable to CGT, but the rights of an insured person may be.

(l) Works of art: s. 258. Exemptions are available on a basis similar to inheritance tax, for which see **20.11.3.1**.

(m) Personal equity plans: FA 1986, s. 39, sch. 8. No CGT within certain limits so long as PEP complies with regulations.

20.10.4 DISPOSALS

Capital gains tax is payable on the disposal of an asset: s. 1. There is no comprehensive statutory definition of a disposal, but it is clear that a disposal occurs when there is a change of ownership, for example by sale, gift, exchange, as the result of a judgment, on making a settlement etc., for example, a taxpayer was held liable to pay CGT on a gift of shares to his children although he got nothing in return (*Turner* v *Follett* (1973) 48 TC 614).

The meaning of disposal is extended to include a part disposal, an indirect disposal etc. see s. 20. If an asset is disposed of for two separate payments there may be two separate disposals for CGT (*Marson* v *Marriage* [1980] STC 177). The destruction or loss of an asset can constitute a disposal: s. 22.

The deriving of capital from an asset is a disposal, including receiving compensation for loss or damage, or for surrender of rights, or the exploitation of the asset: ss. 22–24. This has implications for awards of damages.

Capital derived from a legal cause of action is potentially liable for CGT (*Anders Utkilens Rederi A/S* v *O/Y Lovisa Stevedoring Co. A/B* [1985] 2 All ER 669). This includes sums such as agreed compensation for breach of contract (*Delbourgo* v *Field* [1978] 2 All ER 193) and compensation for wrongfully expropriated property (*Davenport* v *Chilver* [1983] Ch 293). However, it seems that statutory compensation is not liable for CGT (*Davis* v *Powell* [1977] 1 WLR 258).

There are a number of special rules relating to shares, some designed to facilitate commercial transactions and others to prevent tax avoidance: ss. 104–151. Distributions: ss. 122–123. Reorganisations: ss. 126–131. Conversion of securities: ss. 132–134. Reconstructions and amalgamations: ss. 135–40.

20.10.4.1 Time of disposal

Liability to CGT arises at the time of the disposal.

(a) There is a disposal by gift when the gift is legally made.

(b) A sale or other contract is a disposal at the time the contract is made: s. 28, see *Pogson* v *Lowe* [1984] 1 WLR 182, HL, and *Lyon* v *Pettigrew* [1985] STC 369.

(c) A hire purchase or similar agreement is a disposal when use of the asset is given, not when the asset is finally paid for: s. 27.

(d) If capital is derived from an asset, there is a disposal when the capital is received: s. 22.

20.10.5 COMPUTATION OF GAIN OR LOSS

It is the *gain* which is taxable, not the total value of the asset. The gain is calculated by taking the value of the asset on disposal and deducting the value of the asset when it was acquired, and any other allowable deductions. CGT is only payable on the capital part of any payment of mixed capital and income (*Neely* v *Rourke* [1988] STC 49).

20.10.5.1 Value on acquisition and on disposal

If an asset is sold, the amount it is sold for will normally be taken.

If there is a gift, or any other disposal not at arm's length, market value will be taken: s. 17 (see *Harrison* v *Nairn Williamson Ltd* [1978] 1 All ER 608), unless a genuine commercial transaction is involved (*Stanton* v *Drayton Investment Co. Ltd* [1983] 1 AC 501, HL).

Statutory rules provide that anything liable to income tax should not be taken into account: ss. 37, 39, that contingent liabilities should not normally be taken into account: s. 49, and that payment by instalments should not normally be taken into account: s. 280, see *Randall* v *Plumb* [1975] 1 All ER 734.

If people are connected (s. 62), that is in general terms they are related or are partners (s. 63), market value will normally be taken for disposals between them: s. 18.

There are special rules for valuing shares, securities and options: ss. 104–125.

A series of transactions can be taxed together: s. 19.

If arrangements are made whereby the value of an asset is reduced and a benefit conferred on another, the value transferred can be taxed: s. 29.

20.10.5.2 Deductions

Deductions can only be made as allowed by statute: ss. 15, 38.

(a) The initial cost of the asset can be deducted.

(b) Incidental costs of acquisition such as legal and valuation fees can be deducted.

(c) The cost of improvements can be deducted, so long as a capital sum is spent wholly and exclusively to enhance the value of the asset when it is disposed of, so long as the cost is capital rather than income (*Emmerson* v *Computer Time International Ltd* [1977] 1 WLR 734).

(d) Costs of establishing or defending title can be deducted (including legal fees). (See *IRC* v *Chubb's Trustee* [1971] 1 WLR 571 and *Allison* v *Murray* [1975] 1 WLR 1578.)

(e) The costs of disposal, including professional fees, can be deducted.

(f) Certain things are not deductible, such as expenditure allowed for income tax: s. 37; interest payments: s. 40; sums already allowed: s. 52; and sums made good from other sources: s. 50. Only sums actually spent can be deducted (*Oram* v *Johnson* [1980] 2 All ER 1).

20.10.5.3 Part disposals

If the taxpayer only sells part of an asset, only part of the original cost will be deductible: ss. 21, 42. The formula to find what is deductible is:

$$\text{Cost of asset} \times \frac{\text{consideration for disposal}}{\text{consideration for disposal} + \text{market value of rest}}$$

e.g., A buys an asset for £40,000. Sells part of it for £15,000, the market value of the remainder at that time being £35,000. Costs of the sale of the part are £500.

$$£40{,}000 \times \frac{£15{,}000}{£15{,}000 + £35{,}000} = £40{,}000 \times \frac{15}{50} = £12{,}000$$

So from the £15,000 received A can deduct £12,000 and the £500 costs, so he has made a gain of £2,500.

If he later sells the rest of the asset for £50,000, he can then deduct the rest of the original cost. The cost of the whole was £40,000, and he has been allowed to deduct £12,000 on the part disposal so he can now deduct the remaining £28,000. Thus he has made a gain now of £50,000 − £28,000 = £22,000.

20.10.5.4 Taper relief and indexation

For a chargeable asset disposed of on or after 6 April 1998, the chargeable gain may be reduced by taper relief. The rules apply to charge to tax a reduced percentage of the gain accruing depending on the length of time the asset has been owned, and whether the asset is a business asset. The length of ownership or 'qualifying holding period' is the number of whole years for which the asset has been held since 5 April 1998, and maximum relief is reached after ownership of four years for a business asset or ten years for any other asset. From 6 April 2000 taper relief operates as follows:

Gains on disposals of business assets		*Gains on disposals of non-business assets*	
Number of whole years in qualifying holding period	*Percentage of gain chargeable*	*Number of whole years in qualifying holding period*	*Percentage of gain chargeable*
1	87.5	—	—
2	75	—	—
3	50	3	95
4 or more	25	4	90
		5	85
		6	80
		7	75
		8	70
		9	65
		10 or more	60

A business asset includes:

(a) An asset used for the purposes of a trade carried on by an individual, in partnership, or by a qualifying company.

(b) An asset used for the purposes of an office or employment to which an individual is required to devote substantially the whole of his time.

(c) Shares or securities held by an individual in a qualifying company.

A company will be a qualifying company if it is unlisted, if the taxpayer is an officer or employee of the company, or if the taxpayer holds shares entitling him to not less than 5% of the voting rights.

Where an asset was held on 5 April 1998 there may also be indexation relief, which must be calculated before taper relief. The purpose of indexation relief is to try to ensure that a rise in value due to inflation is not taxed. The relief is related to the Retail Price Index, and the total allowable expenditure is multiplied by the indexed rise to give the actual figure deductible. Over time indexation relief will be replaced by taper relief.

20.10.5.5 Rebasing to 1982

CGT was payable on the gain accruing since 1965, but once indexation was introduced this involved complex calculations, so for any disposal made after 1 April 1988, only the gain since 31 March 1982 is taxed: ss. 35–36, schs 3 and 4. These rules may not apply if they will increase a gain or loss, so former rules may still apply in limited cases. (For assets held on 6 April 1965, see sch. 2.)

20.10.5.6 Losses

If deductions exceed value on disposal, there is a loss. Losses in a year are set primarily against gains for the same year. Any unrelieved loss can be rolled forward to future years: ss. 2, 16. Relief for a loss must be claimed (see *Williams* v *Bullivant* [1983] STC 107 and *Larner* v *Warrington* [1985] STC 442).

20.10.6 ASSESSMENT OF TAX

Capital gains tax is assessed on the total gains accruing to an individual in a year of assessment, less allowable losses, less annual allowance: ss. 1–4. The tax year is the same as for income tax. Payment by instalments: s. 280.

Tax is charged at the individual's marginal rate of income tax: 10%, 22% or 40%.

Individuals resident in the UK are chargeable: ss. 2, 9–14. Husband and wife are separately assessed. Disposals between spouses are treated as being at no gain or loss: s. 58.

A gain is not chargeable if it accrues to a charity and is used for charitable purposes: ss. 256–257; see *IRC* v *Helen Slater Charitable Trust* [1982] Ch 49. Companies do not pay CGT, but their gains are subject to corporation tax: ICTA 1988, s. 6.

20.10.7 BUSINESSES

It is important to be aware of these special provisions when advising a business client.

(a) Roll over relief is available on the replacement of business assets: ss. 152–160.

(b) Relief is available on the disposal of a business or an interest in a business by a person over 50, or who retires due to ill health: ss. 163–164. The relief is subject to strict conditions. Full relief on £250,000, plus 50% relief on £250,000 to £1,000,000 is available where the business has been owned for ten years, with proportionate relief for a shorter ownership period. This relief is being phased out from 6 April 1999 (FA 1998), and it will cease to be available from 2003–2004.

(c) A disposal of business assets can attract hold over relief: s. 165.

(d) CGT can be avoided on transfer of business to company: s. 162.

20.10.8 TAX AVOIDANCE SCHEMES

Although tax avoidance schemes are prima facie legal if all the steps in them are legal, a pre-arranged scheme that is a pure sham with no genuine commercial effect may be ineffective. This principle has been evolved in CGT cases, but applies to all taxes.

Duke of Westminster v *IRC* [1936] AC 1: So long as legal, entitled to arrange affairs to pay less tax.
Floor v *Davis* [1980] AC 695, HL: Scheme to avoid tax through company set up for that purpose. Held involved indirect disposition so tax.
See also *Eilbeck* v *Rawling* [1982] AC 300, HL and *Chinn* v *Collins* [1981] AC 533, HL.
W. T. Ramsay Ltd v *IRC* [1982] AC 300, HL: Scheme to manufacture loss to set against gain. Failed as prearranged sham with no real effect.
See also *Furniss* v *Dawson* [1984] AC 474, HL.
Craven v *White* [1989] AC 398, HL: Scheme to defer tax on sale of business. Held effective as all steps not preordained from the start.
Customs & Excise Commissioners v *Faith Construction Ltd* [1989] QB 179: Similar principles apply to other taxes, e.g., VAT.

20.11 Inheritance Tax

20.11.1 INTRODUCTION

The main statute is the Inheritance Tax Act 1984, and references are to that Act unless otherwise stated.

20.11.1.1 Principle of cumulation

Liability for inheritance tax depends on the cumulative total of the chargeable transfers made by a transferor over a seven-year period. Tax liability on any particular transfer involves taking into account all transfers made in the preceding seven years. The current rates of tax are:

Cumulative total	Lifetime tax rate	Death tax rate
£ 0 — 242,000	Nil	Nil
£ 242,000 and over	20%	40%

(Transfers made within three years of death are charged at the death rate.)

20.11.1.2 Grossing up

As tax is charged on the loss to the transferor's estate resulting from the chargeable transfer, if the transferor pays the tax, this will increase the loss to his estate and must be taken into account. This is done by grossing up, to find the sum that after the deduction of the appropriate rate of tax leaves the net value transferred. (Tax is paid on the grossed up value, and the grossed up value must be added to the transferor's cumulative total.)

Statute does not provide a specific method of grossing up, so a variety of methods are used. The Inland Revenue use grossing up tables. One method is grossing up using fractions. If tax due is 20% of total, value actually transferred is 80% of total, so fraction to find tax due is:

$$\text{value actually transferred} \times \frac{20}{80}$$

If Anne has made no previous chargeable transfers and now transfers £250,000 to Brian (net of any reliefs or allowances and assuming it is not a potentially exempt transfer (PET)), there will be no tax on the first £242,000 and tax on the remaining £8,000 will be:

$$\text{£}8{,}000 \times \frac{20}{80} = \text{£}2{,}000$$

The grossed up value of the gift is £250,000 + £2,000 = £252,000. The tax due is £2,000.

There is no need to gross up if the donee pays the tax. If Brian agreed to pay the tax, tax due would be:

$$\text{£}8{,}000 \times 20\% = \text{£}1{,}600$$

20.11.2 TAXABLE ASSETS

Tax is charged on a transfer of value from the estate of an individual: ITA 1984, ss. 1–3. The 'estate' is the aggregate of all property to which the individual is beneficially entitled: ss. 5, 272. Excluded property is not taken into account: ss. 3, 6, 48, 155.

20.11.3 EXEMPT ASSETS AND OTHER RELIEFS

It is important to be fully conversant with the range of exemptions and reliefs to advise a client well.

20.11.3.1 Exemptions

(a) Transfers not exceeding £3,000 in a year are exempt: s. 19.

(b) Transfers between spouses are exempt: s. 18.

(c) Small gifts up to a value of £250 to each individual in a year are exempt: s. 20.

(d) Normal expenditure out of income is exempt: s. 21, so long as;

   (i) it is part of normal expenditure (i.e., is regular),

   (ii) it is from income,

   (iii) it leaves enough income to maintain the normal standard of living of the transferor.

(e) Gifts in consideration of marriage are exempt: s. 22, subject to limits of £5,000 for parents, £2,500 for grandparents or parties to the marriage, and £1,000 for others.

(f) Gifts to charities are exempt: s. 23.

(g) Gifts to qualifying political parties are exempt: s. 24.

(h) Gifts for national purposes are exempt, that is gifts to specified bodies such as the British Museum: s. 25, sch. 3.

(i) Gifts for public benefit are exempt: s. 26. To qualify, the gift must go to a non-profit making body and approval from the tax authorities must be given. Undertakings may be required before approval is given. This exemption is limited to specific categories, such as land, buildings, art collections etc., that are of special interest.

(j) Conditionally exempt transfers: ss. 30–35, sch. 5. Exemption under this head again requires approval, which may be subject to undertakings. It is limited to categories similar to (i) above. This exemption applies only on death or where property has been owned for at least six years, and it is intended to help to preserve assets within a family. Exemption is only conditional, and a charge may arise if the property is disposed of, the person getting it dies, or an undertaking is broken.

20.11.3.2 Potentially exempt transfers

Any gift made during life by one individual to another which is not otherwise exempt will be potentially exempt, and will only be charged if the donor dies within seven years: FA 1986, s. 101, sch. 19. The use of PETs is very important in passing capital assets to relatives while the donor is still likely to live for seven years.

20.11.3.3 Transfers which are not transfers of value

(a) There is no transfer of value, and thus no tax, if there is no intention to confer a gratuitous benefit, and either the transaction is at arm's length between unconnected people, or is such as might be expected at arm's length if it is between connected people: ss. 10, 270. This has very wide practical application. It means for example that there is no inheritance tax on the payment of fines and similar obligations.

(b) There is no transfer of value where there is a disposition for the maintenance of the family: s. 11. The disposition can be to a spouse or a child under 18 or still undergoing education, and can include maintenance on divorce.

(c) Other possibilities: see ss. 12–17.

20.11.3.4 Other types of relief

(a) Business property relief may be available on relevant property, including a business, an interest in a business, assets of a business and shares in a business: ss. 103–104, 113A and B. There are qualifications for relief relating to length of ownership etc.

(b) Agricultural property relief may be available on relevant property, which includes agricultural land and shares giving control of a company which owns agricultural property: ss. 115–124, 124A and B. Again there are qualifications relating to length of ownership etc.

(c) Woodlands: There may be relief on the value of growing timber which forms part of the estate on death: ss. 125–130. There are qualifications for relief, and tax may be charged on a later disposal of the timber.

20.11.4 TRANSFERS

Tax is payable when a transfer is made from an estate. The tax arises on each individual transfer. There is no tax year for inheritance tax.

20.11.4.1 Meaning of transfer

A transfer involves a disposition, but is not otherwise defined: ITA 1984, ss. 1–3. This presumably means that any change of ownership can be a transfer, including a sale, a gift etc. Note that this means that both inheritance tax and capital gains tax may be payable on the same transaction.

Various statutory provisions relate to the meaning of a transfer:

(a) An omission to act can amount to a transfer: s. 3.

(b) Associated operations can be treated as one transfer, to discourage tax avoidance: s. 268.

(c) Voidable transfers will not be taxed once it is shown they have been set aside: s. 150.

(d) Loans of property or money do not necessarily involve a transfer, but may do if e.g., a loan is written off: s. 29.

(e) Future payments, if due more than one year after the original transfer, may be separately liable to tax: s. 262.

(f) Back to back policies of annuity and life assurance may involve a transfer: s. 263.

(g) Close companies may be liable for making transfers: ss. 94–97.

20.11.4.2 Gifts with a reservation

If any interest is reserved, and a donee does not get bona fide possession of a gift, or a donor is not entirely excluded, the property will still be treated as part of the estate of the donor: FA 1986, s. 102, sch. 20. This is to discourage tax avoidance schemes. There are limited exceptions, where for example there is an unforeseen change in circumstances.

The rule may be avoided, e.g., by creating separate legal interests (*St Aubyn* v *Attorney-General (No. 2)* [1952] AC 15). See also *Munro* v *Commissioner of Stamp Duty* [1958] AC 435; *Chick* v *Commissioner of Stamp Duty* [1934] AC 61.

20.11.4.3 Value on transfer

Tax is paid on the loss to the estate of the transferor: ss. 1–3. This will not necessarily be the same as the value of the asset transferred. Note that a sale for full value will not result in a loss.

There are some valuation rules:

(a) The market value will normally be taken in valuing property: s. 160.

(b) Related property, that is all property owned by an individual or by spouses, can be valued together if that gives a higher value: s. 161.

(c) Liabilities can be taken into account: ss. 162, 5.

(d) Restrictions on sale can be taken into account if they are for value: s. 163.

(e) Incidental expenses will be left out of account if paid by the donor (or they would increase the loss to the estate): s. 164. They will be taken to reduce the value transferred if paid by the donee.

(f) Liability to taxes other than inheritance tax will be ignored: ss. 165, 5. However, if any CGT is payable and is paid by the donee, that will reduce the value transferred.

(g) Debts will be assumed to be paid: s. 166.

(h) There are rules for valuing particular assets, such as shares: ss. 167–170.

20.11.5 ADMINISTRATION AND COLLECTION

There is no annual tax return, but a duty to report each chargeable transfer. For details see:

(a) Accounts and information: ss. 215–220.

(b) Assessment and appeals: ss. 221–225.

(c) Payment: ss. 226–232. Payment can be by instalments in limited circumstances: ss. 227–229. Property may be accepted in lieu of tax in limited circumstances: ss. 230–232.

(d) Interest: ss. 233–236.

(e) The Inland Revenue charge: ss. 237, 238. This may attach to property on which tax is due, or property which replaces such property, until the tax is paid or the property passes to a bona fide purchaser, or six years have elapsed from the date the tax was due.

It is always the transferor who is primarily liable to pay tax, unless it has been agreed that the transferee will pay it: ITA 1984, ss. 199–210. However, others may pay the tax by agreement or if there is an Inland Revenue charge, see *IRC* v *Stannard* [1984] 1 WLR 1039 and *Re Clore (No. 3)* [1985] 1 WLR 1290.

20.11.6 TRANSFERS DURING LIFE

It is not always easy for those studying the tax to see how the above rules fit together. The following stages are recommended:

(a) Identify whether a transfer has been made, and if so by whom.

(b) Calculate the loss to the estate of the transferor.

(c) Check whether any exemption or relief may be available. Look for all possibilities, and if there is more than one, decide which is most beneficial.

(d) If the transfer is not exempt, it may be potentially exempt if it consists of a lifetime gift between individuals.

(e) Only if the transfer is actually chargeable, look at the cumulative total of the donor. If the total over seven years exceeds £242,000, tax is payable at 20%.

20.12 Taxation of Real Property

20.12.1 CAPITAL TAXATION

The normal principles for capital gains tax and inheritance tax already outlined will apply. For many individuals, the land that they own will be their main private residence, which will be exempt from capital gains tax during the owner's life. The home will, however, form part of its owner's estate on death, and planning may be needed (for example, when a client buys a house or makes a will) to avoid or reduce a possible charge to inheritance tax. If real property that is not a main private residence may be transferred as part of a divorce settlement, the possible tax implications will need to be considered.

If an individual or a company has a more extensive holding in real property, special rules relating to businesses and/or agricultural property may apply. This may require specialist tax advice.

20.12.2 INCOME FROM LAND

Income from land is taxed under Schedule A: ICTA 1988, ss. 15, 21–24. A knowledge of this area may obviously be useful to the barrister in a landlord and tenant case, or any other case involving land.

20.12.2.1 Definition of income from land: ICTA 1988, s. 15

Any rent or other income from land is taxable under this schedule, including income from leases, rent charges, and payments arising from ownership of land: s. 15. For some exceptions, see **20.12.2.5** below.

Examples of income taxable under Schedule A include money from a right to cut turves (*Lowe* v *J.W. Ashmore Ltd* [1971] Ch 545) and from holiday lettings (*Jefferies* v *Stevens* [1982] STC 639). Capital payments are not taxable under Schedule A.

20.12.2.2 Taxable profits or gains

All income to which the owner is entitled in the tax period is chargeable. There may be some relief if rent is not actually paid: ICTA 1988, s. 41.

Deductions are available for the costs of maintenance, repair, rates etc.: see ICTA 1988, ss. 25–33, sch. 1.

20.12.2.3 Basis of assessment

Tax is charged on the basis of income due. It is charged on a current year basis, so assessments are made on the basis of rent received in the previous year, adjusted later if necessary: ICTA 1988, ss. 21–24.

Tax can be collected from an agent or tenant if it is not paid.

20.12.2.4 Taxation of premiums

Tax on rental income could be decreased by charging a lump sum and charging a low rent, or some similar arrangement. To discourage this, payments made in connection with the grant of a lease, including the value of improvements and the like, can be liable to income tax as 'premiums': ICTA 1988, ss. 34–39, sch. 2.

20.12.2.5 Alternative charges for income from land

As always, it will be an argument of fact which schedule is appropriate.

(a) Schedule D, Case I: Income from any trade involving land can be taxed under this Case, including farming, mining etc. This may be preferable as tax is on a preceding year basis and more deductions may be available.

(b) Schedule D, Case VI: This can apply to furnished lettings for holidays or for students (*Gittos* v *Barclay* [1982] STC 390; *Griffiths* v *Jackson* [1983] STC 184).

20.13 Tax in Particular Types of Case: Loss of Employment

Some types of payment may arise naturally from a loss of employment without any need for legal action to be taken. These will be taxable in the following ways:

20.13.1 PENSIONS

Any pension received will generally be liable to income tax in the same way as other income under Schedule E.

Special tax treatment is offered for approved schemes run by employers, including tax relief for contributions: ICTA 1988, ss. 131, 188–191, 590–659. A personal pension plan can be taken out instead of or in addition to an employers' scheme, also attracting tax relief for contributions: ICTA 1988, ss. 630–659; FA 1988, ss. 54–57

20.13.2 GOLDEN HANDSHAKES

Any payment provided for by a contract of employment will be fully taxable under normal rules: ICTA 1988, s. 131. Thus if a contract specifically provides that £10,000 will be payable if the employee loses his job, this sum will be fully taxable (*Dale* v *De Soissons* [1950] 2 All ER 460). Payments made in connection with varying the terms of employment will also be fully taxed (*McGregor* v *Randall* [1984] 1 All ER 1092), but not a payment made for giving up rights (*Mairs* v *Haughey* [1994] 1 AC 303).

Any payment which is made directly or indirectly in connection with the termination of an office or employment but which is not otherwise taxable will be taxed by statute. However, the first £30,000 of the payment is tax-free: ICTA 1988, ss. 148, 188, sch. 11; FA 1988, s. 74. On this see *Shilton* v *Wilmshurst* [1991] 1 AC 684. It is thus advantageous to agree a payment on leaving a job rather than to provide for it in advance in a contract. The position has, however, been called into question by *EMI* v *Caldicott*, *The Times*, 14 November 1997.

20.13.3 PAYMENTS RELATING TO RESTRICTIVE COVENANTS

A payment made in relation to a restrictive covenant will be taxable by statute, whether or not it is provided for in the original contract of employment: ICTA 1988, s. 313.

20.13.4 DAMAGES OR COMPENSATION FOR LOSS OF OFFICE

If a payment of damages for loss of office is sought, the situation is more complex, in the light of *British Transport Commission* v *Gourley* [1956] AC 185. The relevant principles are:

(a) A claimant should not be overcompensated. Lost earnings and benefits would have been liable to tax, so it is only for the loss net of tax that the claimant should be compensated.

(b) Damages for loss of earnings are not taxed on the same basis as the original earnings would have been taxed. The original earnings would have been taxed in separate tax years with appropriate personal allowances etc. each year. Damages will be taxed as a single lump sum in a single tax year, but the first £30,000 will be tax-free.

(c) General principles for damages such as reductions for mitigation and for accelerated receipt will apply.

These principles mean that a calculation of damages for loss of employment has to be carried out in the following stages:

(a) The gross loss for all heads of damage (including wages, bonuses, commission, fringe benefits etc.) should be established.

(b) The actual net loss after tax should then be calculated (this needs to be done reasonably accurately and may well require the assistance of an accountant).

(c) The net loss must then be grossed up to find the figure that, after deduction of the tax payable by the claimant on the damages, leaves the net loss. (This needs to take into account that £30,000 will be tax-free, and also that above that figure the damages will be taxable. Again the assistance of an accountant may well be required.)

This process should of course be outlined to the client so that the client does not get confused between the gross and net figures, and so that the client does understand that the damages will be taxable on receipt. A relatively simple example of how this approach works can be seen in *Shove* v *Downs Surgical plc* [1984] 1 All ER 7.

The above approach applies where the damages exceed the £30,000 that is free of tax (*Bold* v *Brough, Nicholson and Hall Ltd* [1964] 1 WLR 201). If all the damages fall within the £30,000 tax-free figure, only the net loss will be awarded (*Parsons* v *BNM Laboratories Ltd* [1964] 1 QB 95). The full resources of the plaintiff will not necessarily be taken into account in making calculations (*Beach* v *Reed Corrugated Cases Ltd* [1956] 1 WLR 807). On taking deductions into account see *Lyndale Fashion Manufacturers* v *Rich* [1973] 1 WLR 73, and on the relevance of tax rebates see *Hartley* v *Sandholme Iron Co. Ltd* [1975] QB 600.

These rules can be illustrated in the following example:

Yolanda Smart is bringing an action for breach of contract against her employers, Videopro plc. Two years ago she entered into an agreement to work for them for five years as a computer programmer, but she has recently received a letter informing her that the company 'has reviewed its staffing requirements and is giving her the freedom to explore her potential in a wider market'. Her contract provided that she was to earn £40,000 a year for the first three years, then £60,000 a year. She had fringe benefits of a company car and private health insurance.

Her gross loss would be her salary for the last three years of her contract plus the value of her fringe benefits for that period, a figure in excess of £160,000.

From this gross loss, tax and national insurance contributions that she would have paid for the three-year period will need to be deducted to calculate her net loss, which might therefore be somewhere in the region of £100,000. Appropriate reductions for mitigation and accelerated receipt would also have to be made.

If her net loss were £100,000, the first £30,000 would be tax-free, but the remaining £70,000 would be liable to tax. Tax on this figure could be around £30,000 (if it is taxed at top rate as she has no unused allowances). She would therefore need to be awarded about £130,000 to cover her net loss.

Strictly speaking these rules only apply in full to an award of damages made by a court, but in practice they would need to be kept in mind in negotiating a settlement. Damages received as a result of a negotiated settlement would be liable to tax.

20.14 Tax in Particular Types of Case: Damages and Compensation

20.14.1 INTRODUCTION

Although this area is important for the barrister, it is very difficult to provide a very simple guide. This is because the Inland Revenue, the courts and individual lawyers have different roles to fulfil and their individual approaches to a case do not easily fit into an overall pattern. Also the case law is not very full or coherent. In some cases relevant tax points have either not been raised or have not been fully argued or understood.

In the past it has been thought that tax law was not really the province of lawyers and could just be ignored when assessing damages. In the modern world such an approach is not realistic and does not provide a full and practical service for a client. Even in relatively straightforward contract and tort cases tax can be relevant to the assessment of damages, and it might be professionally negligent to fail to take this into account. If the position is simply that damages will or may be taxable when the client receives them, the client should be advised of this so that he or she can consult an accountant or tax adviser.

20.14.2 APPROACH OF THE INLAND REVENUE

When a claimant receives damages, the Inland Revenue will subject the amount received to tax whenever the damages fall within the normal principles of income tax or capital tax. There is no general principle that damages are exempt from tax. The fact that damages will be subject to tax on receipt will not normally be relevant to assessing damages and presenting a case in court (subject to the principles outlined below), but it may be important to advise the client of the potential tax liability to avoid any misunderstanding about the ultimate outcome of the case.

20.14.2.1 Income tax

Essentially any figure for damages or agreed compenstion that represents lost income which would have been taxable will itself be subject to tax. For example, damages for lost trading income will be liable for tax under Schedule D Case I (see *Donald Fisher (Ealing) Ltd* v *Spencer* [1989] STC 256; *Thompson* v *Magnesium Elektron Ltd* [1944] 1 All ER 126; *Creed* v *H. & M. Levinson Ltd* [1981] STC 486).

In general terms, damages for lost employment income will be subject to tax under Schedule E. Damages or compensation directly arising from the terms of the contract of employment will be taxable in full (*Dale* v *De Soissons* [1950] 2 All ER 460). Any sum agreed as compensation for the loss of any rights under a contract of employment is also liable for income tax (*Holland* v *Geoghegan* [1972] 1 WLR 1473). Compensation for loss of office is taxable, though the first £30,000 will generally escape tax: ICTA 1988, ss. 148, 188 and sch. 11. Note, however, that damages for the surrender of personal rights may escape tax, and statutory redundancy payments are not taxable.

The same principle applies to other types of lost income, so that damages for loss of rent or other income from land will be taxable under Schedule A or Schedule D Case VI. Damages for loss of interest are taxable under Schedule D Case III (*Riches* v *Westminster Bank Ltd* [1947] AC 390). Interest on damages may also be taxable under Schedule D Case III, except interest on damages for personal injury: ICTA 1988, s. 329.

Damages or compensation will not be liable for income tax if the payment is ex gratia rather than arising directly from a legal right (*Simpson* v *John Reynolds & Co. (Insurance) Ltd* [1975] 1 WLR 617). Nor will the figure be liable to income tax if it is capital (though it may of course be liable for capital tax which may be better or worse for the client!) (see *Higgs* v *Olivier* [1952] Ch 311; *Van den Berghs Ltd* v *Clark* [1935] AC 431).

20.14.2.2 Capital tax

Damages will only be liable to inheritance tax where the damages form part of the estate of someone who has died. This could happen where, for example, damages for loss (though not for pain and suffering) suffered by the deceased prior to death are claimed in a fatal accident case.

The possibility of damages attracting capital gains tax is much wider. As a general principle the receipt of damages or compensation for damages to a capital asset is potentially liable to capital gains tax: TCGA 1992, ss. 21–24. It has been held specifically that any damages or compensation from a legal right of action are potentially liable to capital gains tax (*Zim Properties Ltd* v *Proctor* (1984) 58 TC 371 (where a contract for the sale of property was repudiated and it was held that the £69,000 for which the action was compromised was potentially liable to CGT); see also *O'Brien* v *Benson's Hosiery (Holdings) Ltd* [1980] AC 562).

Having said this, the basis upon which CGT may be payable in different types of case is still not entirely clear, and it is important for practitioners to be generally familiar with Extra-statutory Concession D33 which is reproduced below. This suggests in general terms that the tax position will depend upon the 'underlying asset' in the case.

The way in which the taxable gain will be calculated is also not beyond dispute. The *Zim* case left this point open, and the problem is illustrated by *Pennine Raceway Ltd* v *Kirklees Council* [1989] STC 122, were the court felt that a damages figure might be liable for capital gains tax, but felt unable to say in any detail how that tax might be assessed. A variety of arguments may be available for avoiding or reducing CGT liability:

- Compensation for loss of office or employment is not liable for CGT: TCGA 1992, s. 52.
- Damages for personal injury are not liable to tax: TCGA 1992, s. 51.
- Sums obtained as compensation or damages for any wrong or injury suffered by an individual in his profession or vocation are not liable to tax: TCGA 1992, s. 51.
- If damages or compensation are used to repair or replace the capital asset damaged or lost, CGT liability can be avoided: TCGA 1992, ss. 23 and 24.
- The costs of a legal action may be deductible.

20.14.3 EXTRA-STATUTORY CONCESSION D33: CAPITAL GAINS TAX ON COMPENSATION AND DAMAGES

Introduction

1. A person who receives a capital sum derived from an asset is treated for the purposes of capital gains tax as disposing of that asset. The case of *Zim Properties Ltd* v *Proctor* (1984) 58 TC 371 has established that the right to take court action for compensation or damages is an asset for capital gains tax purposes. It follows that a person who receives compensation or damages, whether by court order or arbitration or by negotiated settlement as a result of a cause of action may be regarded as disposing of the right of action. A capital gain may accrue as a result.

The strict position

Cost of acquisition

2. A capital gain will accrue if the capital sum received as compensation exceeds the amount which may be deducted as the cost of acquiring the right of action. A right of action will almost invariably be acquired otherwise than by way of bargain made at arm's length. Special rules for determining the cost of acquisition apply in these circumstances. Where the right of action was acquired on or before 9 March 1981, it is deemed to have been acquired for a sum equal to its market value on the date of acquisition. Where it was acquired on or after 10 March 1981 and there was no disposal of the right of action corresponding to the claimant's acquisition of it, then where — as is usually the case — the taxpayer gave no consideration to acquire it, it is treated as having been acquired without cost.

If the cause of action was held on 31 March 1982 and disposed of on or after 6 April 1988, it will, in accordance with the rebasing rules, be deemed to have been disposed of and immediately reacquired at its open market value on 31 March 1982.

If a right of action passes on the death of the claimant, it is treated as acquired at its open market value on the date of death.

In computing the gain or loss, a deduction may be made for any legal and professional fees incurred in pursuing the claim. If the action in respect of a claim of substance fails, or if the expenses exceed the compensation, a capital loss may accrue.

Date of acquisition
3. A right of action accrues and so is acquired by a person for capital gains tax purposes when, for example, as a result of a breach of contract or the negligent actions of another person (tort) he or she suffers actual loss or damage.

Market value on acquisition
4. In practice, where relevant, the Board of Inland Revenue will be prepared to accept a valuation which gives rise to neither chargeable gain nor allowable loss.

Date of disposal
5. The right of action is treated as disposed of when a capital sum derived from it is received, and if a series of capital sums is received, each receipt is the occasion of a separate disposal.

Rebasing to 31 March 1982
6. If an asset which was held on 31 March 1982 is disposed of on or after 6 April 1988, the gain or loss is normally computed as if it had been disposed of and immediately reacquired at its open market value on 31 March 1982. If an underlying asset were held on 31 March 1982, but a right of action related to that asset were acquired after 31 March 1982, the rebasing provisions would apply on the disposal of the underlying asset but not on the disposal of the right of action.

Reliefs and exemptions
7. Some forms of compensation are specifically exempted from liability to capital gains tax (see paragraph 12 below) and these remain exempt despite the decision in *Zim Properties*. But other statutory reliefs and exemptions are not available where the receipt of the compensation is regarded as giving rise to a disposal of the right of action, not of any underlying asset to which the relief or exemption might apply. These include deferment relief for compensation applied in restoring or replacing an asset, roll-over relief for the replacement of business assets, retirement relief and private residence relief.

Relief concession
8. Where a gain arises on the disposal of a right of action, the case may alternatively, by concession, be treated in accordance with the following paragraphs of this statement.

Underlying assets
9. Where the right of action arises by reason of the total or partial loss or destruction of or damage to a form of property which is an asset for capital gains tax purposes, or because the claimant suffered some loss or disadvantage in connection with such a form of property, any gain or loss on the disposal of the right of action may by concession be computed as if the compensation derived from that asset, and not from the right of action. As a result a proportion of the cost of the asset, determined in accordance with normal part-disposal rules, and indexation allowance, may be deducted in computing the gain. For example, if compensation is paid by an estate agent because his negligence led to the sale of a building falling through, an appropriate part of the cost of the building may be deducted in computing any gain on the disposal of the right of action.

The gain may be computed by reference to the original cost of the underlying asset, with time-apportionment if appropriate if the asset was acquired before 6 April 1965, or by reference to its market value at 6 April 1965. For disposals on or after 6 April 1988, the gain may be computed in appropriate cases by reference to the value of the asset on 31 March 1982.

Other reliefs and exemptions

10. If the relief was or would have been available on the disposal of the relevant underlying asset, it will be available on the disposal of the right of action. For example, if compensation is derived from a cause of action in respect of damage to a building suffered by reason of professional negligence, and the compensation is applied in restoring the building, deferment relief under s. 23, TCGA 1992 will be available as if the compensation derives from the building itself and not from the right of action.

Other reliefs which may become available in this way include private residence relief, retirement relief and roll-over relief. The Board of Inland Revenue will be prepared to consider extending time limits in cases where because of a delay in obtaining a capital sum in compensation, the normal time limit allowed for a relief has elapsed. If the right of action relates to an asset which is specifically exempt from capital gains tax, such as a motor car, any gain on the disposal of the right of action may be treated as exempt.

No underlying asset

11. A right of action may be acquired by a claimant in connection with some matter which does not involve a form of property which is an asset for capital gains tax purposes. This may be the case where professional advisers are said to have given misleading advice in a tax or other financial matter, or to have failed to claim a tax relief within proper time. Actions may be brought in relation to private or domestic matters. Where the action does not concern loss of or damage to or loss in connection with a form of property which is an asset for capital gains tax purposes, the approach in paragraph 9 above of treating the compensation as deriving from the asset itself is not appropriate. In these circumstances any gain accruing on the disposal of the right of action will be exempt from capital gains tax.

Other points

Personal compensation or damages

12. Section 51(2), TCGA 1992 provides that 'sums obtained by way of compensation or damages for any wrong or injury suffered by an individual in his person or his profession or vocation' are not chargeable to capital gains tax. The words 'wrong or injury' include breaches of contractual duties and torts (in Scotland, delicts). If the exemption would have applied to damages received for any wrong or injury, it also applies to any compensation for professional negligence in relation to an action in respect of that wrong or injury.

The words 'in his person' are to be read in distinction to 'in his finances' but they embrace more than physical injury so that distress, embarrassment, loss of reputation or dignity may all be suffered 'in the person'. Compensation or damages for unfair or unlawful discrimination suffered 'in the person' and for libel or slander (in Scotland, defamation) would thus be included. Similarly the words 'in his profession or vocation' refer to compensation or damages suffered by an individual in his professional capacity such as unfair discrimination, libel or slander (in Scotland, defamation) as distinct from 'in his finances'. If the compensation is received by the members of a partnership, each member, in Scotland as elsewhere, is treated as receiving a share of the compensation. The exemption is extended by concession to such compensation received by an individual in his trade or employment.

The exemption also extends to compensation received by a person other than the individual who suffered the wrong or injury, such as relatives or personal representatives of a deceased person. It also extends to compensation for emotional distress caused by the death of another person, and compensation for loss of financial support.

It does not apply to compensation for any other wrong or injury suffered by any person other than an individual.

Indemnity payments

13. The principle in *Zim Properties Ltd* is not regarded as applicable to payments made under a warranty or indemnity included as one of the terms of a contract of purchase and sale. If after the completion of the sale a payment is made under a

warranty or indemnity by the vendor to the purchaser, the purchaser's cost of acquisition in the event of a further disposal is reduced by the sum received, and the sale proceeds of the vendor are adjusted under s. 49, TCGA 1992. Where such a payment is not made in accordance with the terms of the contract, the principle in *Zim Properties* may apply and the sums received by the vendor or purchaser as appropriate may be identified as capital sums derived from the asset, or from the right of action, depending on the facts of the case.

20.14.4 APPROACH OF THE COURTS

In assessing damages a judge will try to compensate the claimant properly, following basic principles for assessing damages:

(a) If what has been lost was not taxable, and the damages will not be taxable on receipt, the judge will ignore tax (and the legal adviser can too).

(b) If what is lost would have been taxable, and the damages will be taxable on the same basis, the judge will ignore tax (but the legal adviser should advise that tax will be payable on the damages).

(c) If there are different taxation rules for what has been lost and for the damages to be awarded, the judge should take tax into account or the claimant will not be properly compensated (see *British Transport Commission* v *Gourley* [1956] AC 185). The legal adviser should therefore take tax into account in preparing the case, in quantifying damages and in advising the client.

Note in addition to these main principles:

- The same principles should apply whether the case goes before a judge or some other tribunal, or is settled out of court. Even if the case is settled, the lawyers should bear in mind what award would be likely to be made in court (see *Anders Utkilens Rederi A/S* v *O/Y Lovisa Stevedoring Co. A/B* [1985] 2 All ER 669, which was compromised pending an appeal).
- No judge can actually assess and demand payment of tax. The Inland Revenue will assess what tax is actually payable only after damages have been assessed and paid. This means that both lawyers and the judge will need to consider theoretical calculations about the amount of tax that may be payable. This is unsatisfactory but unavoidable.
- One part of a damages award may be taxable and another not, or one part may be liable to income tax and another to capital tax, so each part of an award should be considered separately (see *Delbourgo* v *Field* [1978] 2 All ER 193).
- Although an accountant can assist with preparing theoretical calculations lawyers and the judge may need to consider the implications of the calculations themselves.
- Where tax is relevant to proper compensation, appropriate evidence should be obtained, and full arguments prepared. Without clear evidence and calculations tax arguments will not be taken into account (*Hall & Co. Ltd* v *Pearlberg* [1956] 1 WLR 244). You are entitled to details of the tax position of the other side if this is relevant (*Phipps* v *Orthodox Unit Trusts Ltd* [1958] 1 QB 314).
- The court will normally use current rates of tax and allowances and will not theorise about the future (*Daniels* v *Jones* [1961] 1 WLR 1103). Differences between rates of tax in different countries may not be relevant (*Julien Praet & Cie S/A* v *H. G. Poland Ltd* [1962] 1 Lloyd's Rep 566).

20.14.5 ROLE OF THE BARRISTER

The lawyer should never assume that tax is irrelevant, and should become familiar with the types of case in which tax implications may need to be taken into account.

20.14.5.1 Advising a claimant

If damages may be liable to income tax or capital tax on receipt then the lawyer should advise the client of this, whether in an opinion or in a conference, and should advise the client to seek the advice of an accountant if necessary. The fact that damages may be taxable on receipt may also be used in negotiating a settlement of a case.

If tax is actually relevant to the proper calculation of damages it is vital that the lawyer takes this into account and ensures that proper theoretical calculations of the likely effect to the claimant are made. This is most likely to arise:

- in a claim for damages for loss of employment,
- in a claim where capital damages for loss of an intangible right or intangible property are claimed (see *Zim Properties Ltd* v *Proctor* (1984) 58 TC 371),
- in a claim where the quantification of loss of income or capital for a business is complex.

20.14.5.2 Advising a defendant

Where the actual quantification of damages may be affected by tax considerations it is important that the defendant's lawyer ensures that proper calculations are prepared, or at least that the claimant's calculations are properly checked.

If a defendant is paying damages from taxable income from a trade or profession it may be possible to claim the damages as a deduction for tax purposes: ICTA 1988, ss. 198, 74. For example, it is possible to deduct the cost of getting rid of an unsatisfactory employee (*Mitchell* v *B. W. Noble Ltd* [1972] 1 KB 719). It has been held that a hotel proprietor could not deduct the cost of damages for personal injury caused by his negligence (*Strong & Co. Ltd* v *Woodifield* [1906] AC 448), but in practice the Inland Revenue may allow payments of damages for personal injury to be deducted. It is unlikely that paying damages for capital loss can be deducted by the defendant, unless the payment is really an income expense for the defendant.

20.14.6 TYPES OF CASE

20.14.6.1 Contract and tort: claims for loss of profit

Generally lost profits would have been taxable, and damages will have to be entered into business accounts as income and be taxed (see *Donald Fisher (Ealing) Ltd* v *Spencer* [1989] STC 256). This has been held to be so in a case involving a car hire business (*Price* v *Elwood* (1964) 108 SJ 583), in a case involving a ship repair business (*Burmah Steamship Co. Ltd* v *IRC* (1931) 16 TC 67), and in a Lloyd's underwriting case (*Deeny* v *Gooda Walker Ltd (No. 2)* [1996] 1 WLR 426). This does not affect the quantification of damages but is relevant to advising the client. However, there may be circumstances in which the tax position is not identical for the lost business income and for the damages so that tax is actually relevant to the taxation of damages. This was argued in *John* v *James* [1986] STC 352 where profits from licensing agreements were improperly retained and the defendant said that damages should be reduced because the profits would have been taxable in the claimant's hands, therefore reducing his loss, though the argument did not succeed on the facts. However, in *O'Sullivan* v *Management Agency and Music Ltd* [1985] QB 428 is was said that the incidence of tax should be taken into account where a contract between a musician and his manager was held to be void and the manager was ordered to account for profits. The possibility of taking tax into account was also discussed in *Tate and Lyle Food and Distribution Ltd* v *Greater London Council* [1983] 2 AC 509, where the defendant caused a river to silt up and the claimant claimed damages to include the cost of dredging the river, but there was some dispute over what this would actually cost the claimant after tax was taken into account.

Note the need to distinguish capital and income, and the possible problems if it is not clear whether a figure for lost business will be liable for income tax or capital gains tax

(*Pennine Raceway Ltd* v *Kirklees Council* [1989] STC 122, where it was held simply that damages should be paid gross as it was not clear which tax was payable). The importance of distinguishing capital and income when considering tax implications is also illustrated in *London and Thames Haven Oil Wharves Ltd* v *Attwoll* [1967] Ch 772, where a jetty was damaged due to negligence, and it was found that damages for sterilisation of the capital asset were not taxable, but damages for loss of profit were.

20.14.6.2 Personal injury

Damages for loss of earnings, damages for injuries, and damages for loss of dependency need to be distinguished as different principles apply to each of them. Damages for injuries are not liable to income tax or capital tax, but tax may be relevant to damages for loss of income under the principles already outlined.

There are problems in trying to take possible future tax rates and inflation into account when assessing long-term loss. Some cases suggested that future tax rates might be relevant in assessing loss, see *Taylor* v *O'Connor* [1971] AC 115 and *Cookson* v *Knowles* [1979] AC 556, HL. However, in *Hodgson* v *Trapp* [1989] AC 807 it was held that this is not appropriate as it involves too much guesswork and very difficult calculations. This problem may be alleviated by the increased use of structured settlements, which can spread payments over time, allowing some future changes to be taken into account, and which in any event receive favoured tax treatment if set up properly.

Note that in a fatal accident case, damages for loss of dependency go to the dependents not to the deceased, and will therefore not form part of the estate for inheritance tax purposes.

20.14.6.3 Ownership and use of land

Normal principles will apply as regards any loss of commercial income, for example, under a lease (*Raja's Commercial College* v *Gian Singh & Co. Ltd* [1977] AC 312; *Diamond* v *Campbell-Jones* [1961] Ch 22).

Capital gains tax and inheritance tax may be of particular importance in cases involving land, though cases involving a main private residence will escape capital gains tax. The case of *Zim Properties Ltd* v *Proctor* (1984) 58 TC 371 should be noted. The action was based on the repudiation of a contract for sale of land and it was held that compensation for this repudiation was potentially liable for CGT.

There may be problems in cases involving a restriction on the use of land or compulsory purchase. In *Stoke-on-Trent City Council* v *Wood Mitchell & Co. Ltd* [1980] 1 WLR 254 it was argued that tax should be taken into account in assessing compensation, but it was held that, on the evidence before the court, profits would have been taxed and compensation would be taxed, so tax should be ignored. However, in *West Suffolk County Council* v *W. Rought Ltd* [1957] AC 403, on similar facts, it was held that the compensation would not be taxed, so tax should be taken into account in assessing the loss. A similar decision was reached in a case involving compensation for presenting the exploitation of mineral rights, *Thomas McGhie and Sons Ltd* v *British Transport Commission* [1963] 1 QB 125, where it was held that the income from the rights would have been taxed, but the compensation would not, so tax should be taken into account.

20.14.6.4 Trusts

The normal principles do not apply here due to the strict rule that trust property must be restored in full (*Re Bell's Indenture* [1980] 1 WLR 1217). In that case there was a misappropriation of trust funds and it was held it was the duty of the trustee to account for the full loss with no reduction for any tax that might have been payable on the funds misappropriated. There was a similar decision in *Bartlett* v *Barclays Bank Trust Co. Ltd* [1980] Ch 515, where trust property was mismanaged. However, note that once the property has been returned to the trust it will be taxable in the hands of the trustees on normal principles (*Schulze* v *Benstead* (1915) 7 TC 30).

20.15 Exercises

20.15.1 EXERCISE 1

Problem
You represent Norman and Deidre Morton, who are in business in partnership as grocers, specialising in the sale of organic vegetables. Mr and Mrs Morton come to see you in conference regarding a negligence action they are bringing against Build It Ltd, the basic facts being that Build It were demolishing the premises next to the Mortons' shop and did so negligently causing damage to the Mortons' shop.

It seems that negligence will be admitted, but damages are still in issue, and your advice is sought on damages and related tax issues. Consider what advice you should give to the clients, and what issues you may need to prepare to present in court.

The damage to the shop will cost £20,000 to repair, and damage to the Mortons' flat above the shop will cost £15,000 to repair. Trading income of £15,000 has been lost. Vegetables worth £1,000 had to be thrown away. Mr and Mrs Morton also claim that the business has suffered some loss of goodwill, and that Mr Morton has suffered distress at the events. You advise that damages may not be recoverable under all these heads, but are asked what the tax position would be if they could be.

Solution
The £20,000 for the repair of the shop and the £15,000 for the repair of the flat are capital sums derived from a legal right of action, and are therefore potentially liable to capital gains tax (TCGA 1992, s. 22). The sum with respect to the flat would appear to relate to the claimants' main private residence and would therefore be exempt. If the money is in fact used to repair the premises, it would escape any immediate charge to tax and tax would only be charged on any gain when the premises are eventually sold (TCGA 1992, s. 23). If for any reason the claimants were to pocket the money and sell the shop in its damaged state, the £20,000 could be liable to capital gains tax on receipt.

The £15,000 for loss of trading income will need to be put into the trading accounts of the claimants as income and will be charged to income tax when their annual accounts are drawn up. The £1,000 for vegetables thrown away will need to be put into the trading accounts in the same way (but the original cost of these vegetables is deductible).

If a sum is recovered for loss of goodwill it will be potentially liable for capital gains tax (as in *Kirby* v *Thorn EMI* [1988] 1 WLR 445). There is no obvious way in which this figure can escape this charge to tax, and it may therefore be advisable to claim a figure sufficient to cover the loss of goodwill plus the CGT that is likely to be payable.

If damages for distress are recovered, they will not be liable to tax as they relate to personal injury.

20.15.2 EXERCISE 2

Problem
You represent Elizabeth Martin, who is suing a builder, Sound Construction Ltd, whom she employed to work on her house. Advise her whether any capital tax may be payable, and if so, discuss the principles on which the taxable amount may be assessed.

Elizabeth's home suffered substantial damage when one of the builder's workmen used a blowtorch negligently and set fire to the house. The damages sought include £40,000 for damage to the house, £20,000 for damage to an adjoining cottage, £18,000 for damage to furniture, £5,000 for personal injury to Elizabeth, who was hurt when the ceiling collapsed due to the fire, and £2,000 for shock and distress suffered by Elizabeth.

What would your advice be if Elizabeth had been killed in the fire, and you were bringing an action claiming £10,000 for the pain and suffering of Elizabeth prior to her death, and £80,000 for loss of dependence on behalf of her son Edward?

Solution
The £40,000 for the damage to the house, the £20,000 for the damage to the cottage and the £18,000 for the damage to furniture are all potentially liable to capital gains tax as being sums derived from capital assets. The £40,000 for the house is likely to escape tax as relating to her main private residence, but this will not apply to the money for the cottage unless on the facts this is also part of her main private residence (which is unlikely). The £20,000 for the cottage and the £18,000 for the furniture may escape tax if the damages are used to repair the cottage and replace the furniture, though tax would be payable on any gain when the cottage or the furniture is eventually disposed of. Other exemptions might be claimed with respect to the money for the furniture, such as the exemption for chattels (TCGA 1992, s. 262).

The damages for personal injury and for shock will not be liable for tax (TCGA 1992, s. 51; Extra-statutory Concession D33).

If Elizabeth had died, the £10,000 for loss prior to death would pass into her estate and therefore could be relevant for inheritance tax on her estate. The £80,000 for loss of dependency would not attract any tax immediately (though if invested, it could attract income tax and capital tax in the future).

20.15.3 EXERCISE 3

Problem
Your client is Francis Fanshaw who contracted to buy a house, Red Dene, but the sale was repudiated by the seller, George Green, Francis commenced an action for specific performance on your advice, but is now prepared to settle this action for a sum of £60,000. Would this sum be liable to tax if he accepts it?

How would your advice be different if Francis pursued his action for specific performance and became owner of Red Dene, which he then made his home?

On the basis that Mr Fanshaw accepts the £60,000, he buys an alternative property, Field Manor, but then finds that it has severe structural defects. He wishes to sue the surveyor, Harold Henson, on whose report he relied in purchasing the property, for failure to use reasonable care and skill, claiming damages of £50,000. Would these damages be liable to tax?

If Mr Fanshaw is so upset that he writes to the local paper saying that Mr Henson is totally incapable of doing his job and Mr Henson successfully sues him for libel, would the damages recovered by Mr Henson be liable to tax?

20.16 Separation and Divorce

It is vital for the barrister to consider the relevance of income tax and capital gains tax when advising on maintenance for a spouse, or a financial settlement on divorce. The relevant principles are outlined in the ***Family Law in Practice Manual***.

20.17 Tax on Death

The barrister may be called in to advise an executor or personal representative, or to advise on tax planning before death. Knowledge of this area is particularly important for those going into Chancery practice.

20.17.1 INCOME TAX

For estates in administration see: ICTA 1988, ss. 695–701; TMA 1970, ss. 67–90. The tax liability of the deceased for the year of death must be settled. There will be a full personal allowance. There are some special rules, e.g., for the discontinuance of a business.

Any income accruing to the estate while it is being administered will be taxable at basic rate. Broadly, when an asset is passed to a beneficiary, the beneficiary will be reassessed for income tax if necessary, with credit for any tax paid during administration.

20.17.2 CAPITAL GAINS TAX

Capital gains tax is not generally payable on death, because the primary liability is to inheritance tax: TCGA 1992, s. 62. However, executors or personal representatives will be liable for any CGT due on disposals prior to death in the year of death: ss. 64, 65: see *IRC* v *Richards's Executors* [1971] 1 WLR 571. From 1998–99 the executors or personal representatives have an annual allowance for gains accruing in the year of death and the following two years: FA 1998.

20.17.3 INHERITANCE TAX ON DEATH

Inheritance tax is the primary tax payable on death.

20.17.3.1 Estate on death

The estate on death will include everything the deceased is beneficially entitled to immediately before death: s. 4. However, changes occuring by reason of death such as the loss of personal goodwill for a business can be taken into account: s. 71. Property will devolve according to the will of the deceased or the rules of intestacy.

Note that in the case of a fatal accident, damages payable for pain, suffering and loss of the deceased will form part of the estate. Damages for loss of dependency go to the dependants and are not part of the estate.

20.17.3.2 Exemptions and reliefs on death

Some exemptions and reliefs apply on death, but not all. For example, no annual allowance or small gifts exemption can be claimed.

20.17.3.3 Charge to tax

The value of the estate on death will be added to the cumulative total of the seven years prior to death, and tax assessed accordingly at 40%; the executors or personal representatives are liable to pay the tax: ss. 141, 200, 211. Any potentially exempt transfers (PETs) made in the seven years before death will be taxed at death rates: FA 1986, sch. 19.

20.17.3.4 Transfers within seven years of death

These will be subject to death rates of tax, with tapering relief for transfers four to seven years before death: ss. 131–140.

20.17.3.5 Reliefs on valuation

If shares, land or related property are sold within a limited time of death for less than their value on death, the lower value may be taken to assess tax due: ss. 176, 178–189, 190–198.

20.17.3.6 Changes in the distribution of the estate

Some changes are deemed to take place on death and will therefore attract no extra tax, e.g., provision from the estate: ss. 17, 142–147. Deeds of variation may be made within two years of death, will be deemed to take effect on death, and can be very important in lessening the burden of inheritance tax on an estate. It is only possible to have one deed of variation for an estate (*Russell* v *IRC* [1988] 1 WLR 834), unless the second merely rectifies the first (*Lake* v *Lake* [1989] STC 865). A deed that is a sham simply for tax avoidance may be invalid (*Fitzwilliam* v *IRC* [1993] 1 WLR 1189).

20.17.3.7 Incidence of tax

The incidence of tax can be provided for in the will, otherwise it falls primarily on the residue, or if that is insufficient, on specific bequests equally: ss. 36–42.

20.17.3.8 Planning

Planning to decrease possible liability to inheritance tax on death is best carried out during life. The larger the estate, the earlier planning is advisable. No single plan will apply to all individuals, but the following general points can be taken into account:

(a) All exemptions and reliefs should be fully used.

(b) £3,000 can be transferred each year without tax, and in addition £242,000 can be transferred every seven years within the nil rate band.

(c) PETs should be used, making gifts of assets to children etc. while the donor is likely to live at least seven years.

(d) An estate may be divided between a husband and wife, with no tax on transfers between them, to make full use of the allowances of both.

(e) Disposals during life are to be preferred to disposals on death, as the tax rate is 20% instead of 40%.

(f) Where possible, the estate on death should be reduced so that when added to transfers in the seven years before death it does not exceed £242,000.

(g) A donor should beware retaining an interest in property.

(h) Beware leaving everything to a spouse on death. Although it will escape tax at the time, tax will be payable when the surviving spouse dies.

(i) Make regular checks on a will to see it remains tax effective.

TWENTY ONE

INSOLVENCY, RAISING CAPITAL, CAPITAL STRUCTURES

21.1 Introduction

One of the considerations in suing for a debt or damages is whether the person sued will have the money to pay. In advising clients you will need to have a basic understanding of what insolvency means and the money available to satisfy those claiming against an insolvent person. When suing a business, you will also need to understand the basic capital structures of the different forms of business associations.

21.2 Raising Capital, Capital Structures

21.2.1 INTRODUCTION

All trading associations require money to trade and the methods of raising the necessary finance are:

(a) owners' investment — owners' capital,

(b) long-term loans usually with security — mortgages and charges,

(c) short-term borrowing — a bank loan or agreed overdraft,

(d) trade credit — including purchasing goods on credit sale, conditional sale, hire purchase, retention of title clause, leasing agreements.

All these methods are available to all forms of business but the first two differ according to the type of business association and these differences are set out below.

21.2.2 SOLE TRADER

A sole trader may finance the business from his or her own pocket or raise a long-term loan. However, the security which a sole trader can provide is limited to fixed assets which he owns (i.e., mortgaging his property, business or residential). The goods which are traded (stock-in-trade) are not available to give security for a loan. (A company can borrow against such goods — see below.) Provided the business is successful, the sole trader will have a saleable investment in that the business, including any goodwill, could be sold at any time and the money invested elsewhere.

21.2.3 PARTNERSHIP

Partners will usually each invest a certain amount of money (capital) in the business. The return on this investment will depend on the partnership agreement and provisions in the Partnership Act 1890 (PA 1890) and will include a say in the management of the business, a share of the profits, a share in any partnership property and, on dissolution where the money is sufficient, a return of the share together with any surplus. Under PA 1890, s. 24, which is subject to contrary agreement, the partners have no right to pay or interest on their capital but have a right to be indemnified for payments or liabilities incurred and share equally in the profits, both income and capital. They also have equal liability for losses.

The property used in the business, e.g., offices, equipment, may be partnership property or the personal property of one or more of the partners, which is merely being used by the firm for the business. It is important to distinguish between these two because the partnership property must be used exclusively for the firm's purpose (PA 1890, ss. 20 and 29); any increase or decrease in its value is a profit or loss of the firm; and on dissolution it will be used to pay creditors before any surplus is distributed to the partners. In addition, on insolvency the partnership assets will be used first to pay the firm's debts, and personal assets of the partners will be used first to pay personal debts. Determining what is partnership and what is the personal property of one or more of the partners can be difficult. Sections 20 and 21 of PA 1890 contain provisions to assist.

Partners are in much the same position as sole traders in their ability to give security for any loan. Note, however, the effect of PA 1890, ss. 2 and 3, by which the rights of a lender who receives a share of the profits, or interest varying with profits, under a written loan contract are postponed to other creditors.

21.2.4 COMPANY

21.2.4.1 Owners' investment: share capital

A company raises money by issuing shares, whose buyers become part owners (shareholders) in the company. The company decides the nominal (face or par) value of the share (i.e., the amount written on the share certificate) and whether it wishes to charge the initial shareholder more than this nominal value (i.e., a premium). Liability on the shares issued is limited to the company receiving this nominal amount plus any premium charged. Thus if the first owner of a share pays this, subsequent owners will have all the rights of the first owner but have no liability to make further contributions (they will pay whatever price their seller seeks to the seller not the company). It is important to distinguish the different types of share capital; authorised (the amount the company is authorised by its memorandum to issue), issued or allotted (the nominal amount actually issued at any time), paid up (the amount so far paid on shares which have been issued), uncalled (the amount unpaid which the company is entitled to call for). Most shares are now issued fully paid and it is rare to have partly paid shares with the resulting uncalled capital.

A company's issued share capital is seen as a guarantee fund for its creditors. This is necessary as the creditors can pursue only the company for its debts, the members' liability being limited to payment of the nominal value plus any premium. The 'creditors' buffer' must be maintained and not returned to the shareholders. The company can use it to trade and carry on business, as that is the purpose for which it has been raised, but there are strict maintenance-of-capital rules on otherwise reducing it or returning it to shareholders, including prohibitions against the company issuing shares at a discount (i.e., for considerably less than the nominal value), purchasing its own shares, giving financial assistance to purchase its own shares, reducing its capital or paying dividends out of capital. As sole traders and partners generally have unlimited personal liability for the business debts, there are no such capital maintenance rules for them (although if there are limited partners they cannot withdraw their capital: Limited Partnerships Act 1907, s. 4(3)).

Shareholders' return on their investment is by selling their shares at a profit and (until they sell their shares) receiving their share in the profits. Rights to transfer will depend on the articles of association, the general rule being that shareholders have a right to transfer unless restricted. Public companies generally do not restrict the right (and cannot if listed on the London Stock Exchange). Private companies, particularly small ones, may restrict transferability so as to ensure that shares remain among a closed group of people, e.g., a family, either by having pre-emption rights (i.e., shareholders must first offer the shares to existing shareholders) or empowering the directors to refuse to accept the transfer. Rights to receive dividend (which must be out of distributable profits as defined in the CA 1985) will be set out in the articles or terms of issue. The two most common classes of share are ordinary (equity) shares which are the vast majority of shares and will have the usual rights without special definition, and preference shares which usually have preferential rights to dividend of a fixed percentage of the nominal value of the share (e.g., 10%). Where profits are low there may be just enough to pay preferential shareholders, with ordinary shareholders receiving nothing. Alternatively if profits are high, the preferential shareholders will still only get their 10%, but ordinary shareholders may get much more.

21.2.4.2 Borrowing money: loan capital

Virtually all companies rely on borrowing to raise money. A long-term loan to a company is a form of investment whereby the creditor's return is the interest. The loan contract is called a debenture and the lender/creditor is a debentureholder. Whereas a shareholder is part owner of the company with rights under articles (e.g., to vote at meetings) who receives a dividend only if there are sufficient profits and one is declared, a debentureholder is a creditor (an outsider) whose interest is a debt due from the company, payable even if there are no profits. The maintenance-of-capital rules apply only to share capital.

There may be a single debenture (e.g., to a bank to secure an overdraft), a series of debentures in identical form all ranking equally for repayment, or debenture stock, which is a single debt in which each lender has a holding of a specified value (e.g., through an offer to the public a loan is raised from a large number of lenders). The loan contract must (for debenture stock) and may (for series of debentures) take the form of a debenture trust deed whereby trustees are appointed who are, in effect, the creditors of the company, but who hold as such for the true lenders, the beneficiaries of the trust, with the duty to enforce the terms of the contract with the company and protect the lenders' interests.

A company may provide security for a loan by giving the lender a fixed charge over its fixed assets, e.g., buildings, land, in the same way that sole traders or partners may mortgage property. The charge, which may be legal or equitable, attaches to the property when it is created, with the result that the company cannot deal with those assets without the consent of the lender. A company may also provide security by giving the lender a floating charge over assets which, by their nature, change frequently, e.g., stock-in-trade. This type of charge is not available to individuals and means companies have more collateral against which to raise loans. A floating charge has been defined as an equitable charge over a class of assets which change from time to time and which the company uses to carry on its business and may dispose of in the ordinary course of business (at which point the charge ceases to attach to those assets) until the charge crystallises. On crystallisation, the charge attaches to all items within the class of assets charged owned by the company at the date of crystallisation or acquired thereafter. Crystallisation occurs if a receiver is appointed, on commencement of winding up or on any event specified in the debenture, e.g., failure to pay or keep the value of the assets at the level promised. Whether a charge is fixed or floating is determined by its characteristics and not the label attached to it.

A company can create a number of charges over the same property. In general, priority of registered charges is fixed charges in order of creation and then floating charges in order of creation. A creditor with a floating charge may insert a prohibition in the debenture against the company creating subsequent charges with priority, but this is difficult to enforce as the holder of the subsequent fixed charge must have actual notice of the prohibition.

21.3 Insolvency

Insolvency proceedings are now governed by the Insolvency Act 1986 (IA 1986) and rules made thereunder, principally the Insolvency Rules 1986 (IR 1986) (as amended) and the Insolvent Partnerships Order 1994. In addition the Company Directors Disqualification Act 1986 is important in respect of penalising those who have run their businesses to the prejudice of creditors. There is no single definition of insolvency and indeed the word is used in different ways throughout the Act and the Rules.

21.4 Individual Insolvency

If an individual is unable to pay debts the possibilities are:

(a) composition or deed of arrangement under the Deeds of Arrangement Act 1914;

(b) administration order under the County Courts Act 1984;

(c) voluntary arrangement under IA 1986;

(d) bankruptcy.

21.4.1 DEEDS OF ARRANGEMENT ACT 1914

A deed of arrangement is an alternative to bankruptcy whereby a debtor may agree with creditors as to how debts will be paid. Two principal types of arrangement are possible. First, a composition with creditors by which a debtor agrees with creditors, and the creditors agree with each other, that all creditors will accept a percentage of the debt owed in full satisfaction. Secondly, a deed of arrangement whereby a debtor by deed assigns his property to a trustee on trusts declared to use it for the benefit of creditors. Any such arrangement is void unless registered with the DTI (s. 2) and assented to by a majority in number and value of creditors (s. 3). It is binding on those who assented but not on those who did not assent.

21.4.2 ADMINISTRATION ORDERS, COUNTY COURTS ACT 1984, ss. 112–117

Under CCA 1984, s. 112, where a debtor is unable to pay forthwith a debt, the county court may make an order providing for the administration of the debtor's estate. While the administration order is in effect no creditor may, without leave of the court and subject to certain exceptions, have any remedy in respect of any debt covered by the order (s. 114 (to secure equal division amongst creditors)).

21.4.3 VOLUNTARY ARRANGEMENTS, IA 1986, ss. 252–265, AND IR 1986, PART 5

This procedure is to enable an insolvent debtor to have an agreement with creditors which, unless revoked by the courts, is binding on all of them. A debtor may apply for an interim order which prevents any bankruptcy petition from being presented while proposals are being drawn up for paying creditors. An interim order will only be granted if the debtor is an undischarged bankrupt or able to petition for bankruptcy, there has been no previous application for an interim order in the previous 12 months and a nominee who is a qualified insolvency practitioner is willing to act (s. 255). If an order is made, the nominee will obtain a statement of affairs from the debtor, draw up the terms of the proposed voluntary arrangement and present this in a report to the court and a meeting of creditors. The proposal is subject to the approval of creditors which is roughly in excess of three-quarters in value of the creditors, although no approval may affect the rights of secured creditors to enforce their security or preferential creditors without their concurrence. However, if the requisite approval is obtained, the arrangement binds all creditors who had notice of and were entitled to vote at the meeting and the debtor (s. 260). The nominee becomes or selects a supervisor who will then carry out the arrangement. Voluntary arrangements for individuals are similar to those for companies with the principal and vital difference of the moratorium provided by the interim order (see **21.6.4**).

21.4.4 BANKRUPTCY, IA 1986, ss. 264–365, AND IR 1986, PART 6

A debtor or his creditors may petition for bankruptcy (s. 264). However, as with company liquidations, the court will only make an order if a ground set out in the Act is proved.

21.4.4.1 Creditors' petition

Creditors may present a petition only if at the time there is a debt or debts of £750 or more which is unsecured (or the creditor holding the security is prepared to waive it) and payable immediately or at some future time, and the debtor appears unable to pay or to have no reasonable prospects of being able to pay (ss. 267 and 269).

A debtor is unable to pay if:

(a) the creditor has served a statutory demand personally on the debtor requiring, in the case of a debt payable immediately, that the debt be paid, secured or compounded, and in the case of a future debt, that the debtor satisfy the creditor that there is a reasonable prospect that the debtor will be able to pay it when it falls due; three weeks have elapsed since service and the demand has not been complied with; and there is no outstanding application to have the statutory demand set aside; or

(b) in respect of a debt payable immediately, execution of a judgment debt of the petitioning creditor has been returned unsatisfied in whole or in part (s. 268).

Bankruptcy commences on the day the order is made and continues until the bankrupt is discharged (s. 278). A copy of the order is served on the Official Receiver (a civil servant) to whom the bankrupt must submit a statement of affairs setting out his assets, liabilities and creditors (s. 288). The Official Receiver must then decide whether to call a meeting of creditors within 12 weeks (s. 293) and, if not, notice must be given to the court and all creditors. The purpose of the meeting is to appoint a trustee in bankruptcy to replace the Official Receiver. If there is no meeting the Official Receiver becomes the trustee in bankruptcy.

The principal duty of the trustee in bankruptcy (like that of a company liquidator) is to get in, realise and distribute the bankrupt's estate in accordance with IA 1986 (s. 305). Section 283 defines the bankrupt's estate and excludes specific items, e.g., tools etc. necessary for business, and clothing, bedding etc. necessary for satisfying basic needs of the bankrupt and his family. The bankrupt's estate vests in the trustee in bankruptcy immediately the appointment takes effect (s. 306) and any disposition of property between presentation of petition and vesting in the trustee in bankruptcy is void, unless court approval is given (subject to some protection for bona fide purchasers for value and banks) (s. 284). 'After-acquired' property may be claimed by serving notice on the bankrupt (s. 307).

Any creditor wishing to be paid must prove the debt (i.e., formally submit it to the trustee in bankruptcy) (s. 322). The debts are then paid in the order set out in IA 1986:

(a) Preferential debts (sch. 6), PAYE income tax for previous 12 months, VAT (six months), national insurance contributions (12 months), occupational and state pension schemes contributions, employees' pay (four months/£800 per employee) and holiday pay.

(b) Ordinary unsecured creditors.

(c) Deferred debts, including debts owed to the debtor's spouse at commencement of bankruptcy (ss. 328 and 329) and debts under PA 1890, ss. 2, 3, and LPA 1907.

Each group is satisfied before moving on to the next group, and if there are insufficient assets to satisfy any group they abate in equal proportions between themselves.

There are limits placed on a bankrupt's ability to obtain credit, trade or take part in the management of a company. It is an offence to obtain credit, including purchasing goods on hire purchase or conditional sale, or to be paid in advance for goods or services, to the extent of £250 or more without informing the creditor that he is an undischarged bankrupt (s. 360(1)(a)). It is also an offence to engage in business under another name without disclosing the name in which one was adjudicated bankrupt (s. 360(1)(b)). It is also an offence for an undischarged bankrupt to act as a company director, or be part of the management of a company, directly or indirectly, except with leave of the court (Company Directors Disqualification Act 1986, s. 11). If a person contravenes s. 11 he commits an offence (s. 13) and is personally liable for the debts of the company while so acting (s. 15).

A bankrupt is discharged from bankruptcy automatically three years from the commencement of bankruptcy, unless he has been an undischarged bankrupt within 15 years of the commencement of the current bankruptcy (s. 279). Otherwise an application may be made to the court at any time after five years from commencement of bankruptcy for an order discharging the bankrupt (s. 280). The court may refuse, grant the discharge or grant it on conditions. The discharge generally releases the bankrupt from bankruptcy debts but has no effect on the functions of the trustee in bankruptcy so far as they remain to be carried out. There are certain exceptions to this release, e.g., it does not affect the right of any secured creditor to enforce the security (s. 281).

21.4.4.2 Debtors' petition

A debtor may petition for his or her own bankruptcy on the ground of being unable to pay debts (s. 272). The advantage of this is twofold. First, if it is a small bankruptcy (the total of all unsecured debts is less than £20,000 and the value of the bankrupt's estate is equal to or more than £2,000) and the debtor has not been adjudicated bankrupt, entered a composition or scheme of arrangement with creditors within the preceding five years and the court considers it appropriate, it may appoint an insolvency practitioner to report on whether the bankruptcy should be converted into a voluntary arrangement. Even if this is not appropriate, the court may issue a certificate for summary administration of the bankrupt's estate. This is a shorter, simpler form of administration under which the bankrupt is automatically discharged under s. 279 after two years instead of the usual three.

21.4.4.3 Swelling the assets of the bankrupt

There are provisions under which transactions by bankrupts may be set aside by the trustee in bankruptcy, and these are similar to those available to a liquidator on the liquidation of a company (see **21.6.5.4**).

IA 1986, s. 339, provides that transactions at an undervalue (where the bankrupt made a gift, or received no consideration, or consideration significantly less than provided by him, or entered into a transaction in consideration of marriage) may be set aside if entered into within five years of the bankruptcy petition.

IA 1986, s. 340, provides that a preference (a transaction whereby the bankrupt put any creditor in a better position in the event of bankruptcy than he would otherwise have been) will be set aside if to an associate (defined in s. 435 to include relatives, employees, employers, companies under control of the bankrupt) within two years, and to anyone else within six months of the bankruptcy petition.

For both ss. 339 and 340, if the transaction is with an associate nothing further need be proved. If it is with anyone else it must also be shown that at the time of the transaction the person making it was insolvent or became so as a result.

Under IA 1986, ss. 423–425, a transaction at an undervalue may be set aside, if it can be shown that the purpose of the transaction was to put assets beyond the reach of creditors or to prejudice creditors' interests in some other way. The provision is available on the bankruptcy of individuals and liquidation of companies, although there are some limits on its use with companies. Note that there is no time limit for such transactions to be set aside but the difficulty is in proving the purpose of the transaction.

21.5 Insolvent Partnerships

These are governed by the Insolvent Partnerships Order 1994 which applies various parts of IA 1986 and IR 1986 to partnerships. Insolvency proceedings of partnerships contain a mixture of winding up the partnership and bankruptcy of the partners. Some of the basic rules remain, however. Thus the personal assets of partners will be used first to pay personal debts, and joint assets of the firm will be used first to pay joint debts. Only if there is a surplus of both kinds of assets will such surplus be applied in meeting the shortfall in payment of the other debts.

The application of the rules to partnerships is complicated, but there are three main possibilities which are relevant.

(a) Wind up the insolvent partnership only as an unregistered company under IA 1986, Part V, ss. 220–279). The object of this is to get at the partnership assets without personally bankrupting the partners.

(b) Wind up the insolvent partnership as an unregistered company, together with petitioning for the bankruptcy of two or more insolvent partners (or the liquidation of partners which are companies).

(c) Insolvency proceedings against some but not all of the partners without petitioning to wind up the partnership as an unregistered company.

Note that if an insolvent partnership is wound up as an unregistered company (options (a) and (b)), the partners are treated as directors for the purpose of the Company Directors Disqualification Act 1986 and may be disqualified under that Act from acting as directors or taking part in the management of a company.

The Limited Liability Partnership Act 2000 provides that regulations shall make provision about insolvency and winding up of limited liability partnerships by applying or incorporating with such modifications as appear appropriate the provisions relating to the winding up or insolvency of companies or other corporations. The relevant regulations are the Limited Liability Partnerships Regulations 2001 (SI 2001 No. 1090).

21.6 Companies

21.6.1 INTRODUCTION

If a company fails to pay its debts the creditors may:

(a) If secured creditors, enforce their security, usually by selling the assets subject to the charge or appointing a receiver.

(b) Seek an administration order, whereby an administrator is appointed to effect payment of the debts.

(c) Seek a voluntary arrangement, i.e., an agreement with creditors as to how debts will be paid.

(d) Wind up or liquidate the company, which will ultimately dissolve it.

21.6.2 RECEIVERSHIP, IA 1986, ss. 28–49, AND IR 1986, PART 3

Receivership is one of the principal ways in which a chargeholder may enforce his charge. The debenture will usually give debentureholders the power to appoint a receiver. However, if it does not, the court has power to appoint a receiver on the application of the debentureholders in certain circumstances including default in payment of the debt.

The principal effects of the appointment of a receiver are:

(a) directors' powers over the charged assets are suspended;

(b) floating charges crystallise;

(c) notice of the appointment must be given to the Registrar of Companies and put on all documents (s. 39; giving notice to outsiders that the company is in financial difficulty).

The principal duty of the receiver is to take control of the assets subject to the charge and pay off the debentureholders having due regard to the rights of others under IA 1986. Thus the order of priority is:

(a) fixed chargeholders (who may realise the assets subject to their charge);

(b) preferential creditors (who will be paid out of money subject to floating charges if there are insufficient other funds to pay them. These creditors are set out in sch. 6 and are the same as for bankruptcy (see **21.4.4.1**));

(c) floating chargeholders;

(d) ordinary unsecured creditors.

To enable the duty to be carried out, the receiver is given certain powers in the debenture, e.g., to sell the assets subject to the charge. However, if appointed under a floating charge over the whole or substantially the whole of the company's undertaking, the receiver is called an administrative receiver (s. 29) and will have all those powers set out in the debenture plus those in IA 1986, ss. 42, 43 and sch. 1, so far as consistent with the debenture. These powers are very wide and include the power to carry on the business of the company (sch. 1, para. 4). This power is particularly important where the physical assets of the company are not of much value and there is a possibility of trading the company out of financial difficulty or 'hiving down' (by creating a new company, selling the viable parts of the business to the new company in exchange for shares in the new company and then selling the shares in the new company to a willing buyer; the new company thereby having the assets but not the liabilities of the old company). Either of these two alternatives may mean more money for the debentureholders.

The receiver is not concerned with ordinary unsecured creditors as they rank below any secured creditor. However, an administrative receiver now has a duty (s. 47) to obtain a statement of affairs from officers of the company as to the assets, liabilities and creditors and prepare a report as to why he was appointed, the amount due to debentureholders and the amount likely to be available for other creditors. This report must be sent to the Registrar of Companies and all unsecured creditors. A meeting must be called of all unsecured creditors (s. 48) at which the report will be presented, and a committee of creditors may be appointed which may then, from time to time, require information from the administrative receiver as to steps being taken. Thus the unsecured creditors should be kept informed and may, in light of this information decide to take steps themselves, e.g., petition for the liquidation of the company or an administrative order.

21.6.3 ADMINISTRATION ORDERS, IA 1986, ss. 8–27, AND IR 1986, PART 2

This is a new provision inspired by the success of receivers and managers (now called administrative receivers) prior to the IA 1986 in turning round or hiving down companies. It is a procedure whereby a court appointed administrator has much the same (and in fact more) powers as an administrative receiver. The procedure is as follows:

(a) A petition is presented to the court by, *inter alia*, the creditor(s) (secured or unsecured) and served on the company and those debentureholders entitled to appoint an administrative receiver (s. 9).

(b) On issue of the petition there is a freeze on the company in that there may be no:

  (i) order made or resolution passed to wind up the company;

  (ii) security enforced, hire purchase goods (which includes goods under conditional sale and retention of title agreements) repossessed, or legal proceedings taken against the company without leave of the court (s. 10). (However, an administrative receiver may be appointed and a petition to wind up the company may be presented.)

(c) The court will determine whether or not an order should be made. The application must be dismissed unless it is satisfied that the debentureholders who have appointed an administrative receiver consent to it being made. The court may make an order if satisfied that the company is, or is likely to become unable to pay its debts and the order is likely to achieve one of the purposes set out in s. 8 of the Act, e.g., the survival of the company or a more advantageous realisation of the company's assets than on liquidation.

(d) If the court is so satisfied, an order is made with the effect that an administrator is appointed, any administrative receiver in post automatically vacates office and any petition to wind up the company is dismissed. In addition the ban on enforcement of security, repossession of hire purchase goods and proceedings against the company continues, subject to leave of the administrator or the court. In addition all documents must state that the company is being managed by an administrator.

(e) The administrator must obtain a statement of affairs setting out the assets, liabilities and creditors of the company, prepare proposals for achieving the purpose set out in the order (s. 23) and present these to a meeting of creditors (s. 24).

(f) If the creditors approve the proposals, the administrator carries them out.

The administrator has the same wide powers as the administrative receiver, which are set out in IA 1986, sch. 1, plus additional powers, not available to administrative receivers, to remove any director and appoint a replacement (s. 14(2)), to sell property subject to a floating charge (s. 15(1)) and, with leave of the court, to sell property subject to a fixed charge or held on hire purchase (s. 15(2)). The proceeds of any such sale must be used to pay the persons with an interest in the property. Once the purpose of the order has been achieved, the administrator applies to the court for the order to be discharged.

21.6.4 VOLUNTARY ARRANGEMENTS, IA 1986, ss. 1–7, AND IR 1986, PART 1

This is a new provision not previously available to companies to enable them to make binding agreements with creditors. It has not been much used as it is a fairly complicated procedure involving a series of court hearings, does not bind secured or preferential creditors without their consent and contains no provisions for a moratorium while the proposals for the arrangement are being drawn up and considered (unlike administration orders which have become popular, and voluntary arrangements for insolvent individuals in ss. 252–254; see **21.4.3**).

21.6.5 LIQUIDATION, IA 1986, PARTS IV AND VI, AND IR 1986, PART 4

This is the ultimate sanction against a company which fails to pay debts as it will dissolve the company. Liquidation can be voluntary (i.e., the company resolves to liquidate) or compulsory (the court orders that it be liquidated). Either way the effect is the same; a liquidator is appointed to realise the assets and pay off the debts. Once this task has been completed, a return is made to the Registrar of Companies and the company is dissolved and removed from the register of companies (IA 1986, s. 205).

21.6.5.1 Voluntary liquidation, IA 1986, ss. 84–116, and IR 1986, Part 4

This commences by a resolution of members in general meeting and will be a members' or creditors' liquidation. If the directors swear a statutory declaration of solvency (i.e. that the company will be able to pay its debts in full within a specified period not exceeding 12 months (s. 89)) it will be a members' voluntary liquidation in which the creditors play no part. The liquidator is appointed by the members and reports to them.

If the directors are not prepared to swear a statutory declaration, it will be a creditors' voluntary liquidation in which the creditors will play a role. A meeting of creditors will be called within 14 days of the resolution being passed and they will appoint a liquidator (if members nominated a different person the creditors' nominee will act). The liquidator will report to a liquidation committee which is composed of representatives of members and creditors, a maximum of five of each.

If the directors make a statutory declaration without reasonable grounds for their opinion that the company will be able to pay its debts, they commit an offence, and if the company does not pay its debts within the stated period, they are presumed to have had no reasonable grounds for their opinion (s. 89). Hence the incentive for the directors to ensure that the declaration is accurate.

21.6.5.2 Compulsory liquidation, IA 1986, ss. 117–162, and IR 1986, Part 4

This is commenced by the presentation of a petition to the court by the company (rare), the directors, any creditor(s) (most frequent) or member(s) (s. 124). To obtain an order, one of the grounds set out in s. 122 must be proved, which includes the ground that the company is unable to pay its debts. By s. 123 a company is deemed to be unable to pay its debts if:

(a) a statutory demand for a debt exceeding £750 has been served on the company and not paid, secured or compounded within three weeks;

(b) execution of a judgment debt is unsatisfied;

(c) the court is satisfied that the company is unable to pay its debts as they fall due.

The preparation needed for the hearing of a petition is set out in the ***Advocacy Manual*, Chapter 31**.

If an order is made, it relates back to the date of presentation of the petition so any disposition of property or transfer of shares between petition and order are void unless the court otherwise orders (s. 127) (a provision similar to IA 1986, s. 284 for bankruptcy petitions: see **21.4.4.1**).

21.6.5.3 The effect of liquidation, IA 1986, ss. 175–219, 230–246, and IR 1986, Part 4

The effects of the making of an order or passing of a resolution to wind up a company are largely the same. A liquidator is appointed, the company must cease business except as necessary to wind up, all floating charges crystallise, the directors' powers cease and are assumed by the liquidator and all invoices, letters etc. must show that the company is being wound up. The liquidator takes control of the assets, realises them and pays off the debts in the order of priority under IA 1986, which is basically:

(a) fixed chargeholders (who may realise the assets subject to their charge),

(b) preferential creditors,

(c) floating chargeholders,

(d) unsecured creditors,

(e) payments due to members (e.g., unpaid declared dividends),

(f) return of capital to members, and

(g) distribution of any surplus to members in accordance with their rights.

21.6.5.4 Swelling the company's assets

IA 1986 contains provisions to enable the liquidator to swell the assets available to pay the debts of the company by invalidating certain transactions of the company (also available to administrators) or rendering people liable to contribute to the assets.

Invalid transactions
Section 245 provides that a floating charge is invalid, except in so far as consideration is given for it, if given within a specified period before the onset of insolvency (defined as the commencement of liquidation or presentation of petition for an administration order). The period depends on whether the charge was given to a connected person (defined in ss. 249 and 435 to include directors, their relatives and companies under their control), in which case it is two years; or unconnected persons, in which case it is one year. In addition, if the charge was given to an unconnected person it must be shown that at the time the charge was granted the company was unable to pay its debts or became so as a result of the charge.

IA 1986, s. 238, empowers the court to set aside any transaction at an undervalue (i.e., where the company makes a gift or receives consideration significantly less than that provided by the company), unless it was made in good faith on reasonable belief that it would benefit the company. The transaction may be set aside if it was made within two years of the onset of insolvency provided that at the time of the transaction the company was unable to pay its debts or became unable to do so as a result of the transaction (presumed if the transaction was with a connected person).

IA 1986, s. 239, empowers the court to set aside preferences, i.e., any transaction whereby the company puts a creditor in a better position in the event of the company's insolvency than he would otherwise have been, provided the company was influenced by a desire to prefer the creditor (this is presumed if the preference was given to a connected person) and the preference was given within six months of insolvency (if to an unconnected person) or two years (if to a connected person).

Note also ss. 423–425 (see **21.4.4.3**).

Personal liability
The liquidator may obtain a court order that certain persons contribute to the company's assets to assist in paying the company's debts.

IA 1986 s. 212, if on the winding up of a company it appears that an officer or person concerned in the management, promotion or formation of the company has misapplied and retained or become accountable for company property and been guilty of any misfeasance or breach of duty to the company, the court may compel him or her to repay, restore or account for the property or pay compensation for the breach.

IA 1986, s. 213 (fraudulent trading) where on the winding up of a company, it appears to the court that the company has been carried on with intent to defraud creditors, it may declare any persons knowingly parties to it liable to contribute to the company's assets. This provision was taken from an existing provision in CA 1985 which had little success because of the difficulty in proving the necessary intent.

IA 1986, s. 214 (wrongful trading) if on the insolvent liquidation of a company, the court finds that before commencement a director knew, or ought to have concluded, that there was no reasonable prospect that the company could avoid insolvent liquidation, the court may order that director to contribute to the company's assets. However, the court will not make an order if it is satisfied that the director had taken every step she or he ought to have to minimise loss to creditors. The standard by which a director is to be judged under s. 214 contains both objective and subjective elements of knowledge, skill and experience. In *Re Produce Market Consortium Ltd* [1989] 1 WLR 745, the first case on this provision, it was held that, when judging the director, regard should be had to the functions of the director and the nature of the company's business, and the standards should be those of a person fulfilling that function with reasonable diligence. The director is to be treated as possessing information which was capable of being ascertained had the company fulfilled its statutory duties and which the director ought to have ascertained. The directors were found liable and ordered to contribute £75,000. (See now also *Re DKG Contractors Ltd* [1990] BCC 903.)

Note that s. 213 applies to any person party to the fraudulent trading, and s. 214 applies only to directors, although shadow directors (those on whose instructions the board is accustomed to act) are included.

TWENTY TWO

UNDERSTANDING AND ANALYSING BASIC ACCOUNTS

22.1 Need for Accounts

This section of the Manual sets out the basic principles of accounting so that you will be able to understand accounting statements which may be presented to you in the course of your professional work.

To explain why businesses need to produce accounts we need to identify the classes of people who might need information about a business and the information of interest to the members of each class. Thus, for example, the people who might be interested in financial information about a large public company may be classified as follows:

(a) Managers: As they supervise the day-to-day activities of the company, they need information about the company's financial situation to enable them to manage the business efficiently.

(b) Shareholders: They will want to assess how effectively management is performing and how much profit they can afford to withdraw from the business.

(c) Trade contacts: Suppliers who provide on credit will want to know about the company's ability to pay its debts; customers need to know that the company is a secure source of supply and is in no danger of having to close down.

(d) Providers of finance to the company: A bank which permits the company to operate an overdraft, or a lender who provides longer-term finance by granting a loan, will want to ensure that the company can pay the interest and the amounts advanced.

(e) The taxation authorities: They want to know about profits to assess the tax.

(f) Employees of the company: Their future careers and the size of their wages and salaries are dependent on the company's financial position.

(g) Financial analysts and advisers: They need information for their clients, e.g., stockbrokers to advise investors; credit agencies to advise potential suppliers to the company; and journalists for their reading public.

To a greater or lesser extent, accounting information is prepared in financial statements to satisfy the information needs of these different groups. Managers of a business need the most information, to help them take their planning and control decisions; and they obviously have 'special' access to information about the business, because they are in a position to organise the provision of whatever internally produced statements they require. When managers want a large amount of information about the costs and profitability of individual products, or different parts of their business, they can arrange to obtain it through a system of cost and management accounting. In addition to management information, financial statements are prepared and perhaps published for the benefit of other user groups.

22.2 Main Financial Statements

The two principal financial statements drawn up by accountants are the *balance sheet* and the *profit and loss account.*

The balance sheet is simply a list of all the assets owned by a business and all the liabilities owed by a business as at a particular moment. Monetary amounts are attributed to each of the assets and liabilities and, the sum of the assets will always be equal to the sum of the liabilities.

A profit and loss account is a record of income generated and expenditure incurred over a given period. The period chosen will depend on the purpose for which the statement is produced. The profit and loss account which forms part of the published annual accounts of a limited company will usually be made up for the period of a year, commencing from the date of the previous year's accounts. On the other hand, management might want to keep a closer eye on a company's profitability by making up quarterly or monthly profit and loss accounts.

Both the balance sheet and the profit and loss account are summaries of accumulated data. For example, the profit and loss account will show a figure for revenue earned from selling goods to customers. This will be a total amount derived by summing the revenue earned from numerous individual sales made during the period. One of the jobs of an accountant is to devise methods of recording such individual transactions and eventually to produce summarised financial statements from them.

22.3 Accounting Concepts

Accounting practice has developed gradually over a matter of centuries. Many of its procedures are operated automatically by people who have never questioned whether alternative methods exist which have equal validity. The truth is that the procedures in common use imply the acceptance of certain concepts which are by no means self-evident; nor are they the only possible concepts which could be used to build up an accounting framework.

To show the importance in preparing and interpreting financial information, consider the example of a man who purchases a car for £1,000 and sells it one month later for £800. During the month he owned the car he used it to travel 2,000 miles. He estimated that if he had used public transport during that month his travelling costs would have been £230.

One way of recording these facts would be to say:

	£
Proceeds on disposal of car	800
Cost of acquiring car	1,000
Loss on transaction	£ 200

If the man regarded himself as a trader in motor cars, this might be a reasonable presentation of the facts and might lead him to deduce that selling cars would be an unsatisfactory line of business to pursue in the future.

Another way of presenting the facts would be to say:

	£
Benefits of acquiring car:	
(i) Value of travel obtained (measured by the cost of the alternative)	230
(ii) Proceeds received on disposal	800
	1,030
Cost of acquiring car	1,000
Net gain on transaction	£ 30

If the man regards himself as primarily a traveller, he has reason to be satisfied with the outcome of the transaction. The use of a different concept has led to a completely different interpretation of exactly the same facts.

Our next step is to look at some of the more important concepts which are taken for granted in preparing accounts:

(a) the going concern concept;

(b) the prudence concept;

(c) the accruals or matching concept;

(d) the consistency concept.

22.3.1 GOING CONCERN CONCEPT

When preparing accounts, the normal assumption is that the business to which they relate will continue trading for the forseeable future, without closing down or even running down its activities to a significant extent. The effect of this concept on asset values and the measurement of profit may be illustrated by an example.

22.3.1.1 Example

A retailer commences business on 1 January and buys a stock of 20 washing machines, each costing £100. During the year he sells 17 machines at £150 each. How should his profit be calculated, and how should the remaining machines be valued at 31 December, if:

(a) he is forced to close down his business at the end of the year and the remaining machines will realise only £60 each in a forced sale; or

(b) he intends to continue his business into the next year.

22.3.1.2 Solution

(a) If the business is to be closed down, the remaining three machines must be valued at the amount they will realise in a forced sale, i.e., 3 × £60 = £180.

Profit would be calculated as:

	£
Sale of 17 machines (@ £150)	2,550
Forced realisation of 3 machines	180
	2,730
Less cost of 20 machines (@ £100)	2,000
Profit for the year	£730

(b) If the business is regarded as a going concern, the stock unsold at 31 December will be carried forward into the following year, when the cost of the three machines will be matched against the eventual sale proceeds in computing that year's profits. The three machines will therefore appear in the balance sheet at 31 December at cost, 3 × £100 = £300.

The first year's profit will be calculated by reference to the 17 machines sold, as follows:

	£
Sale of 17 machines (@ £150)	2,550
Less cost of 17 machines (@ £100)	1,700
Profit for the year	£850

22.3.2 PRUDENCE CONCEPT

This is the concept which states that where alternative procedures, or alternative valuations, are possible, the one selected should be the one which gives the most cautious presentation of the business's financial position or results. For example, you may have wondered why the three washing machines in **22.3.1.2**(b) were stated in the balance sheet at their cost (£100 each) rather than their selling price (£150 each). This is simply an aspect of the prudence concept: to value the machines at £150 would be to anticipate making a profit before the profit has actually been earned by making a sale.

The other aspect of the prudence concept is that where a *loss* is foreseen, it should be anticipated and taken into account immediately. If a business purchases stock for £1,200 but because of a sudden slump in the market only £900 is likely to be realised when the stock is sold, the prudence concept dictates that the stock should be valued at £900. It is not enough to wait until the stock is sold, and then recognise the £300 loss; it must be recognised as soon as it is foreseen.

22.3.3 ACCRUALS OR MATCHING CONCEPT

This concept states that, in computing profit, revenue earned must be matched against the expenditure incurred in earning it. This is illustrated in example (b) in **22.3.1.2** above: profit of £850 was computed by matching the revenue (£2,550) earned from the sale of 17 washing machines against the cost (£1,700) of acquiring the machines. Although the number of machines acquired and paid for in the year was 20, it would be incorrect to deduct the cost of all 20 in computing profit, because three of them have yet to be sold. They will presumably be sold in the next accounting period and it is then that their cost will be deducted from the revenue earned from their sale.

In this example, the concepts of going concern and matching are linked. Because the business is assumed to be a going concern it is possible to carry forward the cost of the unsold machines as a charge against profits of the next period.

22.3.4 CONSISTENCY CONCEPT

Accounting is not an exact science. There are many areas in which judgment must be exercised in attributing money values to items appearing in accounts. Over the years certain procedures and principles (such as those contained in the Statements of Standard Accounting Practice) have come to be recognised as good accounting practice, but within these limits there are often various acceptable methods of accounting for similar items.

The consistency concept states that in preparing accounts consistency should be observed in two respects:

(a) Similar items within a single set of accounts should be given similar accounting treatment.

(b) The same treatment should be applied from one period to another in accounting for similar items. This enables valid comparisons to be made from one period to the next.

22.4 Accounts of a Sole Trader

We will begin our discussion of financial accounting practice by illustrating how to account for a business's transactions from the time that trading first begins. We will use the example below to illustrate the 'accounting equation', which is the rule that the assets of a business will at all times equal its liabilities.

22.4.1 EXAMPLE

On 1 July 2002, Liza decided to open up a flower stall in the market, to sell flowers and potted plants. She had saved up some money in her building society, and had £2,500 to put into her business. She opens up a business bank account and pays the £2,500 into it.

When the business is set up, an 'accountant's picture' can be drawn of what it owns and what it owes.

The business owns the £2,500 at the bank that Liza has put into it. But does it owe anything? The answer is yes.

The business is a separate entity in accounting terms. It has obtained its assets, in this example cash, from its owner, Liza. It therefore owes this amount of money to its owner. (If Liza changed her mind and decided not to go into business after all, the business would be dissolved by the 'repayment' of the cash by the business to Liza.)

22.4.2 CAPITAL

The money put into a business by its owners is capital. In accounting capital is an investment of money (funds) with the intention of earning a return. A business proprietor invests capital with the intention of earning profit. As long as that money is invested accountants will treat the capital as money which the business owes to the proprietor.

22.4.3 THE ACCOUNTING EQUATION

When Liza sets up her business:

Capital invested = £2,500
Bank = £2,500

Capital invested is a form of liability, because it is an amount owed by the business to its owner(s). Adapting this to the idea that liabilities and assets are always equal amounts, we can state the accounting equation as follows:

Assets = Capital + other liabilities

For Liza, as at 1 July 2002

£2,500 (cash) = £2,500 (owed to Liza) + £0

22.4.3.1 Example continued

Liza uses some of the money invested to purchase a market stall from Len, who is retiring from his fruit and vegetable business. The cost of the stall is £1,800.

She also purchases some flowers and potted plants from a trader in the New Covent Garden wholesale market, at a cost of £650.

This leaves £50 at the bank, after paying for the stall and goods for resale, out of the original £2,500. Liza kept £30 in the bank and drew out £20 in small change. She was now ready for her first day of market trading on 3 July 2002.

The assets and liabilities of the business have not altered, and at 3 July, before trading begins, the state of her business is:

	Assets	=		Capital	+	Other liabilities
	£			£		£
Stall	1,800		Introduced	2,500		Nil
Flowers	650					
Bank £(2,500 − 1,800 − 650 − 20)	30					
Cash	20					
	£2,500	=		£2,500	+	Nil

The stall and the flowers and plants are physical items, but they must be given a money value. This money value will usually be their historical cost.

22.4.3.2 Profit introduced into the accounting equation

Let us now suppose that on 3 July Liza has a very successful day. She is able to sell all her flowers and plants, for £900. All her sales are for cash.

Since Liza has sold goods costing £650 to earn revenue of £900, we can say that she has earned a profit of £250 on the day's trading.

Profits belong to the owners of a business. In this case, the £250 belongs to Liza. However, so long as the business retains the profits, and does not pay anything out to its owners, the retained profits are accounted for as an addition to the proprietor's capital.

	Assets	=		Capital	+	Other liabilities
	£			£		£
Stall	1,800		Introduced	2,500		Nil
Flowers	—		Retained			
Bank	30		Profit	250		
Cash (20 + 900)	920					
	£2,750	=		£2,750	+	Nil

22.4.3.3 Increase in net assets

We can re-arrange the accounting equation to get:

Assets — Liabilities	=	Capital;	which is also
Net assets	=	Capital	

(Net assets is simply the difference between total assets and total liabilities).

At the beginning and then at the end of 3 July 2002 Liza's financial position was as follows:

			Net Assets		Capital
(a) At the beginning of the day:	£(2,500 − 0)	=	£2,500	=	£2,500
(b) At the end of the day:	£(2,750 − 0)	=	£2,750	=	£2,750

There has been an increase of £250 in net assets, which is the amount of profits earned during the day.

22.4.3.4 Drawings

Drawings are amounts of money taken out of a business by its owner.

Since Liza has made a profit of £250 from her first day's work, she might well feel fully justified in drawing some of the profits out of the business. After all, business owners, like everyone else, need income for living expenses. We will suppose that Liza decides to pay herself £180, in 'wages'.

The payment of £180 is probably regarded by Liza as fair reward for her day's work, and she might think of the sum as being in the nature of wages. However, the £180 is not an expense to be deducted before the figure of net profit is arrived at. In other words, it would be *incorrect* to calculate the net profit earned by the business as follows:

	£
Profit on sale of flowers etc.	250
Less 'wages' paid to Liza	(180)
Net profit earned by business	£70

This is because any amounts paid by a business to its proprietor are treated by accountants as withdrawals of profit (the usual term is **appropriations** of profit), and not as expenses incurred by the business. In the case of Liza's business, the true position is that the net profit earned *is* the £250 surplus on sale of flowers, but it is not the retained profit:

	£
Net profit earned by business	250
Less profit withdrawn by Liza	(180)
Net profit retained in the business	£70

Profits are capital as long as they are retained in the business. Once they are appropriated, they are no longer capital. When they are paid out, the business suffers a reduction in capital.

The drawings are taken in cash, and so the business loses £180 of its cash assets. After the drawings have been made, the accounting equation would be restated as:

	Assets	=		Capital	+	Other liabilities
	£			£		£
Stall	1,800		Introduced	2,500		Nil
Flowers	—		Retained Profit	70		
Bank	30					
Cash £(920 − 180)	740					
	£2,570	=		£2,570	+	Nil

The increase in net assets since Liza began trading is now only £70, which is the amount of the retained profit.

22.4.3.5 Introduction of liabilities

Let us now suppose that on the following day, 4 July, Liza purchases some flowers on credit for £200, i.e., Liza, instead of paying £200 cash for the flowers, now owes the supplier £200.

The £200 owed to the supplier is an example of a liability and will have to be paid at a later date.

The accounting equation would now be as follows:

	Assets	=	Capital	+	Other liabilities
	£		£		£
Stall	1,800				
Flowers	200	As before	2,570	Creditor for flowers	200
Bank	30				
Cash	740				
	£2,770	=	£2,570	+	200

All that has happened is that the assets have been increased by £200 by purchasing the flowers, but at the same time the liabilities have increased by £200.

22.4.3.6 The usefulness of the accounting equation

The accounting equation is a useful introductory concept in accounting because it emphasises the equality between assets and liabilities (including capital as a liability). In practice, the accounting equation is rarely used as asets and liabilities are presented in the form of a balance sheet. We shall move on in the next section and see how the equation can be developed into a balance sheet.

We shall then move on and show how a business can summarise its trading performance in a trading and profit and loss account.

22.5 From the Accounting Equation to a Balance Sheet

We left Liza in **22.4.3.5** in the following situation:

	Assets	=	Capital	+	Other liabilities
	£		£		£
Stall	1,800				
Flowers	200	As before	2,570	Creditor for flowers	200
Bank	30				
Cash	740				
	£2,770	=	£2,570	+	200

The accounting equation can therefore be summarised as follows:

Assets	=	Capital	+	Liabilities
£2,770	=	£2,570	+	£200

This could be restated as:

Assets	–	Liabilities	=	Capital
£2,770	–	£200	=	£2,570

Taking this a stage further, the accounting equation could be presented as:

	£
Assets	2,770
Less: Liabilities	(200)
Net assets	£2,570
Capital	£2,570

NB: The brackets mean that the figure is to be deducted.

When the accounting equation is presented in this form it provides the basis of the balance sheet, i.e., a statement of the net assets (assets – liabilities) of the business at a point in time — midnight on 4 July. The balance sheet allows us to show the assets and liabilities that make up Liza's business in more detail. A traditional presentation for Liza's balance sheet would be:

BALANCE SHEET OF
LIZA
AS AT 4 JULY 2002

	£	£
Fixed assets		
Stall		1,800
Current assets		
Stock (Flowers)	200	
Bank	30	
Cash	740	
	970	
Less: Current liabilities		
Creditors	(200)	
Net current assets		770
Net assets		£2,570
Capital		£2,570

22.6 The Balance Sheet Format

In this example the balance sheet we have produced is very simple. No matter how complicated the balance sheet of a business may look, it will basically be made up of the following items.

22.6.1 FIXED ASSETS

A fixed asset is an asset acquired for use over a period of time within the business, with a view to earning income or making profits from its use, either directly or indirectly.

(a) In a manufacturing industry, a production machine would be a fixed asset, because it makes goods which are then sold.

(b) In a service industry, equipment used by employees giving service to customers would be classed as fixed assets (e.g., the equipment used in a garage, and furniture in a hotel).

(c) Less obviously, factory premises, office furniture, computer equipment, company cars, delivery vans or pallets in a warehouse are all fixed assets.

To be classed as a fixed asset in the balance sheet of a business, an item must satisfy two further conditions:

(a) It must be owned by the business — if a building is rented (*not* leased, since leasing can give rise to a fixed asset) or if furniture or telephones are rented, they cannot be assets of the business.

(b) The asset must have a 'life' in use of more than one year (strictly, more than one 'accounting period' which might be more or less than one year).

A tangible fixed asset is a physical asset, one that can be touched. It has a real, 'solid' existence. All of the examples of fixed assets mentioned in the previous paragraphs are tangible.

An intangible fixed asset is an asset which does not have a physical existence. It cannot be 'touched'.

An investment might also be a fixed asset. Investments are commonly found in the published accounts of large limited companies. A large company, A, might invest in another company, B, by purchasing some of the shares or debentures of B. These investments would earn income for A in the form of interest or dividends paid out by B. If the investments are purchased by A with a view to holding on to them for more than one year, they would be classified as fixed assets of A.

22.6.2 CURRENT ASSETS

Current assets are either:

(a) items owned by the business with the intention of turning them into cash within one year; or

(b) cash, including money at the bank owned by the business.

Items which could appear as current assets in the balance sheet are:

(a) Stocks — items unsold at the end of the period (see **22.10.1**).

(b) Debtors — amounts owed by customers.

(c) Prepayments — amounts paid in advance (see **22.12.2**).

(d) Short-term investments — Stocks and shares held in other companies with the intention of selling them in the near future.

(e) Bank and cash balances.

Current assets should be listed in the order shown above. That is with the least liquid of the assets at the top. The least liquid assets are those that would take the longest to turn into cash.

22.6.3 CURRENT LIABILITIES

These are debts of the business that must be paid within a fairly short period of time. By convention, a 'fairly short period of time' has come to be accepted as one year. For the accounts of limited companies, the Companies Act 1989 requires use of the term 'creditors: amounts falling due within one year' rather than 'current liabilities' although in practical terms they mean the same thing.

Examples of current liabilities are:

(a) loans repayable within one year;

(b) a bank overdraft;

(c) trade creditors;

(d) bills of exchange which are payable by the business;

(e) taxation payable;

(f) 'accrued charges': These are expenses already built up by the business, for which no invoice has yet been received, or for which the date of payment by standing order has not yet arrived. An example of accrued charges would be the cost of gas or electricity bills. If a business ends its accounting year on 31 December, but does not expect its next quarterly gas bill until the end of January, there will be two months of accrued gas charges — charges relating to two months' use of gas for which no invoice has been received and no debt is yet 'officially' payable — to record in the balance sheet as a liability. (See **22.12.1**.)

It is often argued that a bank overdraft is not a current liability, because a business is usually able to negotiate an overdraft facility for a long period of time. If an overdraft thus becomes a more permanent source of borrowing, it is really a long-term liability. However, you would normally expect to account for an overdraft as a current liability, since banks reserve the right to demand repayment at short notice.

22.6.4 LONG-TERM LIABILITIES

In Liza's balance sheet no long-term liabilities in the business were included. However, in practice, businesses may well have long-term, as well as current liabilities.

A long-term liability is a debt which is not payable within the 'short term' and so any liability which is not current must be long-term. A deferred liability is a debt due to someone else which has been put off till sometime in the future. In other words, a deferred liability is a long-term liability. Just as 'short term' by convention means one year or less, 'long term' means more than one year. In the accounts of limited companies, the Companies Act 1989 requires use of the term: 'creditors: amounts falling due after more than one year'.

Examples of long-term liabilities are:

(a) loans which are not repayable for more than one year, such as a bank loan, or a loan from an individual to a business;

(b) a mortgage loan, which is a loan specifically secured against a freehold property; if the business fails to repay the loan, the lender then has 'first claim' on the property, and is entitled to repayment from the proceeds from the enforced sale of the property;

(c) debentures or debenture loans. These are common with limited companies. Debentures are written acknowledgements of debt issued by a company at a fixed rate of interest. They are repayable on agreed terms by a specified date in the future. Holders of debentures are therefore lenders of money to a company. Their interests, including security for the loan, are protected by the terms of a trust deed.

22.6.5 CAPITAL

In the Liza balance sheet we showed capital as a single figure of £2,570, representing Liza's investment in the business. There is nothing wrong with this, but in practice we will often analyse movements in capital over the period under review. This could be set out as follows:

	£	£
Capital as at the beginning of the accounting period (capital 'brought forward')		X
Add: additional capital introduced during the period		X
		X
Add: profit earned during the period	X	
Less: drawings	(X)	
Retained profit for the period		X
Capital as at the end of the accounting period (capital 'carried forward')		X

('Brought forward' means 'brought forward from the previous period', and 'carried forward' means 'carried forward to the next period'. The carried forward amount at the end of one period is also the brought forward amount of the next period.)

22.7 Trading and Profit and Loss Account

22.7.1 DEVELOPMENT OF A TRADING AND PROFIT AND LOSS ACCOUNT

We left Liza at midnight on 4 July 2002 with the following balance sheet:

	£	£
Fixed assets		
Stall		1,800
Current assets		
Stock (Flowers)	200	
Bank	30	
Cash	740	
	970	
Less: Current liabilities		
Creditors	(200)	
Net current assets		770
Net assets		£2,570
Capital		£2,570

Let us now develop the example to include a further day's trading:

On the next market day, 31 July 2002, Liza enlists the help of her sister, paying her £20 cash for the day's work.

Liza pays £500 cash for flowers. Liza also has to pay £30 cash to a roofer who is called to repair a hole in the stall roof.

All the flowers are sold that day realising cash of £1,000.

Pleased with the day's trading, Liza takes £100 cash out of the business for personal consumption.

We can summarise the trading performance of Liza for the day in a trading, profit and loss account. In this we will match the revenues earned from selling the flowers with the costs of selling the flowers.

TRADING, PROFIT AND LOSS ACCOUNT
OF LIZA
FOR THE DAY OF 31 JULY 2002

	£	£	
Sales		1,000	
Opening stock of flowers	200		Trading
Purchase of flowers	500		account
Cost of sales		(700)	
Gross profit		300	
Less expenses			
Wages	20		Profit and
Repairs	30		loss account
		(50)	
Net profit		£250	

Notes:

(a) Liza had £200 of flowers purchased on 4 July 2002 but not sold until 31 July 2002 (NB: they were plastic).

(b) The work done on the roof is a repair and must be charged in the profit and loss account as an expense.

(c) Drawings are an appropriation of profit and in this example will be shown as a movement of capital in the balance sheet.

You will see that the trading, profit and loss account has been divided into:

(a) *Trading account*: In this part we basically match the revenues earned from selling the flowers with the costs of those flowers. Liza has managed to sell £700 worth of flowers for £1,000, the difference of £300 is what is known as the gross profit.

The gross profit is a crucial indicator for businessmen as it excludes one-off expenses like the roof repairs. Liza will want to earn as high a gross profit as she possibly can. To maximise gross profit, Liza will try and sell for as high a price as possible, whilst buying goods for as low a price as possible. How successful she is in achieving this, will largely depend on her performance as a businesswoman.

(b) *Profit and loss account*: In this part of the statement we charge the costs which cannot be directly related with the sale, and arrive at the net profit figure.

In our example we have included only wages and repairs, but, in practice, businesses will often face a listing of expenses.

Other business expenses that will appear in the profit and loss account are as follows.

(a) *Selling and distribution expenses.* These are expenses associated with the process of selling and delivering goods to customers, for example, salaries and commissions of salesmen.

(b) *Administration expenses.* These are the expenses of providing management and administration for the business, for example, rent for the premises and telephone costs.

(c) *Finance costs.* These are expenses such as interest paid on loans or on the bank overdraft.

22.7.2 LINK WITH THE BALANCE SHEET

In the previous section, **22.7.1**, we have produced a trading, profit and loss account for Liza. It is important to emphasise at this stage that the trading profit and loss account which we have produced is inextricably linked with the balance sheet. A balance sheet as at 31 July 2002 will look like this:

BALANCE SHEET OF
LIZA
AS AT 31 JULY 2002

	£	£
Fixed assets		
Stall		1,800
Current assets		
Bank	30	
Cash (740 − 500 − 20 − 30 + 1,000 − 100)	1,090	
	1,120	

	£	£
Less: Current liabilities		
Creditors	(200)	
		920
Net assets		£2,720
Capital at start of day		£2,570
Profit earned in day	250	
Less drawings	(100)	
		150
Capital at end of day		£2,720

From this we can see that the increase in net assets during the day must equal the net profit less drawings made during the day.

Increase in net assets in day	=	Net profit	–	Drawings
(£2,720 – £2,570)	=	£250	–	£100
£150	=		£150	

The two statements are therefore clearly linked but both have very different objectives. The trading, profit and loss account summarises trading performance over a period of time. The balance sheet gives a statement of net assets at a point in time.

The next problem you may wish to address is highlighted by the £30 repairs to Liza's stall. We charged the £30 as an expense to the profit and loss account but could it not be argued that it should have been added to the cost of the stall in the balance sheet?

This is the problem we shall look at next.

22.8 What Goes in the Balance Sheet and What Goes in the Profit and Loss Account?

You might by now be a little confused about which items appear in the balance sheet and which appear in the profit and loss account. For example, suppose that a business sells goods worth £20,000 (for cash) during one month, and during the same month borrows £10,000 from a money lender. Its total receipts for the month are £30,000

(a) The £20,000 of sales appear as sales in the trading, profit and loss account.

(b) The £10,000 borrowed will not be shown in the profit and loss account, but will be shown as an asset (cash) and a liability (loan) of £10,000 in the balance sheet.

Suppose again that a business spends £15,000 buying some shares of a public company through the stock market. This company pays a dividend out of its profits, and the business receives a dividend of, say, £1,000 on its investment.

(a) The cost of the shares will not be an expense in the profit and loss account. They will appear as an asset (investment) in the balance sheet.

(b) However, the dividend of £1,000 will appear as income of the business in the profit and loss account.

The two illustrations above are examples of transactions where it is not necessarily clear at first sight whether an item should appear in the balance sheet or trading, profit and loss account. To try to make a distinction we must now turn our attention to the distinctions between capital expenditure and revenue expenditure, and capital income and revenue income. This distinction is also important for revenue law.

22.8.1 CAPITAL EXPENDITURE AND REVENUE EXPENDITURE

Capital expenditure is expenditure which results in the acquisition of fixed assets, or an improvement in the earning capacity of existing fixed assets.

(a) Capital expenditure is not charged as an expense in the profit and loss account, although a depreciation charge will usually be made to write off the capital expenditure gradually over time. Depreciation charges *are* expenses in the profit and loss account.

(b) Capital expenditure on fixed assets results in the appearance of a fixed asset in the balance sheet of the business, either as a new asset (purchase) or as an addition to an old one (enhancement).

Revenue expenditure is an expenditure which is incurred either:

(a) for the purpose of the trade of the business — this includes expenditure classified as selling and distribution expenses, administration expenses and finance costs; or

(b) to maintain the existing earning capacity of fixed assets, such as repairs.

Revenue expenditure is charged to the profit and loss account for a period, provided that it relates to the trading activity and sales of that particular period. For example, if a business buys ten widgets for £200 (£20 each) and sells eight of them during an accounting period, it will have two widgets left in stock at the end of the period. The full £200 is revenue expenditure but only £160 is a cost of goods sold during the period. The remaining £40 (cost of two units) will be included in the balance sheet in the stock of goods held — as a current asset valued at £40.

22.8.2 WHY IS THE DISTINCTION BETWEEN CAPITAL AND REVENUE ITEMS IMPORTANT?

Revenue expenditure results from the purchase of goods and services that will either:

(a) be used fully in the accounting period in which they are purchased, and so be a cost or expense in the trading, profit and loss account; or

(b) result in a current asset as at the end of the accounting period (because the goods or services have not yet been consumed or been made use of).

Capital expenditure results in the purchase or improvement of fixed assets, which are assets that will provide benefits to the business in more than one accounting period, and which are not acquired with a view to being resold in the normal course of trade. The cost of purchased fixed assets is not charged in full to the trading, profit and loss account of the period in which the purchase occurs. Instead, the fixed asset is gradually depreciated over a number of accounting periods.

Since revenue items and capital items are accounted for in different ways, the correct and consistent calculation of profit for any accounting period depends on the correct and consistent classification of items as revenue or capital.

22.9 Introduction of Stocks, Fixed Assets, Accruals and Prepayments

So far we have developed our analysis of the accounting equation to show how the assets and liabilities of a business can be included in a balance sheet. At the same time we have seen how the trading performance of a business can be summarised in a trading, profit and loss account. Let us now move on to include in our analysis, stocks and the cost of sales, fixed assets and depreciation, accruals and prepayments.

22.10 Stocks and the Cost of Sales

A business will not always be able to sell all the goods it has available for sale. Most businesses will find themselves with stocks unsold at their period end.

22.10.1 INTRODUCTION OF CLOSING STOCKS

To introduce closing stocks into our analysis, let's use a simple example.

22.10.1.1 Example 1

Hanley commences trading on 1 January 2002, opening a business bank account with £2,000.

On 2 January 2002, he purchases ten videos costing £150 each. Trade is slow and he does not make a sale until 31 December 2002, when he sells eight videos for £200 each.

22.10.1.2 Solution 1

In this situation, Hanley has generated sales revenues of £1,600 (8 × £200). It would appear that he makes a profit of £100. This analysis would however be incorrect as we would not be applying the matching concept. It is crucial that the revenue from eight videos should be matched with the cost of eight videos, and not ten videos.

The way to do this is to calculate a cost of sales in the trading account. This will take account of the closing stock of videos.

TRADING ACCOUNT
OF HANLEY
FOR THE YEAR ENDED 31 DECEMBER 2002

	£	£
Sales (8 × £200)		1,600
Purchases (10 × £150)	1,500	
Less: Closing stock (2 × £150)	(300)	
Cost of sale		(1,200)
Gross profit		£400

The cost of sale of £1,200 represents the cost of the eight videos sold for £150 each. We have therefore matched costs and revenues in the trading account. The other thing to consider is that Hanley also possesses two videos at the year end which are clearly an asset. We should account for this asset of stock in the balance sheet.

BALANCE SHEET
OF HANLEY
AS AT 31 DECEMBER 2002

	£
Current assets	
Stock (2 × £150)	300
Bank £(2,000 − 1,500 + 1,600)	2,100
Net assets	£2,400
Capital 1 January 2002	2,000
Profit for year	400
Capital 31 December 2002	£2,400

Quite clearly, the two videos in Hanley's closing stock of 31 December 2002 will be made available for sale in the following year, i.e., the closing stock of 31 December 2002 will become the opening stock for the year ending 31 December 2003.

22.10.2 THE INCLUSION OF OPENING STOCKS

Continuing with our example:

22.10.2.1 Example 2

Hanley continues to trade and on 1 January purchases 12 videos costing £180 each. (They are identical to the two in opening stock.)

On 31 December 2002 Hanley sells ten videos for £220 each.

22.10.2.2 Solution 2

Hanley's second year's trading highlights the importance of stocks in the accounts of a business. If we assume that the two videos in opening stock were among the ten videos sold, then Hanley's trading account would be as follows:

TRADING ACCOUNT (FIFO)

	£	£
Sales (10 × £220)		2,200
Opening stock (2 × £150)	300	
Purchases (12 × £180)	2,160	
	2,460	
Closing stock (4 × £180)	(720)	
Cost of sale (2 × £150) + (8 × £180)		(1,740)
Gross profit		£460

This assumes that closing stock is valued on a first in first out (FIFO) basis, i.e., the two videos in opening stock were the first to be sold. This is not an unreasonable assumption and would approximate to good storekeeping.

However, an alternative method of stock valuation would be to assume that the last stock in is the first to be sold (LIFO), i.e., the sales of ten videos were all made from the batch purchased at £180. In this situation the trading account would be:

TRADING ACCOUNT (LIFO)

	£	£
Sales		2,200
Opening stock	300	
Purchases	2,160	
	2,460	
Closing stock (2 × £150) + (2 × £180)	(660)	
Cost of sale (10 × £180)		(1,800)
Gross profit		£400

This highlights the importance of stocks in the accounts of a business. By adopting a different stock valuation, Hanley has seen his profit reduced by £60. The stock figure has a direct impact on profit and it is not suprising that the auditors of a business will often spend most of their time looking at the stock figure.

To complete the analysis, a balance sheet for Hanley at 31 December 2002 with a FIFO stock valuation would be as follows:

BALANCE SHEET
OF HANLEY
AS AT 31 DECEMBER 2002

	£
Current assets	
Stock (4 × £180)	720
Bank £(2,100 − 2,160 + 2,200)	2,140
	£2,860
Capital 1 January 2002	2,400
Profit for year	460
Capital 31 December 2002	£2,860

22.11 Fixed Assets and Depreciation

In **22.5** we identified the market stall used by Liza Doolittle as an example of a fixed asset. That is an asset owned by the business having a life in use of more than one year. In practice, a business is likely to own several fixed assets. These must be disclosed in the balance sheet, the most common being: land and buildings; plant and machinery; motor vehicles; and fixtures and fittings.

We have already considered the treatment of fixed assets in **22.6.1** when we looked at the treatment of capital expenditure. Let us go on and develop the analysis further.

22.11.1 DEPRECIATION

We will develop the idea of depreciation with the following example.

22.11.1.1 Example 1

Fulton purchased a machine for business use for £9,000 on 1 January 2000.

The machine is estimated to have a three-year useful life after which it will be worthless.

Fulton has purchased the machine to use it within the business to help generate revenues over its useful life. The machine is estimated to earn revenues of £6,000 for each of the three years of its useful life.

In the accounts of Fulton we must attempt to match costs with revenues, i.e., charge the cost of the machine to the periods benefiting from the revenues. The way that this is done is to depreciate the machine over its useful economic life. By depreciating the machine we mean that the cost of the machine should be written off, or charged to the profit and loss account over the machine's useful life.

22.11.2 METHODS OF CHARGING DEPRECIATION

There are several methods for charging depreciation on a fixed asset. The most common method and the one considered here is the straight line method. This method depreciates the machine in equal annual instalments over the machine's estimated useful economic life.

In the example of Fulton the annual charge for depreciation would be calculated as:

$$\frac{\text{Cost of the machine}}{\text{Estimated useful life}} = \text{Annual depreciation charge}$$

$$\frac{\pounds 9{,}000}{3\text{ years}} = \pounds 3{,}000.$$

The depreciation rate is often expressed as a percentage, e.g., to divide cost by three years is the same as multiplying cost by 33.3%. Companies often express their depreciation rates as percentages.

22.11.2.1 Example 2

The company charges depreciation at annual rates of 33.3% on cost. So in the example of Fulton:

$$£9{,}000 \times 33.3\% = £3{,}000 = \text{Annual charge for depreciation}$$

The formula can be further developed to take account of any estimated proceeds for the asset at the end of its useful life.

22.11.2.2 Example 3

Fulton anticipates receiving £300 scrap at the end of the machine's three-year economic life.

$$\frac{\text{Cost} - \text{estimated residual value}}{\text{Estimated useful life}}$$

$$\frac{£9{,}000 - £300}{3 \text{ years}} = £2{,}900 = \text{Annual charge.}$$

The straight line method of providing for depreciation is just one of many methods which could be used. It is not necessary to go into the calculation of these other methods in this chapter. It is sufficient to say that they all charge different amounts of depreciation depending on the use made of the machine, or the wear and tear on the machine, in a given period.

22.11.3 DEPRECIATION IN THE ACCOUNTS OF A BUSINESS

When a fixed asset is depreciated there are two things that must be accounted for:

(a) The annual depreciation charge must be included as an expense in the profit and loss account of the business. In this way the revenues which the machine earns are matched with the costs of the machine.

(b) In the balance sheet the fixed asset's value must reflect the cumulative depreciation charged on that asset. The machine is wearing out as it is used and its value is diminishing over time.

In the balance sheet we want to include the machine at its net book value, i.e., at cost – accumulated depreciation.

22.11.3.1 Example 4

Taking the Fulton example and assuming a zero residual value for the machine. We would have the following:

Year ending	31 December 2000	31 December 2001	31 December 2002
	£	£	£
Balance sheet extract			
Fixed assets			
Plant and Machinery at cost	9,000	9,000	9,000
Accumulated depreciation	(3,000)	(6,000)	(9,000)
Net book value	£6,000	£3,000	nil
Trading, profit and loss account			
Sales	6,000	6,000	6,000
Depreciation	(3,000)	(3,000)	(3,000)
Profit*	£3,000	£3,000	£3,000

* This assumes that Fulton has no other revenues or costs (somewhat unrealistic) and that the machine will have a zero residual value.

The example shows quite clearly the dual nature of the depreciation adjustment. The cost of the machine is charged to the profit and loss account over the useful life of the fixed asset whilst the balance sheet reflects the diminution in the value of the machine.

22.11.4 WHICH FIXED ASSETS SHOULD BE DEPRECIATED?

All fixed assets having a finite (limited) useful life should be depreciated. Assets with an infinite useful life, e.g., freehold land, need not be depreciated.

22.12 Accruals and Prepayments

In calculating the profit of a period it is crucial that costs are matched with the revenues earned. It is likely that the business will have to take account of both accruals and prepayments.

22.12.1 ACCRUALS

Accruals or accrued expenses are those which must be charged to the profit and loss account even though they have not yet been paid for.

22.12.1.1 Example 1

Davies prepares accounts at 31 December each year. He rents premises for £500 a month.

For the year ending 31 December 2002 the landlord has been very lax in invoicing Davies, who has not received rent invoices for November and December. As a result the rent has not been paid.

In this situation, Davies has paid 10 months' rent of £5,000 up to the end of October.

At the year end of 31 December 2002 Davies has clearly had the benefit of occupancy in November and December but has not paid for that benefit. In the accounts we should accrue for the two months' rent which we have not yet been invoiced for.

There are two sides to the accounting entry:

(a) The profit and loss should reflect the cost of 12 months' rent as follows:

	£
10 months' rent paid (Jan-Oct)	5,000
Accrual for rent for November and December (2 × £500)	1,000
Total rent charged to profit and loss account	£6,000

(b) The balance sheet must reflect the fact that two months' rent are owed by Davies at the balance sheet date.

Balance sheet extract:

Current liabilities
Accruals £1,000.

22.12.2 PREPAYMENTS

Prepayments are payments which have been made in one accounting period, but which should not be charged to the profit and loss account until a later period.

22.12.2.1 Example 2

Meninga prepares accounts for the year ending 31 December 2002.

On 1 April 2002, he pays his insurance premium of £2,000 to cover 12 months' insurance to 31 March 2003.

At the year ended 31 December 2002, Meninga has effectively prepaid three months' insurance. He will enjoy the benefit of this three months' insurance between 1 January 2003 to 31 March 2003 in the next accounting period. The accounts for the year ending 31 December 2003 should therefore be charged with the cost of that period's insurance. Again, there are two sides to the accounting entry.

(a) The profit and loss account for the year ended 31 December 2002 should only be charged with insurance for the period 1 April 2002 to 31 December 2002.

$$\frac{9}{12} \times £2{,}000 = £1{,}500.$$

The balance should be carried forward as a prepayment and charged to the profit and loss account of the year ended 31 December 2003.

(b) This prepayment of 3/12 × £2,000 = £500 will be included in the balance sheet of 31 December 2002 as follows:

Balance sheet extract year ended 31.12.02

Current assets	
Prepayments	£500

22.13 Accounts of Partnerships

22.13.1 INTRODUCTION

Partnership is defined by the Partnership Act 1890 as 'the relation which exists between persons carrying on a business in common with a view of profit'. In other words, a partnership is an arrangement between two or more individuals in which they undertake to share the risks and rewards of a joint business operation.

It is usual for a partnership to be established formally by means of a *partnership agreement*. However, if individuals act as though they are in partnership even though no written agreement exists, then it will be presumed in law that a partnership does exist and that its terms of agreement are the same as those laid down in the Partnership Act 1890.

22.13.2 THE PARTNERSHIP AGREEMENT

The partnership agreement is a written agreement in which the terms of the partnership are set out, and in particular the financial arrangements as between partners. The items it should cover include:

(a) **Capital:** Each partner puts in a share of the business capital. If there is to be an agreement on how much each partner should put in and keep in the business, as a minimum fixed amount, this should be stated.

(b) **Profit sharing ratio:** Partners can agree to share profits in any way they choose. For example, if there are three partners in a business, they might agree to share profits equally but on the other hand, if one partner does a greater share of the work, or has more experience and ability, or puts in more capital, the ratio of profit sharing might be different.

(c) **Interest on capital:** Partners might agree to pay themselves interest on the capital they put into the business. If they do so, the agreement will state what rate of interest is to be applied.

(d) **Partners' salaries:** Partners might also agree to pay themselves salaries. These are not salaries in the same way that an employee of the business will be paid a wage or salary, because partners' salaries are an appropriation of profit, and not an expense in the profit and loss account of the business. The purpose of paying salaries is to give each partner a satisfactory basic income before the residual profits are shared out.

(e) **Drawings:** Partners may draw out their share of profits from the business. However, they might agree to put a limit on how much they should draw out in any period. If so, this limit should be specified in the partnership agreement. To encourage partners to delay taking drawings out of the business until the financial year has ended, the agreement might also be that partners should be charged interest on their drawings during the year.

22.13.3 HOW DOES ACCOUNTING FOR PARTNERSHIPS DIFFER FROM ACCOUNTING FOR SOLE TRADERS?

Partnership accounts are identical in many respects to the accounts of sole traders. In particular:

(a) The assets of a partnership are like the assets of any other business, and are accounted for in the same way. The assets side of a partnership balance sheet is no different from what has been shown in earlier chapters of this Manual.

(b) The net profit of a partnership is calculated in the same way as the net profit of a sole trader. The only minor difference is that if a partner makes a loan to the business (as distinct from capital contribution) then interest on the loan will be an expense in the profit and loss account, in the same way as interest on any other loan from a person or organisation who is not a partner.

There are two respects in which partnership accounts are different, however.

(a) the funds put into the business by each partner are shown differently;

(b) the net profit must be appropriated by the partners, i.e., shared out according to the partnership agreement. This appropriation of profits must be shown in the partnership accounts.

22.13.4 FUNDS EMPLOYED

When a partnership is formed, each partner puts in some capital to the business. These initial capital contributions are recorded in a series of *capital accounts*, one for each partner. (Since each partner is ultimately entitled to repayment of his capital it is clearly vital to keep a record of how much is owed to whom.) The precise amount of initial capital contributed by each partner is a matter for general agreement and there is no question of each partner necessarily contributing the same amount, although this does sometimes happen. The balance for the capital account will always be a brought forward credit entry in the partnership accounts, because the capital contributed by proprietors is a liability of the business.

In addition to a capital account, each partner normally has: a current account; and a drawings account.

A **current account** is used to record the profits retained in the business by the partner. It is therefore a sort of capital account, which increases in value when the partnership makes profits, and falls in value when the partner whose current account it is makes drawings out of the business.

The main difference between the capital and current account in accounting for partnerships is that:

(a) whereas the balance on the capital account remains static from year to year (with one or two exceptions);

(b) the current account is continually fluctuating up and down, as the partnership makes profits which are shared out between the partners, and as each partner takes out drawings.

A further difference is that when the partnership agreement provides for interest on capital, partners receive interest on the balance in their capital account, but not on the balance in their current account.

The **drawings accounts** serve exactly the same purpose as the drawings account for a sole trader. Each partner's drawings are recorded in a separate account.

The partnership balance sheet will therefore consist of:

(a) the capital accounts of each partner; and

(b) the current accounts of each partner, net of drawings.

22.13.5 APPROPRIATION OF NET PROFITS

The net profit of a partnership is shared out between them according to the terms of their agreement. This sharing out is shown in a **profit and loss appropriation account,** which follows on from the profit and loss account itself.

The way in which profit is shared out depends on the terms of the partnership agreement. The steps to take are:

(a) establish how much the net profit is;

(b) appropriate interest on capital and salaries first. Both of these items are an appropriation of profit and are not expenses in the profit and loss account;

(c) if partners agree to pay interest on their drawings during the year allocate this to their current accounts;

(d) *residual profits:* the difference between net profits (plus any interest charged on drawings) and appropriations for interest on capital and salaries is the residual profit. This is shared out between partners in the profit-sharing ratio;

(e) each partner's share of profits is allocated to his current account;

(f) the balance on each partner's drawings account is allocated to his current account.

In practice, each partner's capital account will occupy a separate ledger account, as will his current account etc. It is customary to represent the details of these accounts side by side, in columnar form, to save time. The examples which follow in this text use the columnar form; they might also ignore the breakdown of net assets employed (fixed, current assets etc.) to help to clarify and simplify the illustrations.

22.13.6 EXAMPLE: PARTNERSHIP ACCOUNTS

Lindner, Kenny and Murphy are in partnership with an agreement to share profits in the ratio 3:2:1. Their accounts for the year ended 31 December 2002 are as follows:

TRADING, PROFIT AND LOSS ACCOUNT OF LINDNER, KENNY AND MURPHY FOR THE YEAR ENDED 31 DECEMBER 2002

		£	£
Net profit (Note 1)			25,080
Less Murphy salary (Note 2)			(6,000)
			19,080
Less interest on capital (Note 3)			
Lindner		2,400	
Kenny		960	
Murphy		720	
			(4,080)
			15,000
Residual in profit sharing ratio (Note 4)			
Lindner	(3)	7,500	
Kenny	(2)	5,000	
Murphy	(1)	2,500	
			(15,000)

Notes:

(1) The actual Trading, Profit and Loss Account will be in the same format as for a sole trader.

(2) The payment of a salary to Murphy is an appropriation of profit and not a business expense.

(3) Interest is paid on capital contributed by each partner.

(4) The balance of the profits are split in the agreed profit sharing ratio.

BALANCE SHEET OF LINDNER, KENNY AND MURPHY AS AT 31 DECEMBER 2002

	£	£
Net Assets (Note 1)		46.130
Capital Accounts (Note 2)		
Lindner	20,000	
Kenny	8,000	
Murphy	6,000	
		34,000
Current Accounts (Note 3)		
Lindner	7,400	
Kenny	1,060	
Murphy	3,670	
		12,130
		46,130

Notes:

(1) The format of the Balance Sheet in arriving at net profit will be the same as for sole traders.

(2) Capital accounts record each parties' initial investment in the firm.

(3) Current accounts record the profits retained in the business by each partner.

22.14 Final Accounts of Limited Companies

22.14.1 INTRODUCTION

The preparation and publication of the final accounts of limited companies in the UK are governed by the Companies Act 1989 which consolidates, and replaces, the provisions of the Companies Acts 1948, 1967, 1976, 1981 and 1985. The general format of the balance sheet and profit and loss account of a limited company will be shown below with some simplifications, in order to introduce certain assets and liabilities which we have not yet considered.

22.14.2 THE FORMAT OF A LIMITED COMPANY BALANCE SHEET

TYPICAL CO. LTD BALANCE SHEET AS AT ....

	£	£	£
Fixed assets			
Intangible assets			
Developments costs		X	
Concessions, patents, licences, trademarks		X	
Goodwill		X	
			X
Tangible assets			
Land and buildings		X	
Plant and machinery		X	
Fixtures, fittings, tools and equipment		X	
Motor vehicles		X	
			X
Investments			X
			X
Current assets			
Stocks		X	
Debtors and prepayments		X	
Investments		X	
Cash at bank and in hand		X	
		X	
Creditors: amounts falling due within one year (i.e., current liabilities)			
Debenture loans			
(nearing their redemption date)	X		
Bank overdraft and loans	X		
Trade creditors	X		
Bills of exchange payable	X		
Taxation	X		
Accruals	X		
Proposed dividend	X		
		(X)	
Net current assets			X
Total assets less current liabilities			X
Creditors : amounts falling due after more than one year			
Debenture loans		X	
Taxation		X	
			(X)
			X
Capital and reserves			
Called up share capital			
Ordinary shares		X	
Preference shares		X	
			X

Reserves		
Share premium account	X	
Revaluation reserve	X	
Other reserves	X	
Profit and loss account (retained profits)	X	
		X
		X

22.14.2.1 Intangible fixed assets

Intangible fixed assets represent amounts of money paid by a business to acquire benefits of a long-term nature. Goodwill and deferred development expenditure are two intangible assets which were discussed in detail earlier.

If a company purchases some patent rights, or a concession from another business, or the right to use a trademark, the cost of the purchase can be accounted for as the purchase of an intangible fixed asset. These assets must then be amortised (depreciated) over the economic life.

22.14.2.2 Tangible fixed assets

As with any other type of business, tangible fixed assets are shown in the balance sheet at their net book value (i.e., at cost less provision for depreciation). Sometimes, a fixed asset, such as a building, might be revalued to a current market value. Depreciation would then be based on the revalued amount, and the balance sheet value of the asset would be the revalued amount less provision for depreciation on the revalued amount.

22.14.2.3 Investments

Investments are fixed assets if the company intends to hold on to them for a long time, and current assets if they are only likely to be held for a short time before being sold.

22.14.2.4 Current liabilities

The term 'creditors: amounts falling due within one year' was introduced by the Companies Act 1981 as an alternative phrase meaning 'current liabilities'. It is therefore likely that you will come across this term frequently.

22.14.2.5 Debenture loans

Limited companies may issue debenture stock ('debentures') or loan stock. These are long-term liabilities described on the balance sheet as loan capital.

When a company issues debentures, it is in effect raising a loan from investors. Although some debentures are irredeemable, which means that the loan does not have to be paid back ever, most debenture stock is redeemable. Redeemable debentures are issued for a given period of time, after which the company must pay back the money it has borrowed.

22.14.2.6 Share capital

Share capital will be split into:

(a) Preference shares which receive an agreed percentage dividend before the ordinary shareholders receive anything.

(b) Ordinary shares which receive the remainder of total profits.

22.14.2.7 Reserves

After accounting for dividends any remaining profits will be transferred to reserves. These reserves may be for a specific reason or merely general in nature.

22.14.3 THE PROFIT AND LOSS ACCOUNT OF A LIMITED COMPANY

This might have a format roughly similar to the one below.

TYPICAL CO. LTD
Profit and loss account for the year ended ....

	£	£
Turnover		X
Cost of sales		(X)
Gross profit		X
Distribution costs	X	
Administrative expenses	X	
		(X)
		X
Other operating income	X	
Income from fixed asset investments	X	
Other interest receivable and similar income	X	
		X
		X
Interest payable		(X)
Profit before taxation		X
Tax		(X)
Profit after tax		X
Dividends: Preference	X	
Ordinary	X	
		(X)
Retained profit for the year		X
Profit and loss account as at the beginning of the year		X
Profit and loss account as at the end of the year		X

22.14.3.1 Allocation of expenses

This format requires the company accountant to allocate his list of expenses to one of the main expense headings. For example, heat and light of the office would go to administrative expenses. No guidelines are given as to which expenses should go where. Clearly consistent treatment from one year to the next is crucial.

22.14.3.2 Taxation

Companies pay corporation tax on the profits they earn. For the financial year 2002, the full rate of corporation tax will be 30%. (See **20.4.3**.)

(a) The charge for corporation tax on profits for the year is shown as a deduction from net profit, before appropriations.

(b) In the balance sheet, tax payable to the government is generally shown as a current liability. This is because corporation tax is normally payable nine months after the company's year end.

Note: Coverage of limited companies has deliberately been kept brief to avoid duplication with other Manuals in the series.

22.14.4 EXAMPLE: COMPANY ACCOUNTS

We can now try to draw together several of the items described in this section into an illustrative example.

The accountant (unqualified) of Wislon Ltd has prepared the following trial balance as at 31 December 2002:

	£'000
50p ordinary shares (fully paid)	350
7% £1 preference shares (fully paid)	100
10% debentures (secured)	200
Retained profit 1.1.02	242
General reserve 1.1.02	171

Freehold land and buildings 1.1.02 (cost)	430
Plant and machinery 1.1.02 (cost)	830
Provision for depreciation:	
Freehold buildings 1.1.02	20
Plant and machinery 1.1.02	222
Stock 1.1.02	190
Sales	2,697
Purchases	2,152
Preference dividend	7
Ordinary dividend (interim)	8
Debenture interest	10
Wages and salaries	254
Light and heat	31
Sundry expenses	113
Debtors	179
Creditors	330
Cash	125

Notes:

(a) Sundry expenses include £9,000 paid in respect of insurance for the year ending 31 August 2003. Light and heat does not include an invoice of £3,000 for electricity for the three months ending 31 December 2002, which was paid in February 2003. Light and heat also includes £20,000 relating to salesmen's commission.

(b) The freehold property was acquired some years ago. The buildings element of the cost was estimated at £100,000 and the estimated useful life of the assets was 50 years at the time of purchase. £36,000 depreciation is to be charged on plant and machinery for 2002.

(c) The debentures have been in issue for some years. The 50p ordinary shares all rank for dividends at the end of the year.

(d) The directors wish to provide for:

(i) debenture interest due,

(ii) a final ordinary dividend of 2p per share,

(iii) a transfer to general reserve of £16,000,

(iv) audit fees of £4,000;

(e) Stock as at 31 December 2002 was valued at £220,000 (cost).

(f) Taxation is to be ignored.

You are required to prepare the final accounts of Wislon Ltd for the year ended 31 December 2002.

Note: When producing the Trading, Profit and Loss Account you should list expenses rather than allocating them to expense headings.

22.14.4.1 Approach and suggested solution

(a) Normal adjustments are needed for accruals and prepayments (insurance, light and heat, debenture interest and audit fees). The debenture interest accrued is calculated as follows:

	£'000
Charge needed in profit and loss account (10% × £200,000)	20
Amount paid so far, as shown in the list of balances	10
Accrual — presumably six months' interest now payable	10

The accrued expenses to be shown in the balance sheet therefore comprise:	£'000
Debenture interest	10
Light and heat	3
Audit fee	4
	17

(b) The misposting of £20,000 to light and heat is also adjusted, by reducing the light and heat expense, but charging £20,000 to salesmen's commission.

(c) Depreciation on the freehold building is calculated as $\frac{£100,000}{50} = £2,000$.

(d) Appropriations of profit must be considered. The final ordinary dividend, shown as a current liability in the balance sheet, is:

$$700,000 \times 2p = £14,000$$

(e) The transfer to general reserve increases that reserve to £171,000 + £16,000 = £187,000.

WISLON LTD
TRADING AND PROFIT AND LOSS ACCOUNT
FOR THE YEAR ENDING 31 DECEMBER 2002

	£'000	£'000	£'000
Sales			2,695
Less cost of sales			
Opening stock		190	
Purchases		2,152	
		2,342	
Less closing stock		220	
			2,122
			573
Less expenses			
Wages, salaries and commission £(254 + 20)		274	
Sundry expenses £[113 − 6]		107	
Light and heat £[31 + 3 − 20]		14	
Depreciation — freehold buildings		2	
— plant		36	
Audit fees		4	
Debenture interest		20	
			457
Net profit			116
Appropriations			
Transfer to general reserve		16	
Dividends: preference (paid)	7		
ordinary — interim (paid)	8		
— final	14		
		29	
			45
Retained profit for the year			71
Retained profit brought forward			242
Retained profit carried forward			£313

WISLON LTD
BALANCE SHEET AS AT 31 DECEMBER 2002

	£'000 Cost	£'000 Dep'n	£'000
Fixed assets			
Freehold property	430	22	408
Plant and machinery	830	258	572
	1,260	280	980
Current assets			
Stock		220	
Debtors		179	
Prepayments (insurance)		6	
Cash		126	
		531	
Creditors: amounts falling due within one year			
Creditors	390		
Accruals	17		
Proposed dividend	14		
		361	
Net current assets			170
Total assets less current liabilities			1,150
Creditors: amounts falling due after more than one year			
10% debentures (secured)			(200)
			£950
Capital and reserves			
Called up share capital			
50p ordinary shares		350	
7% £1 preference shares		100	
			450
Reserves			
General reserve		187	
Profit and loss account		313	
			500
			£950

22.15 Introduction to Analysis and Interpretation of Accounts

At the start of this chapter we identified several groups of people who might be interested in the financial information of a large public company. These different user groups will be interested in the financial information for different reasons. For example, the management of the company will be particularly interested in profitability, whereas the creditors of the company want to know whether or not they will get paid. Whatever their reasons for looking at the financial information, a useful aid to the analysis of financial accounts is ratio analysis.

Ratio analysis involves calculating certain ratios from the information in the accounts. The ratio that is calculated is of little or no use to the user in isolation. The user will want to compare the ratio with:

(a) The same ratio for the same company in previous years.

(b) The same ratio for other companies in the same sector of the economy.

It should be stressed at this point that it is the comparison of the ratio that makes the ratio itself useful to the user. Viewed in isolation, the ratio tells us little about the company. However, comparisons with previous years will help highlight changes in the company's fortunes from one year to the next, and comparisons with competitors will tell users how the company is performing in relation to other similar companies.

There are countless ratios that can be calculated and even different ways of calculating the same ratio. As the aim of this chapter is to gain a broad grasp of the calculation and use of ratios, we shall limit our analysis to a limited number of ratios. To give this analysis some structure, the calculation and use of ratios by three user groups is considered: management; present or potential investors; and lenders and suppliers.

22.16 Analysis and Interpretation for Management

The question we must ask ourselves with each of the different user groups is: Why is the user interested in the accounts? In the case of the management of the company they are primarily concerned with the profitability of the company and the efficient use of the company's assets. The ratios we shall now look at will hopefully assist us in this analysis.

Johnson plc for the years ended 2002 and 2001 is used to illustrate the calculation of the different ratios.

JOHNSON PLC
SUMMARISED PROFIT AND LOSS ACCOUNT

	31 December 2002		31 December 2001	
	£000	£000	£000	£000
Sales		4,000		3,400
Cost of sales		(3,500)		(3,100)
Gross profit		500		300
Distribution costs	(150)		(120)	
Administrative costs	(50)	(200)	(40)	(160)
Operating profit		300		140
Debenture interest paid		(100)		(90)
Profit on ordinary activities before taxation		200		50
Taxation		(100)		(25)
Profit after taxation		100		25
Dividends: Preference	(10)		(10)	
Ordinary	(40)		(15)	
		(50)		(25)
Retained for year		50		—
Retained b/f		450		450
Retained c/f		£500		£450

JOHNSON PLC
SUMMARISED BALANCE SHEET

	31 December 2002		31 December 2001	
	£000	£000	£000	£000
Fixed assets				
Buildings		1,500		1,500
Plant and equipment		500		300
		2,000		1,800
Current assets				
Stocks	650		500	
Debtors	500		400	
Cash	—		50	
	1,150		950	
Current liabilities				
Creditors	(700)		(450)	

Net current assets	450	500
	2,450	2,300
Debenture loans	(950)	(850)
Net assets	1,500	1,450
Ordinary share capital	800	800
Preference share capital	200	200
Retained profits	500	450
	£1,500	£1,450

The market price of the share as at 31 December 2002 is £1.25 (2001: £0.60).

22.16.1 RETURN ON CAPITAL EMPLOYED (ROCE)

Often known as the primary 'ratio' and frequently regarded as the best measure of profitability, indicating how successful a business is in utilising its assets. It is however a ratio that is capable of being calculated in a number of different ways.

For example, there are a number of different ways of interpreting 'capital employed'. In our interpretation we will always take capital employed as being equal to fixed assets plus net current assets. Our formula is therefore:

$$\frac{\text{Profit before deducting interest and tax}}{\text{Fixed assets plus net current assets}} \times 100$$

In this way we exclude the debentures from the denominator and the related interest paid from the numerator. Return on capital employed therefore represents a measure of the return earned by the shareholders:

2002	*2001*
$\frac{300}{2{,}450} \times 100 = 12.2\%$	$\frac{140}{2{,}300} \times 100 = 6.1\%$

In this example the management of Johnson has seen the ROCE double in 2002. On the face of it, this would seem to be a very favourable result. It is however dangerous to draw conclusions from ratios without carrying out further analysis. For example, we would want to look at the ROCE achieved by other similar companies, in our sector of the economy. They may have achieved a trebling of ROCE, making the performance of Johnson look poor in comparison.

Furthermore, the ROCE is a ratio which could be subject to manipulation. A manager who knows he is being assessed on ROCE may be tempted to keep the denominator in the fraction (representing capital) artifically low. This can be done by failing to invest in new, more expensive plant and machinery, and may lead to high returns in the short term. In the long term, investment in new plant is essential and the manager's short-term aims are unlikely to be in the best interests of the business.

22.16.2 PROFIT MARGIN

This is the ratio of profit to sales and is calculated as follows:

$$\frac{\text{Profit before deduction of interest and tax}}{\text{Sales}} \times 100$$

2002	*2001*
$\frac{300}{4{,}000} \times 100 = 7.5\%$	$\frac{140}{3{,}400} \times 100 = 4.1\%$

Another way of looking at this is to say that for every £1 of sales made in 2002, Johnson generates 7.5p of profit before deducting interest costs and taxation. Clearly there has been an improvement in the profit margin of 3.4%. This improvement is largely explained by the fact that Johnson has managed to increase sales by 17.6% whilst at the same time controlling increases in costs.

Increase in sales $\frac{4{,}000 - 3{,}400}{3{,}400} \times 100 = 17.6\%$

Increase in operating costs $\frac{(3{,}500 + 150 + 50) - (3{,}100 + 120 + 40)}{(3{,}100 + 120 + 40)} \times 100 = 13.5\%$

It cannot be determined from the accounts how Johnson has achieved this improvement. Management would have to look closer at the company's operations.

Another important profit margin is the gross profit margin which is calculated as follows:

$$\frac{\text{Gross profit}}{\text{Sales}} \times 100$$

In the Johnson example:

2002	*2001*
$\frac{500}{4{,}000} \times 100 = 12.5\%$	$\frac{300}{3{,}400} \times 100 = 8.8\%$

This again highlights the improvement in the trading performance of Johnson in 2002.

22.16.3 ASSET TURNOVER

This will show how fully a company is utilising its assets. It gives us the ratio of sales in a year to the capital employed (see **21.2.4**). It is calculated as:

$$\frac{\text{Sales}}{\text{Fixed assets plus net current assets}}$$

and is expressed as the number of times a year:

2002	*2001*
$\frac{4{,}000}{2{,}450}$ = 1.63 times a year	$\frac{3{,}400}{2{,}300}$ = 1.48 times a year

Another way of expressing this is to say that in 2002 Johnson plc generated £1.63 of sales for every £1 of capital employed. This compares with £1.48 in 2001. From this we can conclude that Johnson has been using its assets more efficiently in 2002 than in 2001.

To see why the improvement has taken place, management would calculate turnover ratios for all the assets in the balance sheet. This should highlight where the improvements have taken place. It should be stressed that for stock turnover the following formula should be used wherever possible!

$$\frac{\text{Cost of sales}}{\text{Stocks}}$$

This is because stocks are valued at cost and not selling price. To use sales would incorrectly increase the stock turnover.

22.16.4 DEBTOR DAYS

Of crucial concern to management is to ensure that the company is paid promptly by its debtors. This is likely to be the responsibility of the credit control department and obviously management will wish to review the performance of this department.

Debtor days will tell management how long, on average, debtors take to pay the company. We can calculate the average payment period, expressed in days, as follows:

$$\frac{\text{Debtors}}{\text{Sales}} \times 365$$

2002	*2001*
$\frac{500}{4{,}000} \times 365 = 46$ days	$\frac{400}{3{,}400} \times 365 = 43$ days

From this it appears that, on average, debtors are taking three days longer in 2002 to settle their debts. Management may well seek answers as to why the credit period has been extended. Obviously management should consider the credit period given by other similar companies as well as the general economic climate.

22.17 Analysis and Interpretation for Present or Potential Investors

Investors buy shares for two main reasons:

(a) To receive dividends.

(b) To be able to sell the shares for more than they paid for them.

A crucial figure to investors is the 'earnings' figure. Simplifying things slightly this can be taken as profit after tax less preference dividends. So in the case of Johnson:

	31 December 2002	31 December 2001
	£000	£000
Profit after tax	100	25
Less: Preference dividends	(10)	(10)
'Earnings'	90	15

The earnings figure is crucial to investors as the directors of Johnson can do two things with it:

(a) pay it out as an ordinary dividend to shareholders; or

(b) retain and invest it.

Clearly, investors like to receive dividends. However, the retention of the dividend within Johnson, with subsequent reinvestment, should lead to future profit growth and hopefully increases in the share price. The directors of Johnson are therefore faced with something of a dilemma, in that they would like to pay high dividends to keep investors happy in the short term, whilst retaining sufficient funds within the business to meet long-term capital needs. The ideal company obviously has sufficient earnings to do both.

This earnings figure is then a crucial figure and features in three of four investor ratios.

22.17.1 EARNINGS PER SHARE (EPS)

This can be calculated as follows and should be expressed in pence per share:

$$\frac{\text{Earnings}}{\text{Number of ordinary shares in issue}} = \text{pence per share}$$

2002	*2001*
$\frac{90}{800} = 11.25$ pence per share	$\frac{15}{800} = 1.88$ pence per share

This is seen as a very important indicator, and companies listed on the Stock Exchange must show it on the face of the profit and loss account in the published accounts. There has obviously been a big improvement in the EPS of Johnson in 2002 due to the improved earnings figure.

Companies are generally looking to increase their earnings per share. They are keen to show a steady increase of EPS over a period of time.

22.17.2 DIVIDEND COVER

Another important ratio utilising earnings is the dividend cover. This tells investors how safe their dividend is. It can be calculated as follows:

$$\frac{\text{Earnings}}{\text{Ordinary dividends}}$$

2002	*2001*
$\frac{90}{40} = 2.25$	$\frac{15}{15} = 1$

In 2002, Johnson's dividend is said to be at least two times covered. In 2001, all of the earnings are paid out as an ordinary dividend with nothing retained in the business. In 2001 this would suggest to shareholders that their dividend could be under threat as all the earnings are being used to make the dividend payment.

Investors look for a high dividend cover.

22.17.3 PRICE EARNINGS RATIO

This can be calculated as follows:

$$\frac{\text{Market price of one share in pence}}{\text{Earnings per share}}$$

and can be expressed in years. It shows roughly how long it would take to recover the share price out of earnings.

2002	*2001*
$\frac{125}{11.25} = 11$ years	$\frac{60}{1.88} = 32$ years

Generally, a high price earnings ratio is sought by companies as this suggests a high share price in relation to earnings. In the case of Johnson, the price earnings ratio has fallen dramatically in 2002. This is despite the fact that the share price has more than doubled in the year. This doubling of the share price has been more than offset by increased earnings. There are presumably misgivings concerning the future earnings of the company which could be reflected in the share price.

It is very difficult to draw conclusions without more detailed information.

22.17.4 DIVIDEND YIELD

This will give a percentage return on the investment, which can be compared to other alternative investment opportunities. In making the comparison we should remember to compare the yield with other *post* tax returns. The yield can be calculated as:

$$\frac{\text{Dividends in pence}}{\text{Market price in pence}} \times 100$$

and is expressed as a percentage. It must be stressed that the yield calculated is a return net of taxation.

2002	*2001*
$\frac{5^*}{125} = 4\%$	$\frac{1.875^*}{60} = 3\%$

* $\frac{\text{Ordinary dividend paid}}{\text{Number of ordinary shares}}$

These yields could be compared with, say, building society interest rates. Remember, however, that the dividend is not the only reason why investors hold shares.

We should also be aware that any ratio using the market price of shares, may be subject to dramatic fluctuations. As we all know, share prices are subject to day-to-day changes and both the yield and price earnings ratio can be affected.

22.18 Analysis and Interpretation for Lenders and Suppliers

The lenders and suppliers of the business are interested in being repaid. They are concerned about the liquidity of the company. The word liquid means readily converted into cash. A firm's liquidity is measured by its ability to convert its assets into cash, to enable it to meet demands for payments when they fall due.

22.18.1 CURRENT RATIO

This can be calculated as follows:

$$\frac{\text{Current assets}}{\text{Current liabilities}}$$

2002	*2001*
$\frac{1,150}{700} = 1.6:1$	$\frac{950}{450} = 2.1:1$

The ratio compares assets becoming liquid within 12 months with liabilities due for payment within 12 months. Obviously, a company would prefer to have a high degree of cover and historically a current ratio of 2:1, or higher, was considered acceptable.

In the case of Johnson the current ratio is deteriorating and would be a cause of concern to lenders.

22.18.2 QUICK RATIO

This can be calculated as:

$$\frac{\text{Current assets (excluding stocks)}}{\text{Current liabilities}}$$

The thinking here is that stocks cannot quickly be turned into cash and therefore should be excluded from the numerator. For Johnson, the quick ratio would be:

2002	*2001*
$\frac{500}{700} = 0.71:1$	$\frac{400 + 50}{450} = 1:1$

The quick ratio should be viewed in conjunction with the current ratio and clearly the deterioration in Johnson's liquidity is again highlighted.

Historically, a quick ratio of 1:1 is considered acceptable.

22.19 Limitations of Ratio Analysis

In the previous sections we have attempted to draw conclusions from the ratios we have calculated for Johnson. Whilst ratios are a useful analysis tool we should avoid accepting the answers they put forward in too rigid a manner. The following points should be considered.

(a) The ratios calculated must be considered in conjunction with the overall knowledge of the business as a whole. For example, a current ratio of less than 2:1 need not necessarily mean the business has liquidity problems. Organisations such as supermarkets operate on ratios of much less, merely reflecting the nature of their business.

(b) Ratios viewed in isolation tell us little about a business. We must make comparisons of ratios from previous years and with other similar businesses. In making comparisons with other businesses we should ensure, as far as is possible, that their accounts are prepared adopting similar accounting bases.

(c) To be meaningful the comparisons must compare like with like. It may in practice not be possible to get the results of another similar company for comparison. This clearly applies to large public limited companies with several diversified interests.

It is important that we consider the ratios calculated, along with our knowledge of the business and market as a whole. If we do this then we should avoid drawing incorrect conclusions from the ratios.

22.20 Exercise

Problem
Murphy has extracted the following figures from his books of accounts at 31 October 2002. As this is his year end he asks you to help him produce a trading, profit and loss account and a balance sheet.

	£
Land and buildings	71,985
Rent	15,019
Heat and Light	6,324
Advertising	13,765
Wages	44,970
Postage	7,660
Interest paid	5,000
Salaries	19,815
Sales	528,914
Cost of sales	384,457
Closing stocks	14,521
Creditors	37,037
Cash	515
Bank overdraft	3,466
Debtors	27,300
Capital brought forward	51,914
Drawings	10,000

Solution

MURPHY
TRADING, PROFIT AND LOSS ACCOUNT
FOR THE YEAR ENDED 31 OCTOBER 2002

	£	£
Sales		528,914
Less: Cost of sales		(384,457)
Gross profit		144,457
Less expenses:		
Rent	15,019	
Heat and light	6,324	
Advertising	13,765	
Wages	44,970	
Postage	7,660	
Interest paid	5,000	
Salaries	19,815	
		(112,553)
Net profit		£ 31,904

MURPHY
BALANCE SHEET
FOR THE YEAR ENDED 31 OCTOBER 2002

	£	£	£
Fixed assets			
Land and buildings			71,985
Current assets			
Stocks		14,521	
Debtors		27,300	
Cash		515	
		42,336	
Current liabilities			
Creditors	37,037		
Bank overdraft	3,466		
		(40,503)	
Net current assets			1,833
Net assets			£73,818
Capital brought forward			51,914
Profit for year		31,904	
Less drawings		(10,000)	
			21,904
Capital carried forward			£73,818

PART III

PROBLEMS FOR SELF-STUDY AND ASSIGNMENT

TWENTY THREE

CLASS PROBLEMS IN CONTRACT AND TORT

In each of the following problems you are given a brief set of facts. In each case you should advise the client on appropriate remedies, taking as practical an approach as possible.

23.1 Martin Pender

Your Instructing Solicitors act for Martin Pender, whose business is that of car leasing. By a leasing agreement dated 3 January 2000 Mr Pender ('the owner') leased, and Jest Videos Company plc ('the hirer') took, for a term of three years from 1 February 2000, five cars at a rental of £18,000 p.a., payable yearly in advance on 1 February 2000 and the two subsequent anniversaries of that date. Clause 7 of the agreement provided that in the event of default being made in any yearly payment for 14 days or more after the due date, the owner might take possession of the goods.

During December 1999 the owner, in the expectation that the hirer would sign a leasing agreement, bought five new Ford Escort motor cars for £12,000 each which he had painted in accordance with the company's wishes, in company colours. The cost of the modifications was £6,000.

On 1 February 2000 he hirer took possession of the cars and paid the first year's rent.

The hirer failed to pay the rent due on 1 February 2001 and on 16 February the owner repossessed the cars.

Between 16 February and 1 April 2001 the owner carried out at a cost of £3,000 repairs necessary to put the cars in a state fit for releasing, and on the latter date released the cars to Dodgems Incorporated for two years at a rent of £9,000 p.a. Counsel may assume that no terms which would have been more favourable to the owner could have been found, and that it is unlikely that the cars can be leased again at the end of the two-year period, when they will probably be worth about £6,000 each.

As a result of the hirer's default in paying the amount due on 1 February 2001, the owner did not have in hand sufficient funds to fulfil an agreement which he had made to purchase an XYZ990 computer from the manufacturers with delivery and payment set for 1 March 2001. The owner managed to complete this purchase by borrowing £10,000 for six months at 20% p.a. from Grasping Finance Limited. Interest on this loan amounted to £1,000 and Grasping Finance Limited charged an 'arrangement' fee of £300.

Liability is unlikely to be an issue.

Counsel will please advise as to quantum.

23.2 Mr and Mrs Roberts

Mr and Mrs Roberts are the owners of farmland in Northumberland. In 1991 they granted a licence for three years to the Northern Gravel Company ('the Company') to extract gravel from one of their fields. The Company extracted a large amount of gravel, leaving a pit measuring 100 yards by 150 yards with a depth of 40 feet.

On 4 August 1995 Mr and Mrs Roberts entered into a second licence with the Company granting it the right to tip certain types of rubbish in the pit.

Clause 3 of the licence provided:

> *(a) The Company shall tip rubbish up to a level three feet below the natural surface of the pit.*
> *(b) Upon completion of the tipping the Company shall place three feet of top soil evenly over the whole of the pit and such top soil shall be free from all impediments and materials which may turn a plough.*

The Company completed tipping at the pit in September 1998. It then set about complying with Clause 3(b) of the licence. The Company claimed to have discharged its obligation by August 1999. However in October 1999, when the field was being ploughed, the mechanical plough was fouled by an underground obstruction and badly damaged. Mr and Mrs Roberts immediately gave instructions for boring tests to be carried out, which revealed that there is only two feet of top soil and that there is a great deal of rubbish in it, including large concrete blocks.

Unfortunately Mr and Mrs Roberts have only just come to Instructing Solicitors concerning the matter, having relied on their land agent previously to obtain rectification of the position.

If possible Mr and Mrs Roberts would wish to force the Company to place another foot of top soil on the site after the rubbish has been removed from the existing soil. Counsel is asked to advise:

(a) Whether it will be possible to obtain an order for specific performance against the Company.

(b) What will be the measure of damages if specific performance is not ordered and at what date damages will be assessed. The value of the field is now £20,000 but it would have been £30,000 if it were ploughable. The value of the whole farm is £250,000; with the field restored the farm would be worth £255,000. The cost of doing the necessary work to restore the field was £10,000 in 1999 but is now £15,000.

(c) What further damages may be recoverable in any event. As a result of the damage to the plough (which cost £500 to repair), Mr and Mrs Roberts were unable to plough another of their fields in time to sow a winter crop and so lost profit of £3,000. Further they have not been able to use the field in which the Company tipped rubbish for the planting of crops for the last three years, but only less profitably for the grazing of cattle, a loss of £2,000 per annum.

23.3 Newtown Theatre Company

Instructing Solicitors act for Newtown Theatre Company Ltd ('NTC'), a new company set up to run a theatre in Newtown and to tour the surrounding districts.

Counsel is instructed in relation to the employment of two actors, Mr Murray Clive, the well-known film and TV star, and Mr Siegfried Blackstone.

Mr Clive was engaged by NTC on the terms of a letter on NTC notepaper dated 15 September 2002 which reads as follows:

Dear Mr Clive,

This is to confirm the terms of the agreement made yesterday at your meeting with our Mr Selsdon.

1. You will be employed to act for our company from 18 September 2002 to 17 September 2003 at a salary of £1,500 per week.

2. You will act in such roles, and carry out such other duties incidental to the business of the company, as the company's management may direct.

3. You will be entitled to four weeks' paid holiday to be taken in accordance with the direction of the company's management.

4. You will not during the period of the agreement act in any other stage production in the United Kingdom.

Yours sincerely,

Newtown Theatre Co. Ltd.

On 3 October NTC decided that its Christmas production would be 'Aladdin' and cast Mr Clive in the role of Widow Twankey. Yesterday Mr Clive did not turn up to rehearsal, but sent a note saying that he was leaving the company and would be starting new employment with the Grabham Theatre Company in ten days' time.

Mr Blackstone was employed specifically for the production of Aladdin, in which he plays the Genie. His contract runs from 18 September to 31 December 2002. He is paid £500 per week. He has no written agreement, but was engaged orally by Mr Selsdon on behalf of NTC.

NTC has no specific information, but Mr Selsdon has heard a rumour that Mr Blackstone may have accepted an offer from a film company, and will leave their employment shortly before the opening on 1st November. In such an event the company would be forced to abandon the production as it would be impossible to find a replacement, and there would be about £100,000 wasted expenditure on the publicity and settings, as well as the loss of box office profits.

The Company wishes to take proceedings against Mr Clive and wishes to be advised as to its position in relation to both Mr Clive and Mr Blackstone. In particular, it wishes to know whether there is any possibility of preventing Mr Clive or Mr Blackstone from leaving NTC, or, if not, on what basis damages would be awarded.

Counsel is requested to advise NTC what, if anything, can be done to protect its legitimate business interest.

23.4 Gordon Priestly

Mr Priestly previously lived in London with his wife Mary and two children aged eight and six. In 2001 the family decided to move into the country, where they would be able to afford a larger house. They wanted a larger house for two reasons: so that they could provide a home for Mr Priestly's mother, who is getting on in years and not well able to look after herself; and so that they could have a music studio in which to place a grand piano and in which Mary Priestly could supplement the family income by giving music lessons.

They were unable to find just the house they were looking for, but in September 2001 purchased a Victorian house called Mon Repos, Hobbs Green, Sussex, which stood in large grounds and could easily have an extension added.

Mr Priestly engaged Mr James Foyle, an architect, to design a two-storey extension which provided a large living area on the ground floor and a studio and bedroom on the floor above. Mr Foyle delivered the plans and specification in December 2001, and Mr Priestly engaged a local builder, Premier Builders Ltd, to construct the extension, commencing January 2002. He did not employ Mr Foyle or anyone else to supervise the building works, preferring to rely on his own experience as an interior designer.

After the usual delays Premier Builders Ltd completed the extension in June 2002 at a final agreed cost of £45,000. Mr Priestly then employed a local firm of decorators, R. B. Ricketts & Son, to decorate the extension to his design. The decorations included some ornamental plastering on the ceiling of the ground floor of the extension. Before R. B. Ricketts started work, Mrs Priestly's piano was moved into the upstairs studio (suitably protected with dust sheets and plastic wrapping), in order to save storage costs.

On the day they started work, Mr Ricketts senior pointed out to Mr Priestly that the floor of the upper storey seemed very springy and expressed some concern about this, but neither he nor Mr Priestly discussed the matter further. The ornamental plastering was completed, and on 29 June 2002 Mr Ricketts junior, a large man who must weigh about 14 stone, was standing on a ladder while painting in the studio, when suddenly the ladder fell through the floor. He was scarcely able to run out of the way before the piano also fell through the hole, taking most of the floor (and ceiling of the room downstairs) with it.

Mr Priestly called in another architect, Mr Basil Soole, to investigate the damage and supervise the repairs. Mr Soole found no fault with Mr Foyle's design, but reported that Premier Builders Ltd had constructed the floor in breach of the specification, good practice and the building regulations, in four main respects:

(a) The joists to the timber first-floor construction should have been at not more than 600 mm centres in order to comply with Building Regulation B19(3)(i). The joists fitted by Premier Builders were at varying centres, never less than 800 mm and at five places as much as 950 mm centres. There was therefore insufficient support for the floor.

(b) The floorboards should have been of a thickness of not less than 22 mm in order to comply with Building Regulation B21(2)(ii). They were in fact 15 mm throughout the extension.

(c) The specification called for softwood to be Douglas fir, western hemlock, European redwood or Canadian spruce. Premier Builders had used deal, a far inferior softwood to those specified.

(d) Contrary to good practice, Premier Builders had not properly secured the joists to the retaining walls.

The repairs took 10 weeks to complete and were carried out by Crabbe & Co. at a cost of £17,500. In addition Mr Soole's fee was £1,750 and R. B. Ricketts charged £1,000 to redo the ornamental plastering. The piano was beyond repair. It was worth £2,000, but Mrs Priestly had to buy another at a cost of £4,000. She has lost £1,500 income from piano lessons because of the collapse of the floor. Finally, Mr Priestly's mother was not able to move in until three months after she had planned and Mr Priestly had to pay her rent over that period, a total of £750.

Counsel is asked to advise Mr Priestly as to liability and quantum.

23.5 Polly Partridge

Your Instructing Solicitors act for Polly Partridge, who is 45 years old and well-known in the art world. After taking a degree in History of Art at Oxford University, Ms Partridge worked for ten years in various art galleries in France: she then returned to England, where she deals in paintings both on her own account and as agent for various collectors.

In December 1996 Ms Partridge saw advertised in the current catalogue of Quentin Quick Fine Art Limited a drawing described as 'Drawing in pen and ink by J A Dessain, 1921'. Dessain was an artist with whose work Ms Partridge was familiar. After inspecting the drawing, she was satisfied as to its authenticity, and purchased it from Quick for £18,750 on 19 December 1996.

On 1 February 2002 Ms Partridge sent the drawing for valuation to Dr Robert Rawthorne of Rawthorne and Son (Fine Art Valuations) Limited. On 3 February Dr Rawthorne advised Ms Partridge that the drawing was not by Dessain and that it was virtually worthless. He also stated that, if the drawing had been a genuine Dessain, it would have fetched at least £45,000 at auction. Counsel may assume that Dr Rawthorne's advice is correct. At the time it was given, Ms Partridge believed that the only remedies she could have against Quick would be in case of fraud; and Quick's conduct at the time of the sale was in fact entirely innocent.

On 1 May 2002 Ms Partridge offered the drawing for sale by advertisement in art magazines as 'Drawing in pen and ink in the style of Dessain. Artist unknown. About 1920', but received no offer above £250.

On 1 June 2002 Ms Partridge consulted your Instructing Solicitors and was for the first time advised that the remedy of rescission might be available. Your Instructing Solicitors wrote to Quick stating that Ms Partridge was entitled, upon return of the drawing, to the return of the price with interest. Solicitors acting for Quick have responded by saying that it is now too late for Ms Partridge to make any claim and that, in any event, her action in advertising the drawing for sale constituted an affirmation of the contract with Quick so as to deprive her of any right to equitable relief.

Will Counsel please advise Ms Partridge as to her remedies.

23.6 Dreamy Travel Ltd

Instructing Solicitors act for Dreamy Travel Limited ('the Company'). The managing director and principal shareholder is Mr Basil Dream. The Company's business consists primarily of package holidays arranged by the Company, and sold to its customers from a brochure. The Company prides itself on providing a good service to its customers. Every year a brochure is prepared, which is sent out to all previous customers, and to anybody who has expressed interest in the Company's holidays.

For several years, the Company has traded with Greed Hotels Ltd, whose managing director and principal shareholder is Mr Gregory Greed, and which operates several seaside hotels. Each year, the Company takes an allocation of rooms in several of Greed's hotels, and pays a fixed weekly rate for these rooms, on a full board basis, whether or not such rooms are occupied. Of course, in this way, the Company is able to have the advantage of a much cheaper rate than would otherwise be the case. The Company then endeavours to fill these rooms with its customers.

In 1999 Mr Greed informed Mr Dream that he had acquired a valuable site at Brighton, and was building a luxury hotel. On 17 December 2001 Mr Greed told Mr Dream over a lunch at the Greed Hotel, Bournemouth, that the hotel at Brighton was finished and would be available for the 2002 season, from the beginning of April 2002. He said that the Hotel was in the 4-star luxury category, with an Olympic size swimming pool, two saunas, three tennis courts, two large lounges, a bar, discotheque, games room, and smaller writing and television rooms. He said that the hotel was within a five-minute walk from the sea. He supplied Mr Dream with photographs, including a photograph of the swimming pool which looked magnificent. Mr Dream was about to go on a cruise with his wife, and did not go to see the hotel, as he otherwise would have done.

On Mr Dream's instructions the Company wrote the following letter to Greed Hotels Ltd on 7 January 2002.

Dear Sirs,

This is to confirm that we wish to book the following allocation from 1 April to 30 September 2002.

Greed Hotel, Brighton

36 double rooms at £200 per week

12 single rooms at £150 per week

The above prices include room, full board (two persons per double room) all usual hotel services, and to include VAT.

Yours faithfully

Dreamy Travel Limited

Greed confirmed the booking by letter dated 14 January 2002 signed by Gregory Greed to the Company. Payment of the full price (£234,000) was duly made on 22 March, before the beginning of the season.

The Company incorporated in its brochure package holidays based on the Greed Hotel, Brighton, describing it in glowing terms in accordance with Mr Greed's description to Mr Dream, and featuring a reproduction of the photograph of the swimming pool. All the rooms were booked for the whole season and paid for in advance. The Company charged its customers £300 p.w. for a double room and £225 p.w. for a single room.

From the start of the season, the Company received a stream of complaints about the Greed Hotel, Brighton. Mr Dream went down to see for himself on 9 May. The hotel was only partly finished. The builders were still on the premises, and there was considerable noise. The swimming pool was not complete, and it was clear that the photograph supplied to Mr Dream must have been of another swimming pool. One of the saunas was not complete. There was only one lounge. The second lounge was being used as a makeshift dining room, as the dining room was not complete. However, it was not suitable as a dining room, and there was considerable congestion. The games room was not operational as there were builders' tools in it. There was no television lounge. By no stretch of the imagination could the hotel be described as in the 4-star luxury class. Virtually every customer complained.

The Company was obliged to write to all its customers on 10 May. To those who had already stayed at the hotel, or were there at the time and completed their stay, it offered a 50% refund of their money plus compensation for distress and inconvenience and expenses. To those who had cut short their stay it offered a 100% refund plus the same compensation. A 100% refund was automatically sent to those who had heard of the difficulties and cancelled before arriving, even if this was at the last moment. Those customers who had yet to start their holidays were offered three choices: (i) a 50% refund if they took the holiday up; (ii) a 100% refund plus £10 for expenses if they cancelled; (iii) an equivalent holiday at no extra cost at another hotel, if possible in Brighton, otherwise elsewhere on the south coast.

The Company felt obliged to offer these generous terms in view of the volume of complaints from customers indicating that they would never book a holiday with Dreamy Travel again, and in view of some very bad press publicity which must reflect on the future goodwill of the Company.

Mr Dream was able to negotiate with Mr Greed a total cancellation of the booking from 22 July and a full refund of the money paid in respect of the remaining period (£90,000).

A total of £175,000 was paid back to customers by way of refunds, plus a further £23,000 in compensation. The rest of the money received from customers was retained, but the cost of alternative holidays for those customers was £160,000.

In order to make all the rearrangements and offers, the Company incurred postal and telephone costs of £976 and had to employ two extra temporary staff from an agency for two months, at a cost of £10,336.

Counsel is asked to advise the Company as to quantum.

23.7 Peter Boggis

Instructing Solicitors act for Mr Peter Boggis, who is a partner in a firm of architects, Goodhart Boggis & Co. Mr Boggis's car, a Volvo Estate reg. no. V 400 BOG, belongs to the firm, but is exclusively used by Mr Boggis. On about 13 July 2002 he telephoned Rural Motors Ltd and booked it in for service on 20 July 2002. He spoke to the service manager, a Mr Wort.

A few days later, Mr Boggis discovered that he was going to have to go abroad on business on 20 July. Therefore when he took the car in for service on 20 July he asked Mr Wort at the reception desk if Rural Motors could store the car for a few days until he was able to return and collect it. Mr Wort replied, 'OK, I'll store it for you, but if it's for too long we may have to charge you something extra'. Mr Boggis agreed to this.

Mr Boggis then drove his car into the service area, and was just about to leave when Mr Wort pointed out to him that there was a portable laptop computer on the back seat. This was Mr Boggis's personal property. Mr Boggis did not want to take it with him on his business trip, and had no time to return to the office before setting off, so he asked Mr Wort if it would be all right to leave the computer in the car. Mr Wort replied that it 'should be OK'. Mr Boggis accepted this remark without a second thought and left the car with the computer inside it.

As it turned out, Mr Boggis's trip lasted longer than expected and he did not return to collect his car until 3 August. He paid for the service using a cheque drawn on the partnership account. He was not charged for the storage. He then went to drive his car away and noticed that the computer was not inside it. He therefore returned to the reception desk and asked Mr Wort where it was. Mr Wort apologised, and went off to have a look for it. After about 10 minutes he returned empty-handed and said that the only explanation he could give was that 'it must have been nicked'. Mr Boggis told Mr Wort that he held Rural Motors Ltd responsible for the loss, but Mr Wort replied that they were not responsible and pointed out a notice over the reception desk which said:

> Whilst Rural Motors Ltd will endeavour to take every reasonable precaution, it is regretted that no responsibility can be accepted for loss or damage to any property left inside vehicles.

Mr Wort went on to say that the computer might still be kicking around somewhere and that he would keep his eye open for it, but Mr Boggis was obliged to leave without it.

Instructing Solicitors have written to Rural Motors Ltd making a formal demand for the return of the computer, but received a reply from their Solicitors to the effect that (a) the loss of the computer was Mr Boggis's own responsibility since he chose to leave it in the car; (b) that the storage was free of charge and so the garage could not be held liable in any event; (c) that the garage was protected by the notice; and (d) that even if the garage was prima facie liable, Mr Boggis was contributorily negligent.

Counsel is asked to advise Mr Boggis whether he can recover the value of the computer (£3,199) from Rural Motors Ltd.

23.8 Roger Lucas

Roger Lucas was injured on 30 June 1999, on his last day of work for Don Godfrey & Co. Ltd, before starting work as a long distance lorry driver. His date of birth was 1 March 1972. Counsel is asked to advise on quantum.

Roger Lucas will say:

I was very severely injured in the accident, sustaining a paraplegia from which I have been told there is no hope of recovery and my life expectancy has been reduced by about 10 years. I am confined to a wheelchair. Jenny, my wife, has been a wonderful source of support. Before my accident she had two part-time jobs working as a nursing assistant at the nearby cottage hospital for five mornings a week, and as a receptionist/nurse for our local family general practitioner each weekday afternoon. She has given up the receptionist job to look after me and persuaded me to take a positive attitude to my misfortune. From June 2000 to May 2001 at the suggestion of the District Rehabilitation Officer I attended a course at the York Rehabilitation Centre training to become a pharmacy assistant. I passed the end of course exam with flying colours, but unfortunately have been quite unable to get a suitable job. Our local cottage hospital has no vacancy for a pharmacy assistant. Only one assistant is employed and she is still ten years from retiring age. Whether the hospital will still be open in ten years time is a rather uncertain matter. The course organisers have told me that I could almost certainly get a job earning £200 per week net if I were to apply to a big city hospital. But this would entail moving to live in or close to a city which I do not want to do. Neither does my wife, though she too would have no difficulty obtaining employment as she is a trained nurse. We are both country folk born and bred. I have been quite unable to obtain work locally and can see little prospect of ever finding a job which I can conveniently reach from home. I can drive my specially adapted car, but not for distances of more than a few miles.

The losses which I would like to claim arising from my accident are as follows:

(a) Loss of earnings. At Don Godfrey & Co. Ltd I received a net weekly wage of £200. As a long distance lorry driver I would have netted at least £300 per week with a weekend working bonus of £80 net every fortnight. I had never worked weekends while in Don Godfrey & Co. Ltd's employment. He had regular weekend drivers. Before I began my rehabilitation course I received £75 per week incapacity benefit. While on the course I was given a grant of £80 per week. I am now in receipt of £60 per week income support.

(b) The cost of building a ground floor extension to 14 Peel Road which is a three-storey cottage. My architect advises that it is quite impossible to fit disabled person's escalators to this old stone cottage so I am confined to the ground floor. The proposal is to build an extension into the garden which will give me as much accommodation on ground floor level as the cottage has on all three floors. Unfortunately access for contractors is very difficult to the rear of our cottage and the cost of the extension, including professional fees, will be in the region of £50,000. My solicitor points out that I could buy a three-bedroomed bungalow on a new estate about seven miles away for £65,995, but frankly I cannot face living on a new estate. My cottage is presently worth about £70,000.

(c) £150 per week net to my wife for looking after me each afternoon and at weekends. This is what she has lost by giving up her job as a receptionist/nurse on 1 September 1999.

(d) £75 per week to my sister-in-law for looking after me in the mornings. She also comes in most weekends to give my wife a break. She has been doing this since 1 September 1999. I have not been paying anything to my sister-in-law, who is simply a housewife, but would like to do so. Professional nursing attendance for four hours a day, seven days a week, would cost £200 per week. Eight hours a day would cost £350 per week. It would cost another £100 a week to have a nurse on call at night.

(e) The cost of converting my car to enable me to drive it without feet controls. This was £1,000, and this expense will be repeated every, say, five years.

(f) The cost of a special battery-operated wheelchair which I find much more comfortable and versatile than the chair supplied free on the NHS, £3,500. The life of these chairs is about ten years.

(g) The cost of my lost fortnight's holiday in Portugal planned to start on 18 July 1999. The cost was £725 each for my wife and myself, covering flights and accommodation. The flight portion of the holiday was insured and I received £800 from the insurance company when I had to cancel. I had unfortunately decided against insuring the whole holiday which I could have done for an extra £10 premium.

(h) The cost of employing a professional decorator to decorate my lounge, labour charge £350 plus VAT.

23.9 James Davies

James Davies worked as a motorcycle courier until he was injured 1 November 1998. His date of birth was 2 October 1973. Counsel is asked to advise on quantum.

James Davies will say:

I had pains in my right leg and shoulder so I went to the Accident Department of the hospital. A doctor carried out an X-ray and said that there was nothing wrong except rather severe bruising which would heal in a few weeks if I took things easy.

I stayed off work and rested but both my knee and ankle joints remained painful. I went to my GP in February 1999 and he referred me to a Consultant whom I saw on 1 and 15 March 1999. On the second occasion she told me that the results of my test were not certain, but that I had potentially serious injuries to both knee and ankle joints. My leg was put in plaster for three months. In June 1999 I was then told I should exercise the joints as I had some form of rare necrosis and might have to have an arthrodesis operation to pin the joints into a fixed position. My exercises and physio-therapy treatment were not successful, however, and in January 2000 an arthrodesis was performed to both joints. As a result, I cannot now bend my right knee, nor move my right ankle.

I have had to give up motorcycling and cannot undertake any physical work. I was earning £200 per week net when I stopped work. For a year after my accident I received £75 per week unemployment benefit and thereafter received £40 per week income support until I ceased to be eligible in May 1999. I had to sell my bike and my gear. I received £2,000 for the bike and £500 for the gear which were good prices, but I had paid £4,000 and £750 respectively for these items originally.

Before I was injured I used to play the saxophone with local bands for fun and to earn extra money, almost £50 per week. I was unable to earn anything from saxophone playing between the date of my accident and 1 May 2000 when I resumed playing. Between 1 May 2000 and November 2001 I earned on average £100 per week. While off work I practised a great deal and improved considerably. In November 2001 I became a professional. I now earn about £400 net per week. I travel considerably for my work now and have to use public transportation which I estimate costs me at least £1,000 per year more than the cost of going by motorcycle.

There is however no job security in being a professional musician. If times get hard the work may dry up and nobody wants to employ an ex-musician. I am worried that I will find it very hard to gain alternative employment.

EXTRACT FROM MEDICAL REPORT OF MR KENNETH BRAND of 100 Harley Street, London W1:

Opinion: ... in conclusion the trauma of the relatively minor injury to both knee and ankle joints sustained by Mr Davies on 1 November 1998 was responsible for the necrosis which so affected the joints that there was no alternative to Mr Davies's medical advisors but to carry out an arthrodesis of both these joints.

23.10 John Simms

John Simms was injured in an explosion on 1 February 2001. His date of birth was 5 March 1947. Counsel is asked to advise on quantum.

I was in St George's Hospital, Tooting for a month. My head and neck were extremely painful and, despite physiotherapy treatment, I continue to suffer serious headaches and a lack of mobility in the neck. I have been declared unfit to drive fork lift trucks. My employers took me back on 1 August 2002 as a warehouse clerk which is a job I can manage, provided I do not have a serious headache. I get these about once a fortnight, and lesser headaches about three times a week. For about six months after the accident my sleep was regularly disturbed by headaches. I have been advised that I have a 10 per cent chance of suffering from post-traumatic epilepsy. From about six months after my accident I began to feel seriously depressed. I also found that I became very easily irritable and inconsiderate, whereas before the accident I had an easy-going affable personality. Although I have had treatment for this condition, I feel quite frankly that it has been of little use. My temper has been a problem at work and I have got into trouble with the warehouse foreman. I am presently on a final warning and I am worried that I may soon lose my job.

As a fork lift driver I took home £220 per week (p.w.). My net earnings as a warehouse clerk are £170 p.w. For 12 months after the accident I received DSS benefits of £80 p.w. and until I resumed work I then had income support of £60 p.w. My other losses are as follows. I am unable to do the home decorating and gardening which I did before the accident. I estimate that this will cost me on average £800 per annum. During the first 12 months after my accident my sister-in-law, Mrs Watkins, came every week-day to look after me as my wife who works as a canteen assistant could not take time off without losing her job. I paid her £20 p.w. but, considering the amount of work she did, I would like to have paid her £75 p.w. and would wish to make a claim for the higher sum.

I am also told that my pension when I retire will be affected. At the age of 65 I would have received a pension (based on my employers's contributions) of £125 per week, but in view of my reduced earnings this is now likely to be only £100 per week, assuming I do not lose my job.

MEDICAL REPORT of MR KENNETH BRAND, FRCS, of 100 Harley Street, London W.1. (Extract) Mr Simms' injuries may therefore be summarised as comprising:

(a) Three inch laceration of scalp over vertex, which has healed well with no noticeable scar.

(b) Head injury with concussion. There have been some complaints of nausea and dizziness. There is an increased risk of post-traumatic epilepsy in the order of 10 per cent. If Mr Simms is to suffer epilepsy it could be anything up to 10 years before this becomes apparent.

(c) Crush fracture of first cervical vertebra. Mr Simms has made a fair recovery from this injury but will suffer permanently from occasional pain and aching in the neck, and from his present 20 per cent limitation in movement.

(d) Depression, irritability. Mr Simms has been seen by Dr Bard, the eminent psychiatrist, but has not responded to treatment. Unfortunately Dr Bard arranged for him to be admitted to the Clapham Hospital for the Mentally Ill for tests and observation, but Mr Simms was so distressed to see his fellow patients that he left immediately. The prognosis is uncertain, but there are reasonable grounds for expecting this aspect of his condition to improve over the next two to three years.

(e) There is no reduction in life expectancy, which remains about 20 years.

23.11 Richard Reshirn

Richard Reshirn was a quantity surveyor who suffered an accident on 1 November 1999. His date of birth was 20 October 1969. Counsel is asked to advise on quantum.

Richard Reshirn will say:

I lost consciousness and came to in the Clifton Royal Infirmary. I was wearing a hard hat and this probably saved my life. My spine was severely injured, however, and I am now a paraplegic, having paralysis of the lower limbs, bladder and sexual function. I am confined to a wheelchair with no hope of recovery. My life expectancy is reduced to about 15 years. I am prone to bladder infections, respiratory infections and pressure sores.

After 10 weeks in hospital I went to the Westport Rehabilitation Centre where I was trained to cope as best I can with my physical difficulties, but I will always need some nursing assistance. This is at present provided by my wife Laura who gave up her job on 1st March 2000 in order to be able to look after me. Her salary was £12,000 p.a. net. However, she is feeling the strain and wants to resume her career. I will need about 35 hours of nursing care per week at a current cost of £7.50 per hour plus a home help at £30 per week.

Before my accident I was earning £34,000 gross, £25,000 net, and had excellent prospects of promotion in 2001. If I had been promoted my salary would have been £30,000 p.a. net. I had a secure job and was likely to have become a partner by the age of 40, when I could have expected substantially higher earnings, typically £60,000 p.a. net. I am now unable to work except at home, because of the amount of care I need. I have been able to develop my artistic talents as an illustrator of children's books and have been earning about £10,000 p.a. net from this work since November 2000.

We have no children. We had planned to have children very shortly after my accident, but this is now uncertain. It might be possible through artificial insemination, but I could not cope with looking after children, so we would either need a full time nanny, or Laura would have to give up work. We would like to have children, but only if we can afford it. I am however very distressed by the thought that I will not live to see them grown up.

As a result of my accident we had to sell our three bedroomed flat which was on the second floor of a block for £80,000 and buy a house so that I could live on the ground floor. This is at present a small terraced house which we bought as a temporary measure for £60,000, but it is unsuitable in the long term, especially if we have a family. We will need to buy a three bedroomed house with downstairs accommodation for me. This is likely to cost £120,000, and a further £20,000 in special adaptation for my needs.

23.12 Albert Corey

Albert Corey died on 17 October 1999, leaving a widow, Barbara, and two children. Albert was a fitter earning £155.34 per week net at the date of his death with additional regular overtime. Albert consistently kept 25 per cent of his take-home pay and 65 per cent of his overtime for himself; the rest he gave to Barbara who spent it on running the household, keeping the family and paying rent and rates. Nothing was saved. Of the money Albert gave Barbara, 12 per cent was consistently spent by Barbara on Albert's upkeep, the rest on herself and the children and on expenditure for the family as a whole which has not diminished since Albert's death. Of the money Albert kept for himself, 5 per cent was consistently spent on gifts and entertainments for Barbara and the children.

Before Albert's death Barbara worked full-time earning £124.30 per week net, but since his death she has had to give up full-time work so as to look after the children. She quit her job on 1 November 1999 and took up part-time work from the date initially earning £65.98 per week net, rising to £68.32 per week net on 1 September 2000, and £73.85 on 1 September 2001. Her salary in full-time work would have risen to £130.06 per week net on 1 January 2000, £137.20 per week net on 1 January 2001 and £141.62 per week net on 1 January 2002. Had Albert not died his earnings would have risen to £167.61 per week net on 1 March 2000, £175.38 per week net on 1 March 2001 and £189.70 per week net on 1 March 2002. Overtime opportunities at Albert's place of work are spread evenly and fitters of Albert's seniority earned an average of £98.40 per month net in 1999, £99.15 per month net in 2000, £106.80 per month net in 2001 and so far in 2002 £89.20 per month net.

Albert used to do DIY work and repair work around the home. Barbara has so far spent £437.20 on workman's bills for work Albert would have done and has done no redecoration or home improvement some of which is now urgent and will cost £575. Barbara has spent more on baby-sitting since Albert's death: an extra £12.50 per week.

What is the total financial loss suffered by Barbara and the children in consequence of Albert's death as at 1 September 2002?

23.13 David Morgan, Deceased

Counsel is instructed by Bruce & Bruce of 14a High Street, Tisborough, Northamptonshire. Your Instructing Solicitors are instructed by Mrs Annette Morgan who is looking after her two grandchildren following the deaths of Mr and Mrs David Morgan. Mrs Annette Morgan has taken out letters of administration of the estates of both her son and daughter-in-law and wishes to pursue a claim on behalf of her grandchildren. Your Instructing Solicitors have been negotiating with the insurers of Manorborn Builders Limited, who have indicated that they might be prepared to pay £90,000, if this is acceptable.

Would counsel please advise on quantum, and in the light of that advice state whether an offer of £90,000 should be accepted.

ARNOLD MANOR will say:

I am the managing director of Manorborn Builders Limited.

Mr Morgan was a good workman who had been with the company for many years. He had a basic pay which after deductions amounted to £13,200 p.a., and in addition he would earn overtime money during the summer months when we were busy. On average I would expect him to work overtime on about 20 weeks of the year. He would then be given approximately £80 in cash for a week's overtime.

ANNETTE MORGAN will say:

I am the mother of David Morgan, his father died in 1998. David was born on 14 September 1974, and followed his father into the building trade, although he did so well at school I always thought he could have done better. In June 1995 he married Daisy Johnson and they had two children, Maxine who was born on 2 May 1996 and Marcus born on 5 September 1998. They lived in 'The Willows' which David was buying on an endowment mortgage costing £320 a month. When he died the insurance company paid off the mortgage. David was killed at work on 5 September 2001. The funeral was on 12 September 2001 and cost £1,100, paid for by Daisy.

Unfortunately, only three weeks after David's death Daisy had a fatal car accident. It was entirely her fault. I then moved into 'The Willows' to look after the children. I was born in 1954 and am very fit so I expect that I shall be able to look after them through school and, if appropriate, college. I have been asked about the family's living expenses before David's death. Fortunately Daisy was a very methodical person. She kept an account of all the family's expenditure. Her books show that over the year before David died the family spent on average £42 p.w. on food and drink, £36 p.w. on council tax, gas, electricity and general household items, £20 p.w. on clothing, and £43 p.w. on the car (which was written off in Daisy's fatal crash), travel and entertainment. In addition, each week David put aside £10 for each of the children into an endowment policy which would be payable when they reached the age of 18. My impression was that David spent very little on himself, not more than £40 per week in addition to the above. And if any job needed doing in the house he would do it.

Daisy did not work after she married David, though I think she wanted to go back to her job as a solicitor's clerk when Marcus went to school in September. I enjoy looking after the children. They were very cheerful souls, but I find it difficult to manage financially. Since Daisy died I find that it costs me about £2,000 a year to pay all the outgoings on 'The Willows', including the gas, electricity, maintenance and so on, and the children cost at least £1,250 p.a. each to feed, clothe and take on holiday. The jobs around the home which David used to do are costing me about £500 a year. Also, as a special gift, I continue the £10 p.w. endowment policies which David started.

23.14 Susanna and Emma Williams, Deceased

Counsel has herewith: Statement of Michael Morley.

Counsel is instructed by Gatwicks on behalf of Mr Michael Morley, the executor of the estate of his late cohabitee, Susanna Williams, who died in a tragic accident on 6 February 2002, together with their daughter, Emma. Probate of Miss Williams's estate was granted to Mr Morley out of the Brighton District Probate Registry on 28 July 2002.

Counsel is requested to advise whether it would be worthwhile bringing proceedings in respect of Emma Williams's death and on quantum.

MICHAEL MORLEY of 18 Carlton Terrace, London SW1 will say:

I was born on 21 November 1972 and have since 1996 been living with Susanna Williams at the above address. We considered ourselves to have a stable relationship, but we never married. We had two children, Mark, who was born on 3 March 1995, and Emma who was born on 12 October 2001. I am presently unemployed, having been dismissed from my job as an investment analyst at the Biological Bank on 1 November 2001.

I had been earning £100,000 per annum. I was given a severance payment of £30,000 and since then I have been unable to find a job and have had no income.

Susanna Williams was born on 14 October 1972. Throughout our relationship she worked as a commodity broker for Bowyers, Pierce and Green. At the time of her death her remuneration package was a basic salary of £80,000 per annum plus annual bonus which, on 1 January 2002 had been £20,000. This financial year her net income would have been about £65,000 net of tax and National Insurance. She had a company car and her employers also paid her private medical insurance (BUPA) subscription of £500 per annum, permanent health insurance premium of £1,000 per annum, fitness club subscription of £500 per annum and car running expenses up to £500 per annum. Our children were looked after by a full-time live-in nanny whom we paid £100 per week plus board and lodging.

Since the tragedy I have felt unable to continue looking for work and I now look after my son, Mark. Had Susanna lived I expect I would have found a job by now at a salary of about £25,000 net, but at present I am just not interested in working. The nanny has left and I have not replaced her. Susanna and I paid all our earnings when we were both working into a joint account out of which we paid all our expenses. The primary expense was our mortgages. We each had a mortgage with interest payments of £1,100 per month. Our other expenses included council tax of £1,000 each, electricity gas and water at about £1,500 per annum and entertainment expenses of about £1,500 per month. Susanna dressed well and I would estimate that she spent about £5,000 per annum on clothes and accessories. Our holidays and out-of-town breaks cost about £5,000 each year.

I now go out very little, though I have bought a car to replace the car which Susanna had as part of her remuneration package. It cost me £6,000. Mark will start at St Michael's Preparatory School, Belgravia this term. The fees are £1,200 per term and would have been paid by Susanna had she lived. I receive £15,000 per quarter from an insurance policy which Susanna took out before her death, and will continue to receive this until October 2032 when Susanna would have been 60 years old. Susanna and Emma are buried in the graveyard of their home village near Brighton. The funerals cost me £1,500 and £750 respectively and I am erecting an ornamental marble tombstone suitable for a woman of Susanna's achievements at a cost of £4,275.

TWENTY FOUR

SHORT PROBLEMS IN VARIOUS AREAS OF LAW

1. Victor Varley, who is aged 21, was in the 'Star and Garter' on 3 June 2001. At closing time, he left and began to walk home. As he walked round the corner from the public house, he saw two people fighting, with a small crowd around them. He was curious and went to look. He saw that one of the two men fighting was Walter Wicks, an acquaintance whom he knew to be aggressive, with a number of convictions for violence. The other man fighting, whom Victor had never seen before, was smaller and younger. Victor grabbed Walter and told him to pick on someone his own size. As he was doing so, the smaller man apparently picked up an iron bar, hit Victor across the face with it, and ran. Victor was knocked unconscious, and taken in an ambulance to hospital, where he was kept for the next two weeks. As a result of the blow, he has lost the sight of his left eye and has a six inch scar on the forehead.

While he was in hospital, he was visited by Detective Inspector Yeats, who was investigating the incident. Victor, partly because he was still recovering from his injury, and partly because he was nervous about the consequences of being frank, told the inspector that he did not know either of the two men. The inspector said 'If you won't help us, there's nothing further we can do.' On 8 July, you are asked to advise Victor as to his remedies and his best course of action.

2. Mrs Smith has been sexually harassed at work by her section supervisor, Mr James. Her complaints, which have now been verified by her employers consisted of: Mr James asking her out, touching her and pressing against her whenever he had cause to come into her office, and telling others in the company that she was free with sexual favours and that when he had finished with her he would pass her on.

Mr James has been dismissed, and Mrs Smith has decided to continue to work for her employers. You are asked to advise her as to her remedies (if any), the best forum in which to pursue them, and the amount of damages which she is likely to receive.

3. Amateur anglers who fish for salmon on the River Tame are angry. The Ministry of Agriculture, Fisheries and Food has given permission (required by existing fisheries legislation) to a number of commercial fishermen to catch salmon at the mouth of the Tame, using nets.

The fish will return from sea to spawn in the Tame. The anglers believe that most of the returning fish will be caught as the nets are very efficient, especially the 'T-net' which is likely to be used. The result, they believe, is likely to be the eradication of salmon from the river and, hence, loss of the pleasure that the anglers get from fishing there.

Existing legislation permits groups like anglers' associations to submit a formal memorandum to the Ministry, arguing the case against such permission being given. In a Bill currently going through Parliament, the Minister for Agriculture has inserted a clause which will remove this right.

What can the Tame anglers do?

4. Four years ago John went to live with Mary, having met her a few months previously. The house in which they lived had been bought by Mary, two years prior to John's moving in, with the help of a mortgage, and it has been registered in her sole name throughout. Both John and Mary had some training in the operation of computers, and together they ran a business from the house, advising those with problems in running their computer software.

A month ago, John and Mary had an argument, and John went to stay with a friend temporarily, leaving a lot of personal property in the house. He has continued to do some work for the business,but has only visited the house a couple of times, and he has not talked to Mary about the future. This morning he saw the house advertised for sale in a local estate agents.

What should John do?

5. Louis is an engineer, working for a British aerospace manufacturing company in the West of England. He lives with his wife and two children, in a village just outside Gloucester. His eldest child is handicapped and attends a rehabilitation centre. The local authority usually gives a grant to students at the centre but refuses to give one to Louis' child as the family are not UK nationals.

What can Louis or his child do?

6. John Julian bought a Ford Escort ('K' registration) from a used car dealer (Swift & Co.) on 6 July 2002. On 27 July, he left it parked outside his home. When he went to drive it to work the next day, he found that it had gone. He contacted the police, who told him they would keep him informed. On 3 August, the police rang him to say that his car had been found, and he should pick it up. He went to the station the following day, and was asked a series of questions about the vehicle's origin. He explained where he had bought it, and showed the police the vehicle registration documents. The police said that they had information that the car had been stolen before coming into the possession of Swift & Co. They would investigate and inform him as soon as possible. Since then, John has rung the police station two or three times a week, asking for his car back. They refuse to return it, saying they are still investigating.

On 1 September, you are asked to advise John as to his remedies and best course of action.

7. Elizabeth is the sole beneficiary of a trust, set up by her father, the property in which was to go to her when she was 30. Elizabeth was 30 a few months ago, and she found that the property she inherited was worth much less than she expected. She is suing the trustee for breach of trust on the following grounds.

(a) The trustee put £50,000 into an unauthorised investment three years ago. The value of this investment has fallen to £10,000, and income from the investment from £6,000 a year to £1,000 a year.

(b) The trustee put £20,000 into shares in X plc five years ago. These shares are now worth £40,000. This was authorised by the trust instrument, but the trustee could have put the money into shares in Y plc which would now be worth £80,000.

What is Elizabeth likely to recover?

8. The ABC Building Society is unwilling to advance money for the improvement of terraced houses without front gardens in an area where members of ethnic minority groups live. Your instructing solicitors have presented you with a copy of a report which states that 86% of ethnic minority families living in that area live in terraced houses without front gardens, and that 46% of white families living there live in terraced houses without front gardens.

Please advise in the following situations on appropriate procedure and remedies, treating each as independent of the other:

(a) A, who owns a terraced house without a front garden in this area, and is a member of an ethnic minority group, believes she has been indirectly discriminated against. The ABC Building Society has refused to advance money on a mortgage for improvements to her home as a result of this policy.

(b) The local Community Relations Council has received a number of complaints from residents in the same situation as A, but who are unwilling to take action themselves as they fear that they will be seen as troublemakers and be denied any chance of a mortgage if they were to do so.

9. Angela visits her elderly grandfather regularly. Some months ago they had a conversation during which the grandfather said that he trusted Angela and wanted her to help him to distribute his money as he did not trust lawyers. Last month Angela found that her grandfather had put £10,000 into her bank account without telling her. Last week Angela questioned her grandfather about this and he said that she could keep £500 for herself, but should divide the remainder between herself and her two sisters on the grandfather's death.

Yesterday Angela got a letter from her grandfather saying that she should only divide the money between herself and her sister Jane, as her other sister, Emma, did not deserve any money. What should Angela do?

10. Fred was convicted at Bow Street magistrates' court of theft on 10 August 2002. A month before his case was due to be heard he told his solicitor about three potential witnesses who could support his proposed alibi defence. On investigation, the solicitor found that two of the people had previous convictions for dishonesty. The third witness did not keep her appointment with the solicitor.

All three attended court for Fred's trial, but Fred's barrister persuaded Fred that they should not be called as witnesses — in the case of the first two, because their past records suggested lack of credibility, and, in the third, because no proof of evidence had been obtained and it was too risky to call her.

Fred is upset about his conviction when he sees you in conference on 3 September 2002. What should you advise?

Would your advice be any different if Fred had been convicted in the Crown Court?

11. Ian Ingram worked for seven years as an electrician at Carnation Construction plc. On 9 September 2002, he was called in by the site manager and told that he was being summarily sacked for dishonesty. He was given no further details as to what he was supposed to have done. He asked upon what information the company had taken its decision, and was told 'That's our business.' He was told to pick up his wages from the cashier, and when he did so, found that he had been given no money in lieu of notice.

On 28 September, you are asked to advise Ian as to his remedies and his best course of action. You are told that he wants, above all, to get his old job back. You are firmly instructed by him that he did nothing dishonest, and that there had been no complaint against him throughout the seven years that he was employed by the company. In addition, your instructing solicitors tell you that they have been contacted by Carnation Construction plc. The company say that they will probably employ Ian again from 1 January 2003. They will not be prepared to do so if he makes a fuss now.

12. Peter Black, a former MI5 officer, has published his memoirs in Canada and the United States of America, but not in England. Many travellers are freely bringing his book to England. An English tabloid newspaper, *The Moon*, has the serial rights for England. It has only managed to print one extract because the United Kingdom (UK) Government has obtained an interim injunction in the High Court. This prevents it from further publishing or commenting on the allegations about the Secret Services mentioned in the memoirs until the outcome of the main proceedings. The House of Lords has just upheld the interlocutory injunction and extended it to cover all media.

It further ordered a restraint on any reporting whatsoever of court proceedings initiated by the UK Government in connection with the publication.

(a) Advise *The Moon* whether they have any remedies outside domestic law.

(b) Would your advice to *The Moon* be different if the UK Government wins the main action in the House of Lords on the grounds that a permanent injunction is necessary:

(i) for reasons of public security; and

(ii) to maintain the principle of confidentiality?

(c) If the UK Government censored all radio broadcasting from Germany to listeners in England which mentioned the Black memoirs, could a German broadcaster invoke any international treaties in the English courts to have the ban lifted?

13. Jane is the beneficiary of a trust set up by her father when he died in 1997, of which Diana is the trustee. A sum of £200,000 was put into the trust when it was set up, to go to Jane at the age of 25. Jane will soon reach that age, and she recently asked Diana what she can hope to inherit. Diana was very vague, and Jane can only gather that some of the money was put into shares in X Ltd, which have gone down in value, and that the rest was put into a business of which Diana's son is the managing director, and in which Diana herself also has shares. It seems that Diana acted on the advice of Eve, a friend of hers who is an accountant.

What can Jane do?

14. One evening Mrs Jones was punched in the face by her husband who has a drinking problem. She suffered a broken nose.

Advise her.

15. Rose and Sam are the trustees of a family trust, the beneficiaries of which are themselves and their two sisters. There is £500,000 in the trust, and they wish to use it to best effect. They have been told by a friend that they should buy shares in Y Ltd, which sells satellite television dishes, as although it is a very new company, the value of the shares is likely to go 'through the roof' within a few years. Rose and her two sisters are quite keen to buy these shares. Sam is not keen, but is prepared to agree to buy them if the others insist.

Advise Rose and Sam what they can do.

16. Bruce Ltd is a Scottish company which makes and sells bagpipes and spare parts for them. Most of its sales are in Scotland, where its products constitute about 80 per cent of annual sales of bagpipes. The rest of Bruce's annual production (about 150 sets of pipes) is sold elsewhere in the UK and the Republic of Ireland (Bruce has 95 per cent of such sales).

Donald Ltd is a very small London business, whose trade is the repair and renovation of old or broken sets of bagpipes. Last year, Donald set up a wholly-owned subsidiary, Chanter Ltd, to make and sell new sets of bagpipes. It had a production target of 150 sets in its first year and hoped to take some of Bruce's sales by undercutting its prices.

In the six months that Chanter has been trading, Bruce has found its sales have fallen slightly. Last week, Bruce sent a letter to Donald, saying that if it did not close Chanter down, Bruce would stop supplying Donald with the spare parts that it needs to carry on its own business. Chanter has insufficient production capacity to replace Bruce as a supplier.

What can Donald do?

INDEX